NO BIRDS OF PASSAGE

NO BIRDS OF PASSAGE

A History of Gujarati Muslim Business Communities, 1800–1975

MICHAEL O'SULLIVAN

HARVARD UNIVERSITY PRESS

Cambridge, Massachusetts & London, England

2023

Printed in the United States of America

First printing

Library of Congress Cataloging-in-Publication Data
Names: O'Sullivan, Michael, 1988– author.
Title: No birds of passage : a history of Gujarati Muslim business communities, 1800–1975 / Michael O'Sullivan.
Description: Cambridge, Massachusetts ; London, England : Harvard University Press, 2023. | Includes index.
Identifiers: LCCN 2023000745 | ISBN 9780674271906 (cloth)
Subjects: LCSH: Ismailites—India—History. | Khojahs—India—History. | Memons—India—History. | Business—Religious aspects—Islam. | International business enterprises—India—History. | Capitalism—India—History. | India—Commerce—History. | Gujarat (India)—Economic conditions.
Classification: LCC HF3786 .O885 2023 | DDC 338.095475—dc23/eng/20230317
LC record available at https://lccn.loc.gov/2023000745

For Giuseppina and Hugh

I am merely the dust on the feet of the *jamaat*. I am its lowly servant.

—Sharif Jivabhai Surti, Twelver Khoja merchant from Madagascar, in an address to the Zanzibar Twelver Shiʿi *jamaats*

The Sheeah, the Soonee, the Khojah, the Mehmon, the Borah, the Mussulman from the Deccan, and he from the Kokan, have all some distinctive Shibboleth, but agree in the two great points of Mahometanism—the unity of God, and the truth of Mahomet's mission as his prophet.

—Unknown author, cited in the May 8, 1852, issue of *Household Words*, the weekly journal edited by Charles Dickens

The philosophy which would keep economic interests and ethical idealism safely locked up in their separate compartments finds that each of the prisoners is increasingly restive.

—R. H. Tawney, *Religion and the Rise of Capitalism*

Contents

Notes on the Text

This book examines sources in Arabic, Gujarati, Ottoman Turkish, Persian, and Urdu. Each of these languages has its own rules for transliteration. The approach here is to transliterate the titles of texts according to their source language. Thus, a hypothetical work in any of these languages titled *The Light of Guidance* will be transliterated as *Nūr al-Hidāyat* if in Arabic, *Nure Hīdāyata* if in Gujarati, or *Nūr-i Hidāyat* if in Persian or Urdu. For Arabic, Persian, and Ottoman Turkish, I use the standards associated with the *International Journal of Middle Eastern Studies;* for Gujarati and Urdu, I use a slightly simplified version of the Library of Congress transliteration system. Gujarati spelling in this epoch varied widely, so I have stuck to the conventions used by individual authors when transliterating titles. Generally, in my transliterations of Gujarati titles I insert what grammarians call the "inherent a," including in loan words, with the exception of English-origin ones. Works in Bohra Lisān al-Daʾwa (Gujarati written in a modified Perso-Arabic script, with substantial borrowings from Arabic, Persian, and Urdu) are translated according to Arabic standards. For religious terms common across these languages, I default to Arabic transliterations. All translations are my own, unless noted otherwise.

As it is too cumbersome, I have not transliterated the proper names of individuals. Because Anglicized renderings of Gujarati Muslim proper names are hopelessly inconsistent (for example, Habib, Habeeb, Hubeeb; Nathabhai, Nathoobhoy, Nathubhoy), I have done my best to standardize them. Double vowels and the Anglicized spelling of the Gujarati honorific suffix *-bhai* (*-bhoy*) have been discarded. An exception is made when discussing a Gujarati Muslim commercial firm, but when referring to the proprietors I revert to my standardized spelling (i.e., Essabhoy Brothers when referencing the company, but Isabhai when speaking of the proprietors).

Because the term *jamaat* (caste corporation) appears hundreds of times in the pages that follow, and *sethias* (merchant princes / caste leaders), *bait al-mal*, *dai*, *sarkar*, and *zakat* nearly half as much, I have decided not to transliterate these terms.

In the word *sethias* I add an English plural "s" to the singular, *sethia* (the singular also appears in sources as *seth*). Other terms long assimilated into English have also not been transliterated, such as *firman*, *imam*, *madrasa*, *sharia*, and *shaykh*.

Onomastics—the study and application of names to individuals and social groups—is a field rife with controversy, not least in the historiography of South Asia. A share of the difficulty lies in the fact that names are not enough to go on: given that the terms *Bohra* and *Khoja* also are commercial terms (*trader* and *master*, respectively), one finds plenty of instances in which Hindus possess the surname Bohra, or Armenians the Persian title Khwajah, which is the origin of the term *Khoja*. Though *Memon* is commonly held to be a corruption of the term *muʾmin* (believer), it is easy to confuse the community with other groups that go by the name Momin (believer; used both by a class of Muslim weavers in North India and, confusingly, by a group of Ismailis in Kathiawar). In the end, attributing a normative identity to historical actors is a thorny issue, and certain judgments must be made that may not please contemporary sensitivities.

A word is also in order for my use of the phrase "Gujarati Muslim commercial castes." There are dozens of Muslim communities with origins in Greater Gujarat who could be categorized by this label, from Ghanchis to Momins. Yet most often the phrase refers to the three business communities that interest us here: the Bohras, Khojas, and Memons. Therefore, I have used it freely throughout this book to denote them exclusively.

A final note on descriptors applied to the three communities studied in this book. There are a variety of Bohra communities, both Sunni and Shiʿa. When I use a name without an accompanying adjective (such as Bohra), I am referring to the Mustali Ismaili Shiʿi Daudi Bohra *jamaat*, whereas when calling attention to non-*Daudi* Bohra constituencies I add what in Arabic is called *nisba*, an adjectival form denoting place of origin (thus, Alavi Bohras, Sulaimani Bohras, Sunni Bohras, etc.). For the Khojas, I have invariably differentiated them: the Ismaili Khojas, Sunni Khojas, and Twelver Khojas. The Memons are all Sunnis, but the distinctions among Halai, Kachchhi, and Sindhi Memon communities are highly consequential, and whenever possible I have used the relevant descriptor. My focus, however, is on the Halai and Kachchhi subbranches. When I speak of "dissenters" I do not make a value judgment on the orthodoxy of such groups, but only use the terminology employed at the time. Out of considerations of space, clarity, and intelligibility, this book does not deal at any length with Ismaili communities in the Middle East and Central Asia, who were nonetheless connected to their fraternal communities in India, the Bohras and Khojas.

The Bohras, Khojas, and Memons used three calendrical systems in the period covered in this book: the Christian Gregorian calendar, the Hindu Samvat calendar, and the Islamic Hijri calendar. For simplicity's sake, I have converted all dates to the Gregorian, confident in the knowledge that the actors themselves would have had no reservations about this.

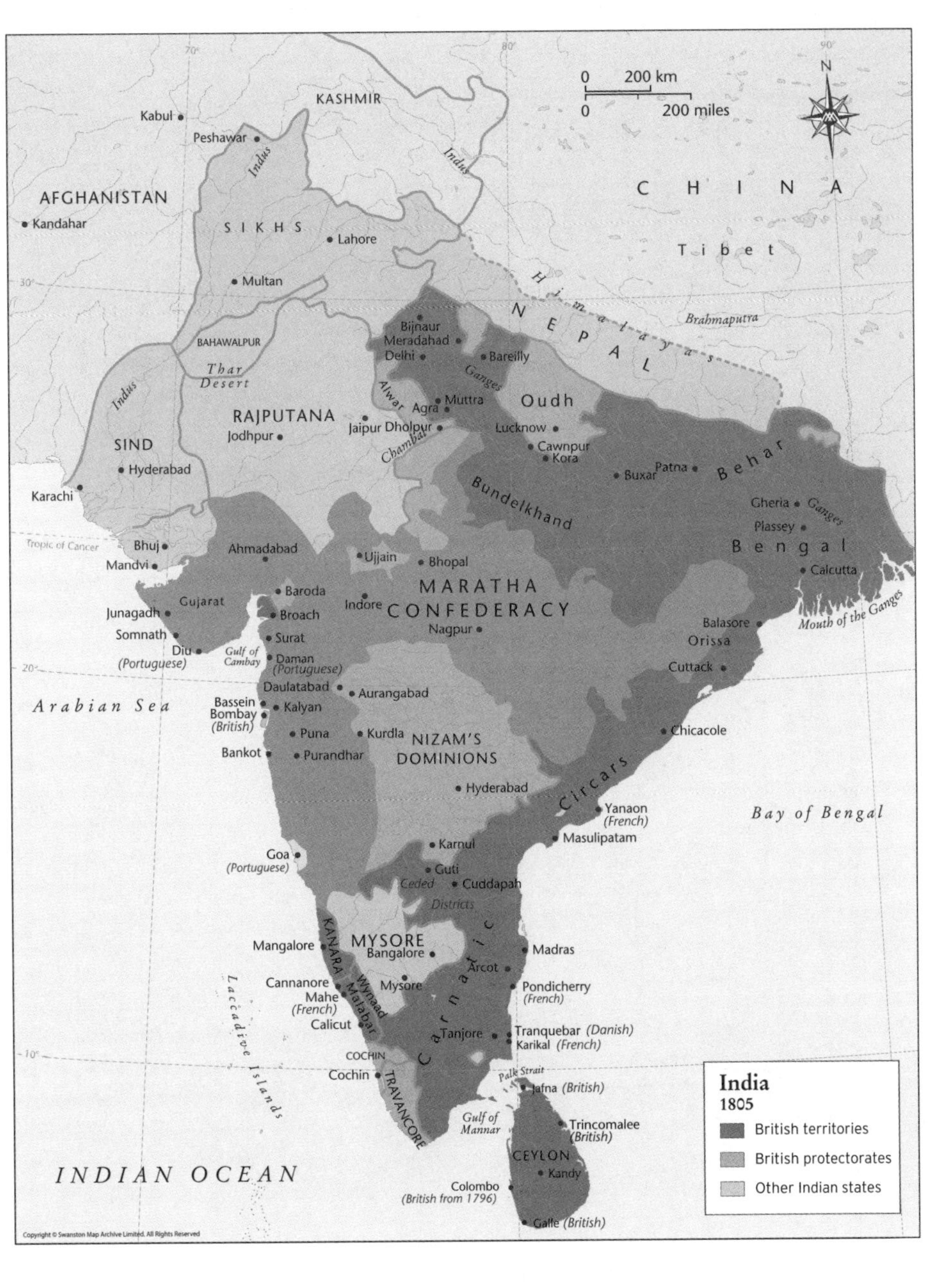
India
1805
British territories
British protectorates
Other Indian states
0 200 km
0 200 miles
N
KASHMIR
AFGHANISTAN
SIKHS
CHINA
Tibet
NEPAL
Himalayas
Oudh
RAJPUTANA
SIND
BAHAWALPUR
Thar Desert
Bundelkhand
Behar
Bengal
Orissa
MARATHA CONFEDERACY
NIZAM'S DOMINIONS
Circars
Ceded Districts
MYSORE
Carnatic
KANARA
Wynaad
Malabar
COCHIN
TRAVANCORE
CEYLON
Kabul
Peshawar
Kandahar
Lahore
Multan
Bijnaur
Meradahad
Delhi
Bareilly
Muttra
Agra
Alwar
Jaipur
Dholpur
Jodhpur
Lucknow
Cawnpur
Kora
Buxar
Patna
Hyderabad
Karachi
Gheria
Plassey
Calcutta
Bhuj
Mandvi
Ahmadabad
Ujjain
Bhopal
Gujarat
Baroda
Indore
Broach
Junagadh
Somnath
Diu
(Portuguese)
Surat
Nagpur
Balasore
Mouth of the Ganges
Cuttack
Gulf of Cambay
Daman
(Portuguese)
Daulatabad
Aurangabad
Arabian Sea
Bassein
Bombay
(British)
Kalyan
Puna
Kurdla
Chicacole
Bankot
Purandhar
Hyderabad
Yanaon
(French)
Bay of Bengal
Masulipatam
Karnul
Goa
(Portuguese)
Guti
Cuddapah
Mangalore
Bangalore
Madras
Arcot
Cannanore
Mysore
Pondicherry
(French)
Mahe
(French)
Calicut
Laccadive Islands
Tanjore
Tranquebar (Danish)
Karikal (French)
Cochin
Palk Strait
Jafna (British)
Gulf of Mannar
Trincomalee
(British)
Kandy
INDIAN OCEAN
Colombo
(British from 1796)
Galle (British)
Indus
Ganges
Chambal
Brahmaputra
Tropic of Cancer
70°
80°
90°
30°
20°
10°

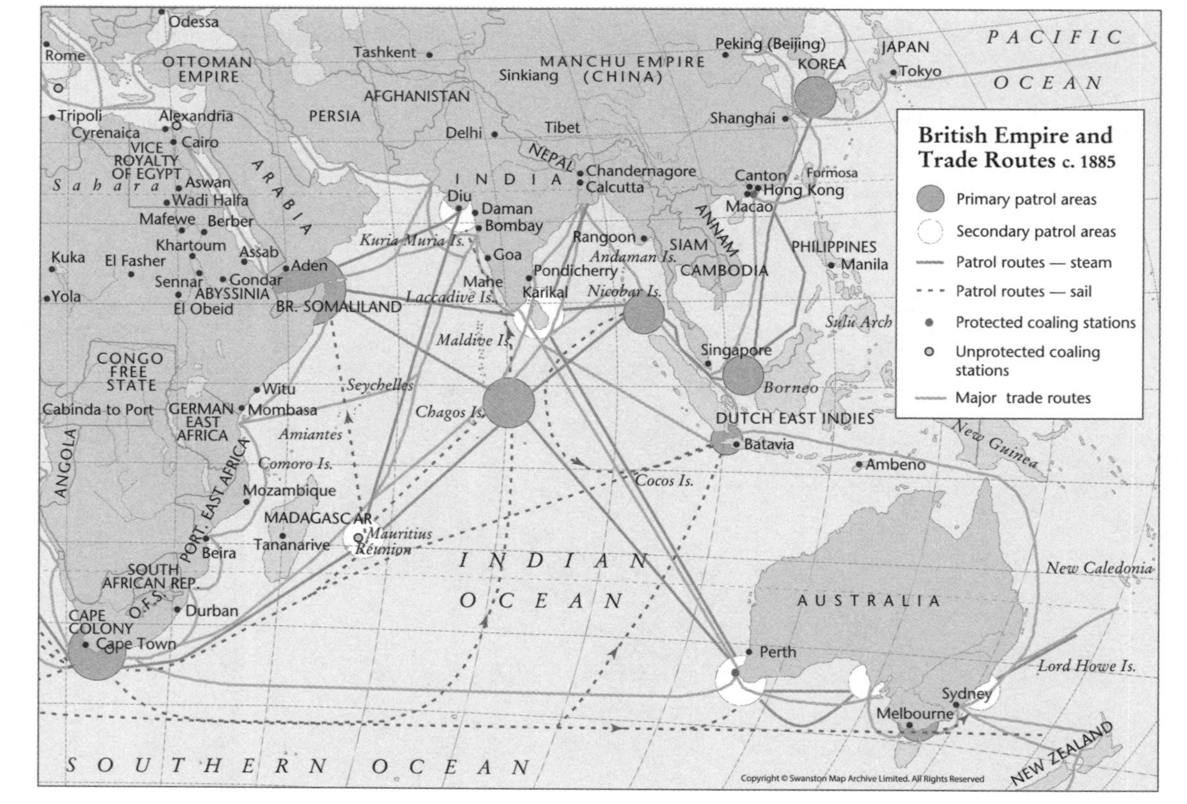
British Empire and Trade Routes c. 1885
Primary patrol areas
Secondary patrol areas
Patrol routes — steam
Patrol routes — sail
Protected coaling stations
Unprotected coaling stations
Major trade routes
PACIFIC OCEAN
INDIAN OCEAN
SOUTHERN OCEAN
OTTOMAN EMPIRE
PERSIA
AFGHANISTAN
MANCHU EMPIRE (CHINA)
INDIA
ARABIA
AUSTRALIA
NEW ZEALAND
DUTCH EAST INDIES
Copyright © Swanston Map Archive Limited. All Rights Reserved

Introduction

From Greater Gujarat to Japan and Beyond

PASSING THROUGH SINGAPORE IN 1909, Abd al-Reşid Ibrahim, a Tatar Muslim scholar and intrepid traveler from western Siberia, met with the directors of an Indian Muslim commercial firm, Essabhoy Brothers. The Isabhai family (Essabhoy being the semi-Anglicized corruption of Isabhai) hailed from the small Gujarati community of Ismaili Shiʿi Muslims called the Daudi Bohras. The company's proprietors were natives of Surat, once Western India's preeminent port and the seat of the Daudi Bohra *dai al-mutlaq* (the chief cleric of the sect) since 1785. From that base, Essabhoy Brothers extended its operations to Aden, China, Hodeida, Japan, Malaya, Singapore, and Zanzibar. Each brother was conversant in Chinese, Japanese, and Malay and knew how to write and speak Gujarati and Urdu. A smaller fraction knew some Arabic and Persian. They were, as Ibrahim remarked, "zealous, to the highest degree, in their religious observances; wherever they have one of their trading branches, if there are ten or twenty servants, there definitely is a leader of their sect, in some places there are even mosques exclusively for them. Among these are mosques solely for their use in Singapore."[1]

Ibrahim used his encounter with Essabhoy Brothers to engage in a digression on the history of the Bohras, fusing praise and polemic in his telling. He acknowledged that throughout India the Bohras had obtained fame as traders. But in keeping with many Muslim commentators before and after him,

Ibrahim's appreciation for the Bohras' commercial prowess was joined with a suspicion of their religious beliefs: "their capital and *jamaats* [corporate caste institutions] are rather excellent, [while] in religion, as possessors of an extraordinary fanaticism, they are bigoted to the utmost degree. They have kept the fundamentals of their sect confidential from days gone by until now. Regrettably, they are Shiʿi Muslims." Eager though he was to caricature Bohra religious beliefs, Ibrahim's jibes buckled in the face of his wide-ranging conversation with the firm's proprietor on Islamic theology. For all that, the Bohras' unmistakable wealth impressed the Tatar traveler most. Upon leaving Singapore and touching down in Calcutta, where Essabhoy Brothers had another branch of their business, Ibrahim marveled at the seeming absence of destitute Bohras, admitting that "in the world the best and most promising Muslim sect are the Ismailis."[2]

As Mustali Ismailis, the Isabhais were from one of the "minority" sects within Shiʿi Islam, of which there are several. Yet this did not prevent the family from supporting Ibrahim, a Sunni scholar of some repute, in his efforts to contact Japan's first Muslims. While in Bombay, Ibrahim received a telegraph from one of the Essabhoy Brothers' directors in Singapore that stated, "A Japanese man named Yamaoka has come from Tokyo. He was sent by Ohara to take refuge with you. Since he is traveling from here today, he requests permission for you to wait for him in Bombay."[3] The Ohara mentioned here was among the first Japanese converts to Islam, and his associate Yamaoka Mitsutarō, another imminent convert, eventually traveled to Bombay to study with Ibrahim, and the two subsequently journeyed to Mecca.[4] In this way, the Bohra firm's commercial contacts helped a Sunni scholar in his bid to Islamize Japan. Ibrahim dedicated the rest of his life to the pursuit of Japan's conversion, later becoming the first imam of the Tokyo Mosque, where he died in 1944.

Essabhoy Brothers had a long-standing association with Japan, beginning operations there as early as 1863. One of the matchboxes produced for the firm in Japan at the beginning of the twentieth century featured two *samurai*, as sure a sign as any of their integration into Meiji era commercial life (see figure I.1). Yet Japan's economic boom brought occasional troubles for the Bohra firm. In 1868, the year of the Meiji Restoration, Essabhoy Brothers was involved in a dramatic commercial dispute in Yokohama, after one of the partners unloaded a box from a British ship without registering it at the Japanese Customs House. After much handwringing in the courtroom over how to

FIGURE I.1 An Essabhoy Bros. matchbox produced in early twentieth-century Japan. Author's personal collection.

administer an oath to the Bohra proprietor (who was initially thought to be a Hindu by British personnel), Isabhai proceeded to swear an oath on the Quran, likely the first Muslim in a Japanese legal forum to do so.[5]

Over the ensuing decades, Essabhoy Brothers endured numerous commercial spats in Japan and other port cities of the Indian and Pacific Oceans. However, its growth was unmistakable. In 1894 one of the brothers financed a Bohra mosque valued at Rs. 40,000 in Calcutta, with another built three years later in Singapore, a city where leading Chinese and Jewish merchants were among the family's closest friends.[6] By 1911 the firm moved into a three-story building in Yokohama and the inaugural ceremony was attended by hundreds of local and foreign dignitaries.[7] That year Tayyib Ali, the manager of the Essabhoy Brothers' Yokohama branch, also attended the opening of the Japanese Diet with a group of Indian and Iranian Muslim intellectuals.[8] In 1912 the Hong Kong branch of the French Banque de l'Indochine loaned the firm $410,000 (Hong Kong dollars) in March alone, covering remittances in Bombay, Shanghai, and Yokohama.[9]

The numbers were deceptive. Shortly after the outbreak of the First World War, Essabhoy Brothers collapsed at alarming speed, one of the many prewar Indian Muslim firms unable to weather the market shocks endemic to the conflict.[10] The subsequent litigation in Hong Kong, Kobe, Singapore, and other port cities underscored the geographic extent of Essabhoy Brothers' obligations—obligations that had once fostered its transimperial business portfolio and now fatally undermined it.[11] The firm's proprietors were socially cosmopolitan, geographically widespread, and invested in broader discourses of Islamic ecumenism beyond their sect. All the while, caste community remained a prominent fixture of the company's portfolio. Its transformation from a humble family firm into a transimperial capitalist corporation is impressive, even more so since it was no singular example. In reality, the firm and the family from which it drew its name are emblematic of the modern history of the three leading Gujarati Muslim commercial castes examined in this book: the Bohras, Khojas, and Memons.

The Gujarati Muslim Commercial Castes

Abd al-Reşid Ibrahim encountered Bohra, Khoja, and Memon capitalists at several points during his travels. He held up their facility in business as an example to other Muslims, but also found their understanding of Islam hard to square with his own. In this he was not alone, for the historical study of these groups remains in its infancy. Each of these communities constitute their own distinct endogamous Gujarati and / or Kachchhi-speaking Muslim trading caste. All three hail originally from a sweep of territories in Western India that this book calls Greater Gujarat.[12] Community narratives maintain that they were the descendants of various nominally Hindu castes converted to Islam by Shiʿi and Sunni missionaries in the mid- to late medieval period. While the Memons are all nominal Sunnis, the Bohras and Khojas are mostly Shiʿi Muslims, albeit of heterogeneous types, with a smattering of Sunni Bohras and Khojas to boot. Tradition relates that their caste names were bestowed on them at their conversion: Bohra (from the Gujarati word *voharā*, trader), Khoja (from the Persian word *khwaja*, master or lord), Memon (a reworking of the Arabic *muʾmin*, believer).[13] Rather than preserving their integrity as three homogeneous communities, each group has been subjected to repeated internal fracturing and differentiation over the centuries, with the rate of fragmentation accelerating in the modern period (see figure 1.2).

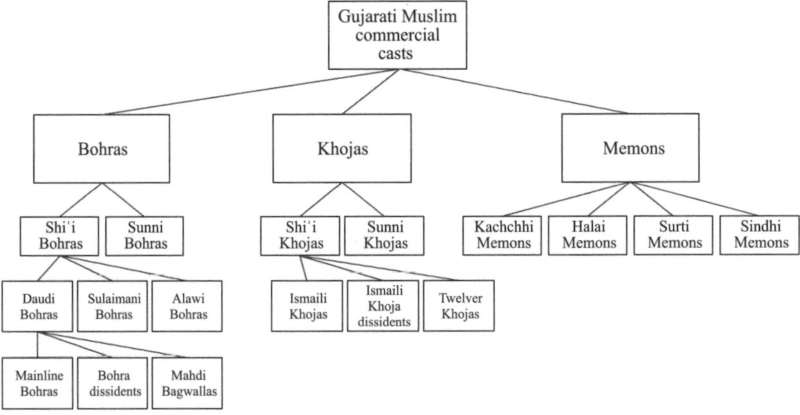

FIGURE I.2 A breakdown of the Gujarati Muslim Commercial Castes. The branches of the Daudi Bohras, Shiʿi Khojas, and Kachchhi and Halai Memons form the main subjects of this book.

Collectively, these three groups have never constituted more than 1 percent of South Asia's total Muslim population.[14] Yet since the beginning of the nineteenth century, all three have acquired an economic prominence well out of proportion to their tiny numbers. This book demonstrates that, since the late eighteenth century, these three Gujarati Muslim communities have been participants in the transformative processes that birthed modern capitalism as an integrated, hierarchical, and coercive system of production and consumption across South Asia and the Indian Ocean. Indeed, between 1800 and 1975, Bohra, Khoja, and Memon firms have ranked disproportionately among the leading Muslim-owned businesses in South Asia and the Indian Ocean region. Like Essabhoy Brothers, these firms generally relied on business contacts both within their communities and outside them. And just as Essabhoy Brothers lent a hand to broader efforts to convert Japan to Islam and built community mosques in several Asian port cities, other Bohra, Memon, and Khoja firms were spirited participants in intra-Muslim religious exchange across Eurasia and Africa.

Even so, many Sunnis and Shiʿis in South Asia and beyond have long regarded the Gujarati Muslim commercial castes—with a mixture of admiration and venom—as Muslims set apart. Colonial officials and Muslim commentators alike have seen them as self-enclosed Muslims, divorced from wider currents of Islam by virtue of their caste institutions and religious doctrines.

In the South Asian popular imagination, moreover, their purported acuity in business has spawned numerous stereotypes. Some were tongue in cheek: as one nineteenth-century Hindustani proverb put it, "Even if the [Memon] goes to Mecca for pilgrimage, he will steal a pair of scales and weights," a dig at the caste's purported stinginess.[15] Others were biting, but toothless: one Indian Muslim historian in 1905 criticized wealthy Memons for not only maintaining "Hindu" customary practices, but also for attending exclusively to the needs of their own community. In a charge often leveled at the Gujarati Muslim commercial castes, he added that the Memons barred the general Muslim public from accessing their caste institutions, hostels, and madrasas.[16] Meanwhile, select Sunni and Shiʿi diatribes against the Bohras and Khojas questioned their credentials as Muslims, framing them as heterodox believers if not outright heretics.[17] The Bohras especially were condemned for keeping their religious books under lock and key and refusing to engage in public debates with other Muslims.[18] In spite of this, several modern Sunni writers have composed stirring tributes to the Bohras and Khojas.[19] Still other Muslim commentators in the colonial period frequently employed the label New Muslims to these communities, a term fraught with polemical overtones.[20] In turn, some of these barbs were internalized and reworked by these communities for their own purposes.[21]

Scholarship on the Gujarati Muslim commercial castes has tended to echo, both implicitly and explicitly, some aspects of these portraits. Two primary narratives dominate the academic study of these groups. The first, propounded by economic historians, treats them as capitalists organized in a coherent trading community or business class for whom religion is immaterial. When religion is invoked, their erstwhile "Hindu" identity is foregrounded and their status as Muslims is regarded as merely incidental or inimical to their success as capitalists.[22] In league with a rich lineage of South Asian business history, their perspicacity in business is seen as a functional outgrowth of their primordial identity as trading castes.

The second narrative, advanced by historians of religion, broadly frames the Bohras, Khojas, and Memons as particularist Muslims of one form or another. Unlike economic history accounts, pioneering religious studies narratives embrace the centrality of Muslim identity in these communities.[23] Many of these accounts situate the modern religious experience of the Bohras, Khojas, and Memons in the paradigm of *Islamization,* which is a byword for the progressive marginalization of "non-Islamic" customary practices and the adoption of "orthodox" Islamic legal norms of belief and practice previously foreign to their normative religious identity. The notion of Islamization is not so much wrong as incomplete in that it ignores the manifold ways in which each community has engaged with diverse traditions of Islamic law for the past several centuries. What is more, by stressing the unidirectionality of each group's religious development, these accounts stand the risk of underplaying the participation of the Gujarati Muslim commercial castes, as both producers and consumers, in broader currents of Shiʿi and Sunni Islam. Taken together, accounts which stress the religious orientation of these groups understandably consign their business activities to the background. Unfortunately, this concedes too much terrain to the economic historians who study these groups one step removed from the vantage point of the colonial archive.

These two literatures, the economic and religious, speak to divergent historical themes, even if there is a remarkable congruence in the portrayal of these groups as either a self-sustaining class of capitalists or as sects of secluded Muslims. But if commercial success ultimately requires transcending the boundaries of one's own community, the Bohras, Khojas, and Memons could never have conformed to the stereotype of a trading caste keeping largely to itself.[24] And the image of them as Muslims set apart begins to fray as soon as one begins to account for the participation of Bohras, Khojas, and Memons in all manner of ecumenical Muslim religious institutions and campaigns.

This book maintains that the economic and religious histories of these three groups cannot be separately told. The ebb and flow of their business activities must be understood in conjunction with the transformations in caste categories, occupational status, and religious norms made possible by the wealth they accumulated through trade and industry. In the realm of economic history, the very stereotypes that characterize these groups as estranged from Islam have effectively obscured the institutional nexus of their commercial activities. In the realm of religious studies, meanwhile, the depiction of these castes as insulated communities has obscured rich and fraught histories of both inter-Muslim and Muslim / non-Muslim religious exchange. By unifying questions of political and religious economy, this book maintains that in all three communities capitalist enterprise and religious exchange have been deeply intertwined from the late eighteenth century onward, although never proceeding in a single direction or to some appointed end, and by no means always acting in harmony. This is best glimpsed when the three communities are studied in unison rather than as separate entities.

The title of this book, *No Birds of Passage*, is meant to evoke the entrenched position of the Bohras, Khojas, and Memons in processes of capitalist and religious enterprise over a period of nearly two centuries. In an 1873 survey of the Indian diaspora in East Africa, the colonial administrator, Sir Bartle Frere, spoke of Indian traders (including, but not limited to, the Bohras, Khojas, and Memons) as "birds of passage," who were as likely to make Africa their home "as a young Englishman in Hong Kong."[25] His words embodied the assumption—held by British officials and indigenous elites alike—that these merchants had no intention of settling down for long: they were transient passers-through, apathetic to local society, whose true and only domicile would always be India. This assumption anticipated many of the aforementioned stereotypes on display in academic accounts of these communities. To be sure, some Indians did migrate to East Africa or Southeast Asia only for temporary periods.[26] However, the Bohras, Khojas, and Memons consistently eluded that trend by planting deep roots in multiple parts of the Indian Ocean region.

Although applied in this instance to Indian traders, Edmund Burke was the first to use the phrase "birds of passage" in the context of British imperialism in a 1785 speech. In one of his many harangues of the East India Company's corrupt administration in India, he rebuked its servants in the following terms:

> Our conquest there [India], after twenty years, is as crude as it was the first day. The natives scarcely know what it is to see the grey head of an Englishman. Young men (boys almost) govern there, without society, and without sympathy with the natives. They have no more social habits with the people, than if they still resided in England; nor indeed any species of intercourse but that which is necessary to making a sudden fortune, with a view to a remote settlement. Animated with all the avarice of age, and all the impetuosity of youth, they roll in one after another; wave after wave; and there is nothing before the eyes of the natives but an endless, hopeless prospect of new flights of *birds of prey and passage*, with appetites continually renewing for a food that is continually wasting.[27]

Burke's description presented the British as predatory and transient "birds of passage," seeking nothing but personal profit and the ruin of India. It is not known if Sir Bartle Frere intentionally drew from Burke's language in his 1873 account of Indian trade in East Africa. What is for sure is that in the twentieth century Indian nationalists weaponized Burke's birds of passage epithet in their critiques of colonial rule.

In the postcolonial period the phrase came back around to describe Indian traders—among them the Bohras, Khojas, and Memons. In Asia as well as Africa, nationalists dismissed these same Indian communities as foreign interlopers uninterested in interacting with local society.[28] Many postcolonial state-builders saw Indian communities—like their erstwhile British overlords—as rapacious migratory birds. To call these groups birds of passage was to imply that they replicated wholesale the voracious capitalism practiced first by East India Company nabobs, and later by European firms in Asia and Africa. It was also to assert that these communities were a world unto themselves, content to feather their own nests, while refusing to interact with other peoples.

The communities studied in this book repeatedly defy these charges. Not only have they been permanent fixtures of numerous localities in the Indian Ocean region, but they have also enjoyed a sustained preeminence in regional circuits of capitalist enterprise. They have thus given the lie to the birds of passage moniker. Moreover, on at least one occasion, a community leader spoke out against such an unflattering label. In 1937, the Agha Khan III, the *imam* of the Ismaili Khojas, proclaimed the following to one of his congregations in East Africa:

> Your position is quite different from that of other Asians. You have made this country your home. I think many a family amongst you have settled in this part for the last 150 years. Since I first visited East Africa in 1899, I don't think any Ismaili has returned to India. You are *not* birds of passage. Your roots are very deep. Your future is tied with Kenya, Tanganyika, Zanzibar and Uganda. Therefore, I am appealing to you to be true, loyal subjects of these countries which you have made your home.[29]

Though spoken ninety years ago, these words are as true as ever, even if the East African expulsions of a half-century ago threatened to prove the Agha Khan III wrong. In the interim, the Bohras, Khojas, and Memons have spread still further across the globe. But while movement was a central feature of their collective experience, their stature in circuits of capitalist and religious interaction was never ephemeral.

The *Jamaats* as Corporations

Abd al-Reşid Ibrahim was right to emphasize the synergies between the economic capital of these communities and their *jamaats*. And it is the relationship between capital and the *jamaats* that invites the central questions pursued in this book. First, how did entrepreneurs from these three tiny communities transform themselves into the leading Muslim-owned commercial firms between 1800 and 1975? Second, how did their caste institutions help or hinder in the acquisition of wealth? And third, how did this wealth become an object of disputation within these castes and between them and other Muslims and non-Muslims? Conveniently, these three strands are integrated in the shared institutional nexus of the *jamaats*.

Throughout this book, the *jamaats* of each community are defined as corporations in three ways: as points of ingress and egress into the wider economic world and depositories of capital; as legal entities straddling the realms of colonial law, Islamic jurisprudence, and caste custom; and as arbiters between the Gujarati Muslim commercial castes and municipal, national, and Pan-Islamic politics. Thus, the model of the corporation employed here is a capacious one, but consonant with venerable definitions of the corporation as a collective association of individuals organized as a single entity and possessing certain legal rights. Understood in this way, the history of the corporation includes a range of institutions, from guilds and religious orders to universities, businesses, and hospitals.[30] It is also a definition sensitive to the ways in which, within South Asian business communities over the past two centuries, the "joint-stock corporation impinged upon a variety of corporate forms, becoming a model for public association, both for profit and for charity."[31]

For all this, to speak of the corporation in South Asia and Islamicate settings is controversial, because the "corporation" in its western European business form did not exist in any recognizable sense in Islamic law before the mid-nineteenth century.[32] According to one line of thinking, this deficiency was responsible for the absence of capitalism in premodern Muslim contexts. For example, the historian Jairus Banaji has recently claimed that "the non-development of capitalism [in the Islamicate world] was less about a failure to emerge than about the failure to acquire a more collective, corporate form that could express and contribute to the solidarity of a class. Capitalists certainly existed in the Muslim world, but they failed to form the kind of collective solidarity implied in the notion of a 'class.'"[33] This notion of capitalists existing in noncapitalist contexts is commonly asserted when scholars speak of the Global South, but it is never satisfactorily explained why the criteria for defining a capitalist should be so radically different from defining capitalism in the round.

Nor do such narratives adequately convey the institutional mechanisms—not least corporate ones—that allowed these capitalists to perpetuate themselves. The definition of capitalism taken in this book is a diachronic one. It is inspired by a long tradition within South Asian studies of seeing commercial capitalism as endogenous to the region, rather than a colonial imposition. And it combines this perspective with new models of commercial capitalism that are inclusive of Islamicate contexts and critical of an older literature that regarded merchant capitalism as an archaic, premodern remnant in the age of modern industrial capitalism.[34] Both of these conceptualizations of capitalism have remained attentive to the transformative aspects of the colonial encounter in South Asia while also taking little from the precolonial period for granted.

It would be wrong to pretend, however, that the corporation can be fit easily into these paradigms. The position taken here is that while the "business" corporation certainly has no formal legal status in Islamic law before the mid-nineteenth century, "corporations" of various types are nonetheless detectable in many Muslim contexts, as historians have long recognized.[35] In a case with particular relevance to this book, previous scholars have made an analogy between the *jamaats* and corporations. Writing over forty years ago, Ashin Das Gupta, a leading economic historian of the early modern Indian Ocean region, entertained the idea that a *jamaat* might resemble a European corporation but confessed that he could find no "evidence to indicate the kind of control that a Muslim [*jamaat*] would have over its members."[36] The best Das Gupta could do was to cite some circumstantial, although enigmatic, examples. Elsewhere he acknowledged that while *jamaats*—and kindred institutions used by Hindus and Parsis—were social organizations at heart, they did perform economic functions in some capacities.[37] But given the dearth of pre-1800 materials related to the *jamaats*, Das Gupta was unable to say what those functions were. Fortunately, as the *jamaats* and their histories become more legible with the mushrooming of post-1800 community and colonial sources—a by-product of the dramatic expansion in commercial and print capitalism in the nineteenth century—one can begin to answer Das Gupta's questions with greater clarity.

Readers might rightly question the utility of framing the *jamaats* as corporations when recent scholarship in business history has done so much to put the corporation "in its place."[38] After all, the once mythic hold the joint-stock company assumed in histories of modern capitalism has been marginalized, and its many disadvantages, not least in colonial India, expertly cataloged.[39] As often occurs in the field of economic history outside modern Western contexts, there is a fundamental problem of stretching analogies to the point of meaninglessness: if all sorts of institutions without an explicitly economic dimension constitute a corporation, then the term loses its explanatory power. But so long as economic history continues to privilege select institutions of Western lineage, applying analogies from the European experience to the non-West is an inevitability. The limits are simultaneously linguistic and empirical. Be that as it may, envisaging the *jamaats* as corporations is a corrective to the tendency to view Indian enterprise through the unchanging category of the family firm.[40] To clarify, a multitude of family firms operated by caste members fell within reach of the *jamaats'* asset portfolio. In aggregate, the interaction of these individual firms coalesced in the space of the *jamaat* and contributed to its identity as a quasi-corporate institution, but this was just one manifestation of the *jamaats'* wider corporate personality.

Finally, defining the *jamaats* as corporations would not have convinced many colonial-era judges in British India. One commentary on a case involving the account books of a Memon *jamaat* reads, "There is no analogy whatever between a Corporation as known to English Law and an Indian caste. The principles governing the rights of members of caste to inspection of accounts of caste properties must be governed by considerations very different from those governing the rights of members of Corporation seeking inspection of the documents of such Corporation."[41] Another compendium on castes in the legal system of British India made this point more extensively, arguing that the case in question underscored that caste properties were "governed by considerations different from those governing the rights of members of corporation, club, society or partnership seeking inspection of documents of them."[42]

Leaving aside the supposed fact that caste had a "socio-religious origin,"[43] all of the functions that the commentator listed to indicate the distinguishing features of caste were actually shared by corporations, clubs, and societies. Thus, even if one acknowledges the existence of ideal legal distinctions between castes and corporations, in practice the *jamaats* muddied the divide between the two. Moreover, from the late nineteenth century onward, the odd European commentator—including the prolific French geographer Elisée Reclus—described these three communities as "corporations."[44] English-Hindustani and English-Persian dictionaries from the early nineteenth century onward also define *jamaat*, among other terms, as a corporation.[45] These historical parallels are enough to justify the conceptualization of the *jamaats* employed in this book.

Corporate Islam and Middle Power

To counter the institutionalist explanations for the supposed lack of corporate capitalism in South Asia and other Muslim settings, and to unify the scholarship on Indian Ocean capitalism, South Asian political economy, and Islamic studies, this book advances the model of *corporate Islam* as a catchall analytical category. As defined here, corporate Islam was a package of institutions and discourses, centered on the *jamaat*, that conceived of capitalist enterprise and the tightly bounded, exclusive religious community as mutually reinforcing, part of a single organizational continuum. To use the language of economics, corporate Islam wove together both private and club goods and services, integrating the private property held by its members in family trusts and companies with the club facilities offered by the *jamaat*. Access to these resources was unequal within the *jamaats*, controlled as they were by vested interests within them.

As subsequent chapters will clarify, corporate Islam took on discrete forms in each Bohra, Khoja, and Memon *jamaat*, shaped both by internal community dynamics and local conditions. The parameters of corporate Islam were never predetermined, but contorted by conflicts in each caste and outside them over how to best organize communal life, manage private and public wealth, and interpret Islam. For this reason, a *jamaat* in 1950 looked quite distinct from that of 1900, let alone that in 1850 or 1800. *Jamaats* thus functioned as individual franchises for the multiple forms corporate Islam assumed in practice.

For all the ambition in this book to disaggregate traditions of corporate Islam and account for community-level specificities, it is still useful to foreground Islam as a distinct institutional package in the portfolio of the individual Bohra, Khoja, and Memon. In so doing, a cue is taken from an economic historian of China, Taisu Zhang, who has argued for the utility of preserving Confucianism as an analytical frame for understanding the links between Chinese kinship practices and the character of Chinese property regimes.[46] As Zhang notes, there is crucial distinction between culturalist and cultural explanations of economic behavior, and to discount the edifice of Confucianism entirely on the grounds that it is culturalist and essentializing is mistaken. One can simultaneously acknowledge that cultural norms are not all-encompassing, inimical to comparison, or unchanging, while also recognizing that to ignore these norms means divorcing historical actors from their everyday frames of reference. Corporate Islam is a category flexible enough to account for a pluralism of behaviors on display in the three communities examined in this book while not losing sight of how the structures of communal / religious life impinged upon the individual.

A common feature of corporate Islam was the valorization of capitalism and religion as the complementary pillars of the overall caste combine. This found expression in each community's intermingling of the *jamaat* and modern capitalist institutions (such as the limited liability company and the bank); sustained intellectual defenses of profit seeking as a resolutely Islamic virtue; and an easy deployment of commercial terminology and advertisements in religious literature. A useful visual expression of corporate Islam can be found in a breakdown of a single *jamaat*'s asset portfolio (see figure I.3), which shows how the *jamaat* functioned as the fulcrum of a much larger institutional basket. The plethora of institutions underpinning corporate Islam were thus centered on the caste corporation while nonetheless remaining bound up with larger circuits of capital and the shifting benchmarks of Shiʿi and Sunni Islam. None of this meant that corporate Islam was a model of economic and religious life universally endorsed by members of the *jamaat*. Far from it; *jamaat* diktat and repression were frequently resisted by constituents who pointed to alternative methods of organizing individual and communal life on offer in the public sphere. The everyday reality of Bohra, Khoja, and Memon associations with noncommunity members posed a threat to the *jamaat* hierarchy's desire to make corporate Islam an entirely self-contained institutional complex.

Traditions of corporate Islam were easier to vindicate in an environment of indigenous political sterilization engendered by colonialism because the

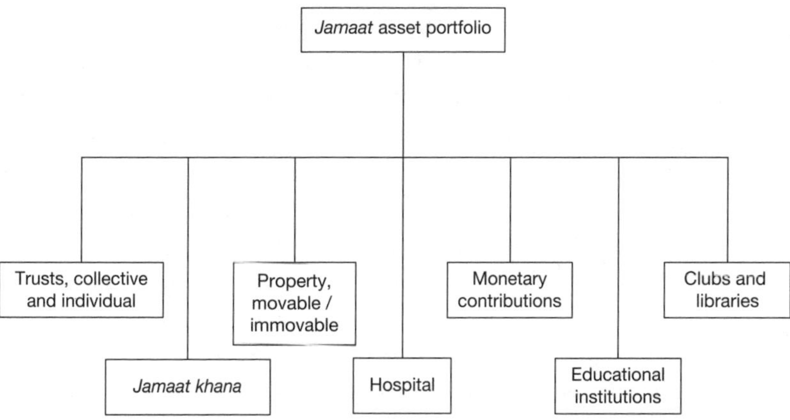

FIGURE I.3 A breakdown of the asset portfolio of a "typical" *jamaat* around the early twentieth century. Though an idealized depiction, it captures the diversity of institutions underneath the *jamaat* umbrella.

caste community—rather than the imagined political nation—was regarded as the highest good in the temporal world. And corporate Islam's capitalist credentials were easier to defend when statist, anti-capitalist economic ideologies were held in check. So long as the demands of Muslim mass nationalism were on a low simmer before the First World War, the self-contained qualities of corporate Islam were not controversial. Yet, with the rise of mass nationalism, traditions of corporate Islam had to be justified as never before. Now, the potential economic advantages accruing to the imaginary Muslim political nation—and not the corporate caste—became the standard for weighing the merits of Gujarati Muslim enterprise and corporate Islam more generally. With special force from the 1920s onward, the corporate Islam associated with the commercial castes faced the attempts of Muslim bureaucrats, socialists, and Islamists in late colonial and early postcolonial South Asia to dragoon the economic resources controlled by these communities and regulate what they perceived as un-Islamic oligopoly and overaccumulation.

In their bid to engineer widespread Muslim prosperity, many Muslim critics of the Gujarati Muslim commercial castes zeroed in on the *jamaats* as institutions simultaneously worthy of replicating and requiring administrative oversight by Muslim political organizations. These debates carried on well into the postcolonial period. By the 1970s, amid the general crises of the postcolonial state in Africa and Asia and the rise of petro-kingdoms in the Middle East, traditions of corporate Islam were eventually delegitimized as an archetype of Muslim capitalism with the rise of "Islamic economics," whose proponents espoused their own notions of what constituted authentic Muslim enterprise.

What follows, then, is a study of corporate Islam in the age of global empire and capitalism and the many intra-Muslim controversies ensuing from its consolidation. As argued throughout this book, corporate Islam was enabled by the Bohra, Khoja, and Memon attainment of middle power within the colonial order. Used here, *middle power* denotes the unique—although by no means exclusive—intermediate position these groups attained in the public sphere of British India and the British Empire in the Indian Ocean region, between white-only colonial authority and high society and the disenfranchised Indian masses. The term therefore encompasses the special position of Bohra, Khoja, and Memon capitalists as representatives of Indian communities—Muslim and non-Muslim—in several ports of the Indian Ocean.[47]

Middle power largely facilitated, but sometimes undercut, the outsized economic success of the Bohras, Khojas, and Memons across empires and their eventual transition into political activism in the early twentieth century. The material frameworks furnished by middle power in turn fostered the expansion of corporate Islam and its caste-centric—though not caste-exclusive—agendas of religious and commercial enterprise. The story told in these pages essentially concerns the making and breaking of corporate Islam, as enshrined in the *jamaats*, on the shifting terrain of Gujarati Muslim middle power.

The Internal Structure of the *Jamaats*

Before embarking upon that story, it is worth examining the internal structure of the *jamaats* in greater detail and then situating them in the larger scholarship on trading networks. Since the eighteenth century, the *jamaats* have functioned as arbiters for many aspects of the public and private lives of their members. Through the *jamaats* the Bohras, Khojas, and Memons have expanded their geographic reach, grown their commercial enterprises, and engaged with currents of global Islam. The *jamaats* are but one manifestation of a multitude of caste and religious corporations that have been a fixture of early modern and modern South Asian history.

An array of Muslim communities in South Asia have long embraced the practice of *jamaat-bandi*, the custom of organizing a caste in a *jamaat*.[48] *Jamaat-bandi* is also observable among non-Muslim groups like the Parsis, an indication of the institutional continuities across Greater Gujarat that both transcend and reinforce caste difference. But the *jamaats* of the three leading Gujarati Muslim commercial castes are distinct not because of their links to kinship or caste as such. Instead they are distinct because they fused precolonial and colonial-era features of caste governance, were adept at re-creating themselves across borders, attained substantial infrastructural capacities, and centralized the comparative wealth of their members in a collective forum.

In terms of their barebones administrative structure, the *jamaats* are similar in the Bohra, Khoja, and Memon communities. Yet over the past two centuries the *jamaats* of each group steadily acquired distinctive features due to patterns of migration, interactions with political power, disparate models of religious authority, and local conditions. As subsequent chapters will reconstruct, these differences became only more magnified over the course of the nineteenth and twentieth centuries as each community's *jamaats* interacted with shifting political and religious economies. To be sure, there were some continuities irrespective of time and place. For one, *jamaat* membership was everywhere regulated by birth and determined key aspects of an individual's life from cradle to grave: where one lived, how one was educated, where one prayed, whom one married, what religious taxes one paid, how one bequeathed wealth, and where one was buried. It need hardly be said that given the diasporic breadth of these communities, the magnitude of *jamaat* authority in an individual life varied based on gender, class, age, and geographic factors.

Like all corporations, *jamaats* are not consentient institutions. To momentarily take the example of the business corporation, there are recurring tensions among ownership, management, and shareholders. Hostile takeovers, mergers, sell-offs, and employee transfers are common. Similar processes occurred at regular intervals in the *jamaats*, but there is also an often-missed paradox at the heart of the *jamaats*. Jean-Claude Penrad, a scholar of the Ismaili Khoja diaspora in East Africa, has explained this paradox well, arguing that the *jamaats*' prosperity "appears as the expression of an ambiguous social behaviour. On the one hand, competition opposed individuals and interest groups of the same *jamaat*, while on the other, the Ismaili network was maintained, reinforced, and regularly valorized."[49]

This quote apprehends the central tension running through these institutions: although comprised of actors intent on individual commercial profit and committed to divergent religious programs, the *jamaats* acquired a robust, collective institutional identity. According to Anas Malik, writing on Memon *jamaats* in Pakistan, the *jamaat* furnishes "the social capital and the information needed to smooth and enable transactions; these in turn facilitate the growth and persistence of collective choice entities."[50] Instead of withering away or morphing into open-source institutions, Bohra, Khoja, and Memon *jamaats* have displayed more pronounced particularism over time. Considerations of distinct *jamaat* lineage maintain their grip on the imagination, working to distinguish groups in diverse demographic settings.[51] As such, each community has witnessed the growth of caste-specific institutions, such as schools, hospitals, funds, trusts, and real estate associations, which steadily differentiated it from neighboring communities, even as its constituents interacted with multiple noncommunity members in a range of other forums. That dialectic is one with which this book grapples at length.

For all this aspiration to work only for the community, the *jamaats* have been part and parcel of intra-Muslim religious competition and mass politics in South Asia for the past two centuries. As recent work on the "religious economy" of global Islam has shown, the *jamaats* were one of many religious "firms" competing for market share among the faithful and generating ever-new forms of socially concrete Islam.[52] And even if the Bohras, Khojas, and Memons were mostly not proselytizing communities, their *jamaats* do confirm the link that scholars of religious economy have theorized between the profusion of rival Muslim firms and business diversification.[53] Moreover, since *jamaats* fashion themselves as one-stop shops for the articulation and inculcation of specific brands of religious identity, they are ideal settings for studying both the consumer and producer sides of religious economy.

Even so, middle power, by raising the Bohras, Khojas, and Memons to such public prominence, guaranteed that the Islam of the *jamaats* was no monolith but was pushed and pulled in varying directions. For all the historiographical emphasis on the Bohras, Khojas, and Memons as closed communities, intellectual boundaries were porous. Undoubtedly, boundary maintenance was upheld, especially in cases of *jamaat* membership and marriage. But the quotidian realities of social interaction and textual circulation guaranteed cross-pollination and comparison. Consequently, it is best to think of the intra-Muslim exchanges that the Bohras, Khojas, and Memons participated in as instantiations of "familiar juxtaposition," to borrow a phrase from the late historian Tony Judt.[54] Familiar juxtaposition is a concept that captures the particularities of Bohra, Khoja, and Memon legal histories while also acknowledging the prevalence of exchanges that violated the boundaries of the *jamaats*. Scholars of Islamic law are accustomed to juxtapositions—Islamic versus human rights law, Islamic versus colonial law, and Islamic versus Jewish law, to name a few. What perhaps is still largely unpursued, and highly relevant to these communities, is an appreciation of how disparate forms of Islamic law interacted in the *jamaats*, corporate institutions that bridged the state and scholarly divide. That ever-growing complex of legal pluralism is integral to the paradigm of corporate Islam examined in this book.

A conception of the *jamaats* as corporations does not negate a view of them as assemblies of individuals, each of whom pursued their own self-interest and frequently contested *jamaat* dictum in matters of religious interpretation. The empirical record is replete with instances in which individuals resented and resisted the "long arm of the *jamaat*." Yet because the *jamaats*' reach was so extensive, and their authority consistently upheld by the colonial courts, they were an unavoidable touchstone, as merchant magnates, destitute women seeking divorce, and many others caste members discovered. Constituents wishing to emancipate themselves from the *jamaats* found the process onerous, expensive, and sometimes dangerous. Only those who could rely on other corporate forms of association or bring a faction of the *jamaat* along in their dissent were able to cut ties.

Another consistent feature was the lack of a clear *jamaat* center within the Bohra, Khoja, and Memon diasporas. True, Bombay became a general headquarters of sorts for all three communities by the later nineteenth century, but the prominence of Bohra, Khoja, and Memon *jamaats* in that metropolis stemmed primarily from the city's economic importance. While the Bohra *dais* (chief clerics) and the Agha Khans eventually took up residence in Bombay, cementing the city's primacy in their respective communities, these figures were remarkably itinerant and regularly visited *jamaats* in the diaspora. In other words, while the interplay among *jamaats* depended on the hierarchies of religious authority in each group, they were always simultaneously local and transregional organizations. No single Bohra, Khoja, or Memon *jamaat* held a monopoly over the other *jamaats* in the community, whether in terms of wealth or interpretation of religious law and caste custom.

Even within a single group the connection of one *jamaat* to another was perpetually being worked out.

Though the Bohras, Khojas, and Memons share the *jamaat* in common, and the questions of corporate governance animating all three communities have a remarkable continuity, this does not mean that the *jamaat* is a monochromatic institution in outline. Disparate geographic, demographic, and religious factors within each community ensure it is not. Even to speak of the Bohra *jamaat*, the Khoja *jamaat*, or the Memon *jamaat* as undifferentiated units is a stretch. When they are spoken of in the singular it can only ever be understood as a discursive fiction. In truth, a choice must be made between when it is suitable to talk of *jamaats* in the plural and when to use the singular *jamaat*. This singular / plural dilemma is compounded by the fact that there was considerable ambiguity over whether the *jamaats* were connected by a hierarchical relationship—with the Bombay *jamaat* serving as the nominal head in each case from around 1900 onward—or whether they were a host of tiny republics staffed by community elders (invariably merchants) and connected to a macroscale diaspora by ties of kinship and religious authority.

The approach taken here is that only the plural form best captures how *jamaats* were simultaneously local and transregional entities. The singular form is used in this book to refer either to individual *jamaats* or to the fiction of a single united *jamaat*. This is not to say that the *jamaats* were not integrated to some degree. As seen throughout this book, conflict in the Khoja *jamaat* in Muttrah (a suburb of Muscat) had reverberations in Khoja *jamaats* in Bombay and Zanzibar; events in a Memon *jamaat* in Calcutta or Rangoon had echoes in Bombay or Karachi; a Bohra legal compendium commissioned by the Dhoraji *jamaat* served as precedent for disputes in other Bohra *jamaats* throughout the diaspora. To appreciate this, one must preserve the tensions endemic to each *jamaat:* those between the individual constituent and the *jamaat;* among *jamaats* of the same community; among the *jamaats* and other corporate entities, Muslim and non-Muslim; and between the *jamaats* and state authorities, colonial and postcolonial.

Though all members of an individual community were considered bound by local *jamaat* rules, the actual decision-making powers of the *jamaats* were the prerogative of the all-male *sethias* (caste leaders; singular *sethia* or *seth*), the wealthiest members of the community (see figure I.4). The *sethias'* ascent from the eighteenth century onward owed in large measure to their

FIGURE I.4 An early twentieth-century photograph of the Agha Khan III seated with the leaders of Karachi's Ismaili Khoja *Jamaat*. The figures surrounding the imam are leading merchants, bureaucrats, and religious scholars, with the portfolios of each likely combining aspects of all three. Reproduced from Ali Muhammad Jan Muhammad Chunara, *Nūram mubīna: Athava Allāhanī pavitrā rassī*, 3rd ed. (Bombay: n.p. [Khoja Sindhi Printing Press], 1951), unnumbered page adjacent to 480.

prominence in the world of regional and global capitalism. Wealth built up through commercial activity likely encouraged *sethias* to vest their fortunes in a single corporate institution, presumably to protect their wealth from arbitrary exaction from state authorities and to ensure its swift intergenerational transfer within families and the caste. Beginning in the late eighteenth century this conglomeration of capital and rights was enshrined in law with the colonial and Princely States' recognition of the *jamaats* as entities possessed of explicit corporate rights.

These *sethias* presided over a committee within the *jamaat* (see figure I.3), whose procedures became more formalized over the decades covered in this book. This committee adjudicated all manner of disputes within the community, from those concerning marriage to property and caste membership. Its rulings did not abide by any formal legal statutes but tended to rely on community custom as a guide to decision-making. It has been argued that the *jamaat* council tended to uphold strict formulations of custom in cases involving inheritance and succession, which over time became binding precedent.[55] It is perhaps more accurate to say that customary options were multiform, shifting within broadly defined parameters and not overly beholden to *jamaat* fiat. The endless controversies within Bohra, Khoja, and Memon *jamaats*, especially after 1850, over what constituted authentic *jamaat* custom—to say nothing of fluctuating ideas of Islamic law—lends credence to this assertion.

Private wealth accumulated by *sethias* and more humble community members was customarily folded back into the *jamaats*, making these institutions both springboards for and beneficiaries of commercial activity. Moreover, collating the capital of their constituents, and partible into independent "franchises," the *jamaats* were as much the entry point into the wider economic world as the point of return. They did not, however, always provide direct economic advantages to their members. Ample evidence suggests that *jamaats* acted as curbs on certain kinds of commercial activity by encouraging explicit mercantile norms and business lines to the exclusion of others, such as interest banking. While the efficiency gains offered by the *jamaats* were multiple, an account of those advantages must be balanced by attention to second-order problems, such as group think, legal ambiguities and rivalries among and within *jamaats*, which mitigated the nominal commercial benefits that they supplied to members. Scrutinizing these second-order problems acts as an antidote to an overemphasis on success in South Asian business history.

As many episodes recounted in this book illustrate, the *jamaats*' role as havens of private and public property generated irresolvable tensions among individual members. Before the nineteenth century, notions of private property in South Asia were vested in corporate groups rather than individuals. This ensured that access to property and the rules pertaining to its alienation, bequest, and inheritance remained unequal and restricted.[56] Problems of individual access became a wellspring of controversy across the nineteenth and twentieth centuries, perhaps none more so than the question of women's access to family and caste property. In the case of the Gujarati Muslim commercial castes, the intractable issues of access and individual rights regularly required both desired and undesired intervention of institutions beyond the *jamaat*, not least the colonial courts. Likewise, access to *jamaat* property by those outside the caste became a highly charged issue in the early twentieth century. From then on, struggles over *jamaat* property intermingled with entrenched disputes over the character of the *jamaats* as corporations comprised of Muslims with community-specific views of Islamic law, custom, and doctrine that were seemingly incommensurate with most other Muslims.

Alongside property, few issues were more divisive in the *jamaats* than questions of community law and custom. In the domain of colonial law and Muslim learned opinion, there was a lasting (mis)perception of *legal exceptionalism* among colonial officials and Indian Muslim learned opinion around the Bohra, Khoja, and Memon *jamaats.* The basis of legal exceptionalism was the conviction that the commercial castes were aberrant among Indian Muslims in possessing Hindu customary laws governing inheritance and succession. In actuality, Indian Muslims adhered to a plurality of inheritance and succession regimes, but the Bohras, Khojas, and Memons were among the few to have their practices recognized by the colonial courts as binding customary law. Colonial actors regarded these as anomalous practices when viewed in the light of the textualist interpretations of Islamic inheritance and succession laws the colonial state applied to most of its Muslim subjects. In time, many other Muslims agreed with this assessment and sought to snuff out Bohra, Khoja, and Memon legal exceptionalism.

Though "colonial knowledge" concerning Hinduism and Islam was more variegated and sophisticated than previously supposed by a generation of scholarship, religious binaries possessed great staying power in colonial discourse across time.[57] And in that binary the inheritance practices of these communities conformed more to the joint family rules common among Hindus than to the complex partible inheritance regimes ordained in the Islamic foundational sources. From the 1840s onward these customs gained the force of binding precedent in the colonial legal system, even if inside the *jamaats* a range of practices were visible. The yoke of precedent ensured that the purported disconnect between such Hindu customs and the otherwise Muslim identity of the Bohras, Khojas, and Memons puzzled colonial officials and Muslim commentators alike until the end of empire.

This legal exceptionalism whereby *caste custom* held precedence over *religious law* is portrayed by economic historians as conveying universal economic advantage to the Bohras, Khojas, and Memons.[58] By this reasoning, these communities were better able to perpetuate their businesses across generations because assets were kept in a joint family (as ordained by Anglo-Hindu law) rather than being dispersed among a legion of heirs (as ordained by Anglo-Muhammadan law). There is an undeniable logic to this argument:

one heir consolidates wealth better than multiple heirs. And it may go towards explaining the unfortunate economic circumstances of some South Asian Muslim communities. Even so, it does not conform to the actual experience of the Gujarati Muslim commercial castes. For one, customary practices pertaining to inheritance were not uniform across all three groups, let alone within each group. There was a spectrum of practices—some resembling ideal Hindu arrangements, others Islamic archetypes—from which it is impossible to deduce positive or negative economic outcomes. To give just one example, a Kachchhi Memon *jamaat* in Bombay followed one formula, while one in Calcutta subscribed to another formula.[59] And the Halai Memon *jamaats* followed a discrete formula from those of their Kachchhi Memon brethren. These subcaste and regional differences must be preserved, revealing as they are of disparate histories within castes, to say nothing of differences among them.

Rather than acting as a guardian of communal autonomy, all too frequently legal exceptionalism invited colonial interference in the *jamaats*. The linkages between the *jamaats* and the colonial courts were in fact so profound that the former may even be called *amici curiarum* (friends of the courts). Arguably, this intimacy produced unwanted secondary economic effects that are difficult to detect when institutions are measured merely by their efficiency. For example, consider the fact that the colonial government—not the Khoja *jamaats*—possessed ultimate powers of escheat when a Khoja man died without heirs, or when a Khoja widow passed away with no surviving relatives on her late husband's side (she already did not have the right to bequeath property to her own relatives because of *jamaat* custom).[60] Legal exceptionalism thus frequently threatened to take wealth and agency away from the *jamaats*.

Ultimately, legal exceptionalism—or any narrative rooted in institutional primordialism, for that matter—is unsustainable as an explanation for the commercial success of these groups. And it can only suffice as an account of their legal history if colonial sources are utilized to the exclusion of community materials. In truth, the colonial legal system was only the uppermost stratum of the legal worlds inhabited by the Gujarati Muslim commercial castes, a place of last resort. Once *jamaat* sources are incorporated it becomes clear that there was endless friction over custom, law, and property beneath the level of the colonial courts. And as *jamaat* councils attempted to exert their authority, individual members repeatedly contested their interpretations. Consequently, ever-more-unmanageable legal pluralism, not uniform legal exceptionalism across castes, is a truer description of the history of these groups in the period surveyed in this book. These qualifications aside, the *perception* rather than the *reality* of legal exceptionalism remained a fixture of colonial and Muslim conceptions of the Bohras, Khojas, and Memons and colored the profile of corporate Islam and middle power alike.

The *Jamaats* and the Scholarship on Network Institutions

One historian has argued that economic history must be studied at three angles: semantics, institutions, and practices.[61] The *jamaats* easily fulfill these three criteria as they have a discursive persona, an institutional core, and actors whose activities are relatively well-documented by the standards of South Asian economic history. In a wider sense, by blending collective and individual perspectives, the framework of corporate Islam speaks to historical puzzles that have preoccupied scholars of networks and diasporas in recent decades. It is essential, nonetheless, to differentiate them from better-known historiographical examples. Like Sephardic Jews of the early modern period, but unlike the New Julfan Armenians or Sindhi traders, the Gujarati Muslim commercial castes inhabited multinodal polycentric networks.[62] In several respects, the most useful points of comparison are contemporary Indian merchant networks, such as the Chettiars, the Marwaris, and the Shikarpuris / Sindworkies. Along with these communities, caste was a central aspect of the mercantile networks of the Bohras, Khojas, and Memons. But caste was regularly transcended, and a variety of institutional forms—religious institutions, family firms, partnerships, joint-stock companies—made up the Gujarati Muslim entrepreneurial basket.[63] Only sparse evidence exists of clustering around individual business lines and professions, as some have argued was the case with the Chettiars in banking.[64]

Perhaps the most useful contrast with the Gujarati Muslim commercial castes are the Shikarpuris and Sindworkies studied by Claude Markovits. While the Shikarpuris had no caste associations (panchayats) in their global diaspora other than in Central Asia, the Sindworkies lacked corporate caste institutions entirely.[65] By contrast, the *jamaats* expanded in lockstep with their individual diasporas and functioned as anchors of community life and enterprise, save an odd location here and there. Arguably, this feature of the Gujarati Muslim experience owed to the greater emphasis within the *jamaats* on an exclusive religious and caste identity, which was not replicated in the cases of the Shikarpuris and Sindworkies. What is more, while the Sindhi communities studied by Markovits relied on a division of labor between the subordinate agent (*gumashta*) circulating across the globe and the stationary capitalist (*shah*) resident in Sindh, this appears to be a less common feature of Gujarati Muslim enterprise. Instead, Gujarati Muslim capitalists themselves circulated throughout their *jamaat* networks, regularly visiting India for brief stints before returning to more familiar haunts in Aden, Mombasa, Rangoon, or Hong Kong.

Because the *jamaats* espoused exclusivist religious identities it is also instructive to compare them to other religious networks. Like the early modern Jesuits, religious affiliation and group identity served as boundary mechanisms for Bohra, Khoja, and Memon networks. Still, there was no Jesuit-style central, bureaucratized "government" to knit the community's fissiparous religious life together in a single apparatus.[66] Similarly, in contrast to the Jesuits, who engaged in proselytization at the global level,[67] religious works, pilgrimage infrastructures, and community trusts created by members of the *jamaats* were intended exclusively for caste members. And while early modern networks of various kinds possessed a range of governance mechanisms and communitarian organizations,[68] arguably none matched the *jamaats'* abilities to formally regulate the commercial and religious behavior of their members. This power stemmed from the stronger infrastructural capacities of the *jamaats*, which had recourse to the mechanisms of law, steam, and print integral to nineteenth-century globalization and empire.

That greater coercive capacity necessarily entailed regular conflict within individual *jamaats* and among *jamaats*. Given this persistence of conflict, they should be framed as institutions that emerged as "the outcome of conflict over the distribution of resources" rather than as primordial outgrowths of unchanging caste society. This accent on the "distributional" character of institutions, first elaborated by a historian of European guilds, corrects the tendency of the new institutional economics to see institutions as merely "efficient solutions to economic problems."[69] The problem with the efficiency argument is that it sees institutions largely as obstructions, rather than as enablers, of economic activity.[70] Undoubtedly, *jamaats* were viable arbiters of commercial life, but they can hardly be described as efficient. The distributional approach permits historians to take stock of the *jamaats'* other functions as lobbyists, cartels, creditors, disciplinarians, and organizations espousing a monopoly of religious interpretation.

The accent on conflict also renders conspicuous the actions of individuals within the *jamaats*, transforming them into three-dimensional actors rather than automatons overdetermined by their network position. It thus offers a solution to reductive interpretations whereby an actor's position within a social network determines their identity.[71] It is therefore not enough to say that the Bohras, Khojas, and Memons were simply "Muslim minorities" or "trading castes," as if those identities were unchanging and constant in the epoch studied in this book. As conglomerates of individuals that constantly negotiated their position in relation to other public institutions, the *jamaats* were, to borrow the inimitable words of scholar of networks Paul McLean, not "automatic trigger[s] for subsequent action" but "congested, and therefore potentially fecund, arenas of persuasive social interaction."[72] Conceiving of *jamaats* as archives of manifold social interactions disrupts both rational-choice theories, which obscure the communitarian context of individual action and fail to account for diverse historical subjectivities, and culturalist interpretations, which rely on essentialist tropes about culture (in the case of these groups, Islam and caste) to explain personal and collective behavior.

That there were caste-specific histories of capital and religion does not mean that there were distinct Bohra, Khoja, or Memon capitalisms separate from other Indian communities.[73] Just the same, to frame the Bohras, Khojas, and Memons as capitalists who just happened to be Muslim, or as purveyors of a cosmopolitan, transreligious Gujarati commercial culture, however well meaning, is to completely miss the plot.[74] In following that line of argument, one is left with a flattened picture of economic life that ignores conflict, divergence, and specificity in its desire to find shared moral economies that cut across religion and caste.[75] Though interactions across caste were legion, in their individual histories the Bohras, Khojas, and Memons turned out to be as different from one another as they were from non-Muslim Gujarati "cognate" groups like the Bhatias, Jains, Lohanas, and Parsis. At the risk of putting too fine a point on it, cognate communities often turned out to be false cognates. The historian's challenge is to attend to group-level distinctions rather than to dissolve all particularities into the monolith of the Gujarati "trading caste."

The emphasis on a singular Gujarati commercial culture also sidesteps a promising historiographical opportunity, for in their fusion of distinct iterations of Islamic interpretive community and capitalist enterprise, the Bohras, Khojas, and Memons contradict a persistent historiographical narrative wherein Islam and modern capitalism are deemed antithetical to one another. Many studies of varying methodological and ideological convictions have attributed Muslims' failure to adapt to modern capitalism to both institutional and intellectual restraints endemic to the Islamic tradition writ large. Institutionally, Islamic law is said to have fostered a commercial environment characterized by static rules governing commercial partnerships, the absence of corporations, the tying up of capital in inalienable pious endowments (*waqf, awqāf*), and the stillbirth of banking.[76] All of these institutional fetters are said to have militated against the advent of capitalism among Muslim populations. Intellectually, Muslim resistance to capitalism is most often attributed to a moral aversion to profit, a suspicion of the commodity form intrinsic to modern capitalism, and a long decline in Islamic intellectual thought that rendered Muslims averse to institutional reforms necessary to compete in modern markets.[77]

The Bohras, Khojas, and Memons do not fit easily into these narratives about Islam and capitalism. For one, they utilized many of the same institutions said to have obstructed Muslims' embrace of capitalism. Intellectual restraints, meanwhile, are a more complicated issue. True, there was the occasional grumble in these communities about excessive consumption and unholy profits, but overall, the Bohras, Khojas, and Memons fully assimilated commercial terminology into their religious discourses, and the pursuit of mercantile profits was seen as nothing less than an Islamic virtue. This reality challenges previous attempts to explain Bohra, Khoja, and Memon commercial success on the basis that they were exceptions to some general Muslim standard of economic lethargy or as beneficiaries of colonial / Western institutions—that is, as closet Hindus or comprador collaborators. To be sure, recent scholarship has focused on how Muslim communities have reconciled themselves to capitalist norms over the past half century or so. Illuminating though these studies are, they often assume that Muslims have no place in histories of capitalism until the last decades of the twentieth century.[78]

A more compelling framing of the history of the Gujarati Muslim commercial castes is not one that pits Islam and capitalism against one another but rather one that foregrounds the largely untold story of intra-Muslim economic divergences in South Asia and other Islamicate contexts. This dimension has been lost in recent scholarship tracing correlations between religious affiliation and economic outcomes in contemporary India. Although this literature sheds important light on the persistence of inequality in India, it pays little heed to differences within religious groups, Muslim or otherwise.[79] To be sure, the histories of the Bohras, Khojas, and Memons do not repudiate narratives of Islamic institutional shortcomings in the round. While economic historians have debated the role of Islamic institutions as contributing factors to Muslim economic diminution over the past three centuries, it is hardly appreciated that many of these concerns were first voiced in the later nineteenth century as a Muslim self-critique.

In fact, Bohra, Khoja, and Memon commentators were among those Muslims who most readily recognized the disadvantages of certain institutional arrangements rooted in the Islamic tradition, especially those stemming from inalienable pious endowments (*waqf, awqāf*). With that said, the regular leveraging of *awqāf* capital for business ventures gives pause to assertions of economic historians that *awqāf* singularly obstructed the flow of credit. However, these practices and the disproportionate wealth acquired by these communities attracted condemnation from a plethora of other Muslim commentators, Abd al-Reşid Ibrahim among them.[80] Attention to these and other aspects of Gujarati Muslim enterprise ensured that the commercial castes have served as a sounding board for other Muslims to debate the reconcilability of capitalist and Islamic institutions. In these discourses the Bohras, Khojas, and Memons figured prominently as archetypes of what was alternatively commendable or reprehensible in the figure of the Muslim capitalist. The analytical category of corporate Islam used in this book is a way of integrating these disparate motifs of intra-Muslim inequality, institutional reform, and autocritique into a larger story of economic and religious enterprise.

The narrative constructed here is thus not a triumphalist one. Rather it takes full stock of how Bohra, Khoja, and Memon commercial efflorescence both challenged and affirmed the viability of Islamic institutions in the context of modern capitalist enterprise. At the same time, the collective saga of these groups also reveals much about the distinct *disadvantages* of colonial subordination and affiliation, factors which commentators have often suggested are the reason for Gujarati Muslim business success. True, colonial power fostered infrastructures of mobility, arbitration, and contracting which benefited all three groups. But intimacies with the colonial state also brought about a magnitude of colonial interventionism in community affairs that was rare among Indian communities. In the final account, however, the economic lifeworlds of the Gujarati Muslim commercial castes were fashioned not by an either / or dichotomy of Islamic versus Western institutions but by an alloy of both. Having said that, the geographic scope of Gujarati Muslim lifeworlds were sharply circumscribed by the constraints of racial prejudice and capital asymmetries intrinsic to Indian enterprise in the colonial era. Corporate Islam was thus never a global brand.

Sources

"You are an expert in the discipline of history, if you inform yourself of their condition, you could put it down in writing and educate the seekers of truth."[81] With these words, the friends of the historian Muhammad Abbas Rafaat Shirvani, writing in the Princely State of Bhopal in 1870, coaxed him into writing a history of the Daudi Bohras. While many recognized that Bohras lived in several provinces of India, Shirvani acknowledged, hardly anything was known of them. Were they from the Arab lands, or Iran, Turkistan, or perhaps even Afghanistan? What was their sect? In the end, Shirvani was only able to answer a subset of these questions. He relied largely on the medieval historiographical tradition concerning the Ismailis, as well as the odd contemporary observation of Bohra life. Diatribe became his key stratagem to fill in the gaps.

In his reflection on sources, Shirvani exhibited a frustration echoed by many other European and Indian Muslim authors of the nineteenth and twentieth centuries, who attempted to situate the Bohras, Khojas, and Memons in Indian and Islamic history. Writing in Persian, Gujarati, and Urdu, their labors were perpetually frustrated by the dearth of available materials, and up-to-date data were typically limited to hearsay and the odd encounter. Memory became an abundant source of polemic, especially regarding issues of lineage and conversion. Of course, historiographic advances in the study of these communities have progressed substantially since Shirvani's day, but several quandaries that he faced continue to confront the historian: What are their origins? How far did their diaspora extend? What is their relationship to Islamic discursive traditions? Did they live separately from other Muslims? How had they amassed such wealth?

Definitive answers to these questions remain elusive given the paucity of eighteenth- and nineteenth-century textual sources related to the Bohras,

Khojas, and Memons. Unfortunately, much remains opaque about their individual histories, especially in the period from around 1750 to 1900. The available source material is an amorphous, disconnected literature produced in a range of languages including Arabic, Gujarati, Ottoman Turkish, Persian, and Urdu. These sources accent the historical specificities of each community and reveal the various ways in which caste, colonial power, Islamic religious authority, and capitalism have interacted in the modern period. This book builds its narrative principally from these sources while also relying on the colonial archive. Overreliance on either community or colonial sources runs the risk of seeing these communities as walled off from those around them. Thus, to tell the full story of the *jamaats* both vantage points must be reconciled. But a third bucket of sources, those composed by a litany of other Muslim and non-Muslim actors about these communities, must also be integrated to attenuate the biases of colonial and community records.

This book is no different from previous histories of South Asian merchant communities in that it must confess to the insuperable limitations of its source material. Although an extensive effort has been made to construct a source base in multiple languages, there are still basic questions of Bohra, Khoja, and Memon corporate life that can only be guessed at. This applies with special force to their economic activities. For that reason, this book makes the case for the use of *paraeconomic* sources—religious treatises, hagiographies, travelogues, and statute books—in the writing of South Asian economic history. As the sources themselves testify, to divide economic from religious concerns is to do a great disservice to the lifeworlds of these three communities. One cannot tell the story of corporate Islam without them.

While these sources may not be explicitly "economic" in content, they contain information on the internal dynamics of the Bohras, Khojas, and Memons not found anywhere else. Unfortunately, except for the odd account book, they largely do not allow for the writing of traditional quantitative economic history (which, anyway, is only one way of writing economic histories). Rather, these sources are compilations of anecdotes that sometimes must be read diagonally. But once gathered, they summon a novel qualitative account of the dramatic effects wealth accumulation and distributional conflicts had in the constitution of corporate Islam and Gujarati Muslim middle power.

* * *

This book tells the story of corporate Islam, and the middle power that made its emergence possible, in two parts. Part I, covering the years 1800–1914, examines its emergence in the conditions of post-Mughal political polycentrism, its consolidation in the colonial legal system from the mid-nineteenth century onward, and its expansion in the context of prewar economic globalization and imperial conquest. Beginning in Western India, the narrative moves freely across borders, to East Africa, the Hijaz, and the South China Sea, while continually returning to India. These chapters aim to tell the histories of all three communities in equal proportion, making note of commonalities and contrasts among them. Only by disaggregating these communities can one appreciate the diverse forms that corporate Islam has assumed.

Part II argues that the remaking of the interwar and wartime colonial order precipitated a crisis in the models of corporate Islam espoused by the Bohras, Khojas, and Memons. Between 1914 and 1947, the rise of mass Indian nationalism in South Asia and other parts of the British Empire and the concomitant politicization of Muslim business placed unique strains on the efforts of the Bohras, Khojas, and Memons to preserve the integrity of their *jamaats*. Pushed as never before between the competing designs of the colonial state and the nationalists, the middle power acquired by these groups in the early colonial era was also subjected to intense pressures. With the advent of the postcolonial order in Africa and Asia the privileges that underwrote middle power were no longer sustainable. Already by the 1920s, the commercial castes' prominent position in the colonial order had damaged the reputation of these groups in the eyes of some Indian nationalists. And with the dawn of decolonization, the special rights bestowed upon these groups by the colonial government were anathema to the programs of political equality and economic leveling preached by postcolonial nationalists of various stripes from Nairobi to Rangoon.

While navigating these novel economic and political conditions, the *jamaats* of the Gujarati Muslim commercial castes also grappled with Indian Muslim political organizations endeavoring to subordinate the panoply of private and caste-level Muslim institutions under an all-India administrative umbrella. The organizers of these efforts believed that stifling private or caste-level institutions was a necessary prerequisite for attaining state power denied to Indian Muslims by colonial rule. In the process, Indian Muslim activists articulated their own statist-economic models of Islam, in which capitalist enterprise was judged—and found wanting—by the standards of the Islamic tradition and contemporary Muslim economic realities. In this vision, Islam was a socioeconomic system in its own right, a viable alternative to capitalism and communism alike.

Chapter 8, encompassing the years 1947 to 1975, tracks the fate of corporate Islam in the burgeoning African and Asian nation-states of the postcolonial order. Initially, Bohra, Khoja, and Memon institutions struggled to acclimatize themselves to the new realities of the postcolonial world. In time they were able to capitalize on the new economic and religious opportunities that decolonization presented. But, between 1965 and 1975, self-professedly socialist states from East Africa to the Middle East and Southeast Asia exacted a wave of violence against the Gujarati Muslim commercial castes and their property. These attacks temporarily prorogued the venerable frameworks of corporate Islam. In Pakistan they cleared the ground for the institutionalization of an "Islamic economy" that departed in important ways from the capitalist ethics that had justified the commercial pursuits of the Bohras, Khojas, and Memons.

Yet despite the attacks on the Bohras, Khojas, and Memons in the late 1960s and early 1970s, their diasporas only became increasingly more global in the ensuing five decades. Ironically, they have attained a prominent foothold in both the former imperial metropole and the white settler colonies of the British Empire, where discrimination once barred them from entry. The unprecedented size of their diasporas, however, invites a return to that moment in the late eighteenth century when their histories as corporate entities first became decipherable. It was then, in the interstices of Mughal and colonial hegemony, that the *jamaats* came into their own as religious and commercial institutions possessed of middle power.

PART I

BETWEEN 1800 AND 1914 THE IDENTITIES OF THE GUJARATI Muslim commercial castes were never pinned down to the point of unwrinkled precision, either inside or outside the *jamaats*. The chief conundrum that colonial officials, other Muslims, and even the castes themselves faced was where the Bohras, Khojas, and Memons stood in relation to other Muslim subjects in colonial India. What kind of Muslims were they, exactly? Should they be governed by the same Anglo-Muhammadan law applied to nearly all other Indian Muslims, or were they exceptions to it? Was their wealth a consequence of those latent Hindu customary practices that not only distinguished them from the supposedly indolent Muslim masses but that also gained official legal recognition from the colonial state? Were the *jamaats* merely bastions of casteism or entities whose largesse could be shared with those outside the community? Who possessed proprietary title over *jamaat* property—the collective, the individual constituent, or the religious cleric? Divisive answers were offered to all these questions, both inside and outside the *jamaats*.

The answers were all the more divisive because of the wealth filtering into the community by means of private capitalist enterprise. Rather than simply mobilizing their supposed immemorial caste identity as traders, the Gujarati Muslim commercial castes acquired expansive economic portfolios over the century covered in Part I, despite the structural shocks to regional economies brought about by the colonial conquest and the advent of a highly unequal, industrialized global economy. A precocious, if fragile, wealth gave them leverage against state authorities in a mercurial political environment. At first, the links to colonial and native states that middle power made possible functioned as an asset, theoretically giving these communities greater leverage than that of most Indian Muslims over their internal affairs. In short order, however, these links to colonial authority in particular became a liability that deprived the Gujarati Muslim commercial castes of substantial communal autonomy.

As the logics of the colonial system crystallized in the last quarter of the nineteenth century, middle power became a structural vise that increasingly determined the parameters of Gujarati Muslim economic and political agency within this system. The contractual nature of middle power compelled these groups to serve as underwriters of colonial conquest in various parts of Africa and Asia. To a large extent, it made their material progress incumbent on colonial good graces. Despite the benefits of middle power, these communities—by virtue of their racialized position in the colonial order—ultimately faced insuperable structural asymmetries compared with European capitalists and white subjects of the British Empire. Middle power was only ever that: middling.

In parallel to this story of interaction with state authorities, the *jamaats* of these three communities served as crucibles for the elaboration of diverse forms of Sunni and Shiʿi law, aided by a general colonial liberal noninterventionism in religious affairs. Here the *jamaats* took center stage by adjudicating disputes, enforcing legal decisions, debating the legitimacy of custom, maintaining caste boundaries, and bridging the realms of colonial law and Islamic jurisprudence. In place of narratives of legal exceptionalism, chapter 1 constructs an alternative narrative of ever-more-unmanageable Gujarati Muslim legal pluralism. If from the vantage point of the colonial courts the Gujarati Muslim commercial castes were reduced to Hindus in all but name, that image falls apart upon inspection of the litany of sources—in Arabic, Gujarati, Ottoman Turkish, Persian, and Urdu—they produced. These relate that the *jamaats* operated as intermediary, corporate institutions straddling the realms of colonial law and the jurisprudential worlds of Islamic scholars. The resulting legal formulas they arrived at were multiplex, differing from one *jamaat* to the next. Their engagement with Islamic law was neither instrumental nor imitative, but constantly modulated by the shifting yardsticks of law and custom as variably determined by the caste corporation, the colonial civic order, and intellectual shifts in Islamic thought.

The Making of Gujarati Muslim Middle Power

Circa 1800–1850

IN 1890 THE BOHRA *dai al-mutlaq* (chief cleric of the sect), Sayyidna Hussain Hussam al-Din, published a series of Arabic verses dedicated to Queen Victoria on the occasion of the visit of her grandson, Prince Albert Victor, to India. These verses were then translated into English and printed in Bombay along with a short treatise on the history of the Bohra *dais*. Praising Victoria in his preface as a ruler worthy of the title Defender of the Faith, the *dai* proceeded in his verses to contrast Victoria's enlightened rule with India's chaotic past: "(Formerly) the countries of India were wild forests, (where) you would find one party fighting with another continually out of malice. Properties were robbed, souls were killed (in so much so) that on account of the prevailing anarchy this nation was threatened with destruction."[1] In drawing a sharp contrast between British justice and Indian tyranny, these lines rehearsed one of the favorite Victorian justifications of empire in India.

Leaving aside the selective memory of the panegyric, the text's true utility is found in the history appended to the eulogy, which elaborated on the Bohras' erratic relations with precolonial rulers and other communities. One episode from the reign of a previous Bohra *dai*, Sayyidna Saif al-Din, was especially poignant. In 1814 the Bohra *jamaat* (corporate caste institution) in Poona was attacked by a group of Pathans. The city was then under the control of the Marathas, a confederacy of Hindu princes vying with the

British East India Company for supremacy in North and Western India. In the ensuing melee, the Pathans besieged the Bohra *dai*'s residence. Catching wind of the *dai*'s predicament, the British governor of Bombay, Mountstuart Elphinstone, sent two of his Indian aides to the Maratha Peshwa, demanding the ruler intervene in support of the Bohras. In haste, the Peshwa dispatched his chief minister, two cannons, and two regiments to the Bohra quarter of the city until the rampage dissipated.[2]

Roughly midway between the 1814 incident and Hussam al-Din's encomium to Queen Victoria, another Bohra *dai* had presented a brief Persian history of his community to the British political agent in Surat. While the treatise also rehearsed the infamous encounters with the Pathans of Poona and the regimental rescue party sent by Elphinstone, it also stressed the Bohras' rapport with Indian rulers. The warm reception granted to a previous Bohra *dai* during his 1595 visit to the Mughal Emperor Akbar's court in Lahore was among the episodes recounted. Happy relations with the Marathas were also advertised. The short sketch ended by stressing the personal bonds between the current *dai*, the prince of Baroda, and the East India Company, and expressed the hope that the future would continue in like fashion.[3]

These two accounts of Bohra interactions with political authorities capture several themes particular to the consolidation of corporate Islam and Gujarati Muslim middle power in the emerging colonial system between 1800 and 1850: the tangled relationship of the Gujarati Muslim *jamaats* with a multitude of political authorities in Western India; the alternatively cantankerous and friendly interactions between the *jamaats* and other communities, Muslim and non-Muslim; the geographic breadth of Gujarati Muslim settlement in South Asia and beyond; the pivotal role of British figures like Mountstuart Elphinstone in the history of these groups and the desire of those same figures to be informed about the history of Gujarati Muslims; and finally the part played by disparate registers of historical memory in shaping the *jamaats*' self-conception. During the half century examined in this chapter, Western India transitioned from post-Mughal to colonial rule—a process that made and unmade the fortunes of a plethora of groups on the subcontinent and reconstituted communities along new lines. Famine, migration, military conquest, and a mixture of economic boom and bust were its hallmarks.

Throughout, the interaction of two institutions helped the Gujarati Muslim commercial castes weather these tempests, gain recognition of their collective identity, and position themselves as the would-be beneficiaries of middle power: the *sarkar* and the *jamaat*. The *sarkar*, a byword for political authority on the subcontinent, encompassed the ruling power of both pre-colonial Indian rulers like the Marathas and the ascendant British East India Company. Although the company became the preeminent power in Western India from 1818, the profile of *sarkar* in the region was marked by a miscellany of overlapping sovereignties until 1947. As argued here, lasting traditions of political pluralism in Western India during this epoch strengthened the corporate status and boundedness of the *jamaats* and other Indian corporate groups across the patchwork sovereignties dotting the region. In this environment, a few Indian merchant communities were able to maintain their control over expanding commodity production throughout Western India, even in the teeth of colonial expansion.[4] Accordingly, the representatives of the *sarkar*, British and Indian, were forced to contend with these corporate privileges and even to compete with one another to recognize them. Pluralism, although never absent of violence and expropriation, permitted the Gujarati Muslim commercial castes to preserve their distinct identities, nebulous and spatially disparate though they were. It also fostered the conditions that enabled the *jamaats* to integrate themselves into the civic order of the *sarkar* and eventually the world of expanding British empire and free trade, which will be examined in chapter 2.

As they were incorporated into the administrative machinery of these states, Bohra, Khoja, and Memon *jamaats* were able to safeguard their collective rights against the machinations of ruling elites. That feat, combined with their ability to sustain their foothold in overseas trade, secured their place among the preeminent Indian merchant communities in the western reaches of the subcontinent. Again, the Gujarati Muslim commercial castes were not entirely exceptional in this regard: in Western India they were but a fraction of the sundry groups all vying for state recognition as corporate entities.[5] Even so, in a preview of still greater strife to come, the *jamaats* in this half century showed frequent signs of fissure over questions of religious authority.

But while debates over religious doctrine assumed great importance in subsequent decades, in this era the access of individuals to property within the *jamaats* was the primary bone of contention. Because the *jamaats* were unable to settle these disputes with their own internal mechanisms of arbitration, the British East India Company *sarkar* was inevitably pulled into the fracas. In particular, the decisions reached by company officials concerning the character of inheritance and succession in these communities, which departed from formulas applied to nearly every other Indian Muslim community up to that point, were motivated by ideological presuppositions and political dynamics singular to the early colonial period in Western India. Thus, it was not so much that the Bohras, Khojas, and Memons were any more "Hindu" and less "Islamic" in their customary practices than the plurality of Muslims in the subcontinent. Rather, for contingent reasons, they were categorized as such by the framers of colonial law in Western India.

The *Jamaats*, Political Polycentrism, and Portfolio Capitalism

The fracturing of Mughal power over the course of the eighteenth century had assorted regional effects throughout the subcontinent, ushering in a volatile mixture of market expansion and rapid political turnover. As historians writing on late Mughal North India have shown, the weakening of central Mughal power fostered the conditions for an assortment of parvenu entrepreneurs and social groups to vie for abundant, albeit hotly contested, political and mercantile resources.[6] Although conforming to patterns seen elsewhere on the subcontinent, Western India was arguably an exceptional case, for there a matrix of corporate merchant power, state fiscalism, and political polycentrism coalesced (and persisted, albeit to a lesser degree, after the colonial conquest), with few parallels in other parts of South Asia.

At the risk of oversimplification, while in the second half of the eighteenth century the Mughal successor states in the north, south, and east of the subcontinent tended to be expansive entities covering large tracts of territory, in Western India the political map was far more disjointed. Alongside the heavies like the Afghans, the Marathas, the Sikhs, and the British East India Company stood innumerable smaller potentates of Rajput origin whose dynasties survived until the end of colonial rule as princes under British suzerainty. Beneath these potentates were the smaller caste combines, able to flex their corporate muscles in the face of grasping state power. To be sure, such groups were scattered across India—for example, in the Gangetic Plain, where Hindu and Muslim corporate groups arose throughout the "rurban" landscape, which was segmented by a hierarchy of markets and occupational structures.[7] These groups were of a piece with the Bohras, Khojas, and Memons in that they never acquired the capacity to seize political power outright but nonetheless were highly active players in the theater of politics. What these Hindu and Muslim corporate combines in interior North India lacked was not only the access to transregional export markets via a presence in overseas shipping. They also lacked the middle power eventually afforded to the Gujarati Muslim commercial castes by way of Western India's idiosyncratic incorporation into frameworks of company rule.

Even before the cementing of company hegemony, the corporate power that Indian merchant communities acquired in eighteenth-century Western India was conspicuous but disconnected. In Surat the preeminent trading entrepôt of the region before Bombay's rise in the early nineteenth century, corporate merchant bodies were pivotal to the functioning of the state taxation system from the late seventeenth century onward.[8] But even in Surat corporate power did not mutate into a single merchant assembly arrayed against state authority, and merchants showed no willingness to emancipate themselves entirely from the boundaries of community.[9] Yet the divide between merchant and state power remained porous into the 1830s. This porousness stemmed from a phenomenon that historians have identified as portfolio capitalism, whereby entrepreneurs blended interests in trade, revenue collection, and kingmaking. The conditions of portfolio capitalism permitted individual entrepreneurs and the corporate bodies to which they belonged by dint of caste origin to shape the flight path of political fortunes.[10] The permeable political / mercantile divide intrinsic to portfolio capitalism persisted throughout the first half of the nineteenth century, until formal colonialism eventually drew a definitive wedge between the political and mercantile spheres.[11] Gujarati Muslim middle power emerged within the interstices of that wedge.

In spite, or perhaps because of, its political fragmentation and volatility, eighteenth-century Greater Gujarat has often been framed as one of the select regions of India that possessed the "sprouts" of a dynamic mercantile capitalism in the precolonial period. Some historians assert that its pre-1800 economic indicators may have even rivaled southern England and southern China in the period before the so-called Great Divergence gathered pace.[12]

None of that preempted Surat, from enduring considerable commercial setbacks in the early decades of the eighteenth century. Muslim-owned shipping is said to have especially suffered, but with the demise of late Mughal-era merchant dynasties, new Indian corporate groups came to the fore, among them the Bohras, Khojas, and Memons.[13] While the latter two groups were still outside circuits of British East India Company rule, the Bohras relied heavily on British ships for freighting to ports in Western Asia, a partnership that foreshadowed a deeper relationship to come. Moreover, regional textile networks—and the broader global "cotton sphere"—continued to serve as a link between Greater Gujarat and various parts of Afro-Eurasia into the twentieth century, even in the face of de-industrializing trends in the first half of the nineteenth century.[14] Surviving examples of these textiles, such as a late nineteenth-century silk garment produced by Memon women, reveal a level of artisanal sophistication which surely contributed to the perpetuation of Gujarati Muslim economic prowess (see figure 1.1).[15]

Just like the textiles they trafficked, the Bohras, Khojas, and Memons were in no sense secluded to Greater Gujarat in the late eighteenth century. Over

FIGURE 1.1 Silk dress made by Kachchhi Memon women, ca. 1883. A testament to Gujarati Muslim artisanal expertise and to the role of women, often invisible in the sources, in networks of production and exchange.
Photograph © Victoria and Albert Museum, London.

centuries of sultanate and Mughal rule they had extended their footprint throughout considerable portions of Central and Western India. By the late eighteenth century, traces of these three groups can be found as far east as Ujjain, as far west as Karachi, as far south as Poona, and as far north as Udaipur. In other words, even within the subcontinent they were scattered throughout Baluchistan, Greater Gujarat, Rajasthan, and Sindh. They thus inhabited a territory that was, by the reckoning of an Indian lexicographer in the 1840s, larger than Great Britain and Ireland, with their shared mother tongues serving as the principal language of business in Central and Western India.[16]

Even if these groups operated across a swath of territories, the problem is locating them in this medley of dissonant sovereignties and attending to their specific trajectories. Unfortunately, so far as is known, source material for these centuries has not survived. Still, one can safely surmise that these groups became part of the increasingly differentiated fabric of Muslim life in Gujarat, which revolved around the twin poles of Sufi orders and sultanic authority.[17]

The Bohra, Khoja, and Memon commercial profile was not exclusively maritime in its contours but operated along the dividing line between agriculture and trade. In a telling case, a Kachchhi Memon *jamaat* was founded in Bhuj in 1799.[18] Bhuj is thirty-odd miles inland from the port of Mandvi, and the decision of Memons to settle there is a reminder that they did not merely hug the coasts of Western India but also operated in the hinterland. Nonetheless, the ability of Bohra, Khoja, and Memon ship captains to maintain their overseas presence—even amid the partial decline of Indian shipping from the mid-eighteenth century onward—was fundamental to the preservation of their precarious economic position in the transition to colonial rule.[19] It meant that the Gujarati Muslim commercial castes were present, albeit in small numbers, in Jeddah, Madagascar, Mocha, Mozambique, Muscat, and Zanzibar by 1800.[20] A Gujarati pilot's map from around 1750 betrays familiarity with the leading commercial entrepôts of the western Indian Ocean, well before formal colonial conquest.[21] British East India Company and Dutch East India Company sources from the eighteenth century reveal passing interactions with Bohras and Khojas.[22] This intimacy with overseas trade was consequential for facilitating Gujarati Muslim interactions with the bricolage of political authorities jostling for supremacy in Western India. But it also partially insulated these groups from the recurring cycles of economic depression that beset agricultural production in colonial India throughout the nineteenth and early twentieth centuries.

For all their commonalities, it is best to attend to the finer points of each community. The Memons materialize on only rare occasions. Community traditions of later centuries state that the Memons moved out of Sindh to the Kathiawar Peninsula in the early fifteenth century. From a supposedly once unified community of Lohana Hindus four umbrella Memon communities emerged in the wake of their conversion to Islam in this period: the Kachchhi (Cutchi), the Halai, the Surti (Surati), and the Sindhi. As they migrated, each developed its own incipient corporate identity based on geographic origin.[23] In the late eighteenth century, Memons began to attain influence over upstart political authorities. An illuminating and representative example comes from the early history of the Dhoraji Memon *jamaat*. According to community traditions, in the early eighteenth century a Memon merchant named Abd al-Rahman settled in Dhoraji. There he was granted worship and trading rights by the Darbar Haloji of Gondal. Some of Abd al-Rahman's descendants stayed in Dhoraji, while others migrated to Bantva, about thirty-two miles away, which became another haven for Memons. By 1780 the population of Memons in Dhoraji had reached critical mass, compelling one Adamji, a grandson of Abd al-Rahman, to establish a Dhoraji Memon *jamaat*. Eventually, the Dhoraji Memon *jamaat* became a vehicle for local Memons to voice their grievances with the local *darbar* (royal court) and to combat what they regarded as the arbitrary power of the mahajans, essentially a guild of Hindu moneylenders.

Perturbed both by the taxation policies of the *darbar* and the influence of the mahajans, the leaders of the Dhoraji Memon *jamaat* decided to migrate as a group in response to these taxation measures. They ended up traveling to Junagadh, which was only some seventeen miles away but was governed by another ruler. In time, however, the Dhoraji Memon *jamaat* was attracted back to Dhoraji by the local ruler, whose revenue had been hard hit by the Memon exodus, and he had decided to reextend privileges.[24] Dhoraji, though witness to occasional scenes of tension between the Memons and local authorities, would be a center of Halai Memon corporate power in Greater Gujarat until 1947. The example of the Dhoraji Memon *jamaat* was repeated among Memons across Western India in the transition from Mughal to colonial rule.

A similar development occurred in Sindh, ruled throughout the eighteenth century by two dynasties, the Kalhora and the Talpur. Community lore maintains that before their conversion to Islam the Memons were clustered in the region of Thatta, an important trading entrepôt in Sindh, but which began to decline in the early nineteenth century.[25] Although many Memons moved outward from Sindh as early as the fifteenth century, an indeterminate body also migrated within the region. In the early nineteenth century, Memon *jamaats* were founded not only in the maritime enclave of Karachi, then only a tiny port, but also far inland in Hyderabad and Sehwan. The latter was an important pilgrimage site for the Sufi saint Shahbaz Qalandar, whose *ʿurs* (death anniversary) saw thousands of pilgrims descend on Sehwan every year. The Memon connection to Sufi saints throughout Sindh remained (and remains) a persistent feature of their religious devotions.[26]

Elusive as the Memons are in the documentary records of this epoch, the movement of Khojas is still harder to trace. The history of the community before the nineteenth century is mired in speculation. For better or worse, later community histories focus inordinately on the succession of Ismaili imams and supply precious little information about the Khoja *jamaats* of this period. It is known that a Khoja *jamaat* was founded in British-ruled Bombay in the 1740s, becoming an early entrant into the realm of the British East India Company *sarkar*.[27] But that fact says nothing about the constellation of other Khoja *jamaats* in Western India existing outside the orbit of the company. Manuscripts in Khojki script detailing prayers recited in a *majlis* (religious assembly) are some of the few documentary materials that survive from this period.[28] To some indeterminate degree, Khojas from Western India journeyed to Iran for the purpose of *darśan / dīdār*, the ritual of seeing the Nizari Ismaili imam in the flesh. This involved an extensive trek inland from the ports of the Persian Gulf to Mahallat, which was the residence of Shah Khalil Allah (the last Nizari Ismaili imam to reside in Iran) after he relocated from Kirman.[29] Consequently, for most Khojas, connections to the imam were largely monetary in nature, with funds dispatched from India at regular intervals.

The emissaries sent by the imam were indispensable in extending an Ismaili Khoja infrastructure in Western India. This trend accelerated in the late eighteenth century, when Ismaili emissaries dispatched from Iran in this period—including Sayyid Ghulam Ali Shah and his successor, Sayyid Muhammad Shah—settled in Western India. These emissaries encouraged the foundation of *jamaats*, gained new converts, composed *ginans* (Ismaili Khoja devotional songs), and established links with local political authorities in Greater Gujarat and Sindh. In the case of Sayyid Muhammad Shah, he not only established close relations with the Hindu Rao of Kachchh, but also acquired a following among Konkani Sunni Muslims, who regarded him as a pir. Suitably, his shrine was built in Bombay, a city fast becoming a haven for both Konkanis and Khojas alike.[30]

Ismaili *dais* were not the only ones who cultivated ties with the holders of *sarkar* in Western India. In exceptional circumstances some Khojas became political officers in the new princely states. This development further redounded to the benefit of the *jamaats* as it heightened the privileges that communities could extract from rulers. One example was Ismail Gangji, who became head of the treasury and master of the mint in Junagadh for some sixty years.[31] According to Khoja tradition, Gangji's father was a servant of the *nawab* (governor) of Junagadh, and Gangji the son followed in the family tradition. By 1821 he had become a revenue administrator in the *nawab*'s bureaucracy, a job that required him to conduct regular tours of Junagadh State. Community narratives also credit him with raising the economic status of the Khojas in the state.[32]

Individual Khojas and Memons were thus social climbers in this period, but because they appear in historical records only in a flicker, caste-wide generalizations about their *jamaats* are hard to come by. It is far easier to reconstruct the movements of the Bohras, who have the most extensive pre-1850 textual records, although one must rely on sources written after 1850 to obtain distilled versions of these materials. Though there is a definitive continuity across these accounts, they often diverge in their details, a testimony to how historical memory in the *jamaats* has been renegotiated over time. Fortuitously, these sources permit the historian to situate the Bohras—or at the very least, their *dais*—in the events of Mughal period following the permanent transfer of the *dai*-ship from Yemen to India in 1567.[33]

Bohra relations with Mughal officials were mercurial. Bohra histories liked to recount an auspicious meeting at Lahore between the Emperor Akbar and the twenty-seventh *dai*, Daud bin Qutb, in 1595. Here the Mughal ruler penned a letter of recommendation for the Bohra *dai* and dispatched it to his lieutenants of Ahmedabad, assuring the latter that the Bohras were a trading and peaceable people to be protected from any harassment.[34] Akbar's successor Jahangir was also said to have intervened in defense of the

Bohras.[35] But these expressions of Mughal patronage were overshadowed by a later infamous episode in 1646 in which the reigning *dai* was executed after being put on trial for heresy by Aurangzeb, then still a Mughal prince.[36] If credence can be given to the polemical account of Ali Muhammad Khan—a Sunni revenue official from Ahmedabad and author of the famous mid-eighteenth-century history of Gujarat, *Mirāt-i Aḥmadī*—the successor to the murdered Bohra *dai* responded by sending out his missionaries to Ahmedabad to collect tithes, free Bohra prisoners, and instruct the faithful. In reaction, the Mughal authorities in Ahmedabad ordered that these Bohra missionaries be apprehended and their heretical teachings combatted by the appointment of Sunni teachers among the "illiterate men and children of their community in this city."[37]

Partially because of these troubles with regional potentates, a succession of Bohra *dais* constantly migrated throughout Western India, visiting their flocks scattered across regional kingdoms and doing their level best to avoid the wrath of potentates, whether Mughal or post-Mughal. They accepted tribute from local *jamaats,* periodically purged the community of "un-Islamic" practices such as smoking and drinking, inculcated sharia norms, and instructed *amils* (officers) in the texts of Ismaili jurisprudence.[38] Bohra religious treatises from this period—written exclusively in Arabic—reveal a sophisticated, albeit understudied, tradition of Ismaili Shiʿism operating at several levels within the learned hierarchy of the *jamaats.*[39]

The transmission of such works occurred against the backdrop of an expanding commercial infrastructure, the product of the labors of *jamaat* and *sarkar* alike. In many locations in the eighteenth century the *dais* reportedly sponsored the construction of bazaars for the sake of the faithful. Community histories also report that *jamaat khanas* (caste assembly hall), which came to possess assets in the value of thousands of rupees, were constructed throughout Greater Gujarat, in places like Burhanpur, Kapadvanj, and Mandvi.[40] The *dais* and local congregations were aided in all this by the special grants bestowed upon them by various Indian rulers. Yet the *dais* and their *jamaats* also frequently became the victims of political intrigues at the hands of these same potentates. One telling example occurred in Surat as far back as 1759–1760 when the Bohras threatened to skip town after a government imam was appointed in their mosques and a special tax levied on them, all supposedly as a sop to the Sunni Muslim population of the city. Almost immediately the local authorities reversed course, spooked by the potentially disastrous effect a Bohra exodus would have on trade.[41] Whatever the occasional setback, by the end of the eighteenth century the Bohras' acumen in trade was discernible enough to catch the roving eye of the famous historian Azad Bilgrami in his panoramic account of Indian Muslims.[42]

Across Central and Western India a vast network of shrines dedicated to Bohra saints slowly materialized. As related in later Bohra calendars documenting the celebration of saints' days, the geography of the anointed stretched from Jamnagar to Wankaner, Ahmedabad, Partapur, Ujjain, Sironj, and other cities across Central and Western India.[43] But to a degree unseen in either the Khoja or Memon *jamaats* in this period, schisms and heresies periodically reared their head in the then more elaborate religious hierarchy of the Bohra *jamaats*. In the sixteenth and seventeenth centuries splintering among the Alavi, Daudi, and Sulaimani Bohras had occurred over the disputed succession to the *dai*-ship.[44] But the most explosive development in the immediate decades before 1800 came in the 1760s with the emergence of a dissident group known as the Hebat Allāhis, whose progenitor claimed to be in communion with the hidden imam.[45] To be in contact with the imam, believed by Bohras to be in occultation until the end times, was an altogether more momentous declaration than a rival claim to the *dai*-ship.

The reigning *dai* and his followers attempted to extirpate what they regarded as a heresy, but traces of the Hebat Allāhis supposedly lived on into the twentieth century. The Hebat Allāhis represented the most important breakaway Daudi Bohra faction until the appearance in the 1880s of the Mahdi Baghwallas, who would also be dismissed by Bohra polemicists as latter-day Hebat Allāhis. They were reflective of the antinomian potentialities within Ismaili Shiʿism surrounding the imamate. But though their eventual numbers were miniscule, the Hebat Allāhis also confirmed the general rule that the survival of a breakaway *jamaat*, common to all the communities surveyed in this book, was dependent on the securing of a critical mass of property and followers.

While internal dissent was isolated in this period, the Bohras endured no shortage of conflicts with other communities and political authorities. This was especially so in Maratha territories throughout Central and Western India. The Marathas were the foremost opponents of British rule in these two regions until their collapse in 1818. In Maratha territories the Bohras enjoyed their own corporate status and were judged according to their own laws. This relationship sometimes elicited the suspicion of the East India Company: in the 1760s the company banned the export of iron from Bombay, which the Bohras had been supplying to the Marathas.[46] Throughout the ensuing decades, the Bohras also relied on Maratha protection. One instance occurred in Baroda around 1817 when it was discovered that a Bohra was selling shoes bearing the names of the first three caliphs on the soles (a curious twist on the storied Shiʿi practice of *tabarra*, the ritual cursing of the Sunni successors to the Prophet, Abu Bakr, Omar, and Othman). Baroda's outraged Sunni community petitioned for the Bohra's execution, but likely in view of the sizable Bohra *jamaat* in the city, the offender was protected by the local *sarkar* in the form of the Gaekwad, a Hindu ruler of Maratha lineage. Nonetheless, the Bohra trader was banished from Baroda with the shoes tied around his neck.[47]

The Bohra *dais* sometimes endured similar indignities. While resident for a time in the Maratha capital of Poona, they were sometimes subjected to harassment by Maratha officers, if later Bohra historians are to be credited.[48] Conveying the insecurity under which the community lived, a Bohra chronicle from the 1880s gave a conflicting picture of the Maratha leader Daulat Rao Sindhia. One series of anecdotes has the Bohras striking up an agreement with Daulat Rao, who granted special privileges to the *jamaat* and praised the virtues of a Bohra *amil* before the retainers of the Maratha court. Elsewhere, however, Daulat Rao was said to have fleeced Bohra *jamaats* of thousands of rupees and confiscated their holdings.[49]

Long before this Bohra tangle with the Marathas, the British East India Company and the Bohra religious leadership had signed an agreement in Bombay around 1771–1772. The full text has proven elusive, but a late-nineteenth century Bohra historian obliquely related some of its contents, which supposedly declared that the Bohras were "well-wishers of the company." The text also highlighted the Mughals' persecution of the "Bohra community" (*qawm-i bawāhīr*) and seizure of their property, an anticipation of Victorian-era bashing of the Mughals that passed over some of the covenants with the Mughals cited earlier in this chapter.[50] When the *dai* moved his temporary residence to Surat a year later, in 1773, the company *sarkar* issued him a passport granting him special privileges in British East India Company territories.[51] For the next several decades, the Bohras drifted still further into the company's orbit as the latter made short work of rival powers on the subcontinent. The company's sepoys even came to the defense of the *dai* and his followers when they were besieged, on separate occasions, by groups of Hindus, Jains, or Sunnis.[52]

The most fateful development in the Bohras' relationship with the company was the decision of the *dai*, Yusuf Najm al-Din ibn Abd al-Tayyib Zaki al-Din, to relocate from Poona to Surat more or less permanently.[53] Continuing to pay frequent visits to *jamaats* across Central and Western India, the Bohra *dais* never remained sedentary in Surat for long. Yet while its status as an economic center was subsequently eclipsed by Bombay, Surat became the religious headquarters of the Bohra *jamaat* until around 1915. From 1810 until today it has remained the site of the preeminent Bohra madrasa, the Dars-i Saifi (now known as the Aljamea-tus-Saifiyah), which trains Bohra scholars in Ismaili law and dispatches them throughout the Bohra diaspora. For all of Surat's continued importance, Bombay catapulted the *dais'* authority in the colonial order to new heights. In 1824–1825, the *dai* became a member of Bombay's Legislative Council. The *dai*'s co-optation into the framework of company rule was an expression not only of the company's meteoric rise over the previous four decades but also of its internal transformation during its conquest of Western India.

Gujarati Muslim Migration and the Company *Sarkar*

As political polycentrism, economic dislocation, and the foundation of *jamaats* spurred the migration and settlement of Bohras, Khojas, and Memons across the breadth of Greater Gujarat, Maratha territory, and Sindh, the British East India Company seized new territories in Western India in rapid succession from the end of the eighteenth century. While historians have debated the extent to which the early colonial state in India marked a continuity or rupture with the past,[54] over the course of its conquests the company *sarkar* in Western India assumed an unmistakably hybrid form. Continuities in Western India were most marked because of the fundamental continuity of Indian merchant communities and notables and the persistence of the broader structures of political polycentrism and portfolio capitalism.

On its end, the company *sarkar* also recognized the indispensable position assumed by these merchant groups in its own financial calculations, especially from the rise of the China trade in the 1780s. By the turn of the nineteenth century, merchant groups in Western India were actively financing the Bombay government's war against the Marathas.[55] Arguably, the financial contributions made by Indian mercantile groups, and their indispensable place in regional commerce, led company officials to show some marked deference to regional caste corporations—in particular, their legal and customary practices.

Notwithstanding the tiny numbers of Bohras, Khojas, and Memons in company territory before 1800, full-scale Gujarati Muslim migration to the possessions of the company *sarkar* was first catalyzed by a wave of famines that struck Western India in the early nineteenth century. To take one example, the famines that swept through the northern parts of Gujarat in 1812–1813 purportedly ravaged half the population, according to one colonial official.[56] Another account saw famine as a major compelling the outward migration of the Gujarati commercial castes: "the emigrants arrived in Guzerat in detached bodies, and for the purpose of convenience spread themselves over the face of Guzerat, from the borders of the Gulf of Kutch to Surat, in many instances even flocking from ports on the coast to Bombay." It was further reported that "native chiefs and opulent merchants [granted] them passages free of charge."[57] Thus, the *sarkar* operated as a pivotal enabler of the migration of the *jamaats*.

The frequency of famine in Western India between 1800 and 1840 encouraged a range of responses from local populations.[58] *Jamaat*-orchestrated migration ranked among these. When discussing this era, Bohra histories speak regularly of famines, and the efforts of the *dais* to formulate a response to them.[59] Another good illustration comes from the history of the Okhai Memon *jamaat* founded in 1810. From its inception, the *jamaat*'s portfolio included a mosque, an assembly house, and an *eidgah* (open-air prayer space). Okha (Okhai is the adjectival form of Okha) was at that time a tiny trading entrepôt under the suzerainty of the Gaekwar of Baroda, though his deputy, the Kamasivdar of Dwarka, was the local ruler. Okha's small stature belied the fact that it was a great pilgrimage center for Hindus, Jains, and Muslims, with the famous *dargah* (shrine) to Haji Kirmani, a Qadiri Sufi, situated across the water from Okha. Just the same, the Okhai Memons' comfortable transition into trade and the respectable fortunes they accrued were not sufficient to insulate them from the drought and famine of 1840.

Eluding the trend of many Memons who moved to Bombay in this period, some one hundred Okhai Memon households settled in Karachi between

1840 and 1880, a foreshadowing of the significant mark the Gujarati Muslim commercial castes would leave on that city. An indeterminate number relocated to Africa (likely Zanzibar) in the same period, while another 150 families stayed in Okha.[60] Some Memons who migrated to East Africa in this epoch reportedly did so to flee the specter of British power: a colonial report written in 1874 noted that many Sindhi Memons who migrated to Mombasa and its environs over the previous two generations were political refugees unsympathetic to the British government, a fact which purportedly distinguished them from local Bohras and Khojas.[61] Like it or not, these refugees were soon incorporated into British imperium, as many Memons who remained in Western India were over the previous half century.

Bombay, the company's prime possession in the region, remained a magnet for Gujarati Muslim relocation in the face of ecological disaster and demographic tragedy. Although nominally under the singular authority of the British East India Company, early nineteenth-century Bombay has been usefully characterized as a "civic heptarchy" of coexisting, albeit rival, corporate bodies.[62] The heptarchy was fertile ground for the growth of *jamaats* and other similar caste institutions. It has already been noted that a Khoja *jamaat* existed in Bombay as early as the 1740s, but this *jamaat* does not appear to have made much of a mark in the documentary record until the sudden arrival of the Agha Khan I in the 1840s.

Compared to the Bohras and Khojas, Memons took slightly longer to reach a quorum in colonial Bombay. There were 3,659 Memons residing in the city as of 1807, according to a survey undertaken for British authorities by a Muslim *qaẓi* (judge). As a later British lawyer put it, the *qaẓi*'s decision to group the Memons in the same table with the male and female prostitutes—and to separate them altogether from Muslim butchers and water carriers—betrayed how little he regarded them.[63] Several slaves and concubines were also listed among the Memon population, a measure of the Memon participation in the slave trade out of East Africa. A more ignominious indication of the Memons' foothold in Bombay was the fact that, in 1818, a British doctor recorded the heavy toll of cholera on Memons, whom he deemed of "lower class."[64]

Other Muslim observers saw the Memons in a more positive light, praising their pursuit of lucrative economic lines. An anonymous Muslim author visiting Bombay in 1816 wrote in his Persian account, *Jān-i Bamba'ī* (The soul of Bombay) that, "on account of selling timber, all Memons make [earnings] above subsistence."[65] The rhapsodic Persian phrase for "above subsistence" (*qūt-i lā-yamūt*) was a sign of the precocious wealth that the Memons in Bombay had accrued by the second decade of the century. While the same author also referenced a Bohra *jamaat* in Bombay, neither he nor other commentators mention the existence of a Memon *jamaat* as such. Supposedly it was not until 1826 that a formal Memon *jamaat*, comprising Memons from Kutiyana, was founded in the city.[66]

Within thirty years of the composition of *Jān-i Bamba'ī*, Memon fortunes had been transformed, thanks in part to their aforementioned foothold in overseas shipping, which included a prominent role in the maritime pilgrimage traffic linking Western India with the Ottoman Hijaz. This is confirmed by one Muhammad Vizir Ali, a North Indian scholar from Moradabad, whose late 1840s travelogue titled *Sirāj al-hujjāj* (The pilgrims' lamp) documented his journey from India to Mecca and Medina.[67] Vizir Ali's account accorded particular attention to Bombay and its material infrastructure, presaging the city's enormous influence in the infrastructure of the Hajj over the next century. While passing through the place, he observed the Memons at length, whom he deemed, along with Konkani Muslims, the wealthiest Muslims in the city (though he did not neglect to mention the Bohras).

No Muslim entrepreneur in Bombay or the western Indian Ocean region piqued Vizir Ali's curiosity more than the Memon commercial magnate Habib Seth Arif Dada Seth. A ship captain who plied the waters between Bombay and Jeddah, Dada Seth undertook the charitable task of transporting pilgrims across the Arabian Sea. He also furnished the capital for the construction of a great mosque at Aden; supplied biryani, pilaf, and other food to pilgrims aboard his ship and to people of Mecca; and established a *waqf* (pious endowment) in Medina for the purpose of accommodating poor pilgrims.[68] This was not a solitary example; many of the most enduring mosques founded in Bombay in this period, such as Haji Zakariyya Masjid, were the bequests of Memon ship captains. Over time these mosques (and the subsidiary trusts their existence fostered) were important suppliers of commercial credit for those inside and outside the *jamaat* but also were subjected to seemingly endless bouts of litigation. They became cornerstones of Bombay's ever-growing Sunni religious economy, sustaining holy men and legal scholars alike.[69] The wealth of Memon shipowners also financed—to the tune of Rs. 20,000 per annum—the contingents of Sufi sayyids from Kachchh and Sindh who descended on Bombay in preparation for the Hajj every pilgrimage season.[70]

As these remittances and Vizir Ali's account corroborate, transactions involving *hundis* (akin to letters of credit / bills of exchange) were a quotidian feature of Gujarati Muslim commercial life. With no exchange banks of the modern type on offer and to mitigate the security problems inherent to transporting large amounts of metallic specie, pilgrims traveling from the western reaches of India to the Hijaz often relied on Memon merchants like Dada Seth for the remittance of funds.[71] These were written in the name of their agents, but pilgrims remained anxious about the time delay and attendant depreciation of their money between Bombay and the Hijaz. In an age before economic overspecialization, banking with letters of credit constituted but one aspect in the portfolio of Gujarati Muslim entrepreneurs. It was an integral feature of an economic world where currencies were multiple, exchange rates ever fluctuating, and markets unevenly integrated. Though the mercantile successors of Gujarati Muslim firms like Dada Seth's continued to use *hundis* well into the twentieth century, they rarely became bankers of the type associated with global high finance from the last quarter of the century, for reasons that will be explored in later chapters.

Dada Seth had his equals in the many Khoja entrepreneurs—some with families in tow—who settled in greater numbers in Mukalla, Muscat, and Zanzibar in this period. For the Aden and Makalla-based Khoja firm of Messrs. Abdoolabhoy and Laljee Soomar, the grain trade and banking business linking Gujarat to Arabia and East Africa had guaranteed a steady expansion since the start of the partnership in 1826.[72] More than a century later the firm was still in operation, albeit on a much grander scale. But the littoral of the western Indian Ocean was hardly the sole stomping grounds of the Bohras, Khojas, and Memons. Migration within India proper was by no means neglected. Poona, where Bohras had already settled in some numbers and where several *dais* lived for brief periods, became the site of an Indian Army cantonment around this time, attracting still more Bohras and cohorts of Memons, who connected with an influential group of Parsi military contractors.[73]

Shortly thereafter, in the 1840s and 1850s, Kachchhi Memons established *jamaats* in Bangalore and Calcutta. Within a few decades of their arrival in Calcutta they even gained trusteeship over the city's Nakhoda Masjid, the latter a term used throughout parts of the Indian Ocean region to denote a ship captain (*nakhoda*). The Memons, said to be the wealthiest Muslims in the northern part of the city, acquired an unmatched stake in the mosque. The first Memon trustee was Haji Zakariya, formerly a leading member of the Kachchhi Memon *jamaat* in Medina, appointed in 1856. His name became so synonymous with the mosque that locals eventually called it Masjid Zakariya.[74] As will be seen in chapter 6, this mosque became a source of a drawn-out conflict among Calcutta's Sunni Muslims during the 1910s and 1920s.

For all this impressive mobility, one sticking point between British East India Company officials and certain Gujarati Muslim entrepreneurs in the 1830s was the latter's illegal trafficking of African slaves into India. Several Bohras were caught in the act, including one Bohra woman who attempted to import a slave into Surat.[75] Bohras continued to dominate the slave trade between Madagascar and Mozambique into the 1870s, when they again earned the ire of British authorities.[76] In some cases Gujarati Muslim entrepreneurs took enslaved concubines for their wives, although the practice of nonendogamous marriage would be a point of controversy for all three groups well into the twentieth century.

These disputes over the slave trade convey how, as the trellis of Bohra, Khoja, and Memon diaspora came into being across coastal India and the Indian Ocean, much remained to be clarified in the relationship between the British East India Company and the Gujarati Muslim commercial castes. For company administrators in Western India the challenge from the 1820s onward was how to govern the new populations falling under their sway. Were these populations to be governed by the same legal arrangements as other Hindu and Muslim populations in other parts of subjugated India? Or were there traits unique to the populations of Western India that had to be accounted for? The next two sections study the intellectual preconceptions that company officials brought to bear on these dilemmas.

Empirical Orientalism and the *Jamaats*

The dialectical pirouette between the authority of the *sarkar* and *jamaats* that was critical to the formation of corporate Islam and middle power also found expression in the assortment of Gujarati Muslim legal disputes that made their way into the colonial courts between 1800 and 1850. By foregrounding the *jamaats*' corporate status, these cases were instrumental in foregrounding the nexus of legal rights and economic power that carried the Gujarati Muslim commercial castes through the colonial period. These cases likewise broadcast how the lobbying power of the *jamaat* as a corporate collective often stood at odds with the will of individual constituents and factions within the *jamaat*, exacerbating conflict and encouraging the intervention of outside entities. As one pursues the domino effects of these cases, shifting perspective from the colonial courts to the *jamaat*, an alternative picture emerges from the neat narrative of colonial incorporation and subordination. What one sees instead is the hollowing out of a middle tier in the colonial system that became more pronounced in the later decades of the nineteenth century.

To repeat, a primary enabling condition for the *jamaats*' legal prestige was the geopolitical context in Western India. As noted earlier, the British East India Company encountered a political world in Western India very much unlike that of Bengal and Madras, where its officials had been the unmistakable overlords from the 1760s. While the company enjoyed footholds in Bombay and Surat, it continued to face the threatening power of Afghans, Marathas, and Sikhs and found itself less able to project power far into the hinterland of Western India. Even after formal annexation of large parts of Western India by the 1830s, company officials had to contend with the legacies of Mughal and post-Mughal *sarkar*, not least the mélange of overlapping sovereignties and the assortment of corporate entities native to the region. They then had to situate the Bohras, Khojas, Memons, and umpteen other communities into this ever-more-viscous legal landscape. The torturous ways in which company officials and other European writers conceived of the Bohras, Khojas, and Memons as Muslims of a peculiar and unfamiliar variety had repercussions for the eventual consolidation of middle power by these groups.

Evidence for this is abundant: the records of the company factory in late eighteenth-century Surat reveal that many officials attempted to understand the array of caste rights possessed by local communities. An entry in the company's Surat diary in 1798 noted the procedures that various communities followed for dispute resolution: "they go to the heads of the caste when there is a dispute to determine the case conformably to the laws of their sects."[77] Such remarks do not mean that company servants always grasped the finer points of caste distinctions. Be that as it may, as the world of political polycentrism and portfolio capitalism in Western India contracted with the ascent of the company *sarkar*, there remained an unmistakable need for company servants to navigate a far denser web of political and corporate power than they had hitherto known in other parts of India.[78] The riddle to come for company officials was what to do once the heads of the caste were unable to agree on the "laws of their sects."

For the new class of company administrators who appeared in the 1810s, the Mughal and Maratha administrative precedents they encountered in Western India supplied a blueprint for understanding local Indian society. These administrators were also motivated by ideological presuppositions quite unlike those that guided their peers and forebears in Bengal and Madras. Company officials in late eighteenth-century Bengal—chiefly Sir William Jones and Warren Hastings, both of whom learned Arabic, Persian, and Sanskrit—had been famously predisposed to textualist notions of religious law in their formulation of Anglo-Hindu and Anglo-Muhammadan law. Moreover, in their attempt to "codify" these two legal traditions, company officials in Bengal had relied on the expertise of Hindu pandits and Muslim *munshis* (clerks) to do the work of interpreting and translating sacred Hindu and Islamic texts, an encounter that has been called "dialogical Orientalism."[79] A strain of political thought that fused Anglicist ideas of liberty with notions of a mythical Mughal constitution also pervaded early company Orientalism in Bengal.[80]

Few of these ideas, especially the archetype of a Mughal constitution, circulated to the company's territories in Western India. Indeed, these archetypes had largely died out in Bengal by 1800. From that moment there was also growing recognition in Bengal that European knowledge of India's Muslims was woefully inadequate. In 1800, Calcutta's Asiatic Society listed an account of the Bohras as a "particularly required" addition to a "connected history" of Indian Muslim communities and other similar "oriental subjects as require further illustration."[81] On the whole, however, company Orientalism in Western India was less textualist in inspiration than its Bengali permutation and more empirical and ethnographic insofar as textual referents assumed secondary importance. The dialogue in which this "empirical" Orientalism engaged was less with Hindu pandits and Muslim *munshis* and more with caste councils. Furthermore, the architects of the colonial legal system in Western India were more cynical about hard and fast divisions between Hinduism and Islam. Their skepticism was reinforced by their interactions with groups like the Bohras,

Khojas, and Memons, who were seen as liminal communities on the borderline between the two religions.

Conceptions of law and governance distinct from those on offer in other parts of British India also sculpted the unique paradigm of company Orientalism in the western part of the subcontinent. In Bengal the company *sarkar* defined the substance and application of Islamic law, making little allowance for the mediating effects of local custom. On the other hand, the culture of law in Western India was a project in which the company *sarkar* recognized the caste customs of Indian Muslim constituencies in a manner that departed from the scripturalist model of Anglo-Muhammadan law conceived in Bengal. An exemplary figure of this brand of the company's empirical Orientalism was Mountstuart Elphinstone. As the governor of Bombay, Elphinstone had intervened on behalf of the Bohra *dai* during the disturbances in Poona in 1814. Suitably, select Bohra histories brim with anecdotes related to Elphinstone.[82] He knew the territories and peoples of Greater Gujarat well, having traveled through them in his capacity as diplomat, ethnographer, and warrior in previous years. He also formulated crucial policy notes with lasting implications for the company *sarkar* and those who fell under its rule. A concise expression of his deference to traditions of political pluralism in Western India was his 1821 work *Report on the Territories, Conquered from the Paishwa*, where he cataloged the inner workings of the Maratha administration that the company had just recently replaced.[83] Instead of sweeping away the institutions of Maratha rule in their entirety, Elphinstone constructed the new edifice of colonial rule in Western India on its vestiges.

Historians of Afghanistan have rightly pointed to the nefarious legacies of the so-called Elphinstonian episteme in propagating an image of Afghan society as atavistically and inescapably tribal in character.[84] By extension, one might argue that, in similar fashion to Afghanistan, Elphinstone glimpsed throughout the breadth of Western India a range of caste subgroups sharing little with one another except their own unique corporate rights. By no means were these ideas exclusive to Elphinstone. From the late eighteenth through the early nineteenth centuries a consistent regard for caste distinction in British East India Company judicial records shows that Elphinstone was not a solitary voice among local officers. Still, his writings came to have enormous sway among both company officials and Indians educated at the institutions he founded in Western India. In time these ideas circulated among the Gujarati Muslim commercial castes by virtue of their residence in Bombay and membership in numerous public associations in the city, including Elphinstone College.[85]

Elphinstone's main contribution to the eventual institutionalization of Bohra, Khoja, and Memon middle power was the concessions he made to the realities of political polycentrism and corporate caste power. His legal philosophy was Janus-faced. On the one hand, he was adamant that any legal code erected in Western India had to be "founded entirely on general principles, applicable to all ages and nations." The basis for this code was to be written texts of Indian scripture or law. But these were to be balanced out by "customs and conditions [that] exist independent of them." Obtaining information about the latter demanded that officers "examine the Shastrees [religious scriptures], heads of castes, and other persons likely to be acquainted either with the law, the custom of castes, or the public opinion regarding the authority attached to each," as well as existing records from local courts of justice.[86] Subsequent efforts to balance out written text and caste custom fostered the conditions for the extension of the corporate powers enjoyed by the Gujarati Muslim commercial castes and other groups in Western India to British territories in India and other parts of the empire.

While Elphinstone does not seem to have written specifically about the *jamaats*, he did reflect at length upon analogous Indian institutions—chiefly the panchayat, or village council.[87] (The semantic distinction matters little, for Gujarati Muslim commercial castes and cognate groups like the Parsis used the term *panchayat* interchangeably with *jamaat*). The panchayat had enjoyed a special status in the Maratha judicial administration, and Elphinstone's reports on Maratha governance made much of the institution.[88] Historian James Jaffe has maintained that the interest of Elphinstone and other British officials harbored for the panchayat "was adjectival, that is, concerned with legal procedure, rather than uncovering the substance of customary law. Implementing their vision, nonetheless, required regularizing *panchayat* procedures, supervising its operation, limiting its jurisdiction, and, in general, incorporating the panchayat into the structures of British judicial administration."[89]

Though the panchayat supplied the ideal archetype in Elphinstone's system for the functioning of native law, it had to be squared with a deeper appreciation for the customs of individual castes. Into the 1830s much remained unknown about the subject populations of Western India. Unsurprisingly, ingrained stereotypes about Hindus and Muslims carried from other parts of India died hard in the face of frequently updated empirical data. So even as the Bohras, Khojas, and Memons began to appear in the dragnet of colonial reportage in the early nineteenth century, they often preempted the efforts of British East India Company officials and European travelers to neatly categorize them. Accustomed to stereotypes of an unbridgeable divide between Hindus and Muslims inherited from Bengal, European observers resorted to all sorts of intellectual somersaults to pigeonhole these three communities. Many of these first impressions persisted, and especially the notion that the Bohras, Khojas, and Memons constituted an indeterminate medial point on the spectrum of Hinduism and Islam. Other, altogether more ridiculous voices deemed them "Mahometan Jews" or even avatars of London's lower-class Jewish population, opinions which had a tenacious hold over the colonial imagination for the next century.[90]

Despite the weight these tropes exercised on the colonial imaginary until 1947, greater sophistication in colonial descriptions of the Gujarati Muslim commercial began appearing in the 1830s. This development owed to increased European intimacy with these communities and a literacy in the history of Western India. One standout commentator was the French explorer Victor Jacquemont (examined in chapter 2 in the context of Bohra economic practices). Another suitable illustration comes from the pen of Henry George Briggs, who undertook a tour of Greater Gujarat and published his findings in 1849. Briggs's volume included an entire chapter on the origins of the Bohras, dedicated in part to refuting earlier European accounts, and his appendix included a translation of a Bohra history written in Arabic.[91] (This period in fact saw the appearance of at least two other Bohra histories written in Arabic, as well as the previously mentioned Persian account given by the *dai* to the British resident in Surat in 1851).[92] Though Briggs did much to clarify the different branches of Bohras, his account concluded with the appeal that much remained to be learned, inter alia, about the Khojas, "who incongruous entwine Hinduism and Muslimism, (fast during Ramadan, maintain the festival of Id, also join in the celebration of the Huli and Divali)" and the Memons, "a corruption of Meman, who have neither a written code nor any established custom, beyond what time and occasion demand."[93]

Several other officials and travelers, such as Richard Burton (later the famous translator of the *One Thousand and One Nights*) and James McMurdo, had preempted Briggs's overture over the past two decades or so, making passing remarks on the Khojas and Memons they encountered throughout coastal and interior Sindh.[94] Some of their commentary is illuminating, such as Burton's claim that the Memons were among the leading supporters of Hanafi scholarship in Sindh. (There probably is some truth to this, as Akhund Azaz Allah [d. 1824], reputedly the first Sindhi translator of the Quran, was a Memon).[95] Unfortunately, other than some scant remarks on religious devotions and customs, these authors offered few of the details Briggs did about the Bohras, an omission likely encouraged by the lack of textual sources on these communities.

European accounts did, nevertheless, grow more elaborate as colonial encounters with the Gujarati Muslim commercial castes became regularized. Sensitivity to caste particularities was not a matter of magnanimous deference, let alone tolerance. The imperatives of colonial rule, and the knowledge regimes that underpinned it, demanded a literacy in the histories of individual communities. There was also a particular urgency present in the case of the Gujarati Muslim commercial castes, for between 1840 and 1850 colonial officials were forced by the intractability of those *jamaat* quarrels that found their way into British courts to come to grips with Bohra, Khoja, and Memon peculiarities. Those peculiarities presented unprecedented challenges to prevailing colonial beliefs about the nature of law and custom among Indian Muslim populations. And the way those challenges were resolved by the *sarkar* determined the eventual shape of Gujarati Muslim middle power in the colonial system.

The Bumpy Legal Integration of the *Jamaats*

With the consolidation of company hegemony around 1830, the world of portfolio capitalism, which permitted Gujarati Muslim and other merchant groups to leverage their economic heft to secure corporate rights from state authorities, narrowed dramatically. Now the object before the British *sarkar* was to subordinate and integrate Indian corporate groups. The process was bumpy. Empirical Orientalism and Elphinstonian deference to Indian corporate privileges in Western India were merely a vague rubric for colonial legal officers operating between roughly 1840 and 1850. The actual work of transmuting these privileges into precedents bearing substantive legal weight fell upon the shoulders of these officers. These figures were typically more solicitous of the particularities of caste custom than Elphinstone, whose interest had predominantly lain in the procedural operation of the panchayat. They also had to grapple with the realm of practice to a degree Elphinstone the legal theoretician never did. Though his 1827 legal "code" gave the impression of permanence, the code's provisions were frequently transgressed in the messy realities of the courtroom. And while Elphinstone sought to preserve aspects of each community's "written law"—by which he primarily meant their religious scriptures—his successors sought to extend the antitextualist strands of Elphinstone's attitudes toward caste custom even further.

It is worth clarifying that Elphinstonian deference to corporate privileges was not simply a top-down, state-driven process. Momentum came from Indians themselves, in the glut of petitions composed from the 1830s onward by communities in Bombay Presidency, and especially the Parsis, who demanded their own substantive law codes that took notice of the fact that they were neither Hindu nor Muslim. Tellingly, Parsis were most adamant about the creation of a code that recognized their specific marriage, inheritance, and succession customs.[96] (The latter two items were the primary points of contention in contemporary Gujarati Muslim court cases). In a reflection of how closely Gujarati-speaking communities observed each other, Parsi activists pointed to legal decisions concerning the Bohras, Khojas, and Memons as a model for redressing their own corporate woes.

The Parsis' bid for legal reform merits a short discussion because it confirms that Gujarati Muslim legal exceptionalism was a watershed moment in the legal history of British India. In 1861 a report was compiled by the Managing Committee of the Parsee Community at Bombay.[97] The committee had been appointed to draw up a series of laws for the Parsi community and to petition the Legislative Council of India for their enactment. Nonplussed by the "powerlessness" of Parsi panchayats to institute community law, the committee complained that the only choice open to Parsis was to follow Hindu or English usages. This owed, the committee held, to not only the corruption of "ancient" Persian laws over the Parsis' long residence in India but also to the "too narrow language of the legislative Acts and Royal Charters which classified all non-European people within India as Mahomedans and Gentoos, or to the too narrow construction which the Courts at an early period (unlike those of the present day when dealing with the Khojas and the Memons) gave to the word 'Gentoos.'"[98] As the Parsi committee correctly surmised, the legal decisions affecting the Gujarati

Muslim commercial castes in the late 1840s had disrupted the enshrined Hindu-Muslim dichotomies that had undergirded company lawmaking in India to that point, and opened up new possibilities for the expansion of community-centric law codes. But if the Parsi panchayat had by mid-century "shed its former role as an adjudicator" and outsourced its duties to the colonial courts,[99] the *jamaats* remained jealous of their autonomy and eager to exercise their voice in the court.

To be sure, the breakdown in the British vision of the Hindu / Muslim binary did not occur in one fell swoop and never disappeared entirely from the colonial judicial record. Despite this, the ultimate consequence of mid-nineteenth-century Indian community petitioning and shifts in colonial conceptions of the Hindu / Muslim divide was that, unlike what was applied to the plurality of other Indian Muslims in Bengal or Madras, the rubric for Bohra, Khoja, and Memon law was not religious scripture but caste practice. The predictably uneven integration of corporate bodies into the colonial legal system—the pretext for which was typically furnished by an internal caste dispute that transgressed the barriers of community—preserved caste specifics to a still more pronounced degree, but with crucial differences among all three groups.

All things considered, of the three Gujarati Muslim commercial castes, the Bohras presented the least confusion to colonial officials. Arguably this was because the company *sarkar* already possessed some recognition of the Bohra *dai al-mutlaq*'s authority thanks to earlier covenants and the Bohras had a network of mullahs and *qazis* across the main urban centers of Central and Western India. Moreover, the Bohra religious hierarchy legitimated its authority on a body of Ismaili law (in the form of regularly recopied manuscripts) unmatched by the Khojas or Memons.[100] (To be sure, colonial and wider Muslim appreciation of the details of Bohra law was never particularly sophisticated, and remained largely the stuff of guesswork, even into the 1940s).[101] Well before other Gujarati Muslims were accorded such privileges, the colonial state recognized the Bohras' special legal culture throughout the western Indian Ocean region. As early as 1839, the estate of one Bohra Shaikh Ali Isabhai—a Daudi Bohra originally from Surat who had died in Muscat after seventeen years' residence—became an object of controversy among his heirs, a local Indian broker, the Sultan of Muscat, and colonial authorities.[102] The affair highlighted the frequent tension between corporate privilege and the ever-more-complex procedures of commercial law, both colonial and Islamic.

After Shaikh Ali died, his Bohra broker in Muscat, Abd Allah bin Badu, took possession of the deceased's estate and sold the effects at public auction. Then the local British representative, an Armenian named Khoja Rubin (whose title is as a reminder of the wider use of *Khoja* as a commercial term connoting "master" throughout Islamicate Eurasia), demanded that Abd Allah hand over Shaikh Ali's books and render an account of the sale. Abd Allah refused, retorting that he would answer only to "the Moollah of the Bohras in Bombay." His response was a precocious attempt to mobilize Bohra corporate privileges against the demands of state power, though it raises the question of the *dai*'s authority since he was then resident in Surat, not Bombay. Subsequently, Khoja Rubin applied to the Sultan of Muscat for assistance, but the sultan refused to interfere in the dispute. For his part, the British political resident in the Persian Gulf was unwilling to accept Abdullah's protest, believing that he had defrauded Shaikh Ali's heirs and creditors to the tune of some two thousand "German Crowns."[103] Despite this, the resident was unable to offer redress, partially because the documents of the estate eluded him, but also because he doubted the legality of dispatching Shaikh Ali's correspondence to the Supreme Court in Bombay. The British resident therefore requested clarification from his superiors in Bombay as to whether, in the future, the local British agent in Muscat had the right to take possession of the estate of a deceased British Indian subject and sell it at public auction.

The episode reflects how procedures of inheritance, succession, and dispute resolution within the diaspora of Bohra *jamaats* were still in the process of formulation at this date. Significantly, the Bohras enjoyed greater freedom of movement in the colonial legal system than either the Khojas or Memons until the 1920s, in large part because they were less beholden to the strict dichotomy drawn by colonial officials between Hindu custom and Islamic law. Still, the fact that the competing parties in the dispute over Shaikh Ali's estate appealed alternatively to Bohra authorities in Surat and Bombay underscores the polycentric character of Bohra legal culture at this juncture. The *dai* in Surat was evidently but one of a coterie of Bohra legal experts across the Western Indian Ocean, and his monopoly over religious authority in the Bohra *jamaats* was not what it would later become.

The centrifugal dynamics of the Bohra diaspora were strengthened by the miseries faced by the reigning *dai*, Sayyidna Badr al-Din, who served in the post from 1836 to 1840. In 1837 an enormous fire in Surat destroyed a multitude of *jamaat* buildings, and the manuscripts of the *jamaat* were only narrowly rescued. This was followed by a flood that inundated the city, which forced the *dai* to establish himself in Poona.[104] Should Bohra histories be any indication, the *dai* was supported in these years by substantial remittances from the Bohra merchant diaspora and by the company *sarkar.*[105] These same histories nonetheless stress the *dai*'s virtues in the face of adversity and the devotion of the *jamaat* hierarchy—including his eventual successor, Abd al-Qadir Najm al-Din—to the needs of Bohra *jamaats* across Gujarat.[106] But these reassuring tones were marred by the mysterious circumstances of the Badr al-Din's death in 1840—from a mixture of hemorrhoids and a dose of crushed diamonds, according to one Bohra historian—and the disputed succession to the *dai*-ship, which had dramatic consequences for the character of religious authority within the Bohra *jamaat,* as covered in chapter 3. The challenge faced by future *dais* was to unify the diffuse Bohra *jamaats* in a centripetal framework based upon their supreme authority.

As byzantine as the Bohras' legal hierarchies proved at this early hour, British jurists found the question of custom and law among the Khojas and Memons more difficult to grasp. Perhaps this owed to the indeterminate position of senior religious authority within both *jamaats* at this moment in time. Likewise, the scarcity of legal and historical documentary materials—especially when compared to the Bohra *jamaat*—meant that there was no textual basis upon which to form judicial precedents. For generations colonial officials were baffled by the complexity of Khoja and Memon law. As one colonial legal commentator, Sir Roland Knyvet Wilson, stated in 1903, "The story of these Khojas and Memons has been told at a length quite disproportionate to their numerical importance, because it illustrates in an unusually impressive manner the inconvenience inseparable from a diversity of uncodified personal laws, especially when differentiated either according to religious profession, or according to varieties of immemorial usage."[107]

Sixty years earlier, in the 1840s, the prospect facing British judges, untutored as they were in the histories of the Khojas and Memons, was far more daunting. Circumstance forced their hand as the integration of the Khoja *jamaats* became an urgent matter of company governance with the sudden irruption of the nominal Ismaili imam, the Agha Khan I, in India in 1843. Accounts disagree as to the precise circumstances of the Agha Khan I's departure from Qajar Iran to India: had he launched a revolt against the

Qajars or was his hand forced by attacks launched against him and his followers?[108] Regardless of the precise causes, the Agha Khan I solidified his place in the constellation of Indian princes by supporting British forces in the First Anglo-Afghan War and in the conquest of Sindh, a move resulting more from improvisation than premeditated opportunism.[109] Going forward, the relationship between the Agha Khan I, British authorities, and the Khoja *jamaats* in Bombay and Greater Gujarat was far from straightforward and is still a subject of debate. For one, the Agha Khan I's close ties to the company *sarkar* by no means guaranteed that his religious authority was correctly understood: many colonial reports in the late 1830s and 1840s continued to erroneously speak of the Agha Khan I as the religious leader of the Ismaili Bohras, not the Khojas.[110] In some sense, the Agha Khan I's troubles with the *jamaats* in these years mirrored those of the Bohra *dais* mentioned above.

The Agha Khan I's relationship with Khoja *jamaats* was indeed confused, and it is their response to his arrival rather than his activities that is the real concern here. As they had done for his father and earlier imams, many Khojas had traveled from India to Iran in order pay homage to the Agha Khan I or sent annual tithes. These connections paid dividends during the Agha Khan I's initial period in India. According to the Persian "memoirs" of the Agha Khan I—which were commissioned by him and ghostwritten by a member of his retinue—published in Bombay in 1861, once out of Baluchistan and Sindh, he journeyed throughout the territories of Kachchh and Kathiawar, establishing ties with the Khoja *jamaats* up and down the land.[111] But contemporary correspondence between the Agha Khan I and British authorities are revealing of a much more fraught relationship between the nominal imam, the *jamaats*, and the *sarkar*.[112] By illustration, when the Agha Khan I and his retinue were sent by British authorities to Calcutta—where he faced extreme pecuniary difficulties—he petitioned the company *sarkar* repeatedly to grant him a stipend and relocate him to Bombay so that he might more easily collect the customary monetary donations made by his followers. The remittance of these funds had recently been interrupted by depredations of the Rao of Kachchh, who was said to have persecuted the Khoja *jamaats* under his jurisdiction. Though they were sympathetic to the plight of these Khojas, British authorities were averse to assisting the Agha Khan I in acquiring these donations.

Moreover, the endeavor by select Khoja *sethias* (caste leaders) to block the collection and relaying of *jamaat* funds made matters worse for the Agha

Khan I. This was done in reaction to what these figures perceived as his usurpation of community resources. This prompted the Agha Khan I to fulminate against two excommunicated members of the *jamaat*, wealthy merchants who had reportedly purchased the loyalty of the poorer members. At this desperate hour some *jamaats* in the embryonic Khoja diaspora in the western Indian Ocean region rallied to the cause of the Agha Khan I. When a Khoja merchant in Langeh, a port on the Persian Gulf, caught wind of Qajar attempts to seize the Agha Khan I on his return to Persian territory, it alerted the Khoja *jamaat* in Muscat. Figures in Muscat then dispatched word to the *jamaat*'s head (*mukhi*) in Karachi, who then passed on the warning to the Agha Khan I in Bombay.[113] Support for the pretensions of the Agha Khan I thus were already dividing the Khoja *jamaats* against themselves at this early date—and beyond Bombay, to boot. The eventual establishment of the Agha Khan I's residency in Bombay and his concomitant declaration to be the living imam and the spiritual leader of the Ismaili Khoja *jamaat* soon ignited a firestorm of controversy in several Khoja *jamaats*.

The Agha Khan I's precise relationship to the Khoja *jamaats* took decades to be worked out, both within the community and in the legal apparatus of the nascent colonial state. In the interim, what needed resolution was the broad character of Khoja and Memon personal law. A binding precedent affecting both communities was delivered simultaneously in a famous judgment by Sir Erskine Perry in 1847. In both cases overseen by Perry, Khoja and Memon widows had cited Islamic inheritance rules as laid out in the Quran to petition for the release of shares that male family members had denied them. For decades to come Bohra, Khoja, and Memon women mobilized readily, if unsuccessfully, around this same issue (see figure 1.2). But, in an early manifestation of what became a common practice in many legal cases involving the Gujarati Muslim commercial castes, witnesses from the *jamaats*—almost universally men—were summoned to testify about what customs prevailed within the community. Their voices almost invariably drowned out those of the women in the *jamaats* who appealed to the strict letter of Islamic law against *jamaat* custom.

From these men Perry learned that the Khojas and Memons had adhered to the custom of depriving females "from time immemorial." Not for the last time did a small stratum of men speak for the whole *jamaat* in the colonial courts. Their viva voce evidence was frequently challenged by Khoja and Memon constituencies for decades to come, but Perry's decision to

FIGURE 1.2 Memon women of Bombay, 1856. From the 1840s, Bombay's Kachchhi Memon women were spirited defenders of their economic rights against caste customs that sought to deprive them of inheritance. In the pursuit of this aim, they and their sympathizers among the men in the *jamaat*, mobilized various Islamic legal formulae to criticize caste custom. Until the interwar period, their periodic protest around the issue came to grief, until Memon (and Khoja) women were granted full inheritance rights before the law with a series of legislative acts.
DeGolyer Library, Southern Methodist University.

accept it as an authentic measure of *jamaat* custom was momentous. In the elliptical conclusion of one historian, Perry's judgment extended the preeminence of caste custom over the written law among the Khojas and Memons, distinguishing them from most other Muslims.[114] To elucidate this point, several of Perry's statements in the case merit special attention. For one, he deliberately distinguished his judgment from earlier precedents governing Hindu and Muslim communities in other parts of India, stating,

> It may be questioned whether one individual in the Legislature—with the exception, perhaps, of Mr. [Edmund] Burke—was aware of the sectarian differences which distinguished Shia from [Sunni]; and not even that great man, we may be assured, was at all conscious that there were millions of inhabitants in India, such as Sikhs, Jains, Parsis, Hebrews, and others, who had nothing, or next to nothing, in common with Brahminical worship. But the policy which led to this clause proceeded upon the broad, easily- recognisable basis of allowing the newly-conquered people to retain their domestic usages. . . . I am, therefore, clearly of opinion that the effect of the clause in the Charter is not to adopt the text of the Koran as law, any further than it has

> been adopted in the laws and usages of the Muhammadans who came under our sway; and if any class of Muhammadans, Muhammadan *dissenters* as they may be called, are found to be in possession of any usage which is otherwise valid as a legal custom, and which does not conflict with any express law of the English Government, they are just as much entitled to the protection of this clause as the most orthodox society which can come before the Court.[115]

Perry's remarks reflect not only a tendency among British officials of this era to look beyond the Hindu / Muslim binary but to see the Bohras, Khojas, and Memons as something akin to a nonconformist breed of Muslims, rather like the Quakers and Methodists. (This was a surprisingly common analogy: in one instance, a contemporary Christian missionary compared Bohras in Muscat to Quakers.)[116] Terms such as *dissenters* and *sectaries* were bandied about frequently by British commentators in reference to these groups. Admittedly, the congregational character of the *jamaats* made these comparisons logical to the British.

Perry's judgment did not rest simply on deference to what the *jamaats*' leaders had to say; instead he maintained that the remit of his ruling extended into the high ethereal realms of "public policy." Initially acknowledging that "public policy would dictate the adoption of the wiser rule laid down by the Koran, by which daughters are allowed a defined share in the succession," he went on to admit that public policy itself was an unruly precedent. Whatever the beneficence of the Quranic injunction, "a custom for females to take no share in the inheritance is not unreasonable in the eyes of the English law." To Perry's mind, then, the existing British procedure for evaluating the authenticity of custom was too idiosyncratic. He asserted that "it is simply absurd to test a Mahomedan custom by considerations whether it existed when Richard I returned from the Holy Land, which is the English epoch for dating the commencement of time immemorial."[117]

Custom thus need not extend back several centuries to be identified as authentic—a useful concession for the Khoja and Memon defendants who were keen to hold up their inheritance practices as bona fide customs in the eyes of both Islamic and common law. All the same, Perry was sensitive to the fact that the custom of depriving women of inheritance directly contradicted the rules for inheritance laid out in the Quran. But alive to what he called his "secular" role as a jurist and the fact that Khojas and Memons lived in areas ruled by "Hindu" sovereigns, he stated that the custom of barring women from a share in inheritance ultimately could not be said to stand in contradiction to either the Quran or English common law. Disparagingly, he concluded that "the attempt of these young women to disturb the course of succession which has prevailed among their ancestors for many hundred years has failed, and, as a price of an unsuccessful experiment, that their bills must be dismissed with costs, so far as the defendants seek to recover them."[118]

The high monetary penalties that Perry's judgment levied on the Khoja and Memon women augured the economic hardships many Gujarati Muslim women endured for generations. Economic historians have argued that the decision did have a potentially beneficial result in that it strengthened intergenerational survival of Khoja and Memon commercial firms by ensuring that inheritance was not parceled out among large numbers of family members. That point will be interrogated in later chapters; for now, it must be emphasized that Perry's 1847 ruling applied to only *one* subgroup of Memons, the Kachchhi Memons of Bombay. Though this may seem like splitting hairs, it is a crucial qualification that historians have tended to overlook. Thus, while Perry's ruling ensured that Bombay's Kachchhi Memon *jamaat* was classified according to "Hindu" custom in matters of inheritance, there was ambiguity for decades to come over whether Kachchhi Memon *jamaats* outside of Bombay were subjected to the same rule.

On the other hand, Perry's ruling held no sway over Halai Memon *jamaats* in Western India, whose inheritance practices conformed more to the injunctions of the Islamic foundational sources. Elsewhere, Sindhi Memons, in the words of Burton, shunned the "heresy so common among their brethren in Bombay, viz., the system of depriving the females of their pecuniary rights in wills and inheritance."[119] Here lies the rub: though some Memon communities followed Islamic inheritance practices and others customary ones, they nonetheless all featured among the leading Muslim business firms. These facts call into question any overt emphasis on the link between "Hindu" inheritance customs as an ingredient in Bohra, Khoja, and Memon business success. Broader inferences about economic performance based on legal classification alone are not supported by the evidence. But while the *jamaats* remained the lead authors of their own legal formulas, it would be an error to ignore legal classification entirely. For as Bombay's Kachchhi Memons and sundry Khoja *jamaats* learned to their near constant frustration, once a legal precedent was set and sealed in the colonial legal system, reform proved intractable.

None of that meant that the Gujarati Muslim commercial castes eschewed the colonial courts. Quite the contrary; despite their exorbitant expenses, these courts were fast becoming a preferred avenue for Gujarati Muslims to seek redress of irreconcilable *jamaat* matters. In 1848 Perry presided over another Khoja case pertaining to property, in which the Agha Khan I was one of the parties. Initially Perry encouraged the dueling parties to settle the dispute within the *jamaat*, though with the aid of court-appointed attorneys. The *jamaat* was unable to settle it to the satisfaction of both parties, and in 1851 Perry heard the case a second time. Here, he urged the leaders of the Khoja *jamaat* to grant all members access to caste property and "the right to decide collectively [how] to dispose of that property."[120] Though the collective allocation of property had been a common operational feature of the precolonial *jamaat*, Perry's injunction to recognize the property rights of all individuals within the Khoja *jamaat* was a clear break with prevailing caste customs, but his 1847 judicial decision had effectively preempted Khoja women from securing meaningful property rights for generations.

In his attempt to mollify Khoja disputes in 1851, Perry drew up what was described as a "Declaration of Rights" for the Khojas, underscoring his hope that it would facilitate the election of a *mukhi* (chief) and a *kamaria* (accountant). Perry saw this constitution of sorts as offering the Khojas a method to settle "caste affairs among themselves, without rendering any further application to the court necessary."[121] Put another way, the *sarkar* was ceding legal authority to the *jamaats*. But notwithstanding Perry's intentions, the Khoja *jamaats*' reliance on colonial courts only heightened from 1851. By that point the Gujarati Muslim commercial castes and the colonial state were locked in a fateful and lasting embrace.

* * *

In disaggregating the distinct histories of the Bohras, Khojas, and Memons, this chapter has deciphered several general trends, each with lasting implications for corporate Islam and the framework of middle power that sustained it. Against the backdrop of ever-shifting political power in Western India, Gujarati Muslim merchants acquired portfolios in remittance banking, overseas shipping, the carrying trade in textiles and opium, and, to a lesser degree, agricultural production. This situated them in a comfortable position to exploit the booming maritime economic opportunities occasioned by the foisting of British imperium on the Indian Ocean region. In parallel to these economic changes, the religious identities of these groups acquired distinct attributes and became more elaborate thanks to the expansion of Islamic textual repertories and interactions with other Muslim groups.

At the same time, Bohra, Khoja, and Memon relationships with various political authorities, British and Indian, oscillated between the collaborative and the antagonistic. Notwithstanding the occasional setback, settlement in a locale typically brought the conferral of specific rights upon individuals and the *jamaat*. The preservation of political polycentrism in Western India after the advent of British East India Company hegemony guaranteed that the company *sarkar* had to follow suit and grant the *jamaats* unique rights. Crucially, in their efforts to clarify the nature of their rule, company authorities approached the legal cultures of these communities through an ideological prism distinct from other parts of British India. Empirical Orientalism and the remnants of Mughal and Maratha rule were the twin pillars undergirding this prism. These three factors—profits, privileges, and polycentrism—were lasting features of Gujarati Muslim middle power for the remainder of the colonial epoch.

The subsequent institutionalization of the *jamaats*' legal exceptionalism between 1850 and 1880—which developed in tandem with the unprecedented commercial success of their constituents—is foundational to understanding the feedback loops between capital and conflict in these three groups. While contemporaries, British and Indian, were wont to chalk up Gujarati Muslim success to their legal exceptionalism, there was far more division than unity within the *jamaats* themselves over questions of legal authority.

2

The Vise of Legal Exceptionalism and Colonial Capitalism

1850–1880

KASIMBHAI NATHABHAI, a self-professed Sunni Khoja merchant who opposed the Agha Khan I's bid for recognition as spiritual head of the Khoja *jamaats* (corporate caste institutions) in the 1850s and 1860s, first made a name for himself in the East Africa trade.[1] The capital he accumulated in turn funded all sorts of *jamaat* schemes in Western India, from the construction of a school in Bombay to Khoja institutions in Navsari in Gujarat.[2] In the late 1830s he pivoted to China, enticed by the promise of enormous profits from the opium trade and the subsequent foundation of Hong Kong in the wake of the First Opium War. Nathabhai's name appears frequently in collective petitions sent by Indian merchants to colonial authorities in Hong Kong, and his firm is listed in many contemporary commercial directories printed in the colony. Nathabhai also frequently corresponded with the founding firm of Hong Kong, the massive Scottish enterprise of Jardine Matheson & Co., signing his name in both English and Gujarati.[3]

In a measure of his firm's precocious performance in the China trade, it sent a Hindu clerk named Damodar Ishwardas to China in 1860. Ishwardas was among the untold, but likely substantial, contingency of noncaste employees working for Gujarati Muslim firms, to say nothing of the Bohras, Khojas, and Memons working as employees of Hindu and Parsi firms or in partnerships with one another. As Ishwardas later reminisced, Nathabhai and his son—along with a host of prominent Indians linked to Bombay's Elphinstonian institutions—saw him off on the day of his departure in April 1860.[4] Ishwardas remained in China for three years as an employee of the firm, returning to Bombay in 1863. That same year Nathabhai senior died, but the firm continued on in the care of his sons. But within a few years, and with little warning, the Nathabhai family's empire swiftly came crashing down in the wake of the Bombay share crisis of 1865–1866. Nathabhai & Sons's bankruptcy was a sober reminder of the precarious nature of the wealth accumulated by the Gujarati Muslim commercial castes. To add insult to injury, in 1866 Nathabhai junior and the other Sunni Khoja plaintiffs lost their famous court case against the Agha Khan I and were deprived of access to the asset portfolio that had hitherto underpinned Bombay's Khoja *jamaat*.

The Nathabhais' firm and others like it were instrumental in the consolidation and expansion of corporate Islam between the 1850s and 1880s. The firm exemplified several salient characteristics of Gujarati Muslim commercial enterprise in this epoch. First, the *jamaats* consistently occupied a backstop position in the institutional portfolio of Gujarati Muslim commercial firms. Although the Gujarati Muslim commercial castes momentously embraced the modern business corporation from the 1840s onward, they did not cease to be members of *jamaats*. In nearly all places where Bohras, Khojas, and Memons settled in numbers, merchants created *jamaats* soon thereafter. Representatives of leading commercial firms invariably staffed the *jamaat*'s upper echelons, and the presence of a *jamaat* encouraged still more merchants from these communities to migrate, all the while easing the burden of relocation. By and by, the *jamaats* became both beneficiaries of this wealth and arenas for contesting it.

A second aspect of Nathabhai's portfolio exhibits the *jamaat* as part of a larger package of economic institutions. So-called weak ties, which fostered sustained links with merchants and other individuals outside the community, were especially prevalent. Yet these ties were not exactly weak: although it was certainly difficult for any Bohra, Khoja, or Memon to operate untethered from the *jamaats*, sometimes ties with noncommunity members mattered more in the making of commercial success.[5] Third, the way that Nathabhai's employees moved among different sites in the diaspora—again, all interlinked by *jamaats*—also speaks to a broader pattern among *jamaats*. Employees from outside the *jamaats*, such as the Hindu, Ishwardas, also made use of these networks. Fourth, Nathabhai's case exemplifies the importance of multilingualism—particularly a knowledge of Gujarati, English and regional languages. Finally, the collapse of Nathabhai's enterprise shows the susceptibility of such firms to rapid swings in capitalist business cycles, which brought many successful concerns crashing down with little warning.

Nathabhai's portfolio was shot through with colonial contacts. Indeed, for those Gujarati Muslim entrepreneurs of his generation who made their names during the first five decades of colonial rule in Western India (roughly 1818–1866), colonial recognition of their corporate and individual rights was decisive in sustaining their enterprises. This was certainly not a partnership of equals. Rather, it was a period characterized by yawning asymmetries of capital and power, which only grew from 1850 onward. Yet colonial factors did recognize the economic power of the *sethia* (caste leaders) like Nathabhai and the *jamaats* they represented. Considering the economic clout of such figures, it was in the colonial's state's interest to do so.

By the 1880s, companies operated by members of the Gujarati Muslim commercial castes had become some of the most successful privately owned Muslim enterprises in the world. Some persisted for generations, while others barely lasted a few years. The *jamaats* were a material, albeit uneven, variable in their success, but they cannot be excluded from the commercial portfolio of any entrepreneur. The *jamaats*' presence was muted in some parts of the Gujarati Muslim diaspora such as China and Japan. But even sites where their footprint was weak, from the Maldives to Australia, were incorporated into Gujarati Muslim networks.[6] Capital generated in all these regions fed into the administration of franchise *jamaats*, alternatively facilitating or undermining the cohesion of the corporate caste.

At the same time, the Nathabhais' (and their fellow Sunni Khojas') tangle with the colonial courts showed how little sway such *sethias* had over colonial judicial decisions affecting the *jamaats*. As the court cases involving Bohras, Khojas, and Memons between 1850 and 1880 evinced, there was no coherent, caste-wide idea about what constituted the authentic custom and law of the *jamaats*. Not even the *sethias* agreed, guaranteeing that the *jamaats* were perpetually host to a range of distributional conflicts—over wealth, status, and religious authority. From the 1850s onward, the *jamaats* were no longer merely the possession of their members; increasingly they became an object of solicited and unsolicited governmental stewardship, first for the officers of the British East India Company *sarkar* (political authority) and, after its implosion in the Indian Mutiny of 1857, the British Raj. Henceforth, corporate Islam was a matrix of contested sovereignties jealously coveted by the *jamaats* and the colonial state.

From Peddlers to Capitalists, 1850–1864

The years between 1850 and 1880 marked the decades when the Gujarati Muslim commercial castes entered the world of the modern capitalist business cycle and began shadowing the routes of colonial expansion. Having previously amassed modest fortunes via family firms and traditional commercial partnerships in Bombay, Western India, and the western Indian Ocean region, these same actors now adopted Western corporate business forms—such as the limited-liability company and the modern bank—as a means of expanding their operations. Henceforth these imported corporate forms then became archetypes for the operation of the *jamaats.* At the same time, older institutional forms nurtured by the *jamaats* and the broader commercial milieu out of which these groups emerged continued to be perpetuated.

The ascent of Gujarati Muslim firms was cleared first by the downfall of the corporation that had slowly gained hegemony in India over the past century: the British East India Company. Many merchant lobbyists in Britain had resented the company's corporate power since the late eighteenth century. In 1813 the monopoly it enjoyed in Asian trade was terminated. And in the wake of its final dissolution in 1858, some British commentators saw the company's downfall as a boon to European colonization and capital alike.[7] What those commentators seemed not to have anticipated was the concomitant boom in Indian enterprise spurred by the company's dissolution. Nowhere was that boom more perceptible than in Bombay and its hinterlands, whence a host of Gujarati Muslim firms extended their operations throughout the Indian Ocean region.

The meteoric ascent of Gujarati Muslim merchants in the decade on either side of 1858 necessitated they undergo an image makeover in the minds of many Europeans. Long dismissed as mere peddlers or hawkers,[8] the Gujarati Muslim commercial castes eventually gained recognition as capitalists of the type who pulled themselves up by their own bootstraps in the *Imperial Gazetteers* of the 1880s.[9] There is indeed a long historiographical tradition of describing Asian merchants as "peddlers," a hangover from eighteenth and nineteenth-century depictions.[10] In the past, the term was used by historians to contrast Asian enterprise with the organizational forms adopted by European trading companies in Asia. A novel way of interrogating the genealogies of this scholarship is to attend to the gradual shift in the discourse around Gujarati Muslim peddling in the first part of the nineteenth century.

Chapter 1 demonstrated how, beginning in the 1830s, European observers began cataloging Bohra, Khoja, and Memon customary practices and religious observances. Some of these figures also devoted special attention to the economic activities of these groups. A revealing example is the French botanist Victor Jacquemont. Traveling through Malwa, a center of opium production in India, Jacquemont described the Bohras as "a Muslim sect that I had never seen before." The Bohras, he noted, "according to their own traditions, arrived in Gujarat from Arabia in the year 1100, and from Gujarat, where their numbers are greater than in any other part of India, they have moved in succession into various parts of India."[11] Jacquemont did relate in passing that "the English attribute a Jewish origin to [the Bohras]." But he was most interested in the Bohras as Muslims who "form a caste as much as a sect" and who rejected many Shiʿi and Sunni articles of faith and inspired the animosity of these two groups.[12] He also supplied some useful ethnographic details. Clad entirely in white, Bohra men had beards that they never cut below the lip; boys and girls alike were circumcised at the age of seven (an early reference to the abhorrent practice of female genital cutting among the Bohras); and they all made a living through trade. His comments on Bohra moneylending practices reveal a ready facility with interest: "They even bank and lend at interest under another name because whereas usury [etc.] is prohibited for Muslims by their religious laws, the Bohras exercise it under the artifice of the [*ḥīla*], that is to say that when they lend money for a fixed time they settle amicably with the borrower the monthly or annual interest, and after having calculated the amount until the end of the repayment, they add this amount to the loaned capital and take from the borrower a receipt of the total.[13]

This facility with moneylending, and the regularity with which Bohras resorted to "expedients" (*ḥīla / ḥiyal*) sanctioned by Islamic legal scholars to circumvent Islam's purported interest ban, is intriguing. Jacquemont's account confirms that the Bohras, along with the other Gujarati Muslim commercial castes, included moneylending in their larger mercantile portfolio. But such practices existed despite the refusal of the Bohra *dais* (clerics) to rule that India was *dār al-ḥarb* (the domain of war).[14] Many contemporary

Indian Muslim scholars—such as the famous Sunni scholar Abd al-Aziz Dehlavi—had made such a declaration, which they saw as permitting Muslims to lend and accept interest when transacting with non-Muslims.[15] The presumption that Bohras frequently bypassed concerns over interest lending can be safely concluded in light of Jacquemont's assertion elsewhere that the Bohras "forbid the trade in tobacco and opium out of religious scruple."[16] Other sources, however, clearly indicate Bohra involvement in the opium trade operating out of Malwa, which had become a key production center for opium bound for China.[17]

Other aspects of Jacquemont's interactions with the Bohras point to their growing economic influence. Anticipating a trope that became common during the last quarter of the century, Jacquemont exclaimed, "Unlike other Muslims[,] [the Bohras'] parsimony is extreme, and contributes, with their industrious habits, to keep them always above poverty. The rich among them hide their wealth. They do not have ostentation common to Muslims." Jacquemont's hackneyed emphasis on Muslim profligacy reflects broader European convictions that frugality and entrepreneurship were inimical to the Muslim character. Notably, he characterized the Bohras as exceptional, possessing "truly European habits of work, order and economy."[18] In the hyperracialized context of the later nineteenth century, the origins for those traits would be found in the Bohras' latent Hinduism rather than their honorary European character.

In the 1850s, European descriptions of Bohras hawking a menagerie of goods were commonplace. Long running anti-Semitic tropes of Bohras as "Jews of India" stayed their ridiculous course.[19] But such depictions coexisted with a recognition of them as full-grown capitalists.[20] Several contemporaries saw the Bohras, Khojas, and Memons as impresarios of a burgeoning Indian commercial ecumene unique to Bombay. In the words of a mid-nineteenth-century Indian writer Narayan Dinanathji, the Bohras, Khojas, Memons, and numerous other groups from Western India were "Gujaratized." By this he probably meant that they became part of a shared Indian commercial milieu composed of castes from the region of Greater Gujarat and with a common Gujarati patois.[21] A shade of exaggeration always permeated such portraits, but Dinanathji correctly noted that the Gujarati Muslims—largely penniless when they came to Bombay—had transformed themselves into leading merchants over the course of thirty years. "If we take a survey of the Memon or Khoja streets," he wrote, "we shall find them lined by large three [or] four storied houses, erected on a rocky and what was considered an almost valueless piece of ground, but which has now become one of the most valuable parts of the Island." By contrast, were one to turn their attention to the areas inhabited by Deccani and Konkani Muslims, these "would not fetch one fourth of the price that an equal portion of land in any of the Memon or Khoja quarters would yield."[22] Evidently, then, the Bohras, Khojas, and Memons had between themselves collectively marginalized the previous generation of Bombay's Muslim commercial magnates, the Konkanis.[23]

Further evidence of Gujarati Muslims' newfound prominence comes from an album of paintings depicting Western Indian commercial actors. The collection was likely completed by an Indian artist for a British military officer in or around 1856. Among those depicted is one Haji Ayub and his nephew. Haji Ayub was an agent of Habib Seth Arif Dada Seth, the Memon ship captain introduced in chapter 1 in connection with his gratis ferrying of pilgrims from Bombay to the Hijaz.[24] The portrait shows Haji Ayub as a white-turbaned agent seated with his *tasbih* (rosary; see figure 2.1). Ayub's dandified nephew is to his left, decked out in a gold-speckled turban and embroidered vest common to Memons, while holding a small volume tied together with string. Other images from that album display Bohra hawkers, a Khoja woman in her sari, and a trio of Memon wood sellers (see figures 2.2–2.5). These are among the earliest visual depictions of figures from the Gujarati Muslim commercial castes. They reflect their subjects in tones not even captured in the earliest photographs of the Bohras, Khojas, and Memons, which date to this same period and are revealing in themselves of changing sartorial habits among these groups in the latter half of the century.[25] They also intimate that women from these communities were active economic contributors to the family firm, a fact concerning which other materials are frustratingly silent.

Vibrant Bombay's business circles may have been, but the city was no self-contained economic world. After all, its commercial boom in these decades was largely a consequence of its links to the China trade. Gujarati Muslims displayed a precocious involvement in that trade even before the foundation of Hong Kong in the 1840s. Representative was the Aden and Makalla-based Khoja firm Messrs. Abdoolabhoy and Laljee Soomar, mentioned briefly in chapter 1. Bucking the Khoja proclivity for westward expansion, in the 1850s a son of one of the proprietors was sent to seek out

FIGURE 2.1 "Hajee Aeb Goomasta of Dadasett. Hajee Aeb's Nephew." Part of a larger album of Indian paintings completed in 1856, this image depicts two agents of the great Memon ship owner, Dada Seth. The portfolios of these Memon entrepreneurs stretched from western India to the Ottoman Hijaz. Reproduction © The British Library Board, Add. Or. 1601.

further opportunities not in littoral East Africa but instead in the South China Sea, where he was deputized to open a branch of the business.[26] The firm's survival over the next century—as was the case for all other Gujarati Muslim firms—was dependent upon a hybrid mix of *jamaat* thrifts and joint-stock corporations.

In pivoting to East Asia, firms like Messrs. Abdoolabhoy and Laljee Soomar encapsulated the new ties between colonial expansion and Gujarati Muslim mercantile opportunity—ties that would reproduce themselves in East Africa a generation later. Though Bohra, Khoja, and Memon migration increasingly mapped onto the geography of colonial expansion, they did not exactly follow the logics of colonial rule. After all, Gujarati Muslim outward migrations had been occurring with some regularity in the mid-

FIGURE 2.2 "Khoja Female. Bombay milk woman." Reproduction © The British Library Board, Add. Or. 1593.

eighteenth century, if not much earlier. The opium trade between Western India and southern China was hardly business as usual, but a harbinger of a new paradigm of colonial capitalism, in which the Gujarati Muslim commercial castes became deeply complicit. Rapidly the South China Sea trade laid the groundwork for a transregional economic network that would augment the commercial fortunes of Gujarati firms with concerns stretching from Zanzibar to Hong Kong. Profits from the China trade almost singlehandedly made Bombay the leading commercial metropolis of the Indian Ocean region in this epoch.

Yet the relative importance of the China trade was rather short-lived for Bombay generally and the Gujarati Muslim commercial castes specifically. Though Indian commercial fortunes continued to be made in China until the end of empire, its heyday ended by 1870 as opium acquired less and less of a share of Bombay's import-export trade. This was the likely reason that the *jamaat* did not function as prominently in the China trade as it did in those ports of the Indian Ocean frequented by the Gujarati Muslim commercial castes. Instead, weak ties, coupled with links to colonial, Indian,

FIGURE 2.3 "Kassim Bora Belgaum supply agent and basket cooly." Reproduction © The British Library Board, Add. Or. 1604.

and Muslim public institutions, mattered more. Perhaps China's greatest contribution in the long term was to serve as a conduit for the Gujarati Muslim entry into Malaya, Singapore, and Japan.

Tiny numbers of Bohras and Khojas were involved in the China trade in the early nineteenth century, operating either in the guise of family firms or larger partnerships. For example, a Bohra named Shams al-Din Rajak was the China agent of the Parsi merchant Cowasji Patel, whose business interests extended to Calcutta, Rangoon, and Malaya.[27] Patel traveled to China on three occasions between 1793 and the late 1830s. In 1844 he published a two-volume Gujarati history of China, though only the first volume seems to have survived.[28] It was the first Gujarati primer about the Chinese empire. Patel's motive for writing his account was, as he stated in the preface, to combat his own compatriots' ignorance of China. Such ignorance was not

FIGURE 2.4 "Bombay Bhatia cloth seller and Bombay Boree prepared cloth seller." Reproduction © The British Library Board, Add. Or. 1591.

merely an academic matter but prejudicial to profit: "Because of [Indian traders'] unawareness of so many things, they have to endure great obstacles in their own profit-making business, and accordingly the European people, on account of their own knowledge [of China], can carry out all their own affairs, while our own people fall behind."[29]

Even if a later nineteenth-century Gujarati account of China insisted that Patel's book was largely ignored, the Bohras, Khojas, Memons, and other Gujarati-speaking mercantile groups benefited substantially from the modest production of Gujarati commercial primers and travelogues from the 1840s onward.[30] Though Gujarati always and everywhere ran a deficit compared to English as a repository of commercial knowledge, for the Bohras, Khojas, and Memons being part of a wider transcommunal Indian commercial society with Gujarati as its lingua franca offered numerous dividends. While Patel's sojourn in China was fleeting, some of his Gujarati

FIGURE 2.5 "Meman woodseller. Servant and wife Memaneeanee selling wood." The image captures the contributions of women, otherwise absent in much surviving material, to the running of family enterprises. Reproduction © The British Library Board, Add. Or. 1584–1621.

Muslim contemporaries stayed for the long haul. Two years before the publication of Patel's account, one Nur al-Din Ibrahim, a Bohra merchant from Surat, established the firm Abdoolally Ebrahim & Co. in Hong Kong. In company lore, the *dai al-mutlaq* (chief cleric of the sect) had ordered Ibrahim to travel to the new colonial outpost on a British East India Company ship.[31] Even if the *dai*'s order did spur his travel, Nur al-Din arrived in a place where Bohra community institutions were nonexistent and it was his responsibility to create them.

To be sure, Bohras and Khojas were present in tiny numbers in Canton before 1839. They began to transfer to Hong Kong after 1842, but no formal *jamaat* was established by either group.[32] A place of worship—something less than a dedicated mosque—was established in the Muslim section of Hong Kong Island in 1843, but this seems to have been a space not dedicated to any particular sect.[33] Somewhat later, in what was probably a singular case in the Gujarati Muslim diaspora, Bohras, Khojas, and Sunnis of various backgrounds were buried in the same cemetery, according to a Memon traveler visiting Hong Kong in the 1890s.[34] Fresh numbers of new entrants replenished the deceased, and by the last two decades of the century the number of Bohras in Canton and Hong Kong numbered several dozen. Abdoolally Ebrahim & Co. became one of the first clients listed in the account books of the Hong Kong and Shanghai Banking Corporation's inaugural branch in Hong Kong and is still registered as a client of the bank today.[35]

For all the staying power of Bohra merchants in Hong Kong, the Khojas were the true stalwarts of the China trade (Memons, though present, never became distinguished players in the region). Two figures, Kasimbhai Nathabhai and Dharamsey Punjabhai, both of whom opposed the Agha Khan I in the 1850s and 1860s, were at the pinnacle of the trade. By the late 1850s Nathabhai was an unmissable fixture in the China trade. His Hindu clerk Ishwardas's subsequent Gujarati travelogue, *Cīnanī musāpharī* (China travels) is best read as an artifact of the Gujarati-speaking commercial milieu inhabited by magnates like Nathabhai.[36] The fact that Nathabhai and other Gujarati Muslim firms had noncaste employees did not ensure that relations were always harmonious among Indian capitalists of different communities. Quite the contrary; the China trade is said to have been the underlying catalyst for the outbreak of communal violence between Khojas and Parsis in Bombay in 1851 and 1874.[37]

Embarrassed Gujarati Muslim capitalists explained away these episodes of communal violence against Parsis as the work of the "lower classes of their co-religionists." In actuality, in the wake of such incidents leaders of *jamaats* were called upon to quell the communal violence, further proof of their corporate power in the colonial system.[38] Crucially, episodes of communal violence never precluded the restoration of trust or the regular employment of those outside the *jamaat*. Easing the processes of reconciliation were the shared vocabularies and moral economy of elite commercial life centered around considerations of *ābarū* (honor and reputation). That often led to a certain snobbish, bourgeois dismissal of communal violence as the work of the ignorant lower classes. Of course, the conceit of classism ignored the occasional communal-inspired violence committed by Gujarati Muslims against one another, such as one infamous episode pitting Memons and other Sunnis against a Khoja and Hindus in the town of Gadhada in the early twentieth century.[39]

Yet the dangers of speculation (*saṭā* in Gujarati), rather than communal violence, was perhaps the greater anxiety in these fitful decades of the mid-nineteenth century. Speculation was the mercantile habit that the moral economy of *ābarū* deprecated most, although many Gujarati merchants,

Muslim and non-Muslim, found speculation impossible to resist. After all, well into the twentieth century many large firms received financing from the share bazaar. For while the bazaar was often framed by Indians and colonial commentators as little more than a den of speculation, in actuality it served as a reservoir of liquid capital for the largest Indian industrial interests.[40] Even so, the capacity of speculation to overwhelm respectable mercantile habits was most visible amid the share mania that rocked Bombay as a consequence of the American Civil War, 1861–1865, which engendered a speculative bubble that later ruined Ishwardas's employer—and many other Gujarati Muslim *sethias* besides.

The Bombay Share Crisis and the Ruin of the Second Generation, 1865–1866

In 1867 an anonymous author published a scathing Gujarati account of the share mania that gripped Bombay in 1864–1865. The author identified himself only as "A Parsi," a wise decision given that he forcefully condemned leading European and Indian capitalists. The book's Gujarati title included a word bound to make an Indian readership uneasy: *saṭā* (speculation).[41] Reconstructing the beginnings of the Bombay share market and following the story of the share mania into cities like Ahmedabad, Calcutta, and Surat, the account supplies singular insight into a moment of bifurcation in the history of Indian banking. By comparison, English-language accounts of the share mania are inclined to be ebullient about the long-term effects of the crisis. An Indian historian writing in 1910 concluded his account of the share mania on the cheerful note that in 1872, once the liquidators finished their job and the rubble of failed companies was cleared away, "a new fabric of credit, commerce and industry, on a sound foundation and of a most substantial character" was established that facilitated the growth of the cotton industry and Bombay's economic might more generally.[42]

That is not how the anonymous Parsi author saw matters in the late 1860s, nor is it the most convincing historical explanation of the share mania if one examines its impact on Indian banking (rather than trade or industry). While unsparing in his tirades against speculative behavior, the author found little comfort in the downfall of Indian firms. In his conclusion he lamented that the only true winners of the share mania were the British agents, directors, and political officers who continued to remit funds to England while Indians (*desis*) lay in ruin. Given its in-depth discussion of individual banks and their proprietors, this narrative offers a rare window into how the effects of 1864–1865 reverberated through subsequent years. It also provides insight into the afterlives of some of the Gujarati Muslim entrepreneurs caught up in the share mania. Though the Parsi author could not have guessed it, in hindsight the most troubling aspect of the share crisis was not the high turnover of Indian firms (a regular enough occurrence in the colonial era) but rather that Indian-owned banks would not again attain the same critical mass until almost two decades *after* 1900.

The structural and racial dynamics of banking on the subcontinent transformed dramatically between the 1864–1865 crisis and the post-1900 reestablishment of Indian-owned banks. Most evidently, the demographic content of the board of directors for the banks changed visibly: in contrast with banks founded in in 1864–1865, those founded in the wake of the crisis reflected a near total bifurcation between European and Indian directorships. This trend, which signaled much larger shifts in the division of labor in Indian banking, remained set in stone well after 1900. The prevalence of European-Indian directorships during the share mania reflected the frenetic character of the speculation in 1864–1865. But once the speculative mania died down, for the three quarters of a century after the crisis, racial bifurcation in Indian banking was almost total.

The rift had its origins in the fallout from 1865, but that only becomes evident when the crisis is evaluated against the long-term trajectories of financial life in colonial India. Part of what made the share mania so extraordinary was its unmistakably global dimensions. In the previous decades, the commercial spread of the Bohras, Khojas, and Memons had extended from the Western Indian Ocean to the South China Sea. By the 1850s select Gujarati Muslim entrepreneurs had even begun traveling to Britain. In 1860 a group of Bombay Memons even set up the appropriately named Memon Company in the hopes of breaking the monopoly of European houses over the import and export trade to and from Britain.[43] For all their ambition, the share mania of 1864–1865 took place on a far grander scale, as the anonymous Parsi author recognized. He understood that the share mania was part of a broader history of financial panics, placing the Bombay crisis squarely in a lineage that began with the Netherlands' Tulip Mania in the seventeenth century, followed by the Mississippi Bubble, the South Sea Bubble, and the Railway Mania, among others.

But as the author recognized, although western Europe and the United States had been down the primrose path of financial ruin several times before, this was a novel phenomenon for India. Until recently, speculation had supposedly been the preserve of Marwaris and only practiced in back alleys of the urban underworld. But while some twenty to twenty-five agents worked in the share market before this period, by 1864 there were hundreds. Soon enough, Bhatias, Englishmen, Jews, Khojas, Parsis, Portuguese, and Vaniyas joined in on the action. In the anonymous Parsi's telling, once these figures began establishing banks intended merely for speculative enterprise, the share mania began in earnest. In time the speculative game assumed regional dimensions and drew a cosmopolitan crowd. But in a foreshadowing of the eventual bifurcation between European and Indian banking, there was also a noticeable gap opening up between European and Indian perspectives on these banks. The two groups even gave them different names: what Europeans called the Bank of India, Indian brokers called the Old Khoja Bank. The East India Bank to the European, similarly, was the New Khoja Bank to the Indian broker. As new firms rapidly formed out of thin air, a new stratum of entrepreneurs followed suit, especially as the middle and lower classes began imitating their social betters. And just as well-demarcated boundaries between classes became blurred, so too did the bounds of language: new English words like *promoter* made their way into Gujarati at this time.[44] Soon enough, so would *liquidator.*

The Khojas were by far the most prominent Gujarati Muslim players in the share mania. The anonymous Parsi's account makes only oblique references to Bohra and Memon figures, but this should not be taken as a sign that they remained immune to speculative temptations. After all, an 1863 account of Bombay spoke of "gangs" of young Khojas and Memons roaming around the city "trying to seduce people into gambling."[45] Moreover, the prominent Sulaimani Bohra lawyer Kamr al-Din Tayyibji (brother of the better-known Badr al-Din Tayyibji) established the India and Continental Financial Association, Ltd., which enjoyed some success thanks to rampant speculation.[46] Still, the Khojas were more critical actors in the share crisis than either the Bohras or the Memons. As early as 1863, Khoja merchants involved in the China trade, like Dharamsey Punjabhai, were drawing up banking schemes with other Indian merchants.[47]

While Khojas and other Indian participants in the share mania showed a proclivity to partner with fellow members of their caste, their decisions were not entirely determined by caste. The Oriental Financial Association, Ltd., was typical in having a mixture of Khojas and prominent merchants from other communities on its board.[48] In this environment, considerations of *ābarū* often counted just as much as caste. Reputation was not simply a code of commercial life shared by elites but rather an avowedly public preoccupation. As contemporaries noted, when the investing public caught wind of a dishonorable character being involved with a firm, the ensuing capital flight was fatal. One entity, the International Financial Corporation, Ltd., began its rapid descent into bankruptcy after the public panicked at the news that the "known thief" Khoja Allah Rakhia Pirbhai had a connection to the institution.[49]

There were Khoja success stories, though *success* was a relative term in the volatile circumstances of the share mania. East India Bank and Eastern Financial Association were two "sister institutions" in which Khojas served as leading directors, alongside several Parsis and Hindus).[50] There was also a certain William Watson, a British manager.[51] All three of the Khoja directors in both concerns had made their fortunes in the China trade: Ala al-Dinbhai Habibbhai and the father-son duo of Kasimbhai Dharamsey Punjabhai and Kasimbhai Dharamsey, the latter said to be "extensive speculators in opium."[52] The son had even traveled to Britain in 1864, where he penned the famous diatribe, the *Voice of India*, against the Agha Khan I. Of the three it appears that Ala al-Dinbhai took the most active part in the share mania, if the anonymous Parsi's account can be trusted.[53]

The Eastern Financial Association founded by these Khojas had an auspicious start. Its (authorized) capital was Rs. 20,000,000, which was divided up into fifty thousand shares valued at four hundred rupees each. The paid-up capital—that is, the amount in which shareholders subscribed in return for stock—amounted to Rs 1,250,000 following the first call of fifty rupees on twenty-five thousand shares. As a later Parsi historian put it, "the capital was employed in buying and selling shares, receiving moneys in deposit, borrowing itself, and entering into those disastrous 'time bargains' which proved to be the ruin of every one of such institutions without exception."[54] The initial reaction to the association was actually tepid. But once a prominent Indian entrepreneur, Pestonji Shroff, purchased one thousand shares with the ambition of stimulating speculation, the share price went stratospheric.

By the close of 1864 the directors reported (illusory) profits of Rs. 2,000,000, with dividends of eleven rupees to be paid out per share and added Shroff to the board.[55] Eventually the premium on the shares soared to sixty-seven rupees. None of this was bound to last, and when Shroff was unable to pay Eastern Financial Association the call on ten thousand shares he had purchased, the firm went into a steep nosedive. Whereas Shroff's fall was Icarian in its angle of descent, the Khoja directors experienced disparate fates. Ultimately, only the father and son duo of Kasimbhai Dharamsey Punjabhai and Kasimbhai Dharamsey remained in good financial standing. Perhaps sensing the shifting tides, Dharamsey Punjabhai withdrew his capital from mere speculation in cotton around the time the share mania morphed into a crisis in 1865. He shifted instead to the industrial processing of it, acquiring the Coorla Mills. In the 1870s he sent his son to England for rubberneck tours of the Lancashire textile industry.[56]

Before jumping ship from his directorships, Dharamsey Punjabhai was appointed one of the liquidators of East India Bank. The audit of the institution turned up some staggering figures. At one point, the amount deposited at the bank totaled more than Rs. 5,600,000, but it eventually suffered a staggering loss. A statement on the institution remarked that the business of the bank was carried out rather shabbily, adding, "Although the bank established branches in Britain [*velat*] and other places, nevertheless the business of hundis, lines, etc. occurred in very small amounts, but most of its time the bank was losing, lending money on rags of shares to speculators." A parting salvo called out both Pestonji Shroff and Ala al-Dinbhai for their disastrous performance at the bank. The report on the Eastern Financial Association, however, related that Ala al-Dinbhai went bankrupt and left Bombay for the city of Daman, roughly halfway between Bombay and Surat. It was hardly a happy retirement; his debt was said to be Rs. 3,000,000.[57] Though likely far smaller in size, it must still have been a crushing amount.

The judicial fallout from the share mania lasted several years, with investigations and lawsuits persisting well into the 1870s. By far the largest of these pertained to the failure of the Bank of Bombay. Many European and Indian witnesses were called to give evidence of the bank's operations. Some of the evidence demonstrated that even in 1864–1865, a division of labor already existed between European and Indian directors, one that grew after 1865. As one Mr. Birch put it, "the practice was, when natives applied for discount, to consult the native directors, because they were supposed to know more of the position, status, and credit of the natives than the mercantile directors could do; therefore the practice was, in the first place, to ask a native director what he had to say about the application, and if he reported favourably, it then went on to a mercantile director, and then to a Government director."[58] After 1865, Indians would be almost entirely demoted from the role of director to those of agent, clerk, or, more typically, that of indigenous banker, or shroff.

Looking back from later in the century, some Parsi authors were understandably inclined to blame the decline of their community's commercial fortunes—and the ascent of communities like the Bohras, Khojas, and Memons—to the share mania.[59] This is certainly an overstatement, but one writer's response in an 1870 issue of the *Athenaeum* is telling. While mostly downplaying the effects of the share crisis on Bombay's "real wealth," the author concluded that 1865 engendered an incalculable "moral shock" in the Parsi community thanks to the ruin of many of its erstwhile leaders. By contrast, that same author emphasized the newfound distinction of Bhatias, Banians, Bohras, Khojas, and Memons in the eastern trade from Bombay, writing that "nowhere in the world is bloated wealth so concentrated as in the part of Bombay emphatically called 'the native town.'"[60]

Be that as it may, as with the Parsis, many of those Gujarati Muslim entrepreneurs who emerged in the 1870s were not in business before the share crisis, as will be examined in chapter 4. This suggests that 1865 heralded the end of the old guard of Khoja traders, particularly those with links to China. Kasimbhai Nathabhai (junior) was among the Indian merchants served with outstanding claims by the liquidators of the Bank of Bombay. Nathabhai (senior) had died around the time the bubble had burst, but his debt long outlived him; as his brother testified to a commission in 1868, the Bank of Bombay held a discount outstanding to the tune of Rs. 1,500,000 against the firm of Cassumbhoy Nathubhoy & Sons.[61] Subsequently, the family fought over the bare bones of the firm, though how much remained after the share mania hollowed out the once thriving enterprise is hard to say.[62]

Just as the cycle of litigation and liquidation occasioned by the bursting of the cotton bubble was gaining steam, the Bombay High Court became the site for the hearing of the 1866 Agha Khan Case. That dispute has been a fixture in all accounts of the Khojas' history, including vernacular accounts written by Khojas themselves, for a century and a half. As such, there is no need to repeat the narrative details covered elsewhere. What follows instead is an effort to situate the case in the longer history of corporate rights in Western India and the fallout from the share mania. It must be recognized that the years on either side of the case had witnessed Bohras, Khojas, and Memons actively renegotiating their corporate status in the colonial system.

Though colonial judges played a preeminent role in the legal dramas that ensued between 1850 and 1866, one cannot discount the lobbying powers of factions from each *jamaat* who mobilized around what they held up as their individual rights in the setting of the corporate caste. Private property—not least the equitable access to it—was invariably the thread connecting all these cases. Property disputes then furnished the opportunity for arguing over the corporate identity of the *jamaat,* from the substance of its religious character to the standards of membership. Since ultimately these were property disputes, it is essential to remember that only a party within each *jamaat* was pleased with the precise formulation of corporate rights granted to it by the colonial state. If anything, corporate rights became a shackle in the eyes of many within each *jamaat* and aggravated, rather than mollified, tensions over law and custom within the Bohra, Khoja, and Memon communities. Frequently those corporate privileges were inimical to the individual rights of constituents.

Recasting Legal Exceptionalism

In a series of pieces written in the 1870s, the Bengali Muslim commentator Dilwar Hussain set out to discover why Muslims were, as a rule, "less industrious than the Hindus," a constant trope, however misplaced, of Indian Muslim writers until the end of empire. To his mind, the culprit for this divergence was Islamic law, and especially the colonial state's eccentric implementation of it in the form of Anglo-Muhammadan law. This, Hussain believed, had obstructed the traditional capacity of Muslim "custom" to shape the character of Islamic law. That conviction comes across clearly in Hussain's analysis of the yawning gap between prevailing customs of inheritance and succession among Indian Muslims and the colonial state's privileging of a form of Islamic law purged of customs and Hindu law alike:

> In many districts of Northern and Eastern Bengal, inheritance and succession among the convert descended Moslems were regulated neither by Mohammadan nor Hindu Law, but by rules derived from both. Daughters obtained no

> share of their father's property except that given away at time of marriage. Younger sons got smaller shares than older sons. In course of time these rules would have acquired the force of law in Bengal as they have done amongst the Bohras, Qhojas [Khojas], or Maemans [Memons] of Bombay. But the English Government established courts of justice in the interior: Vakeels and Moqhtaars appeared and multiplied, ordinary people became acquainted with the laws of Mohammadan inheritance, and succession being determined in accordance with those laws stipulated the excessive division and led to the rapid destruction of property.[63]

Hussain's remarks captured the hardening of Bohra, Khoja, and Memon *legal exceptionalism*—the idea that because the colonial state recognized the supremacy of Hindu custom over Islamic law in their communities, these three groups were not only distinguished from the plurality of Indian Muslims but owed their disproportionate economic success to this classification.

Though unaware of this longer genealogy, historians have followed in the footsteps of Hussain by rooting both the ersatz Muslim identity of the Gujarati Muslim commercial castes and their economic prowess in this supposed legal exceptionalism.[64] Yet even by the time Hussain wrote these words, factions within the Gujarati Muslim commercial castes had long engaged in struggles to change their legal status as defined by the colonial order. Some even called for the repudiation of the very privileges Hussain identified as inherently advantageous to the Bohras, Khojas, and Memons. Discontent was first voiced in a series of public campaigns and vernacular polemics by Bombay's Kachchhi Memon and Sunni Khoja *jamaats*. In one form or another, over the next six decades the relationship between custom and law among these communities became ever more divisive. This discontent operated at several levels: the internal *jamaat* level, the inter-*jamaat* level, and the *jamaat*-state level.

Henceforth, what economic historians might identify as the efficiency gains of having Hindu customary practice recognized over and above Islamic law were frittered away by internal *jamaat* conflicts over legal exceptionalism and subsequent litigation costs in the colonial courts. Exceptionalism thus turned out to be double-edged, threatening to fracture as much as to solidify community and presenting economic advantages of dubious merit. The constituents of *jamaats* felt their corporate autonomy increasingly hemmed in by the colonial legal order, not least because migration offered no escape: while spreading their footprint from East Africa to East Asia, the Gujarati Muslim commercial castes carried the legal status that the colonial *sarkar* in Western India had enshrined between 1847 and 1866. In turn, this exacerbated intracaste factionalism, as members contested the authentic interpretation of *jamaat* custom against shifting benchmarks of Islamic law.

To appreciate this requires a detailed account of Gujarati Muslim legal developments in the fifteen years on either side of the share crisis. Chapter 1 ended with an account of Sir Erskine Perry's famous 1847 decisions governing the Kachchhi Memons and the Khojas. Historians have not sufficiently recognized that objections to Perry's decision began in the immediate aftermath of the case, as Kachchhi Memons mobilized to be reclassified as full Muslims in the realm of personal law. By a stroke of luck, a petition supporting the Kachchhi Memon widow and denouncing Perry's decision has survived.[65] The identity of the petitioners is somewhat opaque. They were likely not exclusively Memon, for they declared themselves devout Hanafis and Shafiʿis, members of the Sunni community, and beneficiaries of Bombay's meteoric rise under British rule. They were nonetheless deeply aggrieved by what they perceived as a shift in colonial legal policy.

Hitherto, the petitioners proclaimed, the Recorder's Court in Bombay had decided all cases pertaining to "inheritance, marriage, divorce, wills, gifts, &c." according to Islamic legal texts and the Quran. This system persisted, the petitioners averred, until the introduction of the Presidency's Supreme Court of Judicature, which led to the abolition of Hindu and Muslim law officers. (Evidently, the petitioners had a long memory, for the Supreme Court superseded the Bombay Recorder's Court as far back as 1823).[66] Until that point, Hindu pandits and Muslim had maulvis served as advisers in the courtroom. Now their expertise was jettisoned by a colonial administration increasingly distrustful of their loyalty and credibility. Undoubtedly, there was some selective memory at work here. In practice, the Recorder's Court in Bombay had been careful to weigh caste custom against "religious usages" in the balance of its judgments.[67]

Still, with the erstwhile Muslim maulvis jettisoned from the Supreme Court of Bombay, the petitioners saw no other way but to deploy their own religious expertise. They accused the all-male defendants in the case of openly violating explicit Islamic legal tenets. Allegedly, the defendants reputedly selected "certain insignificant and illiterate persons" as *muqaddim* (representatives) who, in their capacities as witnesses, became the partisans of the defendants' "infidel views" that contradicted explicit religious injunction. The petitioners argued further that the court had elevated the spurious and invented assertions of these individuals to an unwarranted position above explicit Islamic textual authority. In a telling illustration of the power of print to remake Muslim religious subjectivities, the petitioners drew the court's attention to several English translations of Islamic texts. These included George Sale's translations of the Quran, Sir William Jones's translation of the *Sirajiyya*, and Sir W. Macnaghten's *Digest of Muhammadan Law*, all of which openly asserted, according to the petitioners, "that [customary] usage, legally speaking, is always inoperative in opposition to that which is sanctioned by law."[68]

In short, the petitioners charged that British authority had fatally undermined the one-to-one correspondence between religion and law that had hitherto persisted in the nascent courts. Had it been in their power, the petitioners continued, an appeal would have been filed with the Privy Council. But the cost of such a maneuver was too dear by half, especially because the widow and her supporters had already expended some Rs. 10,000 on the original case. In the end, they demanded that all future cases involving members of the four Sunni legal schools be decided entirely with reference to "the written law" against which "no custom, however old or otherwise proper, ought on any account to prevail."[69] Kachchhi Memons angling for reform in Bombay were to be sorely disappointed for seven long decades.

Like the Memons, the Khojas were enduring legal pangs of their own, but the decisions made by Perry and his successors proved far more momentous for the future of Nizari Ismaili Shiʿism writ large than anything endured by the Memons. The early 1860s had seen the showdown between the self-identified Sunni Khoja *sethias* and the Agha Khan I come to an intractable head. As the share crisis was revving up, leading Khojas capitalists like Dharamsey Punjabhai mobilized against the Agha Khan I's pretensions. The subsequent Agha Khan Case of 1866 marked only the end of the first round of near endless battles between Khoja *sethias* and the Agha Khans. Although there was a clear winner in this dust-up, new challengers would repeatedly arise within the Khoja *jamaats* for almost an entire century.

The Agha Khan Case swung the judicial pendulum to the other extreme from Perry's decisions between 1847 and 1851, inasmuch as the presiding judge, Joseph Arnould, declared that Khoja "religious" law, and not caste custom, was the ultimate determinant of membership within the Khoja *ja-*

maat. Still, both the 1847 and 1866 cases relied predominantly on irreconcilable oral evidence provided by members of the *jamaats*. The net effect of these two rulings, inconsistent as they were in their details, was to carve out a "separate jurisdiction" for caste within the colonial legal system.[70] Above all, two facts have been underappreciated by historians of the Agha Khan Case. For one, though historians have recognized that the Sunni Khoja plaintiffs were merchants, the precise nexus between merchant power and corporate privilege in the case has been underappreciated. After all, the Sunni Khoja *sethias* who penned the famous Anglophone polemic *Voice of India* appear to have been in Britain for business purposes.[71] What is more, the share mania exposed how vulnerable the fortunes acquired by leading members of the Gujarati Muslim commercial castes were to the disorderly business cycles endemic to modern global capitalism. The long-term economic repercussions of the bursting of the Bombay bubble are disputable and will be considered in chapter 4. In the short term, however, it was a devastating blow for many Sunni Khoja merchants, especially because the Agha Khan I's victory almost simultaneously deprived them of access to *jamaat* property.

The other aspect that historians have yet to fully explore in full detail is Arnould's intellectual trajectory. Like Perry before him, Arnould's legal worldview was very much conditioned by Elphinstonian conceptions of caste law. His record as a judge in Bombay during the middle decades of the nineteenth century bears this out. At one point, Arnould led a commission devoted to examining whether the Parsis merited separate legislation in matters of marriage and divorce. He was also a judge in a famous libel suit that pitted the journalist Karsandas Mulji against the religious leaders of the Hindu Vallabhacharya sect.[72] His experiences with the Gujarati Muslims' cognate corporate groups like the Parsis, and Hindu sectaries like the Vallabhacharya, were representative of the unique legal conditions that Western India presented to colonial officials. Undoubtedly these prior experiences with other caste corporations colored Arnould's approach to the Khoja *jamaat* in the Agha Khan Case.

To be sure, Arnould did introduce novel interpretations of the corporate rights of the Khoja *jamaats*, departing from Perry and others in several respects. As previously mentioned, one of the key features of Perry's 1851 decision in the case involving Khoja factions was the so-called Declaration of Rights. Arnould adamantly rejected any insinuation that the declaration was a binding legal precedent. Nevertheless, the rejection of the Declaration of Rights did not entail a wholesale dismissal of the corporate privilege of the Khoja *jamaat*. In fact, Arnould showed careful deference to Perry's conclusion that the Khoja community possessed certain property and rights of its own. Where Arnould saw himself going further than Perry was over the question of "the conditions of full membership in the Khojah community," an issue upon which, Arnould surmised, Perry had never had to adjudicate.[73] To Arnould's mind, membership in the Khoja *jamaat* hinged upon whether the Khojas were Shi'i Imami Ismaili Muslims or Sunnis. His eventual decision that the Khojas were Shi'i Imami Ismaili Muslims effectively meant that the British *sarkar*, in a sharp departure from Elphinstonian precedent, had annexed to its own authority a privilege typically reserved for caste—that is, the decision of who constituted a full member of the *jamaat*.

Despite this, representatives from the Khoja *jamaats* were granted considerable leverage during the trial. While the testimony of Khoja witnesses was often met with all the condescension of colonial hubris, the views of the *jamaats* were weighed in the judicial balance by the court. Testimony was taken from Khoja *jamaats* in Bombay and other parts of Western India. In this way the court was perpetuating the survey methods Elphinstone had advocated throughout the 1820s and 1830s. It is thus only partially right to say that the Agha Khan Case of 1866 marginalized Khoja caste custom by privileging colonial conceptions of "religious law" or that it disregarded the Khojas' "internal dispute-resolving mechanisms" in favor of Anglo-Muhammadan law.[74] Well into the twentieth century, the *jamaats* throughout the diaspora were consulted by authorities in British India and the princely states for their opinion on select legal matters.[75]

To be sure, Arnould's valorization of religious law in 1866 in many ways bore a closer resemblance to the textualist Orientalism of the first generation of British East India Company officials in Bengal than the "empirical" Orientalism which, as argued in chapter 1, was embraced by Elphinstone and other officials in Western India more than four decades earlier. While the company had faded from the scene after the Indian Mutiny of 1857, and the Raj's 1863 proclamation of a liberal noninterventionist policy toward religious groups announced a new ruling disposition,[76] the legal worldview of officials like Arnould blended both an Elphinstonian deference toward the corporate rights of caste and a textualist interpretation of Islam that was hitherto more muted in the colonial legal worldview in Western India.

Although a volte-face in certain respects from earlier judicial precedents in Western India, the Agha Khan Case still arguably upheld the integrity of the corporate status of the Khoja *jamaat* by rooting Khoja "religious law" in the specificities and particularities of the caste corporation rather than in an acontextual, statist version of sharia common in Anglo-Muhammadan law. Even so, Arnould entirely recast the corporate character of the Khoja *jamaat* by conflating its identity with the figure of the Agha Khan I, a conclusion which deprived the Khoja *sethias* of their powers of *jamaat* arbitration in one fell swoop. While this chapter and chapter 1 have argued that the interplay between *sarkar* and *jamaat* supplied the institutional framing for the exceptional character of the Gujarati Muslim commercial castes between 1800 and 1866, it is telling that throughout the case the Agha Khan I was called the *Sarkar-Sahib*, the possessor of the *sarkar*. Among the Ismaili Khojas, the *sarkar* and the *jamaat* were entirely conflated, in Arnould's mind at any rate.

Henceforth, many legal commentators regarded the sovereignty of the succession of Agha Khans as inseparable from the Khoja *jamaats* to a degree never applied to either the Bohra *dai al-mutlaqs* or any of the Sufi pirs and ulama patronized by Memon *jamaats*. Still, it would be wrong to overextend the narrative of religious law's triumph over custom in the Khoja *jamaats* too far or to overstate the scale of the Agha Khan I's victory. The divisive issue of Khoja "law" continued to modulate the colonial state's authority vis-à-vis the Khojas, to propel Khojas into the colonial courts, and even to call into question the Agha Khan I's authority. The wealth pouring into the Khoja *jamaats* ensured this. And the very same year as the Agha Khan Case the status of property owned by a Khoja widow who died intestate and heirless once again taxed the mental energies of colonial judicial authorities.[77]

Even in the immediate aftermath of the case, the Agha Khan I faced difficulties projecting his authority in the Khoja diaspora in the Western Indian Ocean region. For one, the Sunni Khojas organized an appeal to the 1866 case immediately. In the hurried aftermath of Arnould's judgment, several "reformist" Sunni Khojas traveled again to England to, in the words of the *Bombay Guardian*, "see what steps can be taken to deliver their people from a yoke which is even more intolerable than that which the Hindoo Maharajahs lay upon the necks of their victims. . . . Though their battle should prove a Thermopylae, let them nevertheless wage it; victory will spring out of their ashes."[78] If readers can forgive a pun, Khoja rivalries were to prove more a marathon than a Thermopylae. For, as with the Greeks in the wake of the Persian Wars, the Sunni Khoja *jamaat* in years to come ended up more divided against itself over formulas of law and custom than fixated on an external enemy in the form of the Agha Khan I.

Without a doubt, Arnould's 1866 judgment in the Agha Khan Case initiated a new discursive paradigm for the Khojas and became a frequent benchmark for all subsequent Khoja disputes.[79] At the same time, there is much more to be said in subsequent chapters about Khoja court cases in the decades after 1866, which are typically viewed as sideshows or simply affirmations of the Agha Khan Case. To be sure, several historians have hinted that the Khoja inheritance commissions of the 1870s and 1880s embodied traditions of cooperation between the *jamaats* and the colonial state.[80] These readings, however, have generally fueled the assumption that the *jamaats* universally benefited from collaboration with the colonial state. Yet the reception of these legislative changes in the sundry Khoja *jamaats,* where many remained dissatisfied with their outcome, has been overlooked. As with the Kachchhi Memons' agitation against Perry's 1847 decision, attention to the Khojas' reception of the Agha Khan Case and the Khoja Law Commissions reveals that the exceptional formulations of custom and law applied to the community divided Khoja *jamaats* just as much as it united them.

Seeds of discontent found fertile soil far beyond the Bombay *jamaat.* By the 1870s, Muscat was becoming a hotbed of rivalry within the Khoja *jamaat* over the authority of the Agha Khan. In 1872 some four hundred Khojas in Muttrah, a suburb of Muscat, "seceded" from the Ismaili Khoja *jamaat* (though it is doubtful whether they were ever integrated into the post-1866 *jamaat* to begin). They declared that the Agha Khan I had no right to make a proprietary claim on their mosque. As colonial correspondence reveals, the Agha Khan I claimed that the *jamaat khana* had always been "a Public Guest house set apart for members of the Sect of Khojas traveling to and fro between Kerbella and Hindoostan and Africa" and that he had always been its sole owner. He argued further that although these Khojas had indeed seceded, the act of secession led to a forfeit of all liens on *jamaat* property. Leveraging his status as the imam of the Khojas and a British subject, the Agha Khan I protested the Sultan of Muscat's involvement in the affair, declaring unlawful the latter's confiscation and transfer of the property to the secessionists.[81]

In a reflection of the density of Khoja families in the region, which contrasted with the male-only demographics of some Gujarati Muslim trading networks, the Agha Khan I also maintained that, while the husbands had left the *jamaat,* their wives clung stubbornly to the old faith. The secessionists questioned these arguments, holding that the property never served the sole function of the guest house. Since the site had been consecrated as a mosque by the sultan, they argued, it was "bona fide their property, that is inalienable and incapable of desecration by conversion into a Guest House."[82] The sultan, in turn, defended the secessionists and emphasized that he had no wish to interfere with the integrity of the mosque.

The colonial political resident, Colonel Lewis Pelly, found the arguments of the Agha Khan I more persuasive and acknowledged that if the case had been tried within British jurisdiction, the Agha Khan Case of 1866 would have supplied adequate precedent. But since the affair had taken place under the jurisdiction of a "despotic prince," the Sultan of Muscat, the burden of proof (*onus probandi*) fell on the Agha Khan I.[83] Reportedly, the Agha Khan I was not content to rely on legal argument alone. He was even said to have funded two rival potentates, who he hoped would capture Muscat and "confirm his right and title to the musjid [mosque] built by the Khojas in Muttra." When pressed, the Agha Khan I only denied funding one of the two men.[84]

The episode was a reminder of how Gujarati Muslim middle power, first formulated in Western India and expanded in years to come throughout the Indian Ocean region, sometimes became embroiled in the larger game of kingmaking on the frontiers of Britain's empire. It was only the start of a long-running showdown in the Khoja diaspora over the community's religious character and internal organization. Just four years after the Muttrah drama, in a notorious episode in Karachi in 1876, the *jamaat* excommunicated the dissenter Seth Lallan Alladina. After several failed attempts on his life, Alladina was murdered by some Khojas three years later. It was said that he had seized several buildings purportedly owned by the Agha Khan I.[85] A small public relations fiasco for the Agha Khan I ensued but did not detract from the Ismaili Khojas' deepening attachment to the colonial state.

The intractability of Khoja law continued to inveigle colonial officials, who eventually saw fit to form a series of Khoja Law Commissions from the late 1870s to the mid-1880s. These commissions have been dissected elsewhere from the perspective of colonial legislative practice, but the perspective from the *jamaats* has yet to be studied. An excellent window into how the Khoja *jamaats* greeted these reforms is a polemic entitled *Khojā Sunatjamātanā navā kayedā vīrūddha Khojā Abdallā Hājī Alārakhīānā ūrdu copānīāno tarajumo* (Khoja Abd Allah Haji Allah Rakhia against the new laws of the Khoja Sunni *jamaat*), published in both Gujarati and Urdu in 1879–1880.[86] Allah Rakhia's text reveals the vitriol and controversy that ensued when an entrepreneur from these communities attempted to execute a will according to "Hindu custom" or an uncommon interpretation of "Islamic law." While the Kachchhi Memons attempted to do away with the "yoke of custom" by agitating for legal reform, a prominent Sunni Khoja's attempt to invent a new "custom" of inheritance as a prelude to acquiring recognition for an officially codified "law" generated a howl of outrage from the ranks of his own *jamaat*. Allah Rakhia's diatribe underscored that no Gujarati Muslim *sethia* was above community censure for violating what was regarded as the authentic prescriptions of Islamic law.

The target of his animus was the Sunni Khoja merchant and justice of the peace, Ahmadbhai Habibbhai. Habibbhai was a fixture in Bombay public life for close to four decades, and his business empire encompassed some of the largest mills in Ceylon. For a time, his prominence was outshone only by his elder brother, Khan Muhammad Habibbhai, whose mercantile career was stellar by all accounts. As Allah Rakhia recounted in his polemic against Ahmadbhai Habibbhai, when Khan Muhammadbhai Habibbhai died, he left behind a daughter, a wife, and an enormous estate of between fifteen and seventeen lakhs. His will dictated that his brother Ahmadbhai Habibbhai be appointed as "temporary trustee." Immediately, Ahmadbhai Habibbhai began maneuvering to draft a series of inheritance statues for the entire Khoja community that, Allah Rakhia argued, not only contradicted the customs of both the Ismaili and Sunni Khoja *jamaats* but also violated Islam in the round.

According to Habibbhai's formulation, if a male Khoja died without sons, his widow and any daughters had no legitimate claim to inherit the deceased's assets. Rather, in a convenient formulation, given his own circumstances, the brother of the deceased would inherit the estate. Utilizing his friendship with an English judge, Ahmadbhai Habibbhai was granted permission to draw up two petitions outlining the details of the new inheritance bill, which colonial authorities then forwarded to both the Ismaili and Sunni Khoja *jamaats*. According to Allah Rakhia, the Ismaili Khoja *jamaat* convened to discuss the proposal, concluding that "we like our old custom that is in operation, and there is no place for this new law which the government wants to implement." (Yet another reminder that Bombay's Ismaili Khoja *jamaat* was no flunky of colonial power, but jealously defended its corporate privileges). Five thousand Ismaili Khojas then signed a petition maintaining this position and dispatched it to the judge. Meanwhile, at the Sunni Khoja *jamaat*, the facade of consensus masked less than full unanimity.

When Ahmadbhai Habibbhai presented the petition to the Sunni Khoja *jamaat*, its constituents protested that there was no need for a new statute since "for us there is the sacred Quran."[87] Hoping to clear up any ambiguity with colonial authorities, the members of the Sunni Khoja *jamaat* agreed that a missive should be sent to colonial officials all the same, confirming that the inheritance law of their *jamaat* was "commensurate with the Quran and hadith." What they eventually signed was Ahmadbhai Habibbhai's self-serving formula. In Allah Rakhia's telling, when the petitions from the two *jamaats*—the Sunni petition containing around 150 signatures, the Ismaili one five thousand—reached the judge, the Sunni petition was approved as the rule for all the Khojas.

The responsibility of drafting a more formal inheritance law for the Khoja *jamaats* remained unfinished, however. For that reason, a seven-person commission was set up: two Englishmen whose presence so irked Allah Rakhia, the Agha Ali Shah (son of the Agha Khan I, and soon-to-be Agha Khan II from 1881 to 1885), Ahmadbhai Habibbhai, and three Sunni Khojas, Jairajbhai Pirbhai, Dharamshey Punjabhai, and Rahmat Allah Muhammad Sayani. The law that this committee eventually drew up was, according to Allah Rakhia's narrative, rejected as contrary to Islam, both by Agha Ali Shah and the plurality of the two Khoja *jamaats*. That meant that only the two Englishmen and the Sunni Khojas accepted it. Allah Rakhia did his level best to show that the four Sunni Khojas, in drafting this law, had violated several verses of the Quran and canonical hadith, thus rendering themselves unbelievers.

In his conclusion, Allah Rakhia inveighed against the corporate privileges of certain Muslim groups, suggesting that only those who abided by the rules of the larger Muslim community could enjoy its rights. Those who consciously flouted such rules—foremost among them the Kachchhi Memons and Sunni Khojas—should have those rights repudiated. His reflections reveal that the corporate privileges of the Gujarati Muslim commercial castes became a blemish upon their name in the eyes of many of their Muslim peers. What Muslim commentators at the time, and historians of later years, have failed to recognize is that this legal exceptionalism was not universally a badge of honor for all in the *jamaats*. Rather, it was often a source of deep misgivings and dissent.

In the end, Sunni Khoja agitation against the 1866 decision captured the paradox of Elphinstonian deference to caste rights and the administrative legacies of precolonial Indian rulers. Whereas colonial officials assumed they were doing right by the *jamaats* by upholding their corporate integrity, individuals within the Khoja and Memon *jamaats* (and the Bohras, to a lesser extent) were more than willing to disabuse their colonial overlords of that assumption by repeatedly voicing their discontent with the character of their legal classification. Perry's judgments between 1847 and 1851, and Arnould's in 1866, established the parameters for all subsequent legal disputes within the Khoja *jamaats*. In the realm of colonial law, the influence of their decisions should not be underestimated. This said, innumerable other matters of *jamaat* governance—to say nothing of the religious ideas animating its members—had yet to be resolved. Although European and Indian commentators cited both Perry and Arnould ad infinitum over the decades, their decisions were merely a point of reference for polemical combatants, never the final word.

The example of the Gujarati Muslim commercial castes should give pause to the frequent tendency of historians to stress the success of colonial *codification* of Hindu and Islamic law.[88] Some contemporary colonial officials saw codification as an illusion, even when it came to these small Gujarati Muslim commercial castes. This is borne out from the remarks of Sir Courtenay Peregrine Ilbert, best known for the eponymous (and infamous) Ilbert Bill, which, seeking to deprive Europeans in British India of the immunity of being tried by an Indian judge, prompted a "white mutiny" among Europeans in British India. White outrage, in turn, catalyzed the embryonic Indian nationalist movement into organizing itself into the Indian National Congress.[89] Speaking during a less tumultuous occasion on the intractable problems associated with codifying Hindu and Islamic law, Ilbert cited the Khojas as proof that "even in the case of a small community . . . it has, up to this time, been found impossible to frame a set of rules of inheritance on which the leaders of the sect will agree. And any Code not based on general agreement would either cause dangerous discontent or remain a dead letter."[90] Chapter 3, which covers the religious controversies endemic to corporate Islam at greater length, will supply ample corroboration of this statement.

* * *

As suggested herein, the rapid extension of the Bohra, Khoja, and Memon diasporas in the generation after 1865 was not a neat process involving the creation of geographically scattered but institutionally unified *jamaats* across the Indian Ocean region. No single Bohra, Khoja, or Memon formula of law and custom ever materialized. To argue otherwise is to ignore the frequency with which *jamaats* fractured over questions of religious authority. Commercial success and legal exceptionalism thus did not simply enhance corporate Islam but also had the capacity to fracture *jamaats* into ever-greater subunits. Frequently, the supposed efficiency gains acquired by the colonial state's recognition of customary practice over Islamic law—so often cited in attempts to explain the economic success of the Bohras, Khojas, and Memons as compared to other Indian Muslims—were frittered away through internal *jamaat* conflicts. Such were the contradictory effects of Gujarati Muslim middle power.

Around 1880, controversies over religious authority impinged with special force upon the merchant networks operated by Bohra, Khoja, and Memon entrepreneurs, as will be seen in chapter 3. The high water mark of modern globalization, 1870–1914, was characterized by the dramatic multiplication of novel, socially concrete, and irreconcilable forms of Islam. And the Bohra, Khoja, and Memon *jamaats* were lodestones for these competing archetypes.[91] As these archetypes interacted within the *jamaats*, they prompted regular clashes over religious authority. The tensions between a polycentric network of *jamaats* and rival models of religious authority ensured that the Gujarati Muslim commercial castes were never isolated from contemporary currents of both Shiʿi and Sunni Islam. Rather, they were deeply conversant with these currents. And the Bohras, Khojas, and Memons were not only consumers but also producers of novel Muslim religious realities.

Thus, far from being the unitary prototype of the nonintellectual "Muslim trading caste" of many accounts, the three communities were deeply invested in currents of religious scholarship and debate and held within their *jamaats* irreconcilable ideas about Islamic law. Subscribing to disparate accounts of caste ethnogenesis, possessed of disparate traditions of historiography and legal scholarship, and marked by structural discrepancies in their organization of religious authority, it could not have been otherwise. Whether knowledge of the intricacies of Islamic jurisprudence (*fiqh*) was especially complex outside circumscribed circles is another matter entirely. But what can be said confidently is that Islamic law in all its multitudinous forms was appealed to regularly and possessed a semantic valence that buttressed *jamaat* custom rather than universally working against it, as assumed by contemporary colonial officials and Muslim commentators.

3

Clarifying and Contesting Religious Authority

1880–1912

AT KILWA IN 1905, the Agha Khan III, the living imam of the Ismaili Khojas and grandson of Agha Khan I, was involved in a religious disputation supervised by local officials of the German Empire. His adversaries were three newly minted Twelver Khojas: Haji Sulaiman Bhimji, Sharif Nur Muhammad, and Sulaiman Valji, all merchants. Kilwa, some 250 miles from Zanzibar, had been inhabited by Muslim traders since the late medieval period, and became a center of the regional slave trade, with close political ties to Yemen and commercial links to the Red Sea and Gujarat.[1] It fell under imperial German rule in the 1880s during the Scramble for Africa, when it also became host to a variety of Ismaili and Twelver Khojas moving outward from Gujarat and British possessions in East Africa. As Sharif Nur Muhammad recounted in a narrative of the events at Kilwa, he had joined a Khoja commercial firm in Zanzibar as a clerk after a childhood spent in the Gujarati city of Mahuva. In time he found employment at another Khoja firm before opening his own shop in Kilwa in 1890.[2]

Sharif Nur Muhammad's experience with the local Ismaili Khoja *jamaat* (corporate caste institution) was purportedly not a happy one. In his estimation, the local Khojas were less than fastidious in the fulfillment of their religious duties. An element of small-town prejudice seems to have been at work, but Sharif Nur Muhammad was also rankled by far weightier aspects of the *jamaat*'s operation than the personal failings of some of its members.

He was deeply disturbed by assertions within the local *jamaat* that the drinking of *ghat-pat,* the ceremonial water consumed by Khojas (and Brahmins) in their ceremonies, was tantamount to drinking the blood of Imam Hussain. Sharif Nur Muhammad had refused to participate in the ritual, and therefore performed religious exercises at home. Not long after, he was hauled before the *jamaat* for a reprimand. Following this incident, he left the *jamaat* and began to cultivate contacts with the small numbers of Twelver Khojas in Kilwa. One of their first undertakings was the construction of an *imambara* (Twelver Shiʿi worship hall).[3]

Predictably, controversy ensued over ownership of the property. Several members of the Ismaili Khoja *jamaat* filed a case in court against the Twelver Khojas, on the pretext that the site belonged to the Agha Khan and was being used by the Twelvers to insult the imam. The judge eventually ruled that the Agha Khan III had the right to go to both sites. Afterward, the Ismaili Khojas purportedly wrote a letter to the Agha Khan III warning him that the Twelvers, though small in number, were in the ascendant. By the time of the Agha Khan III's visit in 1905, Kilwa reportedly had forty Ismaili Khoja households and twenty-two Twelver Khoja households. In the subsequent debate the Twelver Khojas challenged the Agha Khan III's authority with little sense of restraint. In turn, the Agha Khan III assured his interlocutors that his access to *maʿrifat* (esoteric knowledge) was far above their lowly station, ridiculing one of their number when he admitted he did not know Arabic, English, French, or Persian.[4] This was an assertion of a hierarchical model of corporate Islam in which religious interpretation was the sole monopoly of the apex cleric, the religious leader of the sect.

For every Twelver Khoja merchant who sought to break with the Agha Khans there were many others, like Taria Topan, who supported them. Originally from Kachchh, Topan joined his father's firm in Zanzibar in 1851, quickly becoming a key intermediary for American firms operating in the region. His influence grew to such heights by the 1870s that he was named customs master of Zanzibar. Like Nathabhai, Topan also pivoted to the China trade, and even opened a London branch, though this proved unprofitable.[5] Though he had established himself as a *sethia* (caste leader) long before the Agha Khan I consolidated his position as apex cleric over the Khoja *jamaat,* Topan was a dependable supporter of the Agha Khans from the 1860s to the 1890s. Even if some of Topan's extended family later drifted into the Sunni fold,[6] the capital and surrogate powers that Topan and other Khoja magnates lent to the Agha Khans were decisive in the making of a streamlined Ismaili Khoja *jamaat*. From his towering position in the *jamaat*, Topan continued to use his influence to defend the first three Agha Khans from colonial and Twelver aspersions alike and to inculcate caste-centric norms of inheritance and succession.[7]

The divergent relationships Sharif Nur Muhammad and Taria Topan had with the Ismaili Khoja *jamaats* accent how diaspora, legal pluralism, and wealth exacerbated problems of religious authority and governance in the *jamaats*. Because each *jamaat* was both consumer and producer of diverse iterations of Islam, institutional divergences stemming from the structure of religious authority ensured that the goalposts determining the relationship between Islamic law and *jamaat* custom shifted over the course of the colonial period. In this sense, the religious institutions and discourses underpinning corporate Islam were in a near constant state of flux.

It is useful to recapitulate the main trends of religious change in each community during the period covered in this chapter. Briefly stated, the Bohras embodied one form of the apex cleric model of corporate Islam (figure 3.1). They were increasingly transformed from a decentralized *jamaat*, wherein the position of the *dai al-mutlaq* (chief cleric of the sect) was muted, to a relatively centralized one where law, custom, and pilgrimage networks knit the diaspora together. In these decades, this centralizing impulse owed more to merchant capitalists and religious scholars than to the *dais*, although as seen in chapter 5, the *dai* who eventually obtained power in 1915 aspired to acquire a monopoly over both religious interpretation and community wealth. By contrast, the Memons adhered to the conciliar model of corporate Islam by remaining a decentralized *jamaat*, both because as Sunnis they lacked an apex cleric and because the Sufi saints and ulama they patronized were not native to the group. That did not preclude the Memons from being regularly tied up in conflicts among the range of competing Sunni *masālik* (orientations) that emerged in South Asia in the decades after 1857 (see figure 3.2).

The Khojas, divided henceforth between the Ismaili and Twelver *jamaats*, stood somewhere between the Bohra and Memon *jamaats* when it came to the profile of religious authority. The Ismaili Khoja *jamaats*, by elevating the Agha Khan I and his successors to the status of apex clerics and articulating a publicly confident, streamlined form of modern neo-Ismaili Shiʿism, came to resemble the Bohras. Even so, despite superficial similarities in religious

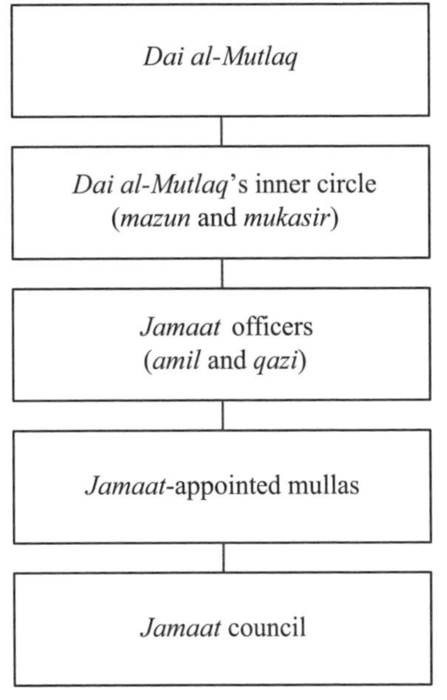

FIGURE 3.1 A depiction of the Bohra "apex cleric" model *jamaat*. It is important for the reader to note that these models are oversimplifications. In reality, the *jamaats* have been the sites of extensive internal conflicts, especially in the case of the "apex-cleric" communities, the Bohras and Ismaili Khojas. The making of an apex-cleric *jamaat* occurred only after periods of hierarchical assertion and elite subordination, and the victory was never total. Furthermore, as discussed in the introduction, the notion of the *jamaat* "collective" is largely a discursive fiction.

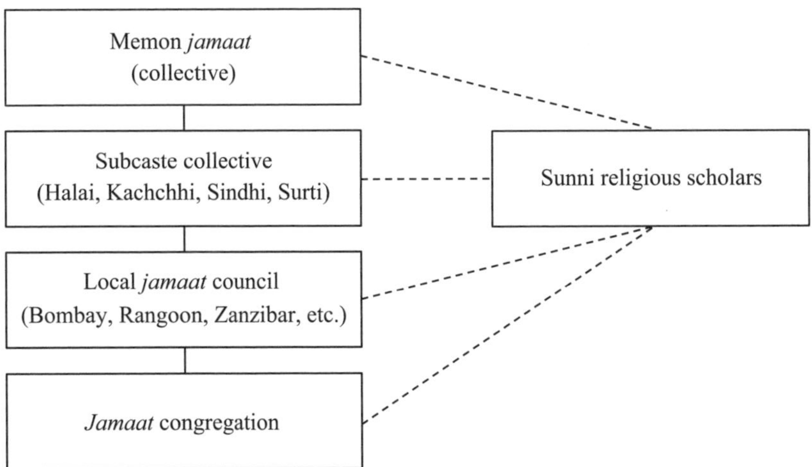

FIGURE 3.2 The Memon conciliar model. A more decentralized model of corporate Islam in which religious authority operates outside the *jamaat*. In contrast to the apex-cleric model, individual religious scholars are patronized by local *jamaats*, a process contributing to inter-*jamaat* differentiation.

organization, the Ismaili Shiʿism of the Bohras and Khojas diverged markedly in this period. Finally, the Twelver Khoja *jamaats* resembled the Memons' conciliar model insofar as they patronized Twelver Shiʿi mujtahids, which allowed the breakaway Twelvers to articulate an alternative, decentralized model of religious leadership to that of the Agha Khan III (see figures 3.3 and 3.4).

To the business historian, a chapter dedicated entirely to religious developments may seem excessive. However, religious dynamics were as fundamental to the story of corporate Islam as the economic capital that perpetuated it, and anyway are impossible to analytically net out from the business history of the *jamaat*. This chapter offers a corrective to those narratives of economic networks that view religious identity as fixed or incidental, or part of the glue that keeps the network coherent across space and time. As this chapter insists, a textured understanding of how conflicting forms of Islam manifested within each *jamaat* conveys that religion had as much potential to cleave the community as to reinforce it. Daily interactions with those outside the *jamaat* and the double role of Bohras, Khoja, and Memon *sethias* as business and religious entrepreneurs intensified these prospects.

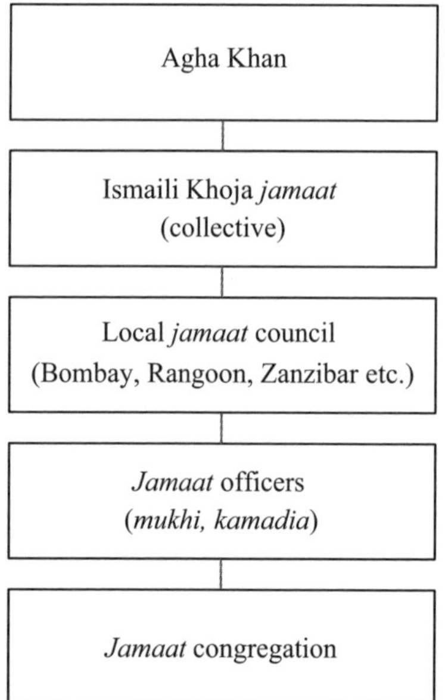

FIGURE 3.3 The apex-cleric model of the Ismaili Khoja *jamaats*. Note that it does not exactly mimic the structure of the Bohra apex-cleric model, with fewer religious scholars in the hierarchy.

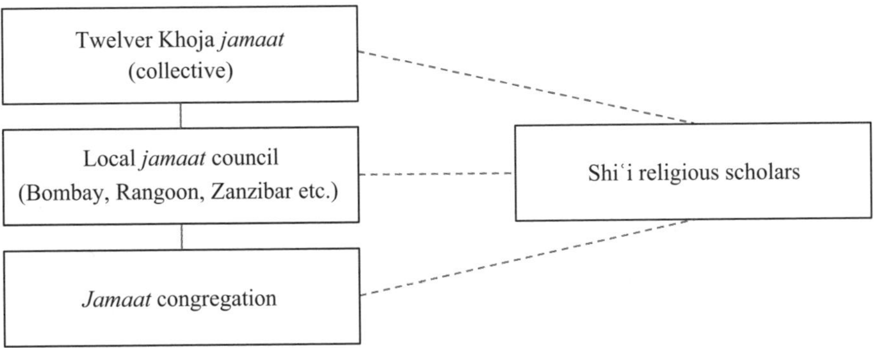

FIGURE 3.4 The Twelver Khoja conciliar model. Like the Memons, this model is more decentralized, with religious authority residing outside the *jamaats*. By the end point of this chapter, however, a substantial body of Twelver Khoja scholars emerged within the *jamaats*. This model was defined in opposition to the Ismaili Khoja apex-cleric model.

The Emergence of the Twelver Khoja *Jamaats*

Just as the Sunni and Ismaili Khojas reached a modus vivendi in the 1870s, a new group of Twelver Khojas emerged to challenge the Agha Khans' pretensions and the integrity of the Khoja *jamaats*. Conflicts between Ismaili and Twelver Khojas erupted across the diaspora, with the center of action shifting violently between Bombay, Karachi, and Zanzibar. To be sure, the number of Bohras, Khojas, and Memons in the leading entrepôts of the western Indian Ocean was still relatively small in 1870. Exact numbers are difficult to come by, and contemporary censuses are inconsistent. One source lists 2,558 Khojas in the greater territory of Zanzibar in 1870, with the vast majority of the 535 households hailing from Kachchh. That same report has 250 Bohras in Zanzibar, 142 in Mombasa, fifty-one in Pemba, and forty-two in Lamu.[8] Another source from the same year records one thousand Khojas residing in Zanzibar, but only fifty Bohras and forty Memons.[9]

The centrality of Zanzibar to all future Khoja disputes bears some explanation. As early as the 1840s, the Khojas were the most conspicuous Gujarati Muslim traders in the region. The profits that they accumulated in East Africa underwrote the expansion of distinct Ismaili and Twelver Khoja geographies from the 1870s onward.[10] (By contrast, colonial records from 1870 state that the Bohras in Zanzibar were "guided by a Moolla and the chief men of the sect, but possess no well-organized Council like that of the

Khojahs. The orders of the Chief of Surat [the *dai*] are in all cases final.").[11] The *mukhi* (*jamaat* chief) and *kamadia* (*jamaat* accountant) performed a litany of fundraising functions in the local Khoja *jamaat*.[12] Such funds were sent by courier or typically by *hundis* (bills of exchange) to Bombay, suggesting that the latter had achieved headquarters status in the broader network of Khoja *jamaats*.

Yet Zanzibar was also becoming a regional hub of its own and continued to possess a unique position in the Khoja diaspora. As a former governor of Bombay, Sir Bartle Frere, summarized matters in his account of the Zanzibar Ismaili Khoja *jamaat*'s administration, the officers of the Zanzibar *jamaat* were elected annually, and the *jamaat* received monetary contributions from Khojas on the coast, Mozambique, and other settlements that did not have a direct relationship with Bombay.[13] Frere had composed this report while touring various sites in East Africa. As he told an audience in Bombay in 1873, the entire stretch of the East African littoral had fallen into the hands of Indian traders in the past fifty years. He judged the Bohras, Khojas, and Memons to be the most numerous, with Khojas in preponderance.[14] Yet, in this world, women remained only minor economic actors, more or less bereft of property rights. Undoubtedly, they supported the business efforts of their male relatives, albeit in the invisible ways common to modern capitalism.

Since the accumulation of wealth accelerated internal conflict within *jamaats*, it was thus scarcely surprising that the Twelver Khoja *jamaat* first took root in Zanzibar. Subscribing to ideas of the imamate irreconcilable with those prevailing in Ismaili Shiʿism, Twelver Khojas rejected wholesale the religious authority of the Agha Khans and their attempts to normalize neo-Ismaili doctrine and practice within the Khoja *jamaats*. The *sethias* of the Ismaili Khoja *jamaats*, whose authority grew substantially in the period of the Agha Khan III's minority (1885–ca. 1895), greeted the advent of Twelver Khoja constituencies as an existential threat to the *jamaat*'s hard-won neo-Ismaili identity. The tendency of Ismaili and Twelver congregations to mix even after the latter's secession only intensified the anxiety of moral pollution among leaders of both *jamaats*.[15]

Nominally, beginning in 1866 the Ismaili Khoja *jamaat* possessed an unambiguous apex cleric whose writ, like that of the Bohra *dai al-mutlaq*, extended universally throughout the community. Though recognizably Shiʿi in the way they embodied Islamic traditions of authority, the Agha Khans were less and less beholden to the traditional corpus of Shiʿi legal theory, Nizari Ismaili and Twelver, from the 1880s onward. As such, the Ismaili Khojas' religious orientation should be called neo-Ismaili, not least because the community did not recover an identifiably Ismaili legal and intellectual tradition until the late nineteenth century.[16] Although Ismaili Khoja ties to the shrine cities of Iraq persisted, the status of Shiʿi Islam's sacred geography was diminished by the Agha Khan from his first tour of Africa in 1899. By contrast, the organization of religious authority in the emergent Twelver Khoja *jamaat* resembled the conciliar model of the Memons: it relied on the legal expertise of a series of decentralized Shiʿi mujtahids, all experts in Shiʿi law, but never univocal in their opinions.

According to community history, the emergence of the Twelver Khojas as a distinct *jamaat* dates to the pilgrimage made by one Haji Devji Jamal to the Shiʿi shrine cities in Iraq in the later nineteenth century.[17] Devji Jamal was a Zanzibar-based merchant who later funded the construction of Zanzibar's first Twelver *imambara* and mosque in the 1880s and 1890s, both of which were managed by the *jamaat*. In fact, sources from the Zanzibar archives show that Jamal's economic network extended north into Lamu and Mombasa, where he purchased substantial plantations (*shamba* in Swahili). He did not manage all these purchases himself, with his agent in Zanzibar in the late 1880s bearing the name Mahmud bin Ali al-Bohri (with *al-Bohri* denoting "the Bohra").[18]

Devji Jamal's pilgrimage to Iraq took place at a moment when the Agha Khans were reevaluating the place of sacred sites like Karbala and Najaf in *jamaat* worship. Following his death in 1885, the Agha Khan II was buried in the family mausoleum in Najaf.[19] Yet his son, the Agha Khan III, would actively downgrade the importance of the two cities from the end of the century. Devji Jamal and other Twelver Khojas pursued the opposite course, and during his pilgrimage he requested that one of the most distinguished Shiʿi mujtahids of the age, Ayat Allah Mazandarani, send a well-trained Shiʿi *ʿālim* (religious scholar) to the Khojas of Western India to educate them in Twelver Shiʿi doctrine. The Ayat Allah chose Mulla Qadir Hussain, who arrived in Bombay in 1873. Qadir Hussain's memoirs relate the many impediments he faced in creating a separate Twelver Khoja *jamaat*. Even his inaugural meeting with Devji Jamal in Karbala was hardly friendly, as he maligned the merchant prince for believing that a pilgrimage to Karbala was worth "seventy Hajj," further encouraging the *sethia* to learn "true Islam" from the sources and branches of the law.[20]

Mujtahids like Qadir Hussain—and the students he acquired in Bombay and the surrounding region—injected new discourses of law and custom into the nascent Twelver Khoja *jamaat*. To be sure, relations were not always harmonious between the Twelver Khoja merchants and their mullah. One spat saw Hussain take umbrage with the tendency of Twelver Khoja *sethias* to accept monetary interest. Riding one day in a carriage with a leading merchant, Jafarbhai Kalyan, Hussain instructed him, "Now you leave dealing in [usury] and make your prayer a true one." Kalyan retorted that it was impossible to conduct business without accepting interest. He added that the practice was made permissible by the ruling of another Shiʿi scholar, one Sayyid Muhammad, who had issued fatwas to several Twelver Khojas endorsing the practice.[21] Hussain found this reprehensible and sought to expunge the custom. At any rate, Qadir Hussain and Sayyid Muhammad were not the only Muslim scholars of this period to disagree over the legality of financial interest, and Khoja merchants perhaps exploited those ambiguities to their benefit.

As part of this attempt to reform the norms and behaviors of the emerging Twelver Khoja *jamaat*, Hussain published several religious works. He also was likely involved in publishing his teacher Mazandarani's ambitious Shiʿi work on ethics, *Zakhīrat al-maʿād* (Treasury of the hereafter), in Bombay in the 1890s.[22] The text likely would have been intelligible to any Twelver Khoja with an intermediate knowledge of Persian. At the time there were very few Gujarati texts for Twelver Khojas to study; that enterprise was left to the coterie of Khoja students trained by Qadir Hussain. The most famous of these was Ismail Ghulam Ali, better known as Haji Naji, who founded a Twelver Khoja newspaper, *Rāhe najāt* (The Path of Salvation) and the Ithnā ʿAsharī Electric Printing Press in Bhavnagar. This press eventually produced more than four hundred religious texts for the Twelver Khoja *jamaat*, and the scholarly legacy of Haji Naji lives on today in the form of a Gujarati website dedicated to his work.[23]

In fact, the desire to inculcate rival neo-Ismaili or Twelver interpretations of Shiʿi Islam in the Khoja *jamaats* dramatically boosted the production of Gujarati religious works from the 1890s. But it first bears emphasizing that that the Bohras, Khojas, and Memons each constituted a multilingual Islamic interpretive community encompassing varying shades of literacy in Arabic, Gujarati, Persian, and Urdu. Nevertheless, Gujarati assumed center stage as a language of religious discourse from the 1880s as the demographics of interpretive community expanded in this era. In truth, the production of texts in Gujarati was a sensitive subject for many Gujarati Muslim commentators from at least the last quarter of the nineteenth century onward, for it revealed both the promise and the peril of a wide readership. Writing in 1894 one Sunni commentator bemoaned the fact that since so many Gujarati-speaking Muslims did not know Arabic, Persian, or Urdu, they were not properly acquiring the tenets of the faith.[24] That deficit also stirred up anxieties. In a preface to a Gujarati translation of an Urdu work on Sunni jurisprudence, one Surat-based scholar issued the following edict: "It is necessary for me to issue a warning to pious brothers: several adherents of the Shiʿi creed, that is Khojas and Bohras, are selling Islamic printed books in Gujarati. And members of the Sunni *jamaat* are buying these books. As such, those who buy books must pay attention to who the printer is. Even if done by mistake, buying these books will accordingly destroy the faith."[25]

Khoja capitalists on either side of the Ismaili and Twelver dividing line were the most enthusiastic producers, consumers, and financiers of such works (although, as will be shown, Bohra authors showed no slack). Their tone diverged widely depending upon the identity of the author. Consider the case of *Ismāilī Prakāśa* (Ismaili Wisdom), one of the earliest primers on neo-Ismaili Shiʿism penned by Mastar Hasham Bogha. Leading merchants of the Rangoon and Zanzibar Ismaili Khoja *jamaats* purchased 246 copies of the book before it was even published. The work deliberately sought to speak in a register of Gujarati understandable to the ordinary member of the *jamaat*, and Bogha hoped that many additional works of Islamic literature would be translated into Gujarati in the future. Presently he assured his reader that explanations of Arabic verses from the Quran and the hadith would be paired with Gujarati explanations.[26]

Whether Bogha's primary audience stopped at the boundary of the Ismaili Khoja *jamaat* seems uncertain. For one, he felt the inclination to explain the meaning of the term "Ismaili" in the distinct theological languages of Muslims and Hindus, asserting further that the Agha Khan III had followers from both communities. Yet, much of the text situated the Agha Khan III's authority in an unmistakably Shiʿi salvation history.[27] The identities of the Ismaili Khoja *jamaats* were thus multiplex, in conversation with contemporary currents of Islamic and Hindu thought. Far from a syncretic blend of the two, however, this was a supersessionary concept of religious community. Suitably, Bogha also turned his hand in these years to the thorny question of Khoja ethnogenesis, a hot topic among Ismaili and Twelver authors who advanced irreconcilable narratives of the Khojas' conversion to Shiʿi Islam.[28]

Bogha was representative of the new breed of Ismaili Khoja religious scholars who emerged in the generation after the Agha Khan Case of 1866 and combined their business and scholarly pursuits with their duties as administrators of the various Ismaili Khoja *jamaat* councils. Serving in an editorial capacity, Bogha encouraged many of these figures to publish their works with the Ismaili Literature Society. Among them was one Jumabhai Alibhai Suratwala, whose 1913 exegetical text *Makasade hakīkata* (The Purposes of Truth) was dedicated to the *ginans* (Nizari Ismaili devotional hymns), the Quran, and sundry Ismaili Shiʿi traditions.[29] The production of religious scholars from within the Ismaili Khoja *jamaat* was a key structural difference from the Twelver Khojas, for the integration of Shiʿi mujtahids into the ballooning network of Twelver Khoja *jamaats* required regular movement outside the network of the *jamaat*.

Ismaili-Twelver rivalry intensified as the Twelver Khoja *jamaats* demonstrated an ability to win prominent public figures to the cause. In 1901 Bombay's leading Parsi newspaper, *Jame Jamshed* (The Chalice of Jamshed), published the names of sixteen Khojas recently excommunicated by the Ismaili Khoja *jamaat*. Having been appointed trustees of a Twelver Khoja mosque then under construction, the group was blacklisted by the leaders of the Ismaili Khoja *jamaat*, who called on all other clandestine Twelvers to identify and excommunicate themselves. Of the sixteen thrown out of the *jamaat*, four were reportedly killed.[30] The Twelvers quickly began printing their own *jamaat* rule book, a proclamation of their separate identity.[31] The incident reflected just how adamant the leaders of the Ismaili Khoja *jamaats* were in their desire to enforce corporate cohesion and loyalty to the apex cleric.

Karachi also furnished fertile soil for Khoja *jamaat* quarrels. The booming port city had witnessed several murders of Twelver Khojas in the 1870s. Over the next decades, ongoing bad blood between the two Khoja *jamaats* sometimes spilled over into other public institutions. The 1906 excommunication of Jaffar Fadu—a well-known journalist, philanthropist, and former member of Karachi's municipal board—was a cause célèbre for the entire city. As one of his subsequent Twelver Khoja defenders recalled, Fadu was from a storied Khoja family. His grandfather, a *jamaat* elder, was one of the many Khojas who moved in midcentury from Kathiawar and Sindh to Karachi, where Fadu was born in 1857. Educated by some indeterminate order of Christian priests, he ended up working as an apprentice in a local hospital. Over the next three decades his achievements included funding a massive dispensary in Karachi (which bears his name to this day).[32] Simultaneously, Fadu was the trustee of various Ismaili Khoja trusts.

Fadu and his family's record of service in Karachi's Ismaili Khoja *jamaat* did little, however, to insulate him from the attacks of Ismaili Khoja *sethias.* In 1906 he received an ominous letter from the chief secretary of Karachi's Ismaili Khoja *jamaat* stating, "It has come to the attention of the Ismaili Council that you are no longer a member of the Shia Imami Ismaili sect, and no longer accept, with obedience, the head of the religion, Sir Sultan Agha Khan, as your imam. That is bad enough, but this is not all." The rest of the letter upbraided Fadu for several offenses, including joining openly with the Twelvers and associating with their *jamaat,* attending the Twelver cemetery and participating in Twelver funerals, failing to bow down to the imam when he visited Karachi, and ignoring the laws and statutes of the Ismaili *jamaat.*[33]

Even after an order of excommunication was passed, public figures like Fadu who refused to play by community rules continued to present a headache to the leaders of *jamaats.* When a disgruntled constituent aired the *jamaat*'s dirty laundry, it did little credit to the institution's image in the court of public opinion. Nevertheless, for every Fadu there were those who remained loyal to the *jamaat* and acted as coercive instruments of its collective will. In Fadu's case, this role was played by Fakir Muhammad Vali Muhammad, a superintendent in Karachi's Municipal Octroi Department who declared the order of excommunication against him.[34] The fact that elite members of the *jamaats* often served in leadership capacities for other corporate bodies within the British Empire tended to alternatively foster or propitiate dissent in the community.

Not beholden to an apex cleric, Twelver Khoja *sethias,* as heads of their respective *jamaats,* exercised considerable authority within the community. This was facilitated, as argued above, by the decentralized character of the Twelver Khojas' conciliar-model *jamaats,* which were structurally distinct from the integrated Ismaili Khoja *jamaats* with their apex cleric and hierarchy of *mukhis* and *kamadias.* Patronage of individual mujtahids did not immunize the Twelver Khoja *jamaats* from fragmentation. In one instance from the early twentieth century, a split tore the Twelver Khoja *jamaat* in Zanzibar into two factions: *Ḥujjat al-Islām* and *Quwwat al-Islām*, each supporting competing Twelver mujtahids.[35] The Khoja businessman Sharif Jivabhai was compelled to travel from Madagascar to Zanzibar to resolve the dispute.[36] Jivabhai had earned his wealth as a trader in Diego Suarez (present-day Antsiranana) on the northern tip of Madagascar. During the French conquest of the island at the end of the century, he moved into the lucrative industry of military provision for the French Army.[37]

It took a figure of Jivabhai's standing to bring the two Zanzibar Twelver Khoja *jamaats* together after previous efforts at consensus had repeatedly failed. Records from the archives in Zanzibar evoke the bitterness of the schism between the two *jamaats.*[38] Both sides leveled heated accusations concerning the credentials of each party to describe themselves as Twelvers, and the authority of the *jamaat* was repeatedly invoked by each to discredit the other. Though Jivabhai was able to resolve the dispute, his time in Zanzibar brought him personal troubles. Not long after his visit, one of the Twelver Khoja residents of Zanzibar, and the editor of the Gujarati newspaper *Jaṃgabāra samācāra* (Zanzibar News), Fazal Jan Muhammad, took him to court for an unpaid bill. Jan Muhammad even charged that the prominent merchant prince of Madagascar was insolvent, an accusation that Jivabhai disputed with documentation.[39] Such suits reflected the intensely litigious character of the Gujarati Muslim commercial castes, uncurbed even by membership in the same *jamaat*. Shared *jamaat* affiliation probably had the opposite effect: rather than abolishing dissensions, its intimacies exacerbated them.

Zanzibar retained its special status as a laboratory of Khoja conflict for decades to come. The same year as the Kilwa dispute, the Agha Khan III and his chief *mukhis* in Zanzibar promulgated a constitution for the local *jamaat*. In the words of one historian, it was intended to "act as safety valve against seceders who might lay claim to communal property."[40] In reality, both sides published *jamaat* handbooks demanding that individual Khojas swear allegiance to their side and threatening expulsion to anyone who interacted with members of the other *jamaat*. These pronouncements only aggravated relations among *sethias*, and their aggravation was likely swollen by the regularity of interactions among Khojas across the sectarian divide throughout the diaspora, something which the Agha Khan III repeatedly discouraged in his firmans. Lacking more and more the mediating function of a single *jamaat*, Ismaili and Twelver *jamaats* relied on the colonial courtroom to mediate their disputes. Such unquenchable litigiousness remained a central feature of corporate Islam among the Khojas for the remainder of the periods covered in this book.

It was one thing for a member of the Khoja laity in Bhavnagar, Kilwa, or Mahuva to contest the proprietary claims of the Agha Khan III, but a far more serious matter when the Agha Khan III's blood relations did so. Worth discussing in that regard is the famous Haji Bibi Case of 1905–1908, in which Haji Bibi, the Agha Khan III's cousin (the daughter of his uncle, Jhangi Shah), sued the Ismaili Khoja imam on the grounds that the charitable contributions he enjoyed were not his alone but belonged to his extended family. Property was by no means the only issue up for grabs, for Haji Bibi also maintained that the family of the Agha Khans were Twelver Shiʿis, not Ismailis. Typically the case has attracted interest for the light it sheds on the history of the Ismaili *ginans*, which were deliberated upon by the court in an effort to grasp the Khojas' religious identity.[41] But in most histories the case is also framed as a rubber-stamping of the Agha Khan III's authority, and even round two of the Agha Khan Case of 1866 inasmuch as it ratified the Khoja *jamaat*'s identity as Ismaili Shiʿi Muslims and asserted that the Agha Khan III was the sole heir of the estate of his grandfather, Agha Khan I.[42]

What that framing misses entirely is the give-and-take of the bitter Khoja conflicts analyzed in chapters 1 and 2. It also misleadingly suggests that colonial officials had already worked out the Khojas' identity to their lasting satisfaction. But this ignores that colonial knowledge of Khoja religious praxis was in a process of constant evolution, though by no means moving toward a greater understanding. In fact, in 1908 the presiding judge, Justice Russell, had to grapple with a more particular question of what kind of Shiʿi the Khojas were. (In the Agha Khan Case in 1866, Justice Joseph Arnould had had to contend with whether they were Shiʿi Imami Ismaili Muslims or Sunnis, and the Twelvers barely factored into the picture.) Finally, the tendency to treat Haji Bibi's suit as just so much a reaffirmation of the 1866 case overlooks the fact that the suit, according to Russell's judgment, took up "the longest time on record" of any case hitherto held in Bombay's High Court.[43] The judgment ran to seventy-odd pages in its "digest" version, suggesting it was not simply the 1866 case redux. During the course of the trial, Russell had forbidden the printing of court proceedings in the press. Still, not long after the trial's conclusion, and even several decades later, rival Khoja authors sponsored Gujarati translations of the case record.[44]

Like many Khoja women over the previous six decades, Haji Bibi asserted that she had been denied her rightful share of her family's estate, and over a dozen other defendants were named in the suit alongside the Agha Khan to corroborate this assertion. One of her more compelling claims was that Islamic rules of inheritance were commonplace in the family of the Agha Khans.[45] While the Khoja community had been understood by colonial officials to have been governed by customary Hindu rules of inheritance since Sir Erskine Perry's judgment in 1847 (see chapter 1), the documents submitted to the court tried to underscore that the Agha Khans' extended family did not follow suit but adhered to Islamic inheritance rules. Haji Bibi then used this presumption to lay claim to 7 / 144 of the Agha Khan I's estate. But, in practice, a range of customary and Islamic practices were followed by the family, with the defendants underscoring that "instead of dividing the said offerings and properties among the persons so entitled to them a custom has grown up in the family ever since the time of the 1st Aga Khan to the effect that the titular head for the time being keeps charge of and manages all offerings and makes suitable allowances to the other members."[46] In this sense, then, the family of the Agha Khans followed its own customary formulations, distinct both from that followed by the Ismaili Khoja *jamaat* and Islamic law.

Ultimately the court rejected most of Haji Bibi's assertions, with Russell complaining that the case had hopelessly mixed up Islamic and Hindu law. The declaration that the Agha Khan III's estate was not jointly held by his extended family but belonged to the imam alone reaffirmed that the *sarkar* of the imam was inseparable from the corporate body of the Ismaili Khoja *jamaat*. Even so, the capacity of Twelver assertions to threaten the integrity of not just the Ismaili Khoja *jamaat* but the imam's personal wealth was remarkable. The Agha Khan III's victory over Haji Bibi, which took over three years to reach its conclusion, was a close-run thing and presaged still greater inter-Khoja struggles to come in the interwar period. For the time being, however, it yet again reaffirmed the straitened economic circumstances endured by Khoja women, itself an integral feature of corporate Islam across all three castes in this book.

Memon Integration into the Rival Sunni *Masālik*

Like their Khoja brethren did with Shiʿi Islam, the Memons trafficked in competing forms of Sunni Islam, conferring the rival Sunni orientations (*masālik*, sg. *maslak*) that emerged in the wake of the 1857 Indian Rebellion with a concentrated infrastructure of institutions—all rooted in the *jamaat*—across the Indian Ocean. These *masālik*—bearing names like Aligarh, Ahl-i Hadith, Ahmadiyya, Barelvi and Deoband—harbored competing notions of what constituted normative Islam, even if there was considerable overlap in some of their positions. They were divided too by contrasting notions of how to manage relations with the colonial state and non-Muslims. Far from being peripheral to these developments, Memons patronized scholars from the various *masālik* and, in turn, were targets of their overtures. Henceforth, Memon identity was a product of dialectic tensions between the institutions of the Sunni *masālik* coalescing from the 1860s and Memon religious life as embodied in the *jamaats*, where venerable attachments to the Hanafi *madhhab* (one of the four Sunni legal schools) and Sufi shaykhs was the norm.

When examining the history of the *masāliks*' interaction with Memon *jamaats*, it is pivotal to differentiate here, wherever possible, between Halai and Kachchhi Memon subbranches. On account of their patronage of rival Sunni *masālik*, Halai and Kachchi Memon differences became more marked. But while Halai Memons were recognized as full Sunni Muslims in the eyes of colonial law, the Kachchhi Memons maintained an ambivalent relationship with their legal status, and that struggle lasted well into the 1930s. A telling indication of the is glimpsed through other Muslims' conflicting perceptions of them during the 1870s and 1880s. For a variety of reasons, Muslim commentators still had trouble seeing Memons as full Muslims. Passing through Bombay on his way to Hajj in 1870, the traveler Muhammad Zardar Khan noted the city's assemblage of affluent merchants. Bombay's Jewish traders were among those to catch his meandering eye. Yet, he continued sourly, "even wealthier than the Jews is the community of the Memons. The Memons are 'new Muslims.' In the region of Kathiawar many of them were shopkeepers, and many fine shopkeepers exist among them now. All the same, their expressions of charity are very great, and en route to sacred Medina one sees many signs of this. Notwithstanding such charity, two defects are very severe among them: the first is lending money at interest [*sūd-khwārī*], the other is the lack of veiling [*bī-pardagī*], which are customs found among the shopkeeping community of Hindus."[47]

Zardar Khan's diatribe certainly would have rankled the growing sensitivity among Memons to the stereotype that they were Hindus in all but name. It certainly contrasted with colonial declarations that the Memon "is strict in his observance of the *Sunna* which commands him to haggle 'till his forehead perspires, just as it did in winning the money.'"[48] Still, even compared to other Sunni Muslim commercial communities distinguished by their wealth, such as the Konkani Muslims and the Navayaths, the Memons were subjected to this unstable mix of admiration (for their business savvy) and reproof (for their supposed hoarding of wealth) by other Sunni commentators. None were more outspoken in their reproof than the Indian Muslim landed gentry, who exhibited much of the antimercantile prejudice of landholding elites the world over. In an early instance, the Islamic modernist Sayyid Ahmad Khan (whose Muhammadan Anglo-Oriental College received generous donations from Memon merchants) lampooned the Memons as a group who "spend a lot of money, but in such a foolish way that they gain nothing, whether spiritually or temporally, except that for a short time people talk of this or that Memons' [madrasa]."[49] In a separate travelogue, Sayyid Ahmad Khan criticized the Memons' penchant for founding individual madrasas that were not coordinated with one another.[50]

Sayyid Ahmad Khan's portrayal conveyed the entrenched assumption that Memons were apathetic to intellectual shifts integral to the making of modern Sunni Islam, too given to "customary" forms of Islam to bother with modern varieties. This erroneous conviction obscured salient aspects of Memon history from 1870, aspects impossible to disentangle from the histories of other Indian Sunni Muslims in this same epoch. One impediment to appreciating the Memons' complex Sunni identity is the lack of sources on their history. From the early twentieth century onward, Memon historians have had to rely on only a handful of sources to tell their own history. One source to which they frequently turned was a text from 1873, written by a curious character named Sayyid Amir al-Din Nuzhat. Nuzhat's compact work, *Ibrāẓ al-ḥāqq* (Presentation of the Truth) proffered documentary evidence of Memon origins unavailable anywhere else.[51] As a later Memon historian put it, the work not only "opened a path for researchers" but saved the history of the Memons from total oblivion.[52]

Unfortunately, Nuzhat revealed little of his background. A native of Burhanpur, Nuzhat was not a Memon himself. According to his own telling, after ten years immersed in the "muck and mire of Bombay" he became familiar with all the city's Muslims, from Bohras to Konkanis. None impressed him more than the Memons, whom he was surprised to learn were the "wealthiest [*āsūda-ḥāl*] of all the Muslims" in Bombay and the surrounding regions.[53] Nuzhat embarked on an extensive search to discover the reason for their prosperity, which he found in an unlikely source: the Memons' spiritual guide, Pir Buzurg Ali of Mundra in Kachchh, a Chisti and Qadiri Sufi shaykh. The Memons attained, Nuzhat wrote later, "the wealth of religion and the world, that is, of Islam and the prestige of material progress, by means of the prayers of their ancestors and the oblations of their guidance."[54] Nuzhat's conviction that the Memons' commercial fortune stemmed from their devotion to their pirs was not merely the enthusiastic musing of a new devotee, for devotion to pirs sometimes did have concrete economic dividends.

Though the Memons' piety garnered Nuzhat's appreciation, Memon self-perceptions often displayed little in the way of self-congratulation. No issue engendered more dissatisfaction than Perry's 1847 ruling that recognized the primacy of Hindu custom over Islamic law in the Kachchhi Memon *jamaat*. Beginning in the 1880s, and continuing for four decades, Kachchhi Memons periodically mobilized around the inheritance issue through petition campaigns and public demonstrations. All were frustrated. The most sustained effort was in 1885, when some leading elements of the Kachchhi Memon *jamaat* in Bombay sent a petition to the government of India after a controversial Memon legal case. As the Parsi newspaper *Kaiser-i Hind* (Emperor of India) reported, on one occasion a massive meeting of Kachchhi Memons was held at the city's Jafariyya Mosque calling for the abrogation of the ruling.[55] Eventually the Memons gained an advocate in the prominent Anglophone Indian Muslim jurist Sayyid Amir Ali. Although Ali was a member of the Imperial Legislative Council, the Memons' petition floundered there.[56]

In assessing the Kachchhi Memons' petition, the colonial government became fixated on the question of whether it represented the unanimous perspective of the *jamaat*. A revision to the *jamaat*'s legal status could only be considered, they reasoned, if the petition were unanimous. Unanimity was a strange precondition for reforming the legal status of a geographically scattered population. Perhaps the requirement was predicated on the notion that unanimity was possible with such numerically small communities. But it ignored the fact that decision-making procedures in the *jamaat* were secluded to a tiny subset of male elites, many of whom preferred the status quo. But maintaining the status quo was no easy feat when ideas of custom and law were constantly in flux. While one later British legal compendia rooted the origins of the Kachchhi Memons' activism in "prickings of conscience as to this deviation from Koranic precepts," a contemporary petition sent to the viceroy made a more generative suggestion. Here the petitioners, led by two prominent Memon merchants, argued that Islamic laws of inheritance were more equitable than Hindu parallels and more commensurate with "the modern systems of Europe, and the Indian Succession Act."[57]

The appeals of 1885 fell on stony ground, and Kachchhi Memon activism around this issue ebbed and flowed over the years. On August 27, 1892, a large group of Kachchhi Memons in Bombay gathered at Jusab Seth's mosque on Muhammad Kambayker Street. Among the meeting's many resolutions was the following: "It is the unanimous opinion of the Cutchee Memon community that the application of Hindu law in matters of succession, inheritance, &c., to the Cutchee Memon community is productive of great hardships to the community and is against the precepts of the Mahomedan religion, and it is necessary that immediate steps be taken to remove the said hardships."[58] *Unanimity,* which became the sine qua non of colonial legal reform of Gujarati Muslim custom, was a term carefully chosen. A commentator in the *Indian Jurist* was deeply skeptical of this claim, believing that the desired reform was antithetical to the Memons' own economic interests; those supportive of the measure, he argued, risked being deprived of their shares in various enterprises.

The author also doubted whether "the Mahomedan law of the books is anywhere observed in its entirety, or with anything approaching scrupulosity, over the greater part of India." Still, the writer was generally sympathetic to the initiative, and noted how unjust it would be for the Kachchhi Memons to remain regulated by "Hindu" law. As a solution, he suggested a registration system in which any Memon wishing to maintain "non-Mahomedan usages" would be forced to declare so openly in an affidavit after the act was passed.[59] Such a declaration, of course, would leave any such Memon open to the charge of not being a true Muslim. It was hardly an appealing prospect, and many Memon men were willing to take the risk in the court of law to ensure a larger share of inheritance.

Irrespective of the weighty precedents governing Memon law and custom that were enshrined by Justice Perry in 1847, the subsequent judicial record shows an odd variance in rulings pertaining to all Memon communities, owing either to the discretion of the judge or a misunderstanding of the precedent's full meaning. Evidently there were rare suits in which Kachchhi Memon women successfully sued the executors of a male family member's will and inherited property they considered rightfully theirs. A certain Aishabhai inherited her grandfather's property in this way.[60] In another case, a Memon widow, Sarabhai Amibhai, obtained recognition of the validity of her husband's will—which recognized her as his executor—when the Privy Council ruled that Kachchhi Memons were beholden to Islamic law in the case of wills.[61]

Most probably, these cases were exceptions. The odds were seriously stacked against Bombay's Kachchhi Memon women who attempted to gain their inheritance shares. At the same time, there is evidence that the Halai Memon *jamaat*, registered as Muslims in all aspects of personal law, played fast and loose with their formal legal status. For example, consider the Bombay government's 1897 announcement that the Memon community was divided into Halai and Kachchhi caste subsets, with the former following Islamic law in all respects. In response, the Halai Memons of Porebunder complained to the administrator that their *jamaat* had long recognized the Hindu law of inheritance.[62] The correction is a crucial reminder that no *jamaat* was entirely of one voice in matters of law and custom but always an assemblage of competing constituencies eager to protect their own self-interests.

Even as their ambitions of colonial legal reclassification ran aground, the Kachchhi and Halai Memons were integrated more deeply into transimperial networks of Sunni Islam. Gravitation toward select Sufi pirs was one aspect of this. Few of the pirs patronized by the Memons outside of India compared to the Naqib al-Ashraf, the custodian of the shrine of the Qadiri Sufi saint, Abd al-Qadir Gilani, whose disciple was said to have converted the Memons in the fifteenth century. Memons are documented at the site, located in Baghdad, since at least the last quarter of the nineteenth century. The Halai Memon *jamaat*'s connection to the shrine was so profound that the Twelver Khoja merchant and author Khoja Lavji Jhina Mastar Banaras—who boasted in a subsequent account of his pilgrimage to Karbala of his links with Memon merchants[63]—completed a Gujarati biography of Gilani and paid a visit to the Naqib al-Ashraf in Baghdad. Like the Bombay proletarian Nuzhat before him, Mastar quizzed the Memons on the origins of their commercial acumen and was told that it was merely the influence of their patron saint. Mastar noted that "in every company and in every shop, some place has been set aside for the sake of [the saint]."[64] Even the dens of capital were suffused with the saint's power.

Halai Memon connections with the Naqibs were far from apolitical. As early as 1877, during the Russo-Ottoman War, the Naqib sent his brother to India to raise money among his followers. Ottoman authorities applauded the move. The Halai Memons' support for the Naqibs was not limited to charity, and their devotion often entangled them in local power politics. As an illustration, in 1914 the would-be successor to the position of Naqib al-Ashraf, Sayyid Ibrahim, fled from Baghdad to Bombay after whispers of his intrigues against his uncle, the current occupier of the post, began making the rounds. While in Bombay, he established close contact with members of the Halai Memon *jamaat*, who had long encouraged Sayyid Ibrahim to venture to the metropolis.[65]

Memon connections with Ottoman authorities, from the Hijaz to Bombay and Rangoon, also contributed to the elaboration of Memon Sunni identities in this period. However, these connections were far from the primary focal point of Memon religious life. In fact, the Memons were active players in the Ottoman religious economy. A notable example is found in a petition sent by a group of Indian Muslims, including a high proportion of Memons, to the Ottoman authorities in Mecca in the 1880s.[66] With their Gujarati and Urdu seals and signatures adorning the bottom of the petition, this clique of merchants, scholars, and pilgrims demanded that the Ottomans expel various "Wahhabis" from the sacred city, seeing them as purveyors of heterodoxy in league with Satan and miscreants who posed a threat to the integrity of the Hanafi *madhhab* (one of the four normative Sunni legal schools). Their Arabic petition was sent to Istanbul, where it was translated into Ottoman Turkish by the Ministry of Internal Affairs. With their appeal, the Memons leveraged their local clout to make Ottoman authorities work at their bidding, and in turn regulated the contours of Sunni Islam as practiced in the Hijaz.

For all this, the Ottoman sultan was mostly a peripheral figure in the lives of most Memon *jamaats*. The *masālik* constituted the true centers of action. Intra-Memon competition over religious endowments throughout the

FIGURE 3.5 The Grey Street Mosque in Durban, South Africa. The mosque, like many other religious institutions in the Memon diaspora, became hotly contested, embroiled in larger disputes over Sunni Islam. Note the dedication to Aboobaker Ahamed & Bros., among the mosque's Memon underwriters.
Author's personal collection.

Indian Ocean was a byproduct Memons' integration into the leading Indian *masālik* at the beginning of the twentieth century. In many cases, competing claims over *awqāf* (pious endowments) and mosques prompted extensive intra-Memon legal battles in the colonial courts. In a remarkable study, the historian Goolam Vahed has reconstructed the conflicts within a Memon *jamaat* in Durban, South Africa.[67] There one faction maneuvered to obtain control over the city's inaugural mosque and its accompanying assets. (Figure 3.5 shows the mosque, the construction of which was financed in part by a Memon commercial firm.) The revisionist faction also sought to inculcate new "reformist" versions of Islam as against the "customary" brand of Sunni Islam hitherto practiced by the *jamaat*. This was not an isolated case; such conflicts occurred frequently in the Memon diaspora.

Another fascinating illustration of this trend comes from Mauritius at the turn of the twentieth century, where Halai, Kachchhi, and Surti Memons became caught up in a litigious battle over the leadership of the mosque in

Port Louis.[68] Writing in 1923, the traveler Maulana Qari Hakim Abd Allah Rashid counted two to four hundred Halai, Kachchhi, and Surti Memons on the island, dating their arrival back to 1835.[69] Despite these small numbers, Memon constituencies in Mauritius were highly fractured, and rivalries among them had lasting consequences for the character of Sunni Islam on the island. A 1912 article from *Revue du monde musulman* (Review of the Muslim world) reflected the stridency of intra-Memon divisions and how commercial competition among Muslim communities on the island precipitated sectarian institutional development.[70]

The court case under consideration began in 1904, when Sulaiman Haji Muhammad (Mamode) filed a motion against the Cutchee Maiman Society. This association, which had some sixty members registered in 1903, was a "benevolent society, formed for charitable and educational purposes, chiefly in connection with the Mahomedan religion."[71] Sulaiman Haji Muhammad was one part of a Kachchhi Memon shipping firm run out of Mauritius and Reunion that became "'a great power" in the sugar, molasses, rice, and timber trade" with India.[72] His opponent in court, the Cutchee Maiman Society, boasted a charter, management committee, secretary, treasurer, and auditors. A society statute asserted that the treasurer must keep strict accounts and that these were liable to inspection by the committee. That statute served as the crux of the dispute, which concerned whether individual members of the society had a right to inspect the account books. Sulaiman Haji Muhammad believed that they did. The court disputed his assertion, averring that the relevant ordinances through which the society was incorporated (which dated back to 1874) made no provision for this. Regardless of the court's decision, the demand among constituent members to inspect *jamaat* account books grew more strident from this point onward.

A more dramatic clash involving the Cutchee Maiman Society and other Memon *jamaats* came in 1906 amidst the former's effort to acquire sole control over a *waqf* (pious endowment) that included the congregational mosque in Port Louis (*mosquée des arabes*) and its adjoining properties. *Revue du monde musulman* valued it some years later at Rs. 350,000.[73] The mosque had been built by Muslim merchants in 1852, and its charter explicitly stated that it could not be alienated. Its revenue was dependent on rent and a rate levied on grain sales by local Muslim merchants. By 1877, however, deeds of purchase appeared that recognized that the property was the sole right of the Kachchhi Memons, with a committee presiding over their administration.

Evidently, when the Cutchee Maiman Society drew up its 1903 charter, it was seeking to undermine the site's status as *waqf* by drawing up deeds that would allow it to sell and lease the site's buildings. This was no one-off: Bohras, Khojas, and Memons alike often tried to circumvent the legal restrictions placed upon *awqāf* by colonial and Islamic law alike.

Such moves were controversial, and both the Surti and Halai Memon *jamaats* attempted to block this ruse. Although they purportedly had been granted the administration of the *waqf* by "tacit consent of all the Sunni Muhammadans," the court asserted that the Kachchhis had acted "ultra vires" when they attempted to obtain perpetual and exclusive management of the *waqf* and to transfer its assets to the society. The court had yet to determine, however, who constituted the founders of the *waqf*, how the rights of the Kachcchi Memon *jamaat* "as a class or caste" affected their status as administrators of the mosque, and whether they held property under the management of the *waqf* in perpetual trust or merely as agents of all Sunni Muslims.[74]

In the follow-up 1906 case, a combination of Halai and Surti Memons sued the Kachchhi Memons. According to the judges' final report, while the Surti and Kachchhi *jamaats* normally held no bad blood toward one another, the latter were contemptuous of the Halais, whom they regarded as inferior. None of this prevented the Kachchhi Memons from accepting a Halai Memon as president of the mosque, the judges continued, but the Halais refused to sign the court's deeds that would have incorporated them into the Kachchhi-run society. The court's final decision ordained that detailed weekly accounts be kept in a manner that clearly displayed the "sums expended and received in connection with the Mosque, and the 'Cutchee Maiman Society' respectively and stating the source of each receipt."[75] The court also ordered that the funds of both the mosque and the society "should be placed to the credit of the Mosque and of the Society respectively at one of the Banks, in the name of such Mosque and Society respectively, and cheques on the Bank shall be signed by the Treasurer and countersigned by the President of the Mosque and Society respectively."[76] Here again, one sees the importance of banks to the management of Memon *jamaat* thrifts, an arrangement that arguably acted as a brake on the development of Memon-owned banks.

Although barred from fully depositing the mosque funds into society coffers, the Kachchhi Memons had secured a predominant position in the management and utilization of the *waqf*'s capital for other enterprises, religious and economic. With victory secured, the Kachchhi Memons increasingly began their ascent in the religious life of Mauritius. They already had a tradition of patronizing Qadiri Sufi pirs on the island, even building a tomb for a certain Sayyid Jamal Shah. Yet from the time the case was settled in 1906, they began to cultivate more formal connections with the scholars of the Barelvi *maslak*, especially in the figure of Abd al-Alim Siddiqi.[77] Meanwhile, the Surti Memon *jamaat* began its turn to Deobandi Islam around the same time. This turn introduced a counterweight in the landscape of Mauritian Islam that continues to have consequences in the religious life of the island to this day.

Yet, as covered in chapter 6, still more conflicts among Mauritius's Memon *jamaats*, occasioned by their deeper integration into the networks of Sunni *masālik*, were just around the corner. By the first decade of the twentieth century, then, declarations in support of one *maslak* had the capacity to deepen Memon contests over Sunni authority. Suitably, beginning on the eve of the First World War, Memon *jamaats* would become involved in a plethora of causes pertaining to Sunni authority, including the campaigns for Ottoman charitable relief in 1912–1914 and the postwar Khilafat movement. Yet long before then, Memons actively participated in the proliferation of Sunni variants of corporate Islam into ever-more-streamlined and adversarial orientations.

The Bohra *Dais* between Merchant Elites and Rival Claimants

The history of the Bohra *dais* in this epoch has been expertly dissected elsewhere.[78] The object here is to fill in some of the narrative gaps with reference to the wider *jamaat*. Although never beset by the same degree of litigation and secession as the Khojas and Memons, the Bohra *jamaats* in this period also experienced a fair share of strain as their constituents attempted to navigate the full import of their more assertive apex cleric model. In some ways, when compared to the Khojas and Memons, the Bohra *jamaats* between 1890 and 1912 displayed an internal coherence upon which contemporaries often commented. These external assessments were partially accurate, but Bohra historians of this epoch and later tend to stress the prevalence of *fitna* (corruption, sedition) within the *jamaat*. Arguably, existing academic accounts have taken these histories too much at their word, ignoring the synergies between Bohra merchant capital and the religious hierarchy of the *jamaats*. Bohra merchants were religious entrepreneurs in their own right, but their ventures most often redounded to the advantage of the *dai*'s authority.

As mentioned in chapter 1, the authority of the *dais* was somewhat equivocal in this period, although Bohra histories disagree substantially on this point. Some accounts maintain that a cloud of ambiguity lay over the authority of *dai* after 1840. That year the reigning *dai* Sayyidna Muhammad Badr al-Din died suddenly—from a mixture of hemorrhoids and crushed diamonds, with whispers circulating that he had been poisoned—before choosing his successor.[79] A controversy arose concerning the legitimacy of his successor, the forty-seventh *dai*, Abd al-Qadir Najm al-Din, specifically over whether he had been designated as *dai* by Badr al-Din in a ritual called *naṣṣ*. *Naṣṣ*, a central but sometimes corrosive feature of Ismaili Islam, denotes the nomination of a successor by the reigning imam or *dai*. In turn, Najm al-Din's successors were bedeviled by persistent claims from within the *jamaat* that they, too, were illegitimate *dais*. That, at least, is the narrative propounded by the later Bohra dissident movement, introduced in chapter 5.

Notwithstanding this inauspicious start to his *dai*-ship, Abd al-Qadir Najm al-Din presided over a period of transformation for the Bohra *jamaat* between 1840 and 1885. He cultivated close ties with British and Indian rulers, and was the first Bohra *dai* since the transfer of the *dai*-ship to India in the late sixteenth century to complete the hajj.[80] What is more, unlike the Agha Khans, his own authority was not called into question in the colonial courts, and the office of *dai* actually was exempt from this. (As future chapters will demonstrate, however, once that privilege was reversed, a deluge of court cases involving the *dais* swiftly followed). All the same, the *dai* was but one religious authority among many in the Bohra *jamaat*, forced by circumstance to contend with the rise of print, capitalists, and rival religious impulses within his own *jamaat*.

The rise of Arabo-Gujarati print and Bohra merchant and religious entrepreneurs in these decades was a watershed for the subsequent history of the *jamaat*. Arabo-Gujarati print had the effect of creating a larger readership among the Bohras, whose reading culture had been based on manuscripts until this point. This print revolution was centered in Bombay and Surat, but it had an important offshoot in Karachi, fast becoming a center of Bohra religious life. The effects of print spread far and wide. In the words of Muhammad Ali ibn al-Majid Jivabhai, the author of three-volume landmark Bohra history published in the 1880s, "in the age of Sayyidna [the *dai* Abd al-Qadir Najm al-Din]—may God perpetuate his dominion—for the sake of the general believers the problems of *fiqh* [jurisprudence] and the sentences of the *akhbār* [statements of the imams] were translated into Gujarati so that all believers could become participants in *ʿilm* (exterior knowledge) and *maʿrifat* (esoteric knowledge) together."[81] Thus, as with the Khojas and Memons, Gujarati print was pushing the boundaries of the *jamaat*'s interpretive community outward. Yet the advent of new participants in doctrinal life was always double-sided, encouraging consolidation of the *jamaat* and rival authorities.

Religious populism had its downsides, as Jivabhai acknowledged elsewhere. In his innuendo-filled account of Najm al-Din's *dai*-ship, Jivabhai underscored that with the death of leading Bohra ulama, the *dai* was left isolated. Lacking loyal subordinates, the *dai* immediately began to face protests from members of the *jamaat*, who as Jivabhai related, expended all sorts of wealth to cause trouble for the *dai*. In the process, traditions of Bohra learning reportedly "went to the termites," and the *jamaat* began to decline. Jivabhai's subsequent account of the controversy over *naṣṣ* stressed that a committee was set up by members of the local *jamaat* in Surat in 1880—the grandiosely-named *ḥilf al-faḍāʾil* (The Alliance of the Virtuous)—without the *dai*'s permission.[82] Evidently, the committee's object was to assume control over Bohra affairs, a distant echo perhaps of the same impulses that drove the Sunni Khojas in their bid to unmake the power of the Agha Khan I several decades before.

Yet, for reasons not satisfactorily explained by Jivabhai, the committee seems to have relented and kept the *dai* in his position of authority. When all was said and done, however, Jivabhai's decision to publicize the controversy over *naṣṣ* in print was a bold decision that signaled the combustible potential of print culture to make rival constituencies in the Bohra *jamaat*. No doubt for this reason the book has a controversial status in the Bohra *jamaat* today.[83] Nevertheless, with its long digressions on British monarchs and the latest technological innovations interspersed within accounts of the *dais*, Jivabhai's history was a fitting monument to the intellectual promiscuities of the late nineteenth-century Bohra *jamaat*. It was also a harbinger of how print would be embraced at the turn of the century by Bohras of all ranks. For all this, until his death in 1885, the *dai* Abd al-Qadir Najm al-Din's preferred mode of expression remained the Arabic manuscript.[84]

Najm al-Din's immediate successors served relatively short periods as *dai*, which probably blunted the force of controversy over succession. Despite this, a most momentous development came in 1891, when the reigning *dai*, Burhan al-Din, declared that he was not the *dai* and claimed no rank save that of *nāẓim* (organizer) of the community, at least according to one influential narrative. This meant he effectively relinquished some of the unassailable religious authority Bohra *dais* had always claimed.[85] All the same, it would be fair to say, as other historians have, that the real motor of life in the far-flung *jamaats* during these decades were not the *dais* but the many Bohra merchant princes who emerged from the ranks to prominent positions in the caste and colonial civic order.[86] The investment of such figures in the *jamaats* and their acceptance of the *dai*'s leadership was of inestimable importance, serving as a cornerstone of that office's legitimacy and an eventual springboard for its assertion of authority over the *jamaat* from 1915.

This said, the Bohras certainly did not lack a scholarly hierarchy that was well versed in law. Bohra legal manuals from the turn of the twentieth century show Bohra scholars and the laity alike engaging with questions of Ismaili jurisprudence, Quranic exegesis, Shiʿi hagiography, and Islamic commercial ethics, including the gnarled question of whether the "rent on money" condemned in sharia applied to all forms of interest, for which there was some debate among contemporary Muslims.[87] These scholars were also delegated with substantial authority by the *dais*. One such figure, Muhammad Ali al-Hamdani, was put in charge of a leading Bohra madrasa in Surat.[88] Upon al-Hamdani's death, a new madrasa was established in his name in Surat, with his son appointed as director. A later prospectus confessed the institution's reliance on donations from "pious gentlemen from our community" and recommended the formation of a managing committee to improve its administration.[89] In due course, such institutions were to be kernels of the Bohra dissident movement.

In the meantime, the Bohra *jamaats* in this period were consumed by a mania for forming committees. These were staffed by leading Bohra *sethias* and *amils*, with the participation of the former of special importance. Yet the Bohra *jamaats* never evolved into a conciliar model of corporate Islam. It was to the *dais*' lasting advantage that figures like the Bohra multimillionaire Adamji Pirbhai (whose business portfolio will be examined in detail in chapter 4) maintained close relations with the Bohra learned hierarchy and became the central prop in the expansion of the *dai*'s influence from the 1880s to the First World War. His Parsi friend Shetji Sahibji drew a sympathetic, if perplexed, portrait of Pirbhai's religious devotionalism in *Vanity Fair:*

> Adamjee is not afraid of the life beyond the grave. He has always been true to his faith as he has been true to his duty. Every Friday he has attended at the mosque and on one occasion he subscribed liberally towards the expenses of the marriage of the Kazi's son. The Kazi [the *dai al-mutlaq*] is the Pope of the Bohra and like His Holiness of Rome he too deals in dispensations. When the Bohra dies he carries with him to the grave a passport enjoining the Angel Gabriel to admit the bearer to heaven. Dear *Vanity*, there are many strange things in this world and one of the strangest is that the shrewd Adamjee should allow himself to be fleeced periodically for the shriving of his sins—what these sins may be the Kazi and he alone know.[90]

Though this portrait reveals clear signs of subservience, Pirbhai seems to have attained a stature in the *jamaat* that exceeded even that of the *dais*. But the *dai*'s bestowal upon him of the title of *Rafīʿ al-Dīn* (The Exalter of the Religion) was a telling indication of the symbiosis between Bohra merchants and the religious hierarchy.

That title was emblazoned on the title page of a Bohra "constitution" printed in Dhoraji in 1899 during the *dai*-ship of Burhan al-Din.[91] The constitution supplies an unrivaled glimpse into the synergistic relationship between merchant power and religious authority in the Bohra *jamaat* in this era. It comprised an assortment of *jamaat* rulings on marriage disputes and community administration. The cases adjudicated by the *jamaat* council extended throughout Greater Gujarat to Bombay and Karachi. Presumably the constitution was circulated in the larger Bohra diaspora, where it would have functioned as a procedural guidebook for *jamaats*. The text is itself a reminder that while a small number of community disputes made it to the colonial courts, the plurality of cases continued to be settled by the *jamaat* itself.

This said, the *jamaat* leaders repeatedly accented that their judgments were in accordance with the laws and customs of the *sarkar* (colonial political authority) and the *jamaat*.[92] Even if this constitution displays less evidence of this input, the higher rungs of Bohra law were heavily conditioned by the towering figures of medieval Ismaili Shiʿi jurisprudence—none more than the tenth-century scholar Qadi al-Numan, whose works were repeatedly copied and commented upon in Bohra madrasas in this age. These three inputs—

colonial, *jamaat*, and Ismaili jurisprudence—constituted the main threads of Bohra legal culture in the colonial era. The latter two acted as alternative legal rubrics to that of the colonial courts, where Bohras were governed by the very different parameters of Hindu custom and Twelver Shiʿi law.

The Dhoraji constitution furnishes unique insight into the Bohra *jamaats*' procedures for legal deliberation, and specifically how *sethias* and *amils* reached a collective judgment. Every case involved a consideration of each party's position, and a final ruling, followed by signatures of the presiding members of the jury. Save the invocation on the title page, the Bohra *dai* does not appear in the text. He need not have, for the monitoring capacities and legal know-how of the council were more than sufficient to the task. Indeed, monitoring capacity was a linchpin of *jamaat* justice, and regularly a separate investigation into the case was undertaken by agents of the *jamaat* council. The coercive capacity of the *jamaats* worked in tandem with these mechanisms of surveillance. Frequently the threat of excommunication and ostracism from the *jamaat* was invoked to compel one party to comply. It was also implemented with a surprising frequency, if the 1899 constitution is any barometer.

Proper methods of accounting were a universal concern in the text, a handmaiden of the conformity Bohra *jamaat* councils sought to kindle within the Bohra diaspora. Indeed, one of the clauses of the constitution made it obligatory for the *amils* of local *jamaats* to remit a portion of their collections to the *dai*.[93] When three members of the Bohra *jamaat* in Dhari were accused of financial malfeasance, a thorough investigation was carried out.[94] Perhaps no other subject in the constitution came under greater scrutiny than dowries, a reminder of just how enmeshed Bohra marriage was in broader proprietary notions intrinsic to corporate Islam. It is fair to say that many of the women who appear in the text are merely viewed as an extension of this accounting, as one-dimensional as the jewelry listed in the asset portfolio of the family estate. It is no revelation, then, to discover that the women of the *jamaat* never represented themselves in these disputes. Husbands and fathers spoke in their stead, and another party of men decided their fate. The *jamaats* were no great emancipators.

Many of these records make for difficult reading. The dispute between one Ghulam Hussain Ibrahmji, a native of Jamnagar, and his father-in-law, Alibhai Jivaji of Rajkot, was typical of *jamaat* life.[95] As Ibrahmji's letter to the *jamaat* recounts, his father-in-law refused to send his wife back home, and he was forced to care for their two young children at great personal cost. On three occasions, several community leaders had traveled from Jamnagar to Rajkot to plead Ibrahmji's case, and that of the children, but to no avail. Alibhai Jivaji's response, as recorded in the *jamaat*'s proceedings, was terse and defiant, unmasking facts that Ghulam Hussain dared not mention in his own letter: "My son-in-law beats my daughter regularly, and it hurts a great deal. Therefore, I will not send my daughter." The *jamaat*'s subsequent decision underscores its capacity to make community members fall in line, even against their better judgment: "Should you hand over the wife of brother Ghulam Hussain, he will not harm you and there will be no grief." In perfunctory fashion the same sentences goes on to record: "With the above decree, Alibhai Jivaji, by taking his son-in-law to Rajkot, handed over his daughter to her husband. Every kind of pledge taken is being handed back to this wife and husband."[96] Lost amid the rigorous accounting, and the magnanimous waiver of legal fees, was a consideration of the human cost of these decisions.

If the Dhoraji constitution represented an attempt to forge something akin to a unitary law code for the Bohra *jamaat*, then the foundation of an impressive transimperial pilgrimage infrastructure in the form of the Faiż-i Ḥussainī was an endeavor to link the scattered *jamaats* more closely together through shared ritual. Connecting Daudi Bohra *jamaats* to Islamic sacred sites in Egypt, Hijaz, Iraq, Palestine, and Yemen, the Faiż-i Ḥussainī serves as another illustration of the close cooperation between Bohra merchants and the *dais* in the late nineteenth and early twentieth centuries. The institution owed its beginnings to two Bohra merchants, Shaykh Isaji Adamji and Alibhai Karimji, who around 1882 first established a reception hall at a Bohra mosque in Karachi. There Bohra pilgrims traveling to the Ottoman domains could obtain comfortable accommodations and avoid the dire conditions of quarantine most travelers experienced while passing from Bombay through Karachi. In 1887, Karimji purchased a site in Karachi for Rs. 35,000 and built a complex for pilgrims, then handing its management over to the Bohra *dai*, Abd al-Hussain Hussam al-Din. By 1897 a ten-person executive committee was established with a president and secretary, thus formally inaugurating the Faiż-i Ḥussainī.[97] The trust's work was further supported by the dissemination of printed texts in Lisān al-Daʿwa and Gujarati that supplied information on pilgrimage waystations and ritual guidance for the individual pilgrim.

For the Bohras and Twelver Khojas alike, the elaboration of pilgrimage infrastructures between India and Iraq in these years supplied a new paradigm of transnational Shiʿi pilgrimage that was both institutionalized and caste-centric. The realization of this infrastructure increased their presence as never before in the sacred terrain revered by all Shiʿis. Though well managed by the standards of the contemporary Hajj, the Twelver Khoja pilgrimage infrastructure paled in comparison to the work of the Bohra Faiż-i Ḥussainī. Contemporaries of various stripes marveled at the operation of that institution and sought to replicate it. One Twelver notable traveling from Hyderabad to Iraq in the 1920s echoed many a contemporary Indian observer when two weeks into his pilgrimage he wrote, "Up until now, only the administration [*intiẓām*] of the Khoja and Bohra *jamaats* merit excessive praise, and, in this specific instance, are worthy of emulation [*qābil-i taqlīd*]."[98]

British officials took the prospect of emulation one step further. One admirer was John Gordon Lorrimer, who managed the Oudh Bequest and Indian pilgrimage traffic in the years before the First World War. In one instance, Lorrimer marveled at the Bohras' work in the shrine cities and acknowledged that "the Oudh Bequest committees might well follow in the [Bohras'] steps by providing suitable hostels for ordinary Shi'ahs [*sic*] at the principal places, and by furnishing guides to interpret for them, make their travelling arrangements, and protect from the thousand and one rapacious harpies to whom they at present fall an easy prey."[99] Even Memon commentators marveled at the workings of the Faiż-i Ḥussainī.[100] Future chapters, nonetheless, will show how capital-intense trusts like the Faiż-i Ḥussainī became hotly contested in the interwar and postcolonial periods.

While the willingness of Bohra merchants and scholars to act as agents of the *jamaats* buttressed the *dais*' authority, the legitimacy of the latter was also aided considerably by the ability of Bohra polemicists to effectively combat the claims of the odd Bohra pretender or two who did appear in this epoch. In truth, the Bohra *dais,* for all the modesty of their position, endured far less truculent rivals throughout the long nineteenth century than the Ismaili and Twelver Khoja *jamaats.* The Khojas were veteran combatants in the discursive battles over whether the imam was hidden or visible, a controversy that became fiercer with the passage of time. By contrast, the Bohras accepted the hidden status of the imam, which aroused deep reverence but not polemical confrontation among the members of the *jamaat.* How unexpected it must have been, then, for many Bohras when a new religious impresario appeared from the ranks of a provincial *jamaat* in Nagpur claiming to have direct access to a living imam.

That impresario was Abd al-Hussain Jivabhai (not to be confused with the Bohra historian mentioned above), also known as H. M. Malak, who became the leader of a Bohra splinter faction in Nagpur later branded the Mahdi Baghwallas by the mainline Bohra *jamaat*. After the controversial election of Burhan al-Din as Bohra *dai* in 1891, Jivabhai and a small group of followers rejected the new *dai*. In time, Jivabhai asserted that he was the rightful successor, and that from 1840 onward four rival *dais* had carried on the true line of succession, the last of which was his father. Jivabhai's religious declarations spoke directly to the eschatology of the Bohra *jamaat* and included the claim that he was an angel (*malak*) and proof of the imam (*ḥujjat al-qāʾim*).[101] These were extraordinary claims for a modest import-export merchant originally from Kapadvanj to make.

Though his movement managed to survive, Jivabhai found it hard to retain his small smattering of followers. Several departed after he reportedly preached sedition against the government.[102] At his death in 1899, Jivabhai's breakaway *jamaat*—sometimes called the Atba-i Malak (Followers of Malak)—split into two factions. The ensuing dispute between the two over *jamaat* property in Nagpur persisted for decades. The succession crisis among the Atba-i Malak, which continues to this day, was evocative of the tendency of onetime splinter factions among the Gujarati Muslim commercial castes to fragment still further over matters of religious authority. As experience repeatedly confirmed, a splinter group's ability to assert control over *jamaat* assets determined its capacity to survive and expand. The faction that managed to secure the *jamaat* properties in Nagpur was headed by one Badr al-Din Ghulam Hussain, who also branded himself H. M. Malak or Mr. Malak. Formerly a merchant in Aden and Bombay until he joined the Atba-i Malak, the latter H. M. Malak was not a *dai* like the vicars of the mainline Bohra *jamaat* but, in an echo of Jivabhai's claim, asserted that that he was a *hujjat al-qaʾim* who served as the "veil" of his predecessor, now purportedly in occultation.[103]

The Atba-i Malak's small property nest egg was a necessary, but not sufficient, guarantee of its survival. Its future also depended upon its capacity to engage meaningfully with non-*jamaat* public institutions, something at which Malak excelled, as underscored by his subsequent (and prominent) involvement with the All-India Muslim League. (For more on the league, see chapter 4.) Even a profile published on the latter H. M. Malak in the *Cyclopedia of India* gave the institution remarkably good press, stressing the genius of its founder (despite his lack of education and his knowledge of no language but Gujarati) and the institution's virtues as a dual religious and industrial entity.[104]

As mentioned above, the size of the Mahdi Bagh Bohra *jamaat* was insignificant. Yet the attention that its progenitor, Jivabhai, garnered in Daudi Bohra polemics was exceptional, for the simple reason that he claimed to be in touch with the hidden imam and set himself up as a rival *dai*. Even if the Ismaili Khojas acknowledged that over the previous thirty years the imam of the time was alive and visible, such a claim was extraordinary for their Ismaili brethren, the Bohras. In company with the Khojas before them, a new breed of Bohra writers at the turn of the twentieth century took up the task of discrediting the arriviste *dai* and his false imam. As the Khoja experience had demonstrated in decades past, the growth of the Bohra *jamaats*' readership required that the faithful be regularly plied with religious literature that conformed to the orthodox line.

Beginning as manuscripts with a curtailed sphere of circulation, the Bohra polemics against Jivabhai entered the realm of print by 1898. They quickly went through several editions and reprints, right up to the moment when the *jamaat* faced its most contentious struggle in 1917. Several of these texts were composed by Muhammad al-Hamdani, the aforementioned manager of a leading Bohra madrasa in Surat, who had a close relationship with several *dais*. Supposedly one of these, Sayyidna Burhan al-Din, had designated Hamdani as the prime polemicist against Jivabhai.[105] Hamdani proved equal to the task, composing three treatises, one of which was eventually printed around the time of his death. The first of these, a manuscript titled "Daʾwa (i)bn Jiwa al-Kaparwanji wa-l-radd ʿalayhi min al-mawla Muhammad Ali al-Hamdani" (The claim of Ibn Jiwa of Kapadvanj and its refutation by Mawla Muhammad Ali al-Hamdani), was written in *Lisān al-Daʾwa* and kept in the private collection of the author and his family until the 1970s.[106] Though the circulation of the manuscript was limited, Hamdani was responding to the demands of a wider readership within the Bohra *jamaats*.

One of the more curious accusations that Hamdani leveled against Jivabhai was that his father ran a business that sold images of the Hindu deities, a trade forbidden to Muslims. Supposedly, Jivabhai had tried to cover up this inconvenient fact.[107] According to one printed text published by a

Bohra author in Surat, Jivabhai continued in his father's path by operating a business that exported pictures of Hindu deities from Glasgow to Bombay, a profession tantamount to the promotion of idol worship. A search of legal cases discloses that Jivabhai was indeed brought before the Bombay High Court in 1892 in connection with his business.[108] Jivabhai was unable to pay back his two Bohra creditors, and the court forced him to dissolve his partnership, Jiwabhoy Hiptula, and seized his "real and personal estate and effects."[109] It is likely that Jivabhai was an agent for Graham's Shipping and Trading Company. This Glasgow-based firm had several branches in India, including in Karachi, and employed a modest Khoja merchant, Punja Jinnah, the father of Muhammad Ali Jinnah. Jivabhai was thus similar to those Gujarati Muslim traders whose fortunes were transformed by their links to European firms like Graham's. Still, Jivabhai's Bohra opponents seized upon his dealing in Hindu religious images as verification that this adversary of the *dai* was no upstanding Muslim.

Although Bohra polemics against Jivabhai were confident that he would vanish in time, just as earlier Bohra heretics had done, the capacity of a relative nonentity to stir up sedition in the Bohra *jamaats* was disquieting. But Jivabhai was representative of the potential for merchant entrepreneurs from within the *jamaats* to transform into breakaway religious entrepreneurs. In a conclusion to one polemic, a Bohra author did not shy away from warning his readers, "From our carelessness at any time, a small thing can assume a large form."[110] This declaration perhaps explains why the text was reprinted in 1915, precisely when the Bohra *jamaat*'s model of corporate Islam, with an assertive apex cleric presiding over a highly hierarchical community, would find itself beset by crises of a far more dramatic order. In that year the autonomy of Bohra merchant princes, the maturity of Bohra print culture, and the percolating controversy over *naṣṣ* converged, with lasting consequences for the integrity of the Bohra *jamaat*.

* * *

As this chapter has shown, merchant wealth and religious authority did not always work in tandem in the space of the *jamaats*. Just as the *jamaats* at the local level had varying influence on commercial activity, so too did their power fluctuate in matters of religious exchange. Nearly everywhere *jamaats* were sites of negotiation, if not outright antipathy, over religious doctrine and praxis. Localized conflicts had the capacity to boomerang throughout the larger network of *jamaats*. These disputes, enlivened by the ever-shifting goalposts of Shiʿi and Sunni Islam, fractured *jamaats* in some instances while strengthening them in others. The interplay of these contradictory processes was a central feature of that nexus of capital and discourse that this book calls corporate Islam. After 1914, these contests over religion became greater still, but increasingly involved Muslim institutions and activists outside the *jamaats*. The great challenge for corporate Islam after 1914 was the encroachment of these players into the once well-demarcated terrain of *jamaat* internal affairs.

The scale of this encroachment was facilitated by the pivot of the Bohras, Khojas, and Memons into politics for the first time in numbers in the generation 1890 to 1912. This shift highlighted the fact that these groups had accumulated wealth far beyond their numbers. In time this prompted searching questions from other Indian Muslims about the *jamaats*' place in the wider Indian Muslim "nation." While the Gujarati Muslim commercial castes experienced something of an economic boom from 1866 to 1890 under the banner of imperial conquest and free trade, the period from 1890 to 1912 ushered in new parameters that compelled them to enter, willingly or not, the embryonic Indian nationalist scene. The parameters were also economic in outline insofar as these two and a half decades saw the advent of a more definitive racial divide in the business culture of the British Empire and a big push among Indian traders into industry. Nonetheless, the move that many Gujarati Muslim entrepreneurs made into industry demanded a delicate balancing act between colonial patronage and the desires of Indian political activists to bring them onside. Despite the precocious rush into industry, banking remained sorely neglected on account of structural constraints endemic to the institutions buttressing corporate Islam and the colonial financial system.

4

Racialized Empire, Thrifting, and Swadeshi

1880–1912

DELIVERING AN URDU LECTURE on Indian trade in 1894, one Sayyid Lutf Ali lamented that India's external and internal commerce was entirely in the hands of Europeans, Hindus, and Parsis and that Muslim economic fortunes were in free fall. He neglected to mention the Bohras, Khojas, and Memons.[1] However, in the afterword to the printed version of his lecture, a colleague reminded the author: "Muslim penury is proverbial in the world today. But even among the Muslims there are those involved in trade. Take a look at the state of the Bohras, Memons, and others. They live in such comfort and ease. Yet it is unfortunate that, because their numbers are so few and far between, their wealth cannot be a salve for the wounds of the [Muslim] community."[2] This rejoinder reflected the tendency among some Indian Muslims to concurrently regard the Bohras, Khojas, and Memons as part of the larger Indian Muslim community but also as Muslims distinguished by their disproportionate wealth and exceptional legal status.

With special force from the 1890s onward, other Indian Muslims increasingly saw the Gujarati Muslim commercial castes as the three most auspicious combines of Muslim capitalists in India. The economic success and public celebrity enjoyed by the third colonial generation of Bohra, Khoja, and Memon entrepreneurs as a result of their post-1865 economic recovery reinforced this impression. Consequently, the North Indian Muslim gentry came to regard the corporate Islam of these groups with both begrudging admiration and simmering contempt. Particularly after the 1906 foundation of the All-India Muslim League, the eventual vehicle for the realization of Pakistan, the gentry voiced resentment at the public prestige of the Gujarati Muslim commercial castes, who were sometimes deemed impure Muslims.[3] One of the league's founders, Muhsin ul-Mulk, a prominent Islamic modernist and member of the North Indian gentry, expressed this sentiment in his work *Causes of the Decline of the Mahomedan Nation*, decrying those "Muhammadans not of pure blood" who dominated business and put "pure-blooded" Arabs, Mughals, and Pathans to shame.[4]

Perceptions of intra-Muslim—to say nothing of Hindu-Muslim—wealth disparities became even more controversial as members of the *jamaats* (corporate caste institutions) entered the realm of nationalist politics between 1890 and 1912. Their activities were not strictly anticolonial but punctuated by varying shades of imperial loyalism and Indian nationalism. Instead of operating at loggerheads, loyalism and nationalism coalesced in the life worlds of many Bohra, Khoja, and Memon *jamaats*. One issue was especially thorny for the *jamaats:* while Indian nationalism drew its rallying power from moral outrage against the economic structures of colonial rule, relative Gujarati Muslim material abundance was also contingent on maintenance of the status quo, namely relationships of mutual convenience with colonial authorities and foreign firms.

This tension certainly did not keep the Bohras, Khojas, and Memons from moving into politics. A shift into politics was made all the easier by Gujarati Muslim middle power, which supplied the positions of public authority necessary for would-be Gujarati Muslim activists to make this move. For example, two Bohra magnates—Alibhai Mulla Jivanji and Adamji Pirbhai, both of whom had been beneficiaries of government contracts—were among the founders of the African branch of the Indian National Congress and the Muslim League. The Agha Khan III, who from around 1900 ascended to the highest echelons of political influence open to an Indian, participated at the forefront of all these organizations until he relocated to Europe in the 1920s. His role as imam of the Ismaili Khojas existed in conjunction with his energetic political activism, which spanned five decades, and his political undertakings also encouraged officers in the Ismaili Khoja *jamaats* to move into politics.

Most constituents in the Bohras, Khoja, and Memon *jamaats*, however, attained no political office. Their entry into politics was conditioned initially by the advent of Swadeshi, the movement for Indian economic autarky. Yet even their experience during the Swadeshi years did not conform to any straightforward brand of anticolonial activism. Rather, it was constrained by the complex links between Gujarati Muslim and colonial / European capital. These links were renegotiated between 1890 and 1912 as a consequence of new colonial policies governing migration and a hardening of anti-Indian animus among European business firms, both of which intensified the racial stratification of economic life in the British Empire.[5] Admittedly, this era saw the intensification of Gujarati Muslim brokerage relationships with European and American firms across the Indian Ocean region.[6] It may be argued, nonetheless, that this did not override the racialization of business, but made economic divisions along the color line more definitive.

These shifts considerably eased the commercial castes' embrace of Swadeshi. Ultimately, the rewriting of the rules governing business and politics occasioned by shifting colonial policies and Indian nationalist confrontation projected the Bohra, Khoja, and Memon *jamaats* into the public spotlight as never before, ensuring that they would become linchpins of various Indian nationalist movements in the interwar period. That primed a much more explosive showdown over corporate Islam in decades to come.

Overtaking the Parsis: The Rise of Comprador Capitalists

Before discussing Gujarati Muslim business in the run up to the First World War, it is imperative to look at the post-1865 economic recuperation, for in the two and a half decades after the Bombay share mania, many new Gujarati Muslim firms got their start. Their proprietors were largely parvenu actors who had made little mark on the pre-1865 mercantile scene, and the business lines they pursued were evocative of the highly uneven quality of the post-1865 recovery. While the dime-a-dozen trading firm flourished, colonial India's indigenous banking sector—in terms of the number of Indian-owned banks in operation—contracted sharply in a manner that can only be described as an involution. With only a handful of exceptions among traders and industrialists, the 1860s marked the end of the Gujarati Muslim commercial castes' involvement in the "formal" banking sector as anything other than clientele.

In the short term, the tide of imperial expansion from the late 1860s to the start of the new century furnished Gujarati Muslim capitalists with new opportunities for capital outlay and migration. These opportunities, which mitigated the problems of financial contraction brought about by the share crisis, began to present themselves, though largely outside the subcontinent. While migrating in this period, these communities tended to settle in *jamaat*-specific clusters in their new habitats. Thus, Bohras from Sidhpur settling in Madras in these years, most of whom owned hardware businesses, congregated in roughly three streets of the city.[7] Without exception, however, the *jamaat* was no barrier to other connections. For example, in contemporary Colombo, Parsis and Bohras maintained their collective grip on trade by jointly forming a Gujarati Chamber of Commerce.[8] Partnerships among Bohra, Khoja, and Memon, and other Gujarati groups, also blossomed in this period. Thus, a Parsi dedicated his Japanese-Gujarati textbook with full sincerity to two dear Bohra friends; a Twelver Khoja father and son in Amreli labored as clerks or accountants for Bohra, Memon, and Parsi firms, while having a bad falling out with the local Ismaili Khoja *jamaat*.[9] As many Gujarati Muslim capitalists discovered, the *jamaat* possessed great powers of coercion over them, despite relationships with those outside the community.

The commercial efflorescence of the Bohras, Khojas, and Memons between 1880 and 1912 increased the corporate power of the *jamaats*. What was the role of colonial states in this development? Arguably, the rise of a new generation of Gujarati Muslim capitalists fostered the advent of comprador *jamaats*. *Comprador* is a pejorative term, suggesting outright collaboration with and subordination to colonial authorities. Accusations by later critics and historians that the Gujarati Muslim commercial castes were monolithically comprador capitalists is overstated, based more on projections from colonial sources than a careful study of community and noncommunity "vernacular" materials. By contrast, an examination of *jamaat* sources reveals that considerations of community and individual self-interest, not colonial rule, were the most proximate motivators of colonial collaboration, if one can use that highly charged, and overdramatized word. The *comprador* label likewise overlooks the fact that most Gujarati Muslim merchants "vacillated between economic security and insolvency" and that few enjoyed explicit colonial support.[10]

With these qualifications in mind, it is still useful to think of the period between 1866 and 1890 as the making of the comprador *jamaats*, both in India and the diaspora. Though the cause of their success cannot be reduced to colonial rule, a close relationship with colonial authorities was a contingent factor in Gujarati Muslim commercial profitability. For better or worse, the Bohras, Khojas, and Memons were bound to the colonial authorities on account of their legal status in the colonial system, their wealth, and their prominence in the civic order of empire. Whether those links always redounded to their advantage is another matter entirely. Ample evidence presented in chapter 2 suggests that they were not. The developments surveyed in this chapter corroborate that supposition still more.

In the economic detritus immediately following the share crisis, those links gained a new lease on life in 1868–1869, amid the litigation arising from the insolvencies caused by the share mania, when large numbers of Gujarati Muslim and other Indian merchants from Bombay provided their ships for a punitive expedition against Emperor Tewodros II of Ethiopia. With names like *Bombay Castle*, *Hippogriff*, *Indomitable*, and *Shah Jehan*, these vessels transported the soldiers of the Indian Army to their disembarkation points and supplied them during the campaign.[11] The participation of these ship captains in the campaign was a testament to the continued vitality of Gujarati Muslim shipping well into the high colonial period.[12] The episode also presaged the role that Indian capital would play in facilitating imperial expansion into East Africa and Burma. It is well known that the growth of Bohra, Khoja, and Memon *jamaats* shadowed the itineraries of imperial expansion. From the late eighteenth century, the Bombay-China trade had set the pattern whereby Indian capitalism clung to the coattails of colonial conquest outside the subcontinent. From the late 1870s onward, and continuing in fits and starts for the next three decades, Burma and East Africa restimulated the dismal relationship between Indian capitalist expansion and colonial subterfuge. Almost immediately the two regions were transformed into the primary stomping grounds for the Gujarati Muslim commercial castes outside of South Asia.

That relationship with colonial capital transformed the Gujarati Muslim commercial castes into exemplars of empire, poster boys for the wisdom of imperial economic policy. In opposition to the growing chorus of Indian economists who faulted Britain's pilfering of the subcontinent for India's poverty, proponents of this view held that all India needed to prosper were communities who shared something of the entrepreneurial spirit of the Bohras, Khojas, and Memons. For example, in 1876 a Parsi lawyer criticized the famous "drain of wealth" thesis that Indian nationalists had advanced from the late 1860s:

> Why is the average income of an individual of this Presidency [Bombay] higher by 50 and 100 per cent. Than that of the sister Presidencies [Bengal and Madras]? Because in this Presidency there are more outlets for employment, there is more energy, more enterprise. Go over the list of joint-stock companies at Calcutta, and you will see management and agencies monopolized by English and foreign firms. Go over the list here and you will see it monopolized by the Natives. That speaks for itself. Why, the average individual income of a Parsee, a Khoja, a Memon, and a Bhattia equals the individual income of favoured nations. Because these people have more energy, more enterprise, and more self-reliance than people on the other side; because these people seek out different outlets of employment, and when they cannot find them they create them. Why, then, not elevate the other communities of India to the level of the enterprise of the small communities I have named? Then the drain the lecturer has been so much complaining of will be a mere bagatelle.[13]

This was the typical cant of purported Bengali lethargy voiced by Dilwar Hussain, the Islamic modernist encountered in chapter 2. Nonetheless, it is a statement that betrays how British and Indian defenders of empire alike pointed to the example of the Gujarati Muslim commercial castes, along with a coterie of non-Muslim trading groups, as apologia for imperial economic policy against the charges of Indian critics of empire like Dadabhai Naoroji.[14]

From the 1870s onward, the Gujarati Muslim commercial castes also became yardsticks for other Indian communities to measure their own commercial standing, none more so than the Parsis. Long prominent in the China trade, by the 1860s the Parsis had been edged out by Gujarati Muslims and other Indian traders. Perceptions of Parsi economic decline, though grossly overstated, became a trope in these years, with the Bohras, Khojas, and Memons acting as a foil. Colonel H. S. Olcott, president of the Theosophical Society, chided his Parsi audience in 1882: "There is a fatal inactivity growing apace among you. Not only are you not the religionists you once were, you are not the old time merchants. . . . And instead of your being as in the olden time the kings in Indian trade and commerce you are jostled by successful Bhattias, Borahs, Maimans, and Khojohs who have accumulated fortunes."[15] Though it was certainly untenable, this zero-sum view of economic exchange is instructive as a measure of Bohra, Khoja, and Memon ascendancy. Notably, it also mirrors the refrain among the Indian Muslim gentry from the 1870s onward that the Gujarati Muslim commercial castes were a band of semi-Islamized, half-Hindu upstarts whose religious credentials left much to be desired.

Polemic aside, historians still struggle to explain the dramatic ascent of select Gujarati Muslim commercial entrepreneurs in a relatively short period after 1865. The regime of political polycentrism in Western India, a continuation of a framework predating colonial hegemony, is one factor to which scholars have pointed. As historian Claude Markovits has argued, "Being legally domiciled in a princely state gave traders of the dry zone a further competitive advantage inasmuch as they could repatriate to their native states, where there existed no income tax, some of the profits made in British India where tax became a permanent fixture from the 1880s onwards."[16] Even so, questions of Gujarati Muslim domicile—such as whether a Kachchhi Memon who emigrated from Bombay to Mombasa was governed by Memon inheritance rights as recognized in Kachchh or Bombay—mystified many colonial officials well into the twentieth century. Instead of domicile or legal category as such, it was the protection and leveraging of Gujarati Muslim corporate rights across British and Princely India that redounded to the benefit of these groups. In the end, what mattered most were institutions capable of reproducing a commercial community over generations and functioning as shock absorbers for twists and turns in the business cycles. As corporate bodies, *jamaats* were foundational in that process, both within India and outside it.

As consequential as the overseas outlet became after 1880, Gujarati Muslims also pursued economic opportunities in South Asia. Ongoing colonial military campaigns in the region gave the third colonial generation of Bohra, Khoja, and Memon capitalists a way to break into industry and establish sustained contractual relations with the colonial state. Consider, for example, the Bohra merchant Adamji Pirbhai. Though his sons were excommunicated by the reigning *dai al-mutlaq* (chief cleric of the sect) in 1915, Pirbhai did more than any other figure to improve the *dais*' muted status in the authority of the Bohra *jamaat*. Born in Dhoraji in 1846, Pirbhai moved with his parents to Bombay to pursue business opportunities.[17] They soon won two government contracts, producing work pleasing enough to their colonial employers to secure preferential treatment for the next three and a half decades. By the time Pirbhai was twenty-one, the family firm had obtained a contract for the Bombay Arsenal which they would hold for decades to come.

The firm really made its name, however, in manufacturing tents for the Indian Army. Colonial armies pitched Pirbhai's tents in Afghanistan in 1878–1880, Egypt in 1884, and the South African War of 1899–1902. During the Afghan campaign, the firm answered the appeal of the commanding officer, Sir Richard Temple, who was desperate for Maltese carts for transport purposes. When other entrepreneurs replied that they could only construct forty to fifty carts every month, Pirbhai produced five hundred in short order, followed by an additional four hundred. This was enough to secure the family a lucrative government contract for four more decades. Even so, a later British military writer was not especially complimentary about the state of the carts: "Supplied by contract, and made from unseasoned wood as quickly as possible, [the carts] readily fell to pieces, owing to the shrinking of the spokes of the wheels."[18]

A poor showing on the frontiers of empire did not prevent Pirbhai's business empire from becoming embedded in larger structures of capital circulation linking London, East Africa, Western India, and southern China. In 1887 he inaugurated a mechanized tannery in Bombay that exported goods to Africa and Europe. The tannery employed around one thousand laborers, who were paid between twelve and eighty rupees per day.[19] Yet despite his many successes, Pirbhai's portfolio was not impervious to the incessant booms and busts of the market. One such victim was the Shah Steam Navigation Co. of India, founded in 1906 after the shipping enterprise of another Bohra firm, Essajee Tajbhoy, ran aground. The initial prospectus of Shah Steam Navigation Co. shows a capital of Rs. 3,000,000, divided into twelve thousand shares of Rs. 250 each.[20] Its directors were, besides Pirbhai and Tajibhai, several other leading Bohra business leaders.

Registered as a limited liability company, Shah Steam Navigation Co.'s aim was to supply Indian merchants with cargo carriers and to break into the Ottoman pilgrimage market. Despite its auspicious beginnings, it was short-lived, as it was unable to compete with industry linchpins. In the wake of repeated losses, Pirbhai withdrew from the firm. After the firm suffered its death blows, the remnants of the fleet were broken up and funneled into new Bohra-led enterprises like the Bombay and Hedjaz Steam Navigation

Co.[21] Still, Pirbhai's other business interests continued to flourish, and as future chapters will show, his firm became a primary supplier to the Indian Army in the South African War.

Although the bursting of the share market bubble in 1865–1866 ruined many of the Khoja entrepreneurs involved in the China trade, small numbers of Gujarati Muslim traders continued to travel to the South China Sea from the 1870s onward. One of these was the Ismaili Khoja, Karimbhai Ibrahim, a stalwart supporter of the Agha Khan III, whose business empire, Currimbhoy, extended outward from Bombay to the far reaches of the Indian Ocean. Born in 1849 into a trading family, Ibrahim was one of the first Muslims to be elected to Bombay's Municipal Corporation in recognition for his charitable endeavors and his services to the colonial *sarkar.* He was eventually knighted, in part thanks to his support of girl's education in Kachchh, an undertaking funded from the proceeds of his mill business.[22] His family's Bombay interests became mainstays of Indian industry until a spectacular collapse during the Great Depression (as covered in chapter 5). By the 1880s, one branch of the firm was a stalwart of Indian business in Calcutta, where its brokers included prominent Marwari firms.[23]

One of Currimbhoy's subsidiaries, E. Pabaney & Co., was a fixture of Indian business in Hong Kong and Shanghai. The firm was a crucial player in the local religious economy of Shanghai, even serving as the chief trustees of a mosque and cemetery in the city's European delegation. As a correspondent for the Indian Muslim newspaper *Islamic Fraternity* (published from Tokyo) later recounted, the muezzin of the mosque was a Chinese Muslim named Hilal al-Din. The mosque even came equipped with modern bathroom and shower facilities.[24] Around the same time, E. Pabaney & Co. requested permission from Shanghai's Municipal Board to establish a new Muslim cemetery; the existing one had become overcrowded, in part due to the interment of the bodies of Indian Muslim sepoys killed during the Boxer Rebellion and Muslim lascars streaming into Shanghai.[25] In its role as a leading trustee, E. Pabaney was earmarked to allot funds for the endeavor.

As E. Pabaney & Co.'s history exemplified, in a multiethnic trading environment, weak ties among Indian merchants were essential—but so was being a subject of the British Empire. In China, Indians' status as British subjects—though subordinated to a second-rate position by dint of racial prejudice—counted for a great deal. For one, it helped combat the aspirations of Chinese merchant corporations to boycott their rivals. This was made plain to E. Pabaney & Co. and another Ismaili Khoja firm, Jairazbhoy Peerbhoy, in 1878, when one such Chinese merchant corporation, the Swatow Opium Guild, decided to "taboo" both firms.[26] The guild's ability to make or break the commercial fortunes of Indian interlopers was a mark of its precocious economic power. In retaliation, the firms Pabaney and Peerbhoy conspired with local British merchants to clandestinely ship their opium under assumed names. In the showdown between Chinese and Indian corporate entities, British subjecthood was a decisive factor.

Magnates like Ibrahim, Isabhai, and Pirbhai were only the uppermost crust of the new breed of Bohra, Khoja, and Memon entrepreneurs to emerge after 1865. Less prominent, but just as important in the story of economic enterprise, were the mid- and low-level entrepreneurs, half-forgotten now, who set out from India between the late 1860s and mid-1880s. Settling in a multitude of locations in the Indian Ocean region, they relied on *jamaat* support, weak ties, and colonial subjecthood to establish their businesses. Many retained connections to their home regions in Gujarat, while a large subset relocated several times in the search for lasting business success and stability. While the fortunes that they accumulated remained precarious, the advent of a global system of free trade, for all its racial injustices, economic inequalities, and liaisons with empire, enabled humble Gujarati Muslim traders to establish multigenerational businesses across broad swaths of Africa and Asia. In so doing they installed *jamaats* in many reaches of the Indian Ocean region where Gujarati Muslim entrepreneurs remain to this day.

By 1880, Aden, Bombay, Jeddah, Kobe, Muscat, Rangoon, Yokohama, and numerous other sites around the world were sufficiently integrated in global transport networks and the economic itineraries of the Gujarati Muslim commercial castes for Haji Sulaiman, a young Memon merchant from Dhoraji, to call at all these ports. This was the beginning of a journey that would take him, in fits and starts, far outside the familiar terrain of Gujarati Muslims. He would eventually travel from Mormon territory in Utah to czarist Russia, and from the Alhambra in Cordoba to Australia—indeed, across nearly the entire globe except for South America, interior Africa, and the northern reaches of Asia.[27] Haji Sulaiman eventually settled in Cape Town, South Africa, home to a substantial community of Memons. Four decades earlier, it would have been unthinkable for a modest Memon trader from Dhoraji to travel around the world. His journey testifies to the meteoric ascent of the Gujarati Muslim commercial castes after 1866, to say nothing of the revolutionized transport infrastructures that made it all possible, but also to the geographic limitations of Gujarati Muslim diaspora in this epoch.

In his movement across the globe, Haji Sulaiman only had recourse to *jamaat* institutions in a few locations: at Jeddah, for example, he stayed at a guesthouse specifically for Memons. The Memon *jamaats*' real contribution to his travels was the role they played as a primary, although not exclusive, audience for his work. In his preface, Haji Sulaiman stated that as the first Memon to circumnavigate the globe, he hoped to have a positive effect on his "caste brothers" and serve as an example to them of the benefits of travel. This said, Haji Sulaiman was not writing only for a Memon audience: his editor, after all, was a close Parsi friend, who later wrote a moving eulogy to his late friend in volume two of the Memon's world travels.[28] Moreover, Haji Sulaiman was also an energetic member of the Anjuman-i Islām, a Muslim "reformist" organization founded in Bombay in the 1860s. Its ranks were filled by Muslims of sundry castes and affiliations, including many Daudi and Sulaimani Bohras, as well as Khojas. Haji Sulaiman's membership in Muslim ecumenical institutions was common among select Gujarati Muslims, but the Memon *jamaats*' stature should not be lost in the shuffle.

Haji Sulaiman had established only a peremptory residence in Burma in 1880. But over the next four decades, the population of Memons—along with smaller but steady numbers of Bohras and Khojas—grew rapidly in Moulmein and Rangoon. As ever, they acquired a public prominence belied by their small numbers. It was only in the 1890s that Rangoon's Memon *jamaat* reached critical mass. By then, the migration of Memon men like Haji Sulaiman to Rangoon from Dhoraji, Gondal, and Upleta was so great that the census takers in Gondal State decided to not include them in the final accounts—not least because the ratio of married Memon women in Gondal was disproportionately high.[29]

Memons also enjoyed a considerable prominence in the contemporary Ottoman Hijaz, as best exemplified by the career of one Abd Allah Arab Memon. Originally from Bombay, Abd Allah made a fortune of some Rs. 200,000 in Calcutta before relocating to the environs of Medina. There he established a fruit orchard business that soon went bust due to lack of cooperation from his Bedouin partners, according to a later commentator.[30] Abd Allah then relocated to Jeddah, splitting his time between there and India. In the 1880s, as part of his bid to enter the steamship market, he paid a visit to a Memon pir in Gujranwala. This pir served as a financier for Memon enterprises in exchange for personal devotion and helped underwrite Abd Allah's scheme.

Throughout his career, Abd Allah Arab Memon was active in various Islamic philanthropic causes in the Ottoman lands and far beyond. In one case, he funded the construction of the Zubaida Aqueduct in Mecca. But this paled in comparison to his collaboration with the American convert, Muhammad Alexander Webb.[31] According to the Ahmadi convert Maulvi Hassan Ali, a figure who styled himself a "Muslim missionary," Abd Allah bankrolled Webb's efforts to propagate Islam in America, pledging one-third of his salary to the cause. However, he was unsuccessful in obtaining subscriptions for Webb's mission from other Indian Muslims, save those in Hyderabad (Deccan) and Rangoon.[32] In all these ventures, Abd Allah sought spiritual direction not only from his pir in Hala Tehsil near Hyderabad in Sindh but also from the Ahmadi messiah, Mirza Ghulam Ahmad, whom Abd Allah visited in the town of Qadian in Punjab. Ahmad purportedly advised Abd Allah on how to best support the spread of Islam in America.[33]

While still residing in the Ottoman Hijaz, Abd Allah was appointed by Sultan Abd al-Hamid II as the Jeddah agent of the official Ottoman steamer line, the Idāre-i Maḥṣūṣa.[34] In turn, the Memon capitalist suggested to Ottoman authorities that the Idāre-i Maḥṣūṣa establish a line for pilgrims between India and Jeddah, which would redound to the benefit of the hajji and the *hazine* (Ottoman treasury) alike.[35] The India-Jeddah line he proposed never materialized, but Abd Allah did eventually earn a medal for the services he rendered ferrying pilgrims.[36] Such transimperial promiscuity occasionally led him into hot water with Ottoman authorities. In one episode it was suspected that he had strung up a Union Jack alongside the Ottoman flag outside the Jeddah headquarters of the Idāre-i Maḥṣūṣa. It turned out the ensign was merely the colors of Abd Allah's commercial firm, but that was enough to get Ottoman authorities to issue a statement that no banner may fly at the same level as an Ottoman flag.[37]

This was not the extent of Abd Allah's dealings with Ottoman authorities. He subsequently was appointed Ottoman consul in Calcutta and labored to import pigeons (*güvercin*) from India to Ottoman Iraq.[38] Such connections did not always pay dividends. In 1895 Abd Allah and the European capitalists for whom he served as agent submitted another manifesto for a Bombay-Jeddah steamer line to Ottoman officials, which, in company with many like-minded endeavors of these years, never materialized.[39] But within a few years Abd Allah's firm was blacklisted by his erstwhile Ottoman patrons for not paying Ottoman customs duties.[40] The fickle relationship between government authorities and private actors was commonplace in the Gujarati Muslim experience. Just as Abd Allah was being nominated to his position in the Ottoman Idāre-i Maḥṣūṣa, the bipartite racial character of the contemporary British Empire was becoming calcified. The crystallization of Britain's "inner" and "outer" empires effectively hemmed in the Gujarati Muslim commercial castes in the interior regions of European empires at the same time as it opened commercial doors for them within that same constrained space.

The Crystallization of the Inner and Outer Empires

By the 1880s, in a fitting reaffirmation of their middle power in legislative and political matters, Gujarati Muslim commercial castes had secured a solid middle-tier status in the economy of the British Empire in the Indian Ocean. There they remained until the end of the empire, only in rare individual cases moving to a higher stratum through economic relationships forged with British, other European, and Japanese firms. Subsequent projects of European empire building both expanded Gujarati Muslim enterprise and pinned it within specific geographic regions. In the last quarter of the nineteenth century, as one historian has usefully argued, the British Empire at the global level had coalesced into two main parts: the outer empire of the white settler colonies, Australia, Canada, New Zealand, and South Africa, and the inner empire comprising Muslim-majority (or high density Muslim-minority) territories in Africa, the Middle East, South Asia and Southeast Asia.[41] The solidification of that bipartite empire ensured that the structure of Indian economic enterprise was increasingly subjected to not only capital disparities but also a racialized division of labor. Racial discrimination was not total, and other divides of caste and religion accentuated prejudice along the color line. Still, a concatenation of factors—insurmountable divisions of labor, capital disparities, and racial asymmetries—conspired to constrain the movement of Gujarati Muslim firms during this period.

The high period of European colonization in Africa after 1885, frequently called the Scramble for Africa, also brought the Gujarati Muslim commercial castes into contact with colonial powers beyond the British Empire. During this period the *jamaats* in Africa were integrated into the administration of other empires, including the French, German, Italian, and Portuguese. French military contracts in Madagascar, Italian colonial partisanship in Somaliland, and Ethiopian government patronage all contributed to the further enrichment of *sethias* and thus to expansion of the *jamaats*.[42] But it was the seemingly endless wars of the late Victorian and early Edwardian eras, which opened new markets and supplied contracting opportunities that served as the primary economic boost for many Gujarati Muslim firms in Africa. The benefits extended to many Gujarati Muslim firms, from the massive Bohra firm of Adamji Pirbhai to the Twelver Khoja firm of Hajeebhoy, Lalji and Co. The former had been a supplier during the British war against the Nandi in 1897–1898, while the latter had rendered "valuable assistance" to colonial armies in Somaliland during the campaigns of 1901–1904.[43] The colonization of Africa was good business for the Gujarati Muslim commercial castes.

By 1890 the third colonial generation of entrepreneurs—those who had appeared in the wake of the 1865–1866 share crisis—had installed themselves in the far reaches of Britain's inner empire in the Indian Ocean region. There they founded *jamaats* and joined other Indian social associations, which became havens for the migration and settlement of fellow caste members. While the vast majority were *replicative* entrepreneurs by virtue of their weak capitalization, some became *innovative* by building connections with a multitude of Indian and non-Indian firms and diversifying their portfolios over the long term.[44] Nevertheless, bankruptcy retained an omnipresent threat for even the most secure businesses, as examples from Bombay and Rangoon to Zanzibar make abundantly clear.

Access to credit was the key determinant of long-term firm survival. While Bombay's share bazaar continued to fund many legally incorporated Gujarati Muslim firms, this was an exclusive club. Moreover, while Indian entrepreneurs after 1865 showed a proclivity for creating various community-level thrifts—funds, savings and loans, and cooperatives—they rarely, if ever, engaged in formal banking to the extent of becoming proprietors of banks. From a purely economic perspective, the great disadvantage of thrifts is that they do not produce the crucial money-multiplier effects that banks do, nor do they furnish clients with the same range of intermediating financial services as banks.[45] Arguably, the "thrifting" of Indian banking after 1865 increased the importance of the *jamaats* as suppliers of credit and other social services to caste members (and sometimes those not in castes).

The *jamaats*' function in this regard can be glimpsed in a Gujarati book detailing the accounts of Bombay's Halai Memon mosque between 1851 and 1881. The work was printed by a certain Seth Hassan Mian Rahmat Allah, one of the mosque's trustees, in 1883.[46] Clocking in at over three hundred pages, the text records in sumptuous detail "the rent of the houses, the purchase of property, repair work, the bills, taxes, and expenditure, etc." of the Halai Memon mosque in Bombay, but its bailiwick covered the sweep of Bombay's Halai Memon quarter. Its coverage of any given year offers fascinating insight into the capital underpinning Bombay's Halai Memon community: loans, funds, warehouses, spinning factories, and residential accommodation. It is hard to assess the typicality of this account book in terms of its demographics and capital, but it can be taken as representative in many respects of the asset portfolios held by *jamaats* and subsidiary trusts. Especially noteworthy are the frequent entries for non-Muslims, affirming the unsurprising fact that individuals outside the *jamaat* also fell under the sway of its capacious economic portfolio, though largely as tenants or debtors rather than direct beneficiaries of its goods and services.[47] Memon or non-Memon, each of these individuals had an account (*khāte*) assigned to their name, and debits and credits registered to the account were fastidiously tracked over time.

Given the mosque's location in Bombay, the economic heart of British India, the accounts for the Halai Memon mosque likely were on a much grander scale than the host of smaller *jamaats* in the Indian Ocean region. With this caveat, its lessons can still be confidently applied to other *jamaats* of the Gujarati Muslim commercial castes. After all, the Halai Memon mosque in Bombay was but one thrift in a broader institutional macrocosm stretching to every corner of the Indian Ocean region inhabited by the Gujarati Muslim commercial castes. But trusteeship over these thrifts became hotly contested precisely from this period onward, with crucial implications for the character of religious authority and wealth in the *jamaats*.

The capital falling under the administrative purview of the Halai Memon mosque leaves open the question of how individuals navigated the wider world of credit. Aflush with capital and condensed Bohra, Khoja, and Memon *jamaats*, Zanzibar offers the best documented archive of credit operations involving actors from these groups. With its dense web of economic ties and legal frictions, Zanzibar was a place where credit cut across the boundaries of these communities and bound their fortunes up with the Africans, Europeans, and other Indians with whom they transacted.[48] Although the circulation of liquid capital kept the island's economy humming, bankruptcy was an omnipresent feature of its commercial life, an attribute it shared with most other parts of the western Indian Ocean. The exclusivity of formal banking and the persistence of thrifting among Indian communities in the British Empire meant that merchants often only had recourse to trade credit or moneylending arrangements when they were barred from utilizing (or exhausted) those first two options.

Colonial banks were highly selective in providing credit to native merchants. With an extensive surveillance network in place to ascertain the credit status of Indian merchants, race was never incidental to lending decisions. At the Bank of Bengal's Rangoon branch, for example, a consortium of well-established Kachchhi Memon traders grouped under the name Hajee Valley Mahomed Hajee Abba were flagged for having precariously imbalanced bill ledgers and were investigated by a local agent.[49] Arguably, these allegations had their source in something other than a concern for scrupulous banking, for even the most prominent Muslim firms were blacklisted and deprived of capital on the pretext that they were overcommitting themselves or selling fake demand drafts tied to no mercantile transactions.[50]

The internal financial resources of the firm—which, in the interests of good bookkeeping, necessitated frequent intra-branch transfers, usually involving hundis, across the Indian Ocean region—and trade credit supplied from European firms were two other means of keeping the internal machinery of many Gujarati Muslim business concerns above board. This latter source of funding, in which the borrowing firm receives the goods up front from the creditor firm and settles its debt at a subsequent date, was another means of propelling a largely unbanked commerce. But like bank credit, trade credit was highly selective, reserved only for firms with a solid reputation, with longstanding commitments to European firms. Paltry cash reserves were a common feature across many transimperial firms, a fact which pushed Gujarati Muslim entrepreneurs into borrowing money at high rates of interest. Taking out high-interest loans was a source of unease, even if these same firms lent money on equally steep terms to those inside and outside the *jamaats*. All the while the financial precarity of the far-flung firm was exacerbated by the unpredictable price fluctuations inherent to commodity trading.[51]

High interest rates only multiplied the webs of overlapping debt obligations that were inimical to long-term commercial survival. One unfortunate merchant who was declared a bankrupt in Zanzibar in 1893, Salah Chatur, was not uncommon in having one bania (a catchall term for Indian merchants of indeterminate caste origin), two European, seven Bohra, and eleven Khoja creditors chasing him for repayments.[52] His debts to his Bohra and Khoja creditors ran the gamut, from fifteen rupees to Rs. 5,000. These sums suggest that the advancing of loans was a constituent part of the commercial portfolio of many Gujarati Muslim entrepreneurs. This said, credit operations varied in orders of magnitude as a proportion of a merchant's portfolio and rarely evolved to the point that Bohras, Khojas, or Memons founded "formal" banking institutions.

Chatur was also representative of the frightening instability of Gujarati Muslim business fortunes. According to the initial bankruptcy case, for some time he had managed a business that consigned goods to Marseilles, among other ports. After his firm endured heavy losses, Chatur was unable to pay off his debts. After a two-year pause in which he was expected to put his financial house in order, another round of litigation brought him yet again before the court, and a full account of his estate and outstanding debts was drawn up. On this occasion his creditors expressed their consternation that Chatur had done nothing in the intervening two years to pay down his obligations.[53] Chatur was no stand-alone figure, and in future decades, Muslim indebtedness became a divisive political issue in India and the diaspora. Eventually, the issue became sectarian as the "Hindu" moneylender took on the status of bogeyman in the Indian Muslim political imagination. Nevertheless, many Muslim commentators were wont to overlook the practices of Muslim moneylenders who imposed high rates of interest on the likes of Chatur and diminished the prospects of a fresh start for debtors.

By no means were Gujarati Muslim traders the immutable victims of their creditors. Writing from Aden in 1877, a British official noted a curious, if unseemly, practice purportedly used by Kachchhi Memons to establish themselves as petty traders in the port.[54] In this setup a trader possessing two hundred rupees in cash would purchase goods, with the help of three months' credit, from a group of other merchants and open a shop. (Note the recourse here to intra-firm trade credit, discussed above). Typically, the trader paid the loan installments for a month or two, but then tucked away the remaining cash, absconded with the goods, and declared bankruptcy. The lenders sometimes had luck in seizing the collateral, but in many instances the Memon borrowers made a break for it and were impossible to track down. Even those Memons jailed for their indiscretion were set free after their erstwhile creditors grew tired of paying their maintenance fees. Such were the unconventional methods to which a largely unbanked world of commercial credit gave license.

The sharp hierarchies between European and Indian banking were a stark feature across the world of inner empire. Only in rare cases did Gujarati Muslims make inroads into Britain's outer empire, but their stay was almost universally a temporary one. Australia offers a pithy illustration of this. An Ismaili Khoja merchant and later a long-serving member of the Bombay Legislative Council, Fazlbhai Visram claimed to have been the first Khoja, and potentially the first Muslim, to visit the colony in 1884, though this is disputable. Deeply literate in Bombay's trade with Mauritius and Zanzibar, Visram spoke at length in his travelogue about the untapped commercial potential Australia presented to Indian traders.[55] For this Ismaili Khoja entrepreneur, Australia was as logical an area of expansion as anywhere in the Indian Ocean. The Memon merchant Haji Sulaiman, discussed earlier, also had an extended stay in Australia in 1893, noting the substantial enclave of Bengali Muslims in the country.[56] Although a mosque was founded in Perth around the time of Haji Sulaiman's visit, Gujarati Muslims were not among the Afghan, Bengali, and Pathan Muslims who constituted the original donors.[57] Any subsequent Gujarati Muslim emigration to Australia would have been exceptionally difficult, as the country introduced anti-Asian legislation in the 1890s. Echoing similar policies in the United States and other parts of the white British Empire, this legislation barred Indian emigrants from entry.[58]

Australia was largely a jumping-off point to other parts of the inner empire for the Bohras, Khojas, and Memons. The Bohra merchant Alibhai Mulla Jivanji is an excellent example. Jivanji had opened a business in Karachi in 1891, which quickly became one of the leading Bohra *jamaats* outside of Bombay and Surat. Yet he soon relocated to Australia, where he gained some success as a small-time hawker and shopkeeper in Adelaide, about 450 miles west of Melbourne. There several British officials encouraged him to shift his business to East Africa, where his fortunes were transformed. After arriving by steamer, Jivanji entered into an agency agreement with Smith Mackenzie & Co. in Mombasa.[59] In remarkably short order, via his role as an agent of the Imperial British East Africa Company, Jivanji was tasked with organizing the emigration of Indian labors, artisans, and police officers to East Africa. The labor pool from which Jivanji's firm drew from sources as far afield as India's Northwestern Frontier provinces, a demonstration of the company's ability to tap into noncommunity labor resources. But if the salaries and contract terms for the managers are any indication, the remuneration and working conditions for these laborers must have been abysmal.[60] Over the next decade, Jivanji became an employee of the East Africa Protectorate and a government-contracted railway supplier, a position that accelerated the British conquest of Uganda and projected him into the highest ranks of the local colonial order.[61] Like many Bohras before him, he also acquired a significant role in overseas shipping.[62]

It is unclear how close Jivanji was to Bohra *jamaats* in these years. One biographer paints Jivanji's 1916 excommunication by the Bohra *dai al-mutlaq* as foreordained by the independence he had shown over the previous two and a half decades.[63] But this may be a retrospective reading of the evidence. As stressed repeatedly in earlier chapters, merchant wealth had paradoxical consequences for the *jamaats*, magnifying either centripetal or centrifugal tendencies. It is probable that a merchant of Jivanji's standing chafed under the authority of the *jamaat*. Even so, it would not be wise to project his later falling out with the Bohra religious leadership onto his earlier life. After all, he personally financed the construction of a Bohra mosque in Mombasa in 1901.[64] And even if Jivanji was eventually excommunicated by the *dai*, along with a host of other Bohra capitalists (a development covered in chapters 5 and 6), his commercial portfolio underwrote the growth of Bohra *jamaat* infrastructure in East Africa.

Beyond his community, Jivanji's political trajectory exemplified how the restrictive labor and capital regimes imposed on the inner empire served to bolster the support of the *sethias* (caste leaders) for Indian nationalism. To be sure, Jivanji remained a linchpin of colonial rule in East Africa for decades to come, helping to expand the economic infrastructure of Indian business in Nairobi. But from 1911 onward he became a vocal opponent of select British policies in the East African Protectorate. During a 1911 visit to Manchester, Jivanji decried attempts by the British government to prevent "the natural flow of Indian capital and labour into the country. British East Africa is being run by the British taxpayer, who is, through this dog-in-the-manger policy, denied the proper return for his money. At the same time the British Indian feels himself under an injustice. He holds that this policy is a deviation from that freedom of trade and intercourse which is characteristic of the British system."[65] This defense of the free movement of Indian capital and labor was a trope in which Gujarati Muslim entrepreneurs often indulged when speaking to British capitalists. Obsequious though these comments were, any threat to free circulation of peoples and capital within the inner empire, such as through the implementation of strict controls on migration, was anathema to Gujarati Muslim business.

A year after his Manchester speech Jivanji condemned a fifteen-rupee "poll-tax" the colonial government aimed to levy on the "non-native" (meaning, British Indian and European) population. If an individual could not pay—a real possibility given that the majority of the Indian population were laborers and artisans—fines or imprisonment awaited. "Historians, ancient and modern," Jivanji wrote, "have with one voice condemned a capitation tax levied in any country and in any time." The levying of the tax would add insult to the many injuries already endured by Indians in East Africa, from unequal treatment to racial discrimination.[66] Racialized policies governing Indian migration thus cajoled a hitherto co-opted Gujarati Muslim capitalist into taking up the cause of Indian nationalism, a move cemented by Jivanji's founding of the East African branch of the Indian National Congress in 1915.

South Africa reveals a similar but more complex process in which Gujarati Muslim capitalists shifted into anticolonial politics. Mohandas Karamchand Gandhi's experience in South Africa is, of course, emblematic, but the Gujarati Muslim *jamaats* followed disparate trajectories. As is well known, he had been brought to South Africa by a Memon firm, Dada Abd Allah, and worked closely with Memon *jamaats* throughout his time in the country.[67] Still, as Gandhi's collected correspondence reveals, he often struggled to bring the Memon *jamaats* onside and to shake them out of what he saw as their complacency with the colonial order. In one case in 1907, he faulted two Memons in Pietersburg for failing to close their shops during a general strike. In the same breath, however, he noted that the two had also been censured by Memons and other Indians in the town.[68]

Sometime later, when members of the Memon *jamaats* betrayed signs of conceding to government pressure during a general Indian campaign against the Immigration Bill, Gandhi asked rhetorically, "Is there among the Memons no brave man who will courageously declare: 'Even if other Memons should go, I certainly will not.'"[69] When a group of Memons caved and obtained permits from the government to reside in the Transvaal as merchants, Gandhi inveighed against the "Perversity of Memons." He lambasted them for accepting "the title-deed of slavery" in order to "carry on their business in peace."[70] A tiny group of Memons eventually bucked the *jamaat* trend and refused to concede to the government, foreshadowing the intra-*jamaat* divisions that the brave new world of mass politics exacerbated in years to come.[71]

Although South Africa was quickly becoming a laboratory for Indian nationalism at the turn of the century, it was simultaneously a site for imperial loyalism, especially during the South African War of 1899–1902. Gandhi, as is well known, volunteered as a medical orderly during the South African War. As was noted earlier in this chapter, Adamji Pirbhai's firm had proven itself to colonial authorities during the Anglo-Afghan War of 1878. But this was small fry in comparison to the South African War, in which the firm supplied the bulk of the tents issued to the British Army, according to later testimony given by his son during the First World War.[72] Suitably, Pirbhai's firm advertised its tents in Gandhi's Anglo-Gujarati newspaper, *Indian Opinion*. Despite these services to the empire, Pirbhai's family was not spared the commonplace racial prejudice that Indians in South Africa experienced—prejudice that ultimately galvanized the nascent Indian nationalist movement. While Gandhi's expulsion from the whites-only train in Pietermaritzburg is a famous moment in the mythology of Indian nationalism, Pirbhai's own son experienced racial discrimination in South Africa in 1900. There he was turned away from four hotels and told that there was "no such thing as an Indian gentleman."[73] In Britain's white outer empire, the social confidence of the Gujarati Muslim capitalist, itself the consequence of the agency afforded by wealth, was not easily accepted.

Rangoon was yet another testing ground of Indian Muslim politics in this era, but it never evolved the assertive nationalism of East and South Africa. At century's end, from the ranks of Rangoon's Memon *jamaat* came one of the leading prewar Indian merchants in Burma: Abd al-Karim Jamal, a man christened by a later Memon historian as the "merchant prince of the Memon community."[74] Considering the density of Memon migration to Rangoon, it is rather surprising that a Rangoon Memon *jamaat* was not registered until 1909.[75] But it also invites the question of whether formal recognition and incorporation as a *jamaat* mattered when all the other criteria of the *jamaats'* corporate power were already in place: a baseline of (male) caste members, madrasas, *awqāf* (pious endowments), and caste consciousness. Additionally, one must remember that individual Memons carried the legal status of their original domiciles with them wherever they went in the diaspora. For this reason, their corporate power was reproducible even in areas where the *jamaats* were unincorporated.

Jamal's career conveys how a Gujarati Muslim entrepreneur's movement into imperial-loyalist politics redounded to the benefit of one's own *jamaat*. His father's business interests brought the family to Burma, where Jamal was educated at Rangoon College.[76] As a profile in the *Moslem World* later put it, when Jamal took over his father's firm in 1882, at the age of twenty, the concern was already "gigantic," with a specialization in piece goods and silk. Under Jamal's watch, the firm diversified into cotton, paddy, and petroleum (to name only a few). He became, by the featurette's reckoning, "the pioneer of industry in Burma" for his role in creating rice and oil mills and ginning factories.[77] Jamal was a cornerstone of colonial society in Burma until his death in 1924. An enthusiastic imperial loyalist, he also invested heavily in the infrastructure of his home region in Gujarat, remitting regular donations to various charities, madrasas, and high schools.[78] His leadership of the Burmese branch of the All-India Muslim League from 1910 onward was just one segment of his sprawling political portfolio. But the league, for all its modest beginnings, soon began to change the rules of the game for Indian Muslim politics.[79]

Eschewing careers in trade, certain sons of Gujarati Muslim entrepreneurs did move into the highest ranks of the colonial legal order during these years—in large part thanks to the legal education that they obtained in Britain. The most famous example was the Khoja Muhammad Ali Jinnah, later the leader of the Muslim League and inaugural president of Pakistan. Jinnah's grandfather, Punja Meghji, was a humble Ismaili Khoja shopkeeper who migrated to Karachi from Kathiawar in 1861.[80] In time he created a firm registered in the name of his son, Valji Punjabhai. Greatly aided by his knowledge of English, Punjabhai then struck up a partnership with Graham's Shipping and Trading Company in Karachi and exported gum arabic to England and Hong Kong.[81] It was a three-year apprenticeship with the company that first brought Jinnah to London for his legal education in 1893.[82] Three years after returning to Karachi and settling in Bombay in 1896, Jinnah had purportedly "converted" to Twelver Shiʿism.[83] His return to India set him up for a legal and political career unmatched by any other Gujarati Muslim; he often represented Bohras, Khojas, and Memons in legal cases, and established close personal relationships with members of all three commercial castes. These relationships would become instrumental in the eventual achievement of Pakistan.

Jinnah was obviously exceptional among Gujarati Muslims in his ability to move with relative ease among the highest of imperial and Indian institutions. For most Bohras, Khojas, and Memons, the *jamaats* were a life-or-death institutional backstop—as terrible events at the turn of the century made plain. In these years, devastating famine and plague brought colossal suffering to large swaths of India. Western India was struck with a ferocity that did not spare even the better-off Indian social groups. The human toll exacted from Indian communities unambiguously signaled the enormous inequalities between European and Indian citizens on the subcontinent. Luckily for the Bohras, Khojas, and Memons, their primary status as traders, rather than agriculturists, spared them the worst consequences of famine.[84]

Famine had catalyzed Gujarati Muslim migration to British territories in the early nineteenth century, as was seen in chapter 1. A century later, in 1900, the famine that fell upon Greater Gujarat and large parts of India once again instigated the migration of numerous Bohras, Khojas, and Memons.[85] The death toll from the famines throughout India around the turn of the century was staggering, encompassing anywhere from eight to nineteen million people.[86] That it was not even worse owed in part to local famine relief efforts. These moments of crisis underscored the *jamaats*' function as providers of social services in a setting where state institutions were weak. Bohra sources relate that Bohra *jamaats* throughout Western India undertook famine relief efforts, and Bohra *sethias* like Adamji Pirbhai remitted funds to destitute areas in Kathiawar.[87]

Developments at Sidhpur proved that the *jamaats* did not only take care of their own. There a host of Bohra magnates paid into a "public fund" for the benefit of all the residents of the area and a special store that sold grain at artificially depressed prices was also set up. Notwithstanding these efforts, the famine spared few, and even ravaged the Bohra *dai*'s seat in Surat, where hundreds of destitute Bohras from the surrounding area descended on the city. While the authorities in Surat had taken some initiative to tackle famine, in other cities the official response was practically nonexistent. Private acts of Bohra charity thus became the only recourse open to victims, if Bohra reports are dependable witnesses.[88]

Gujarati Muslim reactions to combatting plague in these years were more sectarian, with hospitals segregated based on the identity of the plague victim and organized by the *jamaats*. When bubonic plague swept through Bombay, Karachi, and other Western Indian ports in 1897, one Muslim administrator, Sirdar Muhammad Yaqub, initially found the Memon antiplague measures underwhelming. After organizing a series of crisis meetings, however, he was pleasantly surprised to see the Kachchhi Memon *jamaat* spring into action. Nevertheless, the Halai Memon *jamaat* was criticized by Yaqub for initially hesitating to implement antiplague measures. After repeated meetings with the *jamaat* council, Yaqub learned that the holdup owed to "internal discord" in the caste, and once the head of the *jamaat* was replaced the Halai Memons organized their plague response along the lines of the Kachchhis.[89]

Suitably, *jamaat* funds financed community efforts to combat the plague. Expenses for the running of the Kholsa Molla Mahomedan Plague Hospital, built for Halai Memons, were taken directly out of the Halai Jamaat Fund, which collected money via "a sort of income-tax." The Kachchhi Memon Plague Hospital's annual report proclaimed that, with the aid of capital from leading merchants of the community, funds amounting to Rs. 15,000 were raised. With its twenty-four-member committee, the hospital administered to a sizable number of patients in the *jamaat khana* (assembly hall) itself.[90] As for the Bohras, in a bid to bolster Bohra inoculation rates, Adamji Pirbhai convened a meeting of the Bombay *jamaat*. Five thousand people attended. The *dai* was summoned to give a religious endorsement for inoculation, and Pirbhai and his son were administered shots on the spot.[91] Combating vaccine skepticism was thus yet another social cause taken on by the Bohra *jamaats* in this era.

Even so, the human costs of these devastating cycles of plague and famine clearly highlighted the yawning welfare gap between the populations of the inner and outer empires. These events also occurred at the same moment as prominent Indian capitalists and nationalists sought to rewrite the rules surrounding business and politics on the subcontinent. From 1900 onward, India underwent its first experience with nationalist mobilization on a mass scale. Possessed of considerable economic power, the *jamaats* were primary mediators of Gujarati Muslim interactions with the political sphere throughout these years, and *sethias* were at the forefront of political agitation. The bywords for this new era were twofold: *swaraj* (self-rule) and *swadeshi* (self-made).

The Uneven Embrace of Swadeshi, 1900–1912

Swadeshi is typically framed by historians in nationalist terms as a movement built upon anti-industrialism, autarky, and Indocentrism. By seeking to expand Indian industry and combat British economic hegemony, Swadeshi heralded a complete reordering of the colonial economic order that had prevailed since the 1860s. Unsurprisingly, it had dramatic implications for the *jamaats*. Yet the embrace of Swadeshi by Gujarati Muslims was uneven. Industry became the preferred sphere of economic activity, even coterminous with Swadeshi, as the production of Indian-manufactured industrial goods was seen as the only viable means to challenge India's subordinate economic position as a British colony. On the other hand, brick-and-mortar banking, so crucial to the smooth functioning of industrial enterprises, remained sorely neglected by many Indian entrepreneurs in the high years of Swadeshi. Arguably, this was less a consequence of entrepreneurial laxity than the poor performance of banks and the racially and capital-restrictive character of high banking in colonial India. But the neglect of banking had important implications for the subsequent economic history of the Gujarati Muslim commercial castes until the end of empire.

In addition to its economic program, Swadeshi aimed to dramatically expand the scale of political franchise, rejecting the notion that politics was the domain for Indian elites alone. But to appreciate that transformation, and the *jamaats*' role in facilitating it, one must first understand the nature of Gujarati Muslim political participation in the decades before Swadeshi. From the 1870s, the *jamaats* acted as voting blocs in municipal elections in the major cities of British India. They consequently produced numerous justices of the peace, legislators, and representatives. Among these were two of the earliest Muslim university graduates: the Sulaimani Bohra lawyer, Badr al-Din Tayyibji, and the Ismaili Khoja, R. M. Sayani.[92] Gujarati Muslims were largely the product of the port cities in Western India and the Indian Ocean, but their ties to the Indian Muslim gentry of Central and North India remained negligible.

That changed with the birth of the All-India Muslim League. The first session of the league was hosted in Karachi in 1907, bringing together the leading lights of the Gujarati Muslim commercial castes and the North Indian Muslim gentry. Its president on that occasion was the Bohra industrialist Adamji Pirbhai. Also in attendance was the Agha Khan III, whom Pirbhai deemed the "leader of our community," a signal of the growing tendency to conceive of Indian Muslims as a collective body. (The Agha Khan III had been among the foremost critics of the Partition of Bengal in 1905–1906, and his appeals to the viceroy in the subsequent agitation considerably heightened his prestige in the eyes of many Indian Muslims.) During the session, Pirbhai inveighed against sectarian tendencies among Indian Muslims, stressed Muslim commitments to British rule, public service, and communal harmony and held up the Prophet Muhammad as a figure who believed "in the dignity of labour." He also stressed that "In India [the Muslim] has shown special aptitude in industrialism," the sector in which the individual Muslim could "best exert his influence and carve for himself a high position in the Empire."[93]

That line resounded with all the typical tropes of Swadeshi. Even so, Muslim participation in Swadeshi is often assumed to have been negligible.[94] Such a reading, however, ignores the fact that many Muslim commentators saw Muslims as the chief beneficiaries of the movement. One such commentator, Mushir Hussain Kidwai, wrote in 1908 that Swadeshi would supply Indian Muslims with new avenues for productive investment. Homegrown industry, he held, would rescue Indian Muslim capital from the clutches of usurious moneylending that he and many other Indian Muslims saw as the cause of Muslim penury. Kidwai, however, also emphasized that the Muslim form of Swadeshi must not indulge in anticolonial politics.[95] In the decades to come, few Indian Muslim proponents of Swadeshi obeyed that summons.

Select entities owned by Gujarati Muslims played a leading role in various Swadeshi schemes from the first, certainly well out of proportion to their numbers. Predictably, at the forefront were the small concentration of Gujarati Muslim industrialists in Bombay. They were by no means recent entrants into the world of industry. In fact, the ascent of Muslim mill owners began in earnest in the late 1880s, when the Ismaili Khoja Karimbhai Ibrahim led the first foray into the industry. From that date onward, Khoja firms—both Ismaili and Twelver—were some of the most conspicuous Indian industrialists. A solid stratum of Khojas were inducted into the world of

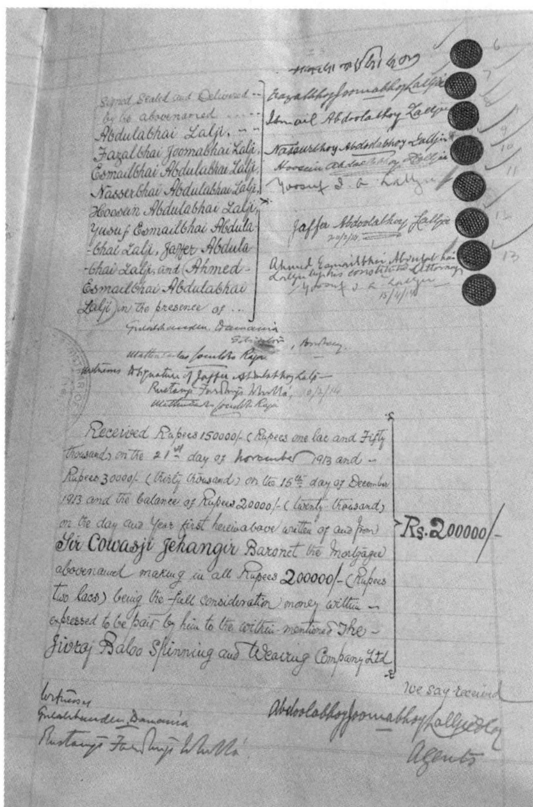

Signed Sealed and Delivered by the abovenamed Abdulabhai Lalji, Fazalbhai Joomabhai Lalji, Esmailbhai Abdulabhai Lalji, Nasserbhai Abdulabhai Lalji, Hoosein Abdulabhai Lalji, Yusuf Esmailbhai Abdula-bhai Lalji, Jaffer Abdula-bhai Lalji, and Ahmed Esmailbhai Abdulabhai Lalji in the presence of ...

Received Rupees 150000/- (Rupees one lac and Fifty thousand) on the 21st day of November 1913 and Rupees 30000/- (thirty thousand) on the 15th day of December 1913 and the balance of Rupees 20000/- (twenty thousand) on the day and Year first hereinabove written of and from Sir Cowasji Jehangir Baronet the mortgagee abovenamed making in all Rupees 200000/- (Rupees two lacs) being the full consideration money within expressed to be paid by him to the within-mentioned The Jivraj Baloo Spinning and Weaving Company Ltd — Rs. 200000/-

We say received

Agents

FIGURE 4.1 Indenture for the sale of Jivraj Baloo Mills to the Twelver Khoja firm of Hajibhai Laljee & Co. Note the reference to the Parsi magnate, Sir Cowasji Jehangir. Author's personal collection.

industry thanks to their appointment as directors to non-Muslim firms, such as Jubilee, Kastoorchand, and Victoria.[96]

As ever, a combination of *jamaat* resources and weak ties smoothed the movement into industry. A representative example is Jivraj Baloo Mills, which was acquired by a Twelver Khoja firm with links to Aden, Hajeebhoy Laljee & Co., from its original Parsi owners in the 1900s.[97] (The signatures of the firm's proprietors can be glimpsed in the indenture seen in figure 4.1.) Although all the leading partners of Hajeebhoy Laljee & Co. were members of Bombay's Twelver Khoja *jamaat*, it was the firm's established relationship with the Parsi firm of Sir Cowasji Jehangir that made the sale possible. The deal was overseen by the Parsi legal firm Mulla & Mulla, whose services were utilized by a range of Bombay's leading entrepreneurs in the late nineteenth and early twentieth centuries. Despite this auspicious acquisition, Jivraj Baloo was one of many mills, including the New Islam Mill and

Noor Mill, that went into liquidation between 1905–1915 because of Japan's competition with Indian yarn in the China market.[98]

Thanks largely to Japanese competition, colonial support for Indian industry in the form of tariffs expanded dramatically in the years around the First World War. Protectionism was most visible in the match industry, which proved to be one of the few industrial sectors where Indian Muslim firms excelled, despite intense competition from European and Japanese rivals. No Muslim-owned enterprise exemplified the marriage of imperial protectionism and Muslim Swadeshi better than Ahmedabad's Gujarat Islam Match Factory. Founded as a joint-stock company in 1895 with a capital of Rs. 100,000, the Gujarat Islam Match Factory became the "largest and most successful match manufacturing company in India."[99] Its proprietor, Fateh Muhammad Khan Munshi, a Sunni Muslim from Ahmedabad of unknown caste origin, was committed to sundry Muslim social causes, including the abolition of purdah. His progressive views, however, did not extend to labor: during the testimony he gave to the Indian Factory Labour Commission in 1908, Munshi noted that the workers were from a variety of castes and included women and children. "There is no effect on the health of adults by working long hours," he argued. Munshi also stressed that children should not have to submit a physical fitness certificate, which would disqualify many from work.[100] In time the commercial ephemera of the company, and other Gujarati Muslim firms like the Bohra entity A. Ebrahim, would regularly employ the central imagery of Swadeshi: a woman spinning yarn at the charkha (see figures 4.2 and 4.3).

Despite Gujarati Muslim capitalists' precocious embrace of industry, the same cannot be said for banking. As has been noted above, the neglect of banking revealed one of the central oversights of the Swadeshi program. There are several possible explanations for the ambivalence of the Gujarati Muslim commercial castes toward banking. Most obviously, Gujarati Muslims may have concluded that most of their credit needs were fulfilled by preexisting exchange banks, moneylenders, and *jamaat* trusts. This said, there was no shortage of complaints among caste members about the *jamaat* trusts. An evocative cartoon published in August 1898 in the satirical newspaper *Hindi Punch* succinctly conveys how, by the end of the nineteenth century, many Indians had come to realize that community funds were bastions of inert capital. The image depicts two men chatting before eight soundly sleeping figures, each bearing the Khoja community's turban on

FIGURES 4.2 AND 4.3 Swadeshi-inspired matchboxes produced by Gujarati Muslim firms.
Author's personal collection.

their head and the name of an Ismaili Khoja fund on their swollen belly. The caption has one of the figures saying, "What bright and sparkling cherubs these would be, if they moved about freely. Why don't you let them play, as they ought to? The blood in them will turn to poison, if it does not circulate, and it will be a pity to destroy such valuable lives. Wake them up, sir, for their benefit and for yours."

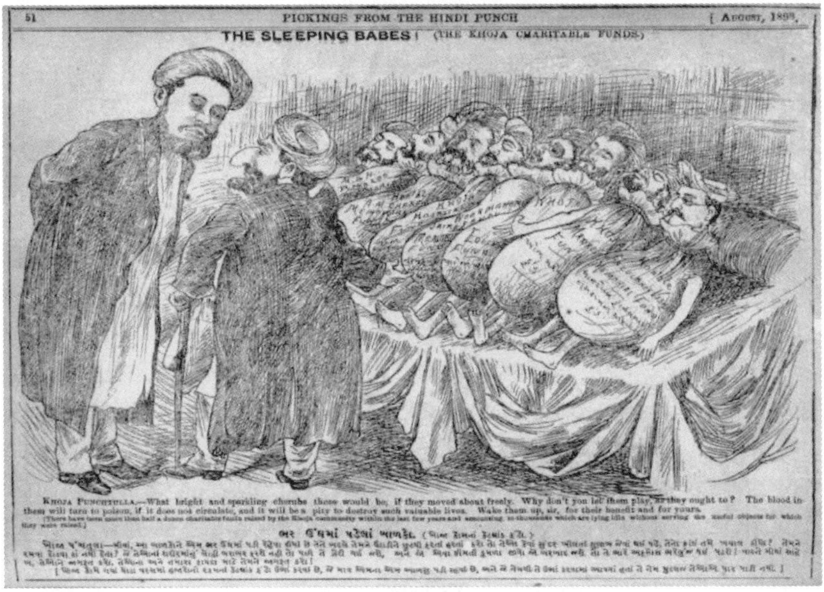

FIGURE 4.4 The Khoja Charitable Funds 1. Both this figure and figure 4.5 capture the late-nineteenth century controversy over the management of Khoja thrifts. As the cartoons convey, they were seen by many commentators as bastions of inert capital, sinkholes for community wealth that could be employed to more productive purposes elsewhere. Reproduced from Barjorjee Nowrosjee, ed., *Pickings from the Hindi Punch for August 1898* (Bombay: Bombay Samachar [?], 1899 [?]), 51.

As the editorial line beneath the caption explains, although funds in the Khoja community had expanded considerably in recent years, the capital within them "are lying idle without serving the useful objects for which they were raised" (see figure 4.4). In another cartoon, also from *Hindi Punch*, three wealthy Khoja gentlemen stand around an emaciated horse, whose trunk bears the words "Khoja Charitable Funds" (see figure 4.5). The contrast between these dignified men and the skeletal stallion serves as a useful allegory for a paradox of Gujarati Muslim commercial prowess: in an environment where capital was prohibitively expensive, how were these communities able to create successful, intergenerational enterprises without banks? This question troubled many Indian Muslims in the last four decades of colonial rule.

It is easy to overstate the idleness of these *jamaat* trusts. Recently, economic historians have hypothesized that Indian institutions must have had an unappreciated hand in early twentieth-century Indian industrialization.[101] *Jamaat* sources and other records partially bear this out, with the capital in these

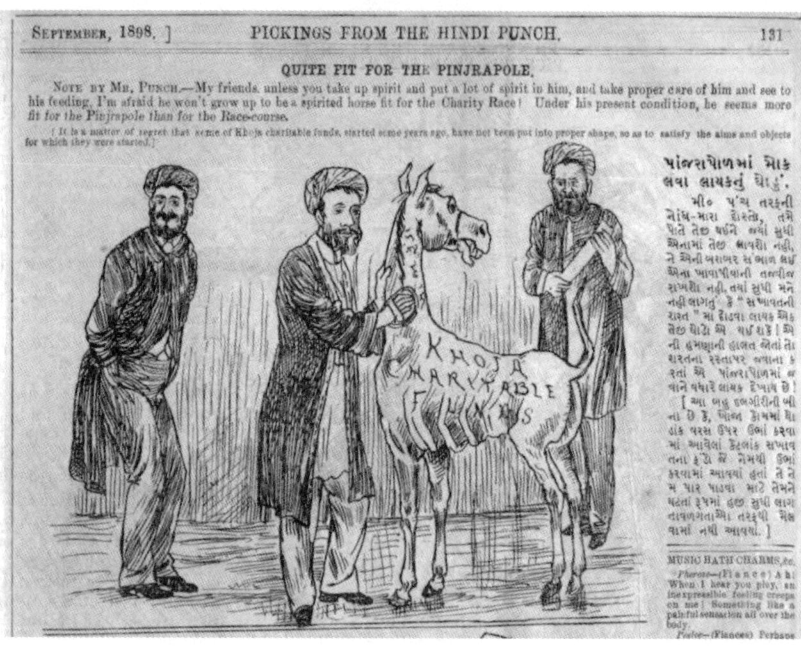

FIGURE 4.5 The Khoja Charitable Funds 2. Reproduced from Barjorjee Nowrosjee, ed., *Pickings from the Hindi Punch for September 1898* (Bombay: Bombay Samachar [?], 1899 [?]), 131.

trusts always lucrative enough to entice leading Gujarati Muslim entrepreneurs to gain control of them. Karimbhai Ibrahim, the Ismaili Khoja proprietor of E. Pabaney & Co. who became one of India's top industrialists by the turn of the century, obtained ownership stakes in nearly all the Ismaili Khoja *jamaat*'s leading funds. The presence of elite Muslim entrepreneurs in the management of these trusts probably made them more, not less, susceptible to adjudication by the colonial courts, liable as entrepreneurs were to take matters to court. This is precisely what happened with one of the trusts, the Jairaj Pirbhai *waqf*, which was overseen by Karimbhai Ibrahim, the proprietor of the massive Currimbhoy industrial concern. The problems of legal interpretation in these cases were dizzying. As the judge in the trial succinctly put it, "And the question is—a very important question, I think, in this town [Bombay]—whether a voluntary settlement during the lifetime of a Khoja Mahomedan of this kind is a valid gift, or if not a gift, whether it is a will, or if not a will, whether it is a *wakf* and in either of the latter characters good and valid."[102] That the legal experts were so confounded suggests that these trusts operated according to principles that did not track with the mutually-exclusive functions assumed by colonial law. In practice, they were charities, props of business, tax shelters, and cornerstones of family maintenance.

But just as trusts were sources of conflict within *jamaats* and confusion to colonial judges, they also became springboards for the creation of rival *jamaats*. In the case of the newly ascendant Twelver Khoja *jamaat*, the Hidayat Fund fused diverse congregations of the Twelver Khoja diaspora around a common institutional core. The trust deed made plain that the fund was envisioned as a site for the safekeeping of the *jamaat*'s capital.[103] All of this indicates that *jamaat*-based funds were able to perform many of the services of a bank and had the infrastructural capacities to extend far beyond a *jamaat*'s geographic base. Any ambition to expand, however, was preempted by the reality that the primary clientele these trusts wished to serve was, naturally enough, the members of their own *jamaat*.

The reliance of Gujarati Muslim entrepreneurs on European banks served as an additional impetus for the further expansion of *jamaat* thrifts. Indeed, the trustees of the Hidayat Fund went one step further and followed a practice typical among Gujarati Muslim trusts: they opened an account at the Bank of Bombay in the name of the manager, Haji Ghulam Ali Haji Ismail.[104] Of course, this allowed the inert capital sheltered in the fund to accrue interest, a fact that would later become highly charged for Indian Muslims. Even so, the gesture once again accentuates a crucial feature of the Indian banking scene after 1865: the division of labor in the credit market between European-run banks and Indian thrifts.

The modicum of support the colonial state supplied to Indian industry from 1900 onward did not extend to banking. Only the cooperative credit movement, which Gujarati Muslims showed some aptitude for beginning in the 1930s, gained outright government support. Partially for this reason, the spate of Indian exchange banks established between 1900–1914 performed poorly, with few exceptions. This was not for lack of effort, for in these years a dense network of new savings banks and cooperative credit societies set down roots in parts of North India. These institutions sought to break some of the deadlock imposed by the slow pace of colonial financial reform and to open new infrastructural possibilities for the mobilization of Indian Muslim capital. They were principally intended as concrete means to untangle the cycles of agricultural poverty and debt traps that the Indian Muslim intelligentsia increasingly pinpointed as the cause of Muslim penury.

Nonetheless, the dismal Gujarati Muslim showing in banking is hard to understand. After all, the embrace of Muslim banking was a phenomenon that extended throughout the contemporary Islamic world. Indian Muslim commentators regarded contemporary Muslim forays into banking in the Russian Empire as a model for their own efforts on the subcontinent. The *Aligarh Institute Gazette*—the mouthpiece of the Islamic modernist educational bulwark, the Muhammadan Anglo-Oriental College at Aligarh (later Aligarh Muslim University)—remarked on May 6, 1908, that Indian Muslim businessmen should follow the example of a recent group of Russian Muslim capitalists. Specifically, they should "increase the material resources of their co-religionists" by setting up a Muslim bank.[105] Adamji Pirbhai, the Bohra industrialist and first president of the All-India Muslim League, was among those singled out. Pirbhai's firm did not take the bait. In this respect, he was representative of his class: while entrepreneurs from the Gujarati Muslim commercial castes after 1900 participated in some Indian-owned banking enterprises as directors and customers, these remained ancillary concerns to their primary interest in trade and industry.

In the end it was a Punjabi Muslim entrepreneur in Lahore, not a member of the Gujarati Muslim commercial castes, who established India's first Muslim-owned bank, the Muslim Orient Bank, which opened its doors in 1908. The bank had a checkered career for the next few decades, failing on several occasions, before permanently shuttering in 1939. Even in the best of times, its performance left much to be desired and its operations paled in comparison to other Indian banks.[106] Yet the fact of its establishment makes the reluctance of the Gujarati Muslim commercial castes to engage in banking even more confounding. To be sure, the Bohras, Khojas, and Memons did establish small cooperative banks around the turn of the twentieth century. Yet these were mostly community-based operations, eclipsed by the far more energetic push for cooperative credit in Punjab.

The few banks in which Gujarati Muslims served as directors after 1900 were joint enterprises with other Indians. Unlike 1864–1865, however, Indian-European joint directorships were entirely absent due to the racialization of banking over the past five decades. The Bombay Merchants Bank, Limited, founded in July 1909, had a total of twelve directors, four of whom were nominal Muslims: Haji Abd Allah Mia Haji Ahmed Khandwani and Haji Ismail Gul Muhammad, both Memons; and Mohammed Hajibhai Lalji and Daudbhai Fazalbhai Pir Muhammad, both Khojas. None of the directors was a fully dedicated banker, and all were prominent members of Bombay's legislative councils and merchant chambers.

This may explain the bank's meek performance in subsequent years. Compared to the banks founded in 1864–1865, its capital base was low (amounting to Rs. 1,000,000). This said, there was substantial public interest in the company, with deposits in the range of Rs. 4,456,774.[107] Echoing the share mania of 1864–1865, the bank was tied to the cotton business, with the directors hoping to open a branch at Ahmedabad for expressly this purpose. The bank's subsequent history was uneven, though it did survive for some two decades. It went into liquidation in September 1929, one month before the Wall Street Crash and the onset of the Great Depression brought low even more Indian banks.[108]

Bohra, Khoja, and Memon dependence on foreign banks was made clear in the campaign for Ottoman charitable relief between 1912 and 1914. International financial control, in the form of the European-run Ottoman Public Debt Administration, had been a fact of Ottoman economic life since the mid-1870s.[109] Since Indian Muslims owned scarcely any banks of their own, European banks in the Ottoman Empire and colonial India acted as intermediaries between the Ottoman government and those Indian Muslim constituencies seeking to remit funds. The affair added an international dimension to Muslim Swadeshi by underscoring intra-Muslim economic divergences and revealing the structural weaknesses, both within Muslim communities and in the colonial system more generally, that obstructed economic improvement among Indian Muslims.

* * *

The generation before the First World War witnessed the outright politicization of business in colonial India and the British Empire. No longer were the Gujarati Muslim commercial castes, or other Indian corporate bodies, able to remain comfortably apolitical as they had over the previous century of colonial rule. The highly constricted realm of indigenous political action that British colonialism encouraged made this an easier stance to sustain. While the interwar years did see tangible commercial successes, the world of free trade and relatively open borders did not survive the outbreak of war in 1914. The ensuing shocks of deglobalization, protectionism, and mass nationalism forced Indian business to play by the rules of the new political game. Those rules were dictated both by colonial policy and the programs of Indian nationalists.

More narrowly, these developments also led to a legitimacy crisis for the middle power of the Bohras, Khojas, and Memons. Henceforth, Indian Muslim public opinion found it inexcusable for such tiny communities to feather the nests of their *jamaats* while allegedly depriving the wider Muslim community of access to their disproportionate wealth reserves. In turn, members of the *jamaats* also grew sensitive on this front and contemplated how to guarantee and defend *jamaat* property. Yet if the interwar period saw the *jamaats* struggling with their position as corporate institutions vis-à-vis other Muslim constituencies, it also necessitated that the *jamaats* grapple with a parallel dilemma: how to manage the internal disputes that threatened their own corporate integrity. Beginning in 1914, these disputes became more ungovernable, as texts and actors from outside the *jamaats* increasingly tread on their jurisdiction.

PART II

THE CENTRAL CLAIM OF THE NEXT FOUR CHAPTERS IS that the First World War and its aftermath imposed unprecedented pressures on Bohra, Khoja, and Memon models of corporate Islam, pressures that showed little sign of abating in the early postcolonial period. Religious authority, collective property, legal interpretation, and the rights of individual constituents in the *jamaats* (corporate caste institutions) became points of division between the Gujarati Muslim commercial castes and other Muslims and non-Muslims for the next fifty years. The dawn of the postcolonial period brought in an additional player: the developmental state, whose architects found much fault in the Gujarati Muslims' legal exceptionalism and acumen for capitalism.

The catalysts for these conflicts were twofold. First, a new paradigm of mass nationalism emerged that made three demands on the Gujarati Muslim commercial castes: that business serve the needs of politics; that *jamaat* trusts be made into "public" entities that were accountable to Muslim supervisory organizations unaffiliated with the caste; and that Bohra, Khoja, and Memon legal exceptionalism be dissolved in a universal Islamic law applicable to all Indian Muslims and unsullied by the particularities of custom. Second, the interwar period witnessed the birth of still new forms of colonial interventionism—both welcome and unwelcome—in the legal and economic affairs of the Gujarati Muslim commercial castes. Transformations in the political economy of colonial governance exacerbated the pressures that nationalism placed on the *jamaats*. In these years Indian Muslims, including those from these castes, frequently used colonial institutions to pursue their vendettas against select practices and personnel within the *jamaats*.

Taken together, these factors recast the nature of corporate Islam and Gujarati Muslim middle power. The capital and discourses underpinning corporate Islam, which prior to 1914 were relatively autonomous and unanswerable to any higher power save the colonial state, now were susceptible to outside interference by Indian Muslim organizations. And whereas the *jamaats*' middle power before this period was largely predicated upon a bilateral relationship with the colonial state, henceforth the Bohras, Khojas, and Memons had to navigate the rules of the game where good relations with antinationalist colonial authorities and anticolonial nationalists had to be held in equilibrium. Maintaining the balance proved especially onerous given that the *jamaats* themselves were susceptible to ever-greater processes of internal fragmentation.

Accelerating those processes was the extensive handwringing over the exact relationship among the *jamaats*' constituents, community property, and religious authority, both living and textual. A great deal of the "religious" property—mosques, *awqāf* (pious endowments), shrines, and the like—held under the aegis of *jamaats*' individual constituents or the *jamaat* collective had been subjected to Islamic and colonial laws of trusteeship from the 1840s onward.[1] While mosques were generally not considered property in colonial India, according to the Sulaimani Bohra legal expert Faiz Badruddin Tyabji in his highly influential account of "Muhammadan Law," the *jamaats* were an exception. The courts "to some extent recognized mosques for the exclusive use or at any rate in the exclusive management of particular *jamaats*," and non-members were not permitted to even enter the premises without express permission.[2] This privilege became harder to justify from the 1910s with the rise of a new breed of Indian Muslim politics. And thereafter efforts were made by influential Indian Muslims to secure outright de facto, if not de jure, proprietary control of these sites, entailing an attempt to circumvent or bend colonial trust law. In this brave new world, Bohra, Khoja, and Memon internal conflicts and property disputes attained material and political stakes well out of proportion to the size of these communities.

In the latter part of the interwar years these conflicts over trusts were subsumed within a larger endeavor by these same Indian Muslim activists to annul Gujarati Muslim legal exceptionalism. If subordinating *jamaat* trusts to pan-Indian Muslim governing bodies was one goal of Muslim nationalists in late colonial India, another was integrating India's Muslims within a common framework of Islamic law that paid no heed to caste, custom, or sect. Predictably, the results were uneven, but the undertaking engendered additional strain within the *jamaats* over the relationship between law and custom. These campaigns went hand in hand with attempts by Indian Muslim political entrepreneurs of various stripes to bring Bohra, Khoja, and Memon entrepreneurs along with them in their schemes to forge either a united India or a separatist Pakistan. Yet, for all the intonations made to this effect, business never became a sectarian affair in late colonial India.

The Second World War and Partition brought new challenges—and opportunities—to each community. Decolonization and de-globalization inaugurated novel paradigms of statehood, subjecthood, and political economy across Asia and Africa. Conducting trans-national business in this environment was no easy task, but the Bohras, Khojas, and Memons found a niche for themselves in the ambitious economic targets set by developmental technocrats in places like Pakistan. Yet from the late 1960s the perception of economic capture by these and other cognate merchant communities—in Pakistan and a half a dozen other countries—led to a fierce backlash that threatened to unmake traditions of corporate Islam for good. Nevertheless, by the late 1970s interventionist state power in some of these contexts had receded and a new world of global migration and relatively open borders associated with the epoch of neoliberalism supplied the environment for the rejuvenation of corporate Islam.

5

Corporate Crises from the Balkan Wars to the Great Depression

1912–1933

THE HALAI MEMON MAGNATE Seth Haji Jan Muhammad Chotani was as improbable a figure as any to throw his weight behind the anticolonial nationalism associated with Mohandas Gandhi and the newly assertive Indian National Congress. For his part, Gandhi had had extensive contacts with Memon entrepreneurs from the 1890s onward. But politics was a new venture for Chotani, in contrast to his Memon peers in South Africa. A beneficiary of lucrative government contracts, Chotani owned acres of timber yards and sawmills in Sewri, a choice area of wetlands in South Bombay. His business imported lumber from America, Burma, England, Japan, Scandinavia, and Singapore. Throughout the First World War, his firm provisioned the Indian Army during its overseas expeditions, services which earned the praise of a British military commander who had participated in the battles in Ottoman Iraq.[1]

Chotani had been happy to supply the Indian Army's campaigns against the Ottomans in the Arab provinces, but the subsequent Greek invasion of Ottoman Anatolia—and the threat that these events posed to the status of the Ottoman sultan-caliph—catapulted Chotani into the realm of anticolonial politics. As early as May 1919, Chotani suggested that a delegation be sent to the viceroy to discuss the issue of Ottoman sovereignty. A trip to the peace negotiations at Versailles in the company of leading Indian Muslim politicians (see figure 5.1) solidified his place in the nationalist hierarchy. Upon

FIGURE 5.1 The Halai Memon magnate, Seth Haji Jan Muhammad Chotani (far right), photographed with other leading members of the Khilafat movement during their mission to the 1919 Paris Peace Conference. Agence Meurisse / Bibliothèque Nationale de France.

returning to Bombay, Chotani helped form the Central Khilafat Committee, on which he served as president and eventually treasurer. Among other activities, he issued appeals to raise funds for Ottoman relief, a continuation of the campaigns that had taken place in India between 1912 and 1914.[2]

Chotani handled these donations in his capacity as the treasurer of the committee. He was also conspicuous for his generous donations to Gandhi. On one occasion, he sent over Rs. 300,000 to Gandhi's Swaraj Fund, a measure of the yeoman's work that thrifts would do for the Indian nationalist movement.[3] Perhaps Chotani's most impressive contribution was his forfeiture of his own spinning wheels and looms to Gandhi in October 1921. Gandhi's own correspondence reveals that Chotani donated as many as 100,000 of these, though the Mahatma noted that "it is not a simple matter to distribute one lakh of charkhas in a useful way."[4] Sometime later, he instructed Chotani to disseminate "the spinning-wheels donated by him among poor Mussalman women in Panchmahals, East Khandesh and Agra."[5] At the same time, Chotani tried to convince Bombay's Halai Memon *jamaat* (corporate caste institution) to accept *khaddar* (homespun cotton cloth), and portioned out spinning wheels among several Halai Memon associations.[6]

Two dramatic episodes brought a swift halt to this happy story of Indian Muslim industrial and political collaboration. The first was a massive fire at the Chotani Saw Mills at Sewri that left close to Rs. 1.5 million worth of damage in its wake.[7] Shortly thereafter, whispers began to circulate that Chotani had diverted funds raised by the Central Khilafat Committee for Ottoman Muslim refugees—to the tune of Rs. 1.7 million—into his private account. Still worse, it soon became public that Chotani was unable to dispatch to Ankara any of the funds gathered on the subcontinent and the Indian diaspora. He defended himself from charges of embezzlement by claiming that he was merely compensating himself for the losses he incurred as a result of his steadfast support for the Khilafat and noncooperation movements. None of his detractors were convinced by such claims, and the result was the liquidation of his firm, a process overseen by the Central Khilafat Committee.

The saga of Chotani and his firm is a cautionary tale for how the Gujarati Muslim commercial castes' formal entry into anticolonial politics after the First World War put hitherto unknown stresses on their capital and communities. Henceforth, Bohra, Khoja, and Memon *jamaats* as collectives—not merely individual constituents—had to walk an uncomfortable line between Pan-Islam, Indian nationalism, and imperial loyalism from 1914 until the end of empire. For the first time, Gujarati Muslim capital was not only subordinated to the demands of Indian Muslim politics but also subjected to a legion of Muslim accountants and activists eager to ensure that it was used for the good of the entire Indian Muslim community.

Even if many Gujarati Muslim capitalists wanted to throw their capital and expertise into the war effort, many found, to their chagrin, that the colonial state obstructed rather than facilitated their ambitions. This new stage in the relationship between the colonial state and Indian capital was a central development of the First World War. Total war on a global scale necessitated the redrawing of economic relations among the constituent parts of the empire, with lasting implications for Indian commercial firms. For each community there was slight variation. While Bohra merchant elites, the colonial government, and the Bohra *jamaat* had operated roughly in sync before the war, the war's outbreak inaugurated a new, highly strained relationship among all three.

The Agha Khan III's prominence in global politics only increased from the war, but his own *jamaat* was subjected to dramatic internal problems. The Twelver Khoja *jamaats*, bolstered by cohorts of new converts from the Ismaili *jamaat*, attained a substantial public profile across the British Empire. Meanwhile, the Memons were pushed and pulled as never before between an assertive brand of Muslim politics and a desire to remain politically quiescent.

Pan-Islam, Humanitarianism, and New Imaginaries of Muslim Capital, 1912–1914

Gujarati Muslim participation in Indian campaigns for Ottoman humanitarian relief between 1912 and 1914 were a bridge between the developments covered in chapter 4 and those covered here: anxieties over Muslim capital and the paucity of Muslim banks, the rise of Indian Muslim political organizations, and changing relationships between Indian elites and colonial authorities. Connections between the Ottoman government and various members of the Gujarati Muslim commercial castes had increased in the last decades of the nineteenth century. Since pockets of Bohras, Khojas, and Memons had settled in the outer reaches of the empire—in the Hijaz, Iraq, and Yemen—they appear with some frequency in the Ottoman archival record. The relationship was not always cordial. Ottoman officials remained suspicious of the ties between British authorities and Gujarati Muslims, as even the Bohra industrialist Adamji Pirbhai discovered during his pilgrimage to Ottoman Iraq in 1905.[8] But this did not prevent Gujarati Muslim capitalists like Pirbhai from having a direct hand in the negotiation of Ottoman relief and the subsequent Ottoman bond drive.

The outpouring of support for the Ottoman government in 1912–1914 was spurred by the contemporary Pan-Islamic moment. Historians have written extensively about Pan-Islam and Indian Muslims, but often frame the movement as a singular enterprise orchestrated from Istanbul or Cairo. Fittingly for a geographically dispersed and temporally sporadic ideology, Pan-Islam was many things to many Muslims. Though it had anticolonial overtones, it was not straightforwardly so. Moreover, plenty of imperial loyalists among the Gujarati Muslim commercial castes were committed to Pan-Islam in one form or another.

In the subcontinent, the origins of Pan-Islam date to no earlier than the Russo-Turkish War of 1877, when Indian Muslims raised substantial charitable sums for the Ottoman government. Indian Muslims had formed fund-raising organizations of their own, such as the Indian War Fund Commission, which remitted £4,500 to the London branch of the Imperial Ottoman Bank. In turn, the Ottoman consul general in Bombay was ordered to express the Ottoman government's gratitude to the commission for a gesture "resulting in the protection of Islamic unity."[9] Even so, the language of unity only obscures the range of Indian Muslim constituencies involved. More than 150 Muslim associations sent aid to the Ottoman government, raising some O.L. 124,843, an equivalent to some £113,000, or Rs. 1 million. Their contributions were collected in *Defter-i ʿIāne-i Hindiyye* (The inventory of Indian contributions), a 115-page work compiled for the Ottoman sultan Abdülhamid II.[10] The geographic breadth is tremendous, ranging from Himalayan hill stations to *mohallas* (neighborhoods) in Bombay and small principalities in Punjab. Bohra and Memon shipping captains stand out, as do the heads of leading princely states like Bhopal and Hyderabad, and the rectors of the newly founded Sunni seminary at Deoband.[11]

For the next several decades, Gujarati Muslims and the Ottoman government courted one another for economic opportunities. In March 1888 an anonymous Khoja wrote to the Gujarati Muslim newspaper *Kāside Mumbaī* (The Messenger of Bombay) calling upon Bohra, Khoja, Konkani, Memon, and "Mughal" (a word used for Bombay's Iranian population) merchants to pledge their capital to the Ottoman government.[12] Ottoman commentators also wrote glowing dispatches on Gujarati Muslim industrial enterprises in the beginning of the twentieth century. The Tatar Muslim Abd al-Reşid Ibrahim—whose meeting with Essabhoy Bros. served as the opening anecdote of this book—was fulsome in his praise of the same when he visited Bombay in 1908–1909, but he was not alone.[13] In a report on Bombay's trading institutions, S. M. Tevfik, a journalist for the Pan-Islamic newspaper, *Sebil al-Reşad* (The Path of Righteousness), singled out Fazlbhai Karimbhai among the city's strata of Muslim factory owners. Tevfik made note not only of the scale of the Currimbhoy enterprise but also the fact that Karimbhai was knighted by the colonial government and an elected member of state councils.[14]

For all the difficulties Ottoman authorities had with the likes of the Memon ship captain Abd Allah Arab Memon (see chapter 4), until the outbreak of the First World War they continued to employ Indian Muslim capitalists in their Indian Ocean consular service.[15] Yet another Memon, Mulla Ahmad

Daud Efendi, was chosen as Ottoman consul general in Rangoon in 1913. On his appointment, a document sent by the Ottoman foreign minister to the grand vizier described Daud Efendi as both a native of Medina and "among the notables of Rangoon city." (The mention of Medina is hardly surprising, for pockets of Memons resided in the Ottoman Hijaz from the last quarter of the nineteenth century). The Ottoman foreign minister further stressed that, given Daud Efendi's support for the Ottoman caliph and his charitable donations, his nomination would generate "positive effects" in Rangoon.[16] The remark reflects how Ottoman authorities saw individuals like Daud Efendi: as instruments of soft-power diplomacy whose devotion to the Ottoman sultan could be utilized in a campaign to win imperial legitimacy outside the empire.

Pan-Islamic mobilization in India acquired an unprecedented intensity from 1911 onward. The initial catalyst was the Italian invasion of Ottoman Libya. Yet the movement acquired true momentum when a confederation of Balkan states declared war on the Ottoman Empire, nearly pushing the Ottomans entirely out of southeastern Europe within weeks. As a result, a new paradigm of Indian Muslim politics was born. Both the Ottoman Archives of the Prime Minister's Office and the archives of the Turkish Red Crescent testify to this development, as they contain thousands of documents detailing the immense outpouring of Indian Muslim charity in response to these events. These same sources reveal the intermediary role played by European exchange banks of various stripes. These institutions, and the banking literacy of select Indian Muslim activists, mitigated the unbanked status of most Indian Muslim donors.

Memons were highly energetic participants in the Ottoman relief campaign, both as individuals and in *jamaats*. Seth Haji Abd Allah Harun, a Memon businessman based in Karachi, managed Sindh's Red Crescent branch, corresponding regularly with the Ottoman Red Crescent and government.[17] In these letters, Harun urged the Ottoman government to acknowledge receipt of his regular bank transfers and gave advice on how to better prosecute the war in the Balkans. From Gujarat to Burma, *jamaat* sessions served as opportunities to both raise and remit funds. In one instance, the Ottoman journalist S. M. Tevfik recorded Bombay's Kachchhi Memon *jamaat* as having dispatched three installments totaling Rs. 135,000.[18] Other Ottoman sources disclose that the Memon *jamaat* of Byculla (south of Bombay) remitted Rs. 2,000, while those in Tankara in the Princely State of Morvi, and in Bantva, sent Rs. 690.18 and Rs. 600, respectively.[19] It is unlikely that these were singular donations. Meanwhile, in Rangoon, several young members of the Memon *jamaat* raised subscriptions for Ottoman relief. They also passed a series of resolutions, one of which stated that all those in positions of service must pay one-fifth of their salaries to the fund.[20]

The fact that Rangoon's honorary Ottoman consul general, Daud Efendi, was a Memon merchant considerably facilitated fundraising initiatives in the city. During the Balkan Wars, the Memon magnate sent regular charitable remittances to the Ottoman Red Crescent.[21] An image produced in Ottoman newspapers at the time shows Daud Efendi and an assemblage of leading Muslim denizens of Rangoon who comprised that city's Ottoman relief committee.[22] But with the outbreak of the First World War and the subsequent entry of the Ottoman Empire a little over a year later, Daud Efendi and many other Memons in Rangoon found declarations of Ottoman support impossible to reconcile with older traditions of imperial loyalism.

By no means did Bohras and Khojas sit out the campaign on account of their Shiʿism. In fact, at meetings held at Bombay's Anjuman-i Islam, the Ismaili Khoja industrialist Karimbhai Ibrahim, alongside the industrialists Seth Chotani and Kasim Mitha, pledged their own capital.[23] Ottoman records relate that Karimbhai Ibrahim and Kasimali Pirbhai, the latter the Bohra magnate and son of Adamji Pirbhai, jointly contributed enormous sums throughout November and December 1912 totaling a staggering Rs. 547,600.[24] It is unclear how much of this money was their own capital, as opposed to funds they had collected from other Muslims for purposes of remittance. Pirbhai's firm also donated 1,050 pairs of hospital slippers to the Ottoman Red Crescent.[25] The Agha Khan III and his good friend, the retired Twelver Shiʿi judge Sayyid Amir Ali, were among the chief organizers for Ottoman relief in London—further proof of the Shiʿi contribution to Ottoman aid.

Of course, Gujarati Muslims certainly were not the only participants in an affair that mobilized constituencies across the subcontinent—nor were charitable remittances the only issue at stake. While remittances flowed out of India, several Indian Muslim activists envisioned a scheme whereby the Ottoman government would circulate treasury bonds throughout the subcontinent. These interest-bearing five-year bonds would be purchased by Indian Muslims, who would profit handsomely from their new status as bondholders. As opposed to the onetime remittance, bondholding evinced

FOR THE SAKE OF ISLAM!

OR, THE INDIAN KHICHREE FOR THE HUNGRY TURK.

BIRADAR MOSLEM (of India)—In the name of Allah! For the sake of Islam!

BIRADAR—A thousand thanks! May Allah reward you for all this trouble and kindness!

[The Indian Mahomedans are taking up a good portion of the five per cent. Ottoman Treasury Bonds of £ 5,000,000 issued by the Porte.]

["*Hindi Punch*," *Feb., 1913.*]

FIGURE 5.2 Cartoon from *Hindi Punch*, February 1913.
Reproduced from Barjorjee Nowrosjee, ed., *Cartoons from the Hindi Punch for 1913* (Bombay: Bombay Samachar, 1913), 25.

one's true devotion to the Ottoman cause. Capturing the spirit of Indian Muslim participation in the bond drive, a marvelous cartoon published in *Hindi Punch* in February 1913 portrayed an Indian Muslim cook pouring a hefty serving of *khichdi* (lentils and rice) onto the plate of a suppliant Ottoman high official (see figure 5.2).

Predictably, the sheer volume of Indian Muslim interlocutors exacerbated some of the confusion around Ottoman bonds. To alleviate some of the unease brought on by these affairs and to encourage more bond purchases, the Agha Khan III stepped into the fray with an article on the benefits of buying Ottoman bonds, writing, "It may be asked whether the Mussalmans of India will find two or three millions. I think the Mussalmans all over the country have money in various banks and in various kinds of securities, and where will they find better investment than transferring their holdings to the 5 per cent. Turkish Bonds? Personally, I would not hesitate to get out of every investment that I possess and that does not bring me more than 5 per cent. and buy the 5 per cent. Turkish Bonds." He then asserted that if Indian Muslims contributed generously, the Ottoman government could rely on an additional £12 million per annum—an amount nearly equal to what it drained every year from its "Asiatic" provinces for the defense and maintenance of its European holdings. With that money, he continued, Indian Muslims could contribute to the rapid development of Mesopotamia, a region that would be "what the Argentines have been for Europe," with a commercial value greater than "five East Africas."[26] Indian Muslim capital was to be a vehicle for Ottoman progress in its "backward" regions, and by implication, a vehicle for Indian colonization. True to his word, the Agha Khan III eventually purchased some Rs. 90,000 (£6,000) in Ottoman bonds. Despite this, his pronouncements in 1913 that the Ottomans should evacuate their European provinces incurred calls for his expulsion as president of the All-India Muslim League. He duly obliged, though he cited his frequent absences in Europe as the reason.[27]

In the end, even if Indian Muslim charitable remittances to the Ottoman government were enormous, the Ottoman bond drive was a comparative failure. The bond drive had revealed the extent to which the vast plurality of Indian Muslims were unbanked and capital poor. None of the capital reserves of Indian Muslim capitalists, whether Gujarati or otherwise, was sufficient to mitigate these realities. At the same time, the campaign, which brought Indian Muslim capitalists and political activists into a single institutional continuum in numbers for the first time, once again highlighted the enormous disparities between Gujarati Muslim merchant groups like the Bohras, Khojas, and Memons and other Indian Muslims outside the circuits of elite business. In the two decades that followed, these disparities transmogrified into a central issue of Indian Muslim politics.

Bad Options in an Age of Total War, 1914–1918

The war years partially foreshadowed the tumult that would befall these three communities in the conflict's immediate aftermath. Dependable Gujarati

Muslim loyalism shielded the Bohras, Khojas, and Memons from the worst excesses of state violence, for the most part. Still, there were instances in which Gujarati Muslims engaged in outright sedition against colonial authorities. In one case, select members of the Memon *jamaat* in Rangoon—which, as was seen in the previous section, contributed substantially toward Ottoman relief—attempted to bankroll the massive mutiny of an Indian Muslim regiment in Singapore. The mutiny was brutally crushed by the British, with nearly one thousand sepoys executed in one of the most egregious episodes of mass violence committed in the history of the British Empire.[28]

According to colonial reports, in December 1914 one of the regiments in Singapore sent a letter to Mullah Ahmad Daud Efendi, the Memon merchant of Rangoon and honorary Ottoman consul general, requesting that he find a means for Ottoman authorities to send a warship to Singapore. In turn, some Rs. 15,000 in subscriptions were raised by a secret society in Rangoon, with the headmaster of the city's Memon Muhammadan School serving as one of its leaders, helping to smuggle guns into the country and drawing up rules for the society.[29] After correspondence between Rangoon and Singapore was intercepted, British authorities foiled the plot in November 1915 and interned the conspirators. Yet outright resistance was the exception. Other Memons in Rangoon, such as the city's leading Indian industrialist, Abd al-Karim Jamal, were avid supporters of the British war effort.

A useful barometer of Gujarati Muslim support for the British war effort was their participation in the war loan drives. Bohras, Khojas, and Memons subscribed in sizable numbers to these campaigns. Successive collection drives were held throughout British India. For example, in Bangalore, Haji Ismail Sait, a highly successful Kachchhi Memon businessman and director of Mysore Bank, donated Rs. 10,000—amounting to half of his bank's fixed deposits—to the war loan.[30] When contrasted with the Ottoman bond drive of 1912–1914, the popularity of the Indian war bond drive shows just how many Indian Muslims regarded their capital as bound up with the British imperial enterprise. To be sure, not all Indian Muslim mercantile consortiums responded with equal enthusiasm. Even the Agha Khan III, who supported the war loan, expressed his frustration with the steady flow of contributors to the campaign—given that in earlier years, his attempts to raise funds for a Muslim university had progressed at a glacial pace.[31] The Surti Memon *jamaat* of Rangoon withheld its capital out of an aversion to accepting interest.[32] By contrast, according to one count, the Bohras subscribed to the war loan in 1918 to the tune of Rs. 181,300.[33] A leading Bohra explained that "as the taking of interest was against the tenets of their religion, no interest would be drawn on the amount subscribed by them."[34] The reluctance to accept interest on war loans was not universal among Muslims and would become highly divisive issue later in the interwar period. But at the height of the war bond drive in 1917 at least one commentator—a certain Maulvi Sayyid Al-i Ahmad—advocated its permissibility in an Urdu pamphlet on the subject.[35]

Within two years, such open support for the government and insistence on the legitimacy of accepting interest would become nearly indefensible in the court of Muslim public opinion. By the time the Khilafat movement was launched in 1919, the popularity of the war bond drive was so pervasive that abstinence from participating in war loan campaigns was one of the many conditions for joining (other conditions included abdicating government titles and boycotting government offices). Contrary to Al-i Ahmad's narrative, Indian nationalists asserted that the war loan had been a forced levy and a contributing factor to the drain of wealth from India to Britain. Both Gandhi and the leaders of the Central Khilafat Committee encouraged Indians to stop subscribing to the war loans. And Jamāʿat-i ʿUlamāʾ-i Hind, a new consortium of Indian Muslim scholars founded in 1918, even felt compelled to issue a fatwa against subscribing to war loans.[36]

Fealty to the empire was no guarantee of material security or communal integrity. The Bohras exemplified how the war years ushered in both uneven prosperity and schism. As scholars have long asserted, two developments initiated this sea change in the life of the *jamaats:* the death of the Bohra multimillionaire and government contractor, Adamji Pirbhai, in 1913 and the accession of Tahir Saif al-Din to the position of *dai al-mutlaq* (chief cleric of the sect) in 1915. A showdown between the heirs of Pirbhai and the *dai* ensued in these years as Bohra merchant elites and the *dai* put forward irreconcilable visions of *jamaat* governance, particularly over the management of community trusts. To put it in terms of the models employed in this book, it was a clash between the conciliar model of *jamaat* governance (espoused by the dissidents) and an apex cleric model (espoused by the *dai*).

This is a more useful way of understanding the conflict that arose during the First World War between the mainline and dissident Bohras than its typical framing by the Bohra dissident movement—that is, as a duel between an obscurantist priestly class and progressive "reformers." According to the oft-quoted Bohra reformist dissident Mulla Abd al-Hussain, originally from Burhanpur but writing from Rangoon in 1921, the wicked actions of the Bohra "priestly class" in the immediate past had led to the *dai*'s centralization of wealth and the establishment of various subscriptions and funds that squeezed the community to the last drop.[37] Yet, as will be shown in the chapter 6, this polemical explanation ignores the extent to which many non-Bohra Muslims defended the *dai*'s authority from the dissidents.

The showdown between the *dai* and the leading merchants of the *jamaat* was not the only calamity that beset the Bohra *jamaat* during the First World War. Disaster came in late 1914, when groups of Sunni Muslims attacked Bohra businesses in the Princely State of Bhopal, supposedly on account of the Bohras' professed loyalty to Britain in its war against the Ottomans. In turn, representatives of the Bohra *jamaat* demanded compensation from the Bhopal durbar. They received only individual reimbursements from Sultan Jahan, the Begum of Bhopal.[38] In the aftermath of the Bhopal riots, Adamji Pirbhai's son Ibrahim published an Urdu treatise that laid bare the divisions in the Bohra *jamaat*, especially between Tahir Saif al-Din and leading elites.[39] In Pirbhai's telling, the cause of division was the *dai*'s purported unwillingness to either obtain restitution for his followers from the court of Bhopal or allow the Pirbhai clan to supply financial assistance to Bohra refugees.

The attack on Bhopal's Bohra *jamaat* had occurred before Tahir Saif al-Din's accession to the rank of *dai*, and he came into his office only after the legal controversies had intensified. The chief dilemma he and leading Bohra *sethias* (caste leaders) faced was what to do with the many Bohras who had fled to Bombay, Burhanpur, and Ujjain. As Pirbhai recalled, the Bohra refugees in Ujjain repeatedly ignored the *dai*'s calls to return to Bhopal and open their shops, fearing for their safety and demanding compensation for their losses. The *dai*'s anger with the refugees' recalcitrance was unrelenting, but so was their refusal to budge. Over time they accumulated their own grievances against the *dai*, decrying his interference in the court case and his many unfulfilled promises of aid. In turn, influential figures in the *jamaat* became disillusioned with the *dai*'s leadership, which eventually prompted their excommunication between 1915 and 1917. The Pirbhais were among the most prominent victims of the expulsions. Lesser members of the community had certainly been cajoled and coerced by the threat of *salam bandh* (excommunication), as shown in the 1899 constitution from Dhoraji examined in chapter 3. The expulsions of 1915–1917, however, thrust many prominent members out of the caste in one fell swoop, including pillars of the *jamaats*. As will be shown in chapter 6, this group became the nucleus for the budding Bohra reformist (or dissident) movement.

The *dai* and his loyal followers experienced substantial problems of their own during the later years of the war. Two years after he became *dai* in 1915, Tahir Saif al-Din published an Arabic treatise titled *Dauʾ nūr al-ḥaqq al-mubīn* (The Brilliance of the Light of Transparent Truth). There he not only underscored his monopoly over religious interpretation but also directed some snide remarks at Sunnis and Shiʿis. Two years later, once the book gained a wider readership beyond the confines of the Bohra community, a public campaign against the *dai* and his followers engulfed several cities in Gujarat. Gujarati and Urdu handbills challenged the *dai* to a disputation and called for his censure, while Arabic, Persian, and Urdu fatwas decried his recourse to *takfir* (excommunication of one Muslim by another). Bohra commentators, such as the editor of the Gujarati newspaper *Islam*, defended the *dai*'s actions by stressing that *Dauʾ nūr al-ḥaqq al-mubīn* was meant to be read only by the Arabic-literate Bohra religious hierarchy. Unable to pronounce an order of excommunication against those outside the *jamaat*—which became his weapon of choice against Bohra dissidents in years to come—the *dai* was nonetheless fortunate to have several capable polemicists inside and outside the *jamaat* who rose to his defense.[40]

To add insult to injury, the war years also saw leading Bohra magnates like the Pirbhais lose out on lucrative government contracts that had sustained them for many decades. Since the 1870s, Gujarati Muslim firms—including Adamji Pirbhai's—had been suppliers to several British military expeditions, from Afghanistan to Ethiopia, Somaliland to South Africa. Pirbhai's sons continued to supply equipment to the Indian Army until their father's death in 1913. But the outbreak of war in 1914 threatened to undermine ties between the firm and colonial authorities. The firm showed no hesitation in making its displeasure known. In 1917 Karimbhai Pirbhai, eldest son of the late Adamji Pirbhai, asserted before the Industrial Commission that the government had shown unwarranted favoritism toward European companies in the distribution of government contracts throughout the war.[41] According to Pirbhai, while European firms were given orders of between fifteen hundred and two thousand tents, Indian firms had to be content with only fifty to seventy-five. The consequences for Indian industry were unsurprisingly disastrous. Pirbhai's testimony caused a sensation in the Indian press, not least because of his testy exchange with the investigative committee of the Industrial Commission. Members of the committee took umbrage with the charge and disputed Pirbhai's account.

When one member read out from a list of government contractors and discovered more Indian than European firms, Pirbhai challenged him to state the ratio of materials in the contracts given to Indian companies as opposed to European ones. The presiding member refused. Pirbhai repeatedly attempted to go into further detail, even seeking to delay the proceedings so that he could bring his business papers to the commission. To protect the reputation of the colonial officials that Pirbhai mentioned, the president of the commission tried to muzzle him and keep the affair out of the public eye.[42] Pirbhai refused to comply, and thereafter leaked the minutes to the press. The exchange was a portent of worse matters to come, and indeed the next few years were not joyous ones for the Pirbhai clan. Most of the assets of the family business were liquidated, family infighting over inheritance was rife, and their relationship with colonial authorities continued to fray.[43]

The First World War and its aftermath also had momentous effects on the Ismaili and Twelver Khoja *jamaats,* even if they were calmer years in comparison with the Bohras. From the outbreak of war, imperial loyalism came easier to the Ismaili Khojas, given the Agha Khan III's rank in the stratosphere of Indian princes. The Agha Khan III's fealty to the imperial cause was lauded in the British press, and these articles were reproduced in Ismaili Khoja publications.[44] In a firman promulgated shortly after the outbreak of war, the Agha Khan III bid the Ismaili Khoja *jamaats* to keep those fighting for the empire in their prayers.[45] But the Ismaili imam's prestige in the colonial order and in Muslim political circles ensured that he exercised a degree of political influence that transcended mere imperial loyalism. At the war's end, in an echo of his actions during the Balkan Wars, he spoke adamantly in defense of the Ottoman caliph. Nevertheless, the Agha Khan III (who by this time lived primarily in Europe) and some of his chief lieutenants in Bombay sometimes found themselves in awkward positions during the Khilafat and noncooperation movements (1919–1924). Wishing to be both stalwart defenders of empire and supporters of Indian nationalist aspirations, they at least had the benefit of an apex cleric who had the ear of both the colonial state and Muslim political activists.

In fact, the Agha Khan III's immense prestige in the colonial order meant that he was party to various schemes of imperial geopolitics. His *India in Transition*, written in 1918, had foreseen the age when India's imperial borders would stretch "from Aden to Mesopotamia, from the two shores of the [Persian] Gulf to India proper."[46] It was perhaps for this reason that the British Foreign Office suggested the Agha Khan III as a potential leader of Iraq in 1919, though his name was quickly dropped from the list of candidates.[47] Still, rumors of his appointment as Iraq's ruler remained ubiquitous—so much so that one leading member of the Ismaili Khoja *jamaat* in Bombay had to publicly deny it in a lecture to members of the *jamaat*.[48] Once the nascent Turkish nationalist movement in Ankara showed signs of abolishing the caliphate in 1923, the Agha Khan III and his longtime London-based collaborator, Amir Ali, both Shiʿi Muslims, were dismissed by several members of the Turkish Grand National Assembly as "heretics of heretics," absurdly charged as the ringleaders of a British-backed plot to crush the Turkish nationalists and restore the Ottoman caliph.[49]

Bizarre as these accusations were, the Agha Khan III did indeed encourage his followers to relocate to Mandate Iraq after its conquest by British and Indian armies. Barring some pre-war merchants in Basra, the modest influx of Ismaili Khoja merchants into Iraq began in earnest with Britain's conquest of Ottoman Iraq in 1917–1918. The site for the first Khoja Ismaili *jamaat khana* (assembly hall) was the Basra offices of Messrs. Pesan Allana Bros., led by a merchant who migrated from Karachi to Iraq after hearing the Agha Khan III encourage Ismailis to seek business opportunities in the country.[50] The Agha Khan III's declaration was actually disseminated as a firman in Karachi. As the imam stated, "Those *murīds* (followers) who are not running a business here go to Mesopotamia, so as to make very good profits. . . . Now, this is nothing new, twenty or thirty years ago in Africa, Burma island, etc., no businesses of *murīds* were in operation. They were begging us in such a way, then we gave an order to go to Africa, Rangoon, Burma Island, etc., and in turn our *murīds* became millionaires. Similarly, if you are not running a business here [Karachi], go there [Mesopotamia], and you will make very good profits. *Khānāvādān* [May your house be blessed]."[51] Although the Ismaili Khoja *jamaat* in Iraq did grow somewhat as a result, Iraq held a secondary importance in the pilgrimage landscape of Ismaili Khojas in this period.

Twelver Khojas also migrated to Mandatory Iraq from 1918. Lacking an apex cleric, individual entrepreneurs instead initiated these efforts, though *jamaat* resources were pivotal in their success. Iraq had been a key site of interaction between Twelver mujtahids and Twelver Khoja merchants from the 1870s, but the latter do not appear to have established either branches of their commercial enterprises or *jamaat khanas* in numbers until the turn of the century. A small uptick was apparent following the British conquest of Iraq. Jethbhai Gokal, among the Twelver Khojas who set up a business in Karachi during the Khoja controversies of the 1890s, moved his operations to Basra in 1918 after the British conquest of the city.[52] There he opened a shipping business and became the head of the Twelver Khoja *jamaat*.

Gokal's easy leap from Karachi to British-controlled Basra was a move that became politically difficult for Indian Muslim entrepreneurs from the very moment he made it, for in 1919 the Khilafat movement inaugurated yet another turn in the axis of Indian Muslim business and politics that effectively ended the apolitical stance of Gujarati Muslim commercial firms.

Khilafat and Noncooperation, 1919–1924

The political and business atmosphere inhabited by the *jamaats* changed irrevocably with the end of hostilities in 1918 and the onset of the Khilafat and noncooperation movements. The emergence of mass anticolonial nationalism and outright opposition to British rule disrupted the modus vivendi that the Gujarati Muslim commercial castes had long enjoyed with the colonial state. By 1919 there were also difficult economic conditions compelling the Bohras, Khojas, and Memons to embrace Swadeshi: the fall in the exchange rate to the detriment of the rupee (the consequence of the colonial government's deliberate fixing of the rate), a general depression in trade, and a dramatic reduction of Indians' purchasing power during 1918–1919.[53]

An early indication of the difficult choices that now had to be made by the *jamaats* came from the public missive published by Karachi's Ismaili Khoja *jamaat*—no stranger to public controversy since the 1870s—in 1919. There the leaders of the *jamaat* condemned disloyalty to the government and professed their own dedication to the king-emperor.[54] During the First World War, there was a need to declare open support for the empire, but now the *jamaats* faced the far harder predicament of staking their positions vis-à-vis both the colonial state and Indian nationalists. Each of the three commercial castes followed its own course, but the Memons were the most fulsome in their embrace of anticolonial politics, even if some refused to be taken in by the onrushing tide. Haji Ismail Sait, one of the leading merchants of Mysore, owner of a famous whiskey-bottling business in Calcutta, and the head of Bangalore's Kachchhi Memon *jamaat,* learned firsthand what happened to those who clung stubbornly to the imperial stern: the heads of fifteen mosques in Bangalore attempted to excommunicate him for not giving up his titles, despite the fact that he had donated generously to the Khilafat Funds.[55] Memon magnates who adopted a collision course with colonial authorities, however, discovered that the consequences were far graver than excommunication from the *jamaat.*

Umar Sobhani was the scion of a pioneering Memon industrialist firm, which had purchased the Elphinstone Mills around 1900. Upon his father's death, Umar expanded the family's operations. In 1919 the mills had been converted into a joint-stock company with a capital of Rs. 5 million, subdivided into twenty-five thousand ordinary shares and twenty-five thousand preference shares, each at one hundred rupees. While Muslim business ventures faced the perennial problem of undersubscription, this oversubscribed venture proved the exception.[56] Sobhani's commitment to the Khilafat and noncooperation movements was born of a broader desire to stimulate domestic production in India and to make Swadeshi a viable economic program. At a meeting in Allahabad on June 1, 1920, a "Swadeshi sub-committee" was created, consisting of Gandhi, Seth Chotani, Umar Sobhani, and numerous other Hindu and Muslim businessmen and dignitaries.[57]

In company with other Indian magnates, Sobhani was willing to put his own business on the line for this cause. In 1921 his works at Parel in Bombay became the site for an enormous bonfire of foreign cloth, an event attended by some 200,000 people.[58] Sobhani worked actively to raise money for the Swaraj Fund by canvassing mill owners in Bombay, from whom he hoped to collect Rs. 2 million. Should he fail to raise this sum, he promised to pay the difference himself.[59] Other members of the Sobhani family also became involved in the Khilafat movement. Mrs. Haji Yusuf Sobhani founded a spinning school for girls in 1921. At the opening ceremony, she enjoined the audience to heed the saying of the Prophet Muhammad that ordered Muslims to "teach women spinning." She also urged the pupils to follow the example of Umm Salama, one of the Prophet Muhammad's wives, who spun regularly and supposedly once said that "Satan runs away from the charkha."[60]

Beginning in 1921, Umar Sobhani began to advocate the outright boycott of British goods, heading a committee dedicated to that cause.[61] Thereafter, colonial authorities were compelled to turn against Sobhani. According to one account, the viceroy deliberately flooded Bombay with cotton to undermine Sobhani's mills. In time, Sobhani had to pay out losses of Rs. 3,640,000 and his business went into liquidation.[62] Tragically, he died by his own hand in 1926.[63] His brother Osman, a leading member of the Indian National Congress, took up boycotting British goods in the late 1920s; he served several stints in prison for his trouble. Osman was also one of the leading lights of Bombay's Kachchhi Memon *jamaat,* a position commensurate with his political activism.[64]

Seth Chotani also lost his business due to his participation in the Khilafat movement, albeit for reasons more to do with his own malfeasance than state expropriation. While in London in 1919, Chotani advocated sending arms to Ottoman troops fighting against the Greeks in Anatolia and issued appeals for the raising of funds for Ottoman relief.[65] He handled these visits in his capacity as the treasurer of the Central Khilafat Committee. To remit the funds to Istanbul, Chotani worked primarily through the Netherlands Trading Society.[66] Nevertheless, he landed in trouble when the lines between his business accounts and those of the Khilafat Funds became blurred. Memon journalists rallied to defend their own, with one declaring that "certain jealous and Satanic individuals" had impugned the great name of Seth Chotani and overlooked the services that Memons had rendered to fellow Muslims during the Tripoli, Balkan, Khilafat, and noncooperation campaigns.[67]

By October 1922 Chotani was forced to hand over his mills as compensation to the Central Khilafat Committee. The valuation of these mills proved to be a source of considerable conflict between Chotani and the committee, which had a difficult time disposing of them over the next three years. The committee was convinced that Chotani had overinflated the value of his mills at Rs. 1.8 million, in part because he had failed to account for the depreciation of machinery.[68] As a result, in 1923, Umar Sobhani was commissioned to conduct an independent audit. His efforts were chronicled by Muhammad Ali Jauhar's paper, *The Comrade,* which a decade earlier had been the primary advocate for the purchase of Ottoman bonds by Indian Muslims. Sobhani's audit concluded that the total property owned by Chotani amounted to no more than Rs. 800,000–900,000, less than half the amount Chotani proclaimed. Sobhani also contested many of Chotani's assertions concerning his assets and his plans to compensate the Central Khilafat Committee—including a proposal to float a new joint-stock company, which Sobhani found ridiculous.[69] This was no mere intra-*jamaat* dispute: a leading Kachchhi Memon industrialist had unreservedly reprimanded a leading Halai Memon industrialist in a foremost Indian Muslim periodical. In this sense, Sobhani's report shows just how much the Khilafat movement transformed the stakes of Gujarati Muslim business, for by subordinating Muslim capitalists to Muslim political organizations, the Khilafat movement made these figures susceptible to public audits. These audits not only aired the dirty laundry of leading capitalists but also measured their commitment to the nationalist cause.

As if proper valuation was not difficult enough, Muhammad Ali Jauhar told a session of Jamāʿat-i ʿUlamāʾ-i Hind that it was impossible to convert the Rs. 1,650,000 in Chotani's possession into liquid cash.[70] Wood is an especially difficult commodity to price, which perhaps explains why Chotani, the auctioneers, and the Central Khilafat Committee came to such divergent conclusions about the book and market values of his assets. None of that complexity redounded to the credit of Swadeshi enterprise.[71] As the archives of the Turkish Red Crescent reveal, Turkish republican authorities and the Central Khilafat Committee negotiated extensively over how to wind down Chotani's business empire. These negotiations dragged on until June 1925, when teak from Burma, *mai yang* from Siam, and pine from Oregon were finally sold at auction.[72]

Other Muslim politicians on the Central Khilafat Committee speculated about how to use the funds accruing from the liquidation of the mills. Shaukat Ali adamantly advocated for the creation of a Saw Mill Fund, which would be utilized to purchase a permanent office in Bombay for the committee. Abu al-Kalam Azad and the Aligarh Muslim University–educated journalist Maulana Ghulam Rasul Mehr objected, stating that "according to the law and custom of public opinion" the Angora funds could only be utilized for the work of the Central Khilafat Committee.[73] In the end, the Angora Fund remitted only O.L. 55,439, less than one-fourth the sum that Indian Muslims sent to the Ottoman Red Crescent during the Balkan Wars.[74] Amid these events, relations soured between the Khilafatists and the emergent Turkish nationalists. In February 1924, colonial authorities reluctantly granted a Turkish Red Crescent mission permission to journey to India to raise funds for Muslim refugees flooding into Anatolia at the end of the Ottoman Empire. However, the abolition of the caliphate forced the delegation to return shortly after arriving in Bombay.[75] Subsequently, Chotani—on hajj in the early 1930s—told the prominent scholar Maulana Abd al-Majid Daryabadi that he regretted that the amounts raised for the Angora and Smyrna Funds were never dispatched to Turkey.[76]

For both Chotani and Sobhani, participation in the Khilafat and noncooperation movements came at a prohibitive cost. Neither of their businesses survived the end of the Khilafat movement in 1924. The demise of two Memon merchant princes encapsulated the great costs of political confrontation with the colonial state. But it also exhibited the drawbacks of collaboration with Indian Muslim political institutions, which had distinct financial repertoires and demanded a level of transparency in account keeping that many entrepreneurs were hard-pressed to gratify. Other Muslim industrialists, like Haji Ismail Sait, certainly attempted to take a middle path: giving generously to the Khilafat Funds while refusing to renounce support for the colonial government. While they, too, faced consequences, these were usually limited to a tarnished reputation within their communities. Entrepreneurs like Chotani and Sobhani, meanwhile, risked their entire personal fortune in allying closely with nationalist schemes. The tensions visible during the Khilafat movement presaged many more to come, both within individual *jamaats* and among *jamaats* and noncaste Muslim organizations.

The Collapse of the Loyalist Old Guard, 1924–1932

Chotani, Pirbhai, and Sobhani were not the last Gujarati Muslim industrialists to meet their end in the interwar period. Even dependable imperial loyalists were not insulated from the market volatility of the 1920s and 1930s. Most notoriously, Jamal Bros., the enormous entity run out of Rangoon by A. K. A. S. Jamal, collapsed between 1924 and 1925. As late as 1922, a featurette in the *Calcutta Review* had praised Jamal: calling him "the Rice King of Burma," the author noted that he was equal to industrialist Jamsetji Tata and "an object lesson to many capitalists having their wealth locked up either in Government papers or in jewellery or in landed property."[77] Yet Jamal's death in 1924 struck a mortal blow to the firm, and his family's speculation on the rice market supplied the knockout punch. According to one narrative, the European firm with which Jamal Bros. had long cooperated, Steel Brothers and Company, Ltd., came to the rescue by taking over both the Jamal Bros. sales offices and its managers.[78] Contemporaries saw matters in another light, however. In 1935, one nationalist commentator asserted, "We know how Jamal Brothers were ruined by their own partners and how gradually their business passed into the hands of the British merchants who were settled down there."[79] This was a measure of just how politicized Indian business had become over the past decade.

There were warning signs that one of the largest Muslim-owned enterprises worldwide stood at risk. In 1921 a fire destroyed the firm's rice mill at Kanaungto, which instigated a staggering loss of Rs. 2 million. The next year, another conflagration destroyed the firm's new paper mill.[80] The firm's failure was so dramatic that it stirred up numerous rumors about the liquidity of the Central Bank of India, one of the largest indigenous exchange banks, managed by the Bombay Parsi Sir Sorabji Pochkhanawala. The Central Bank had extended an enormous amount of loans to Jamal Bros., likely with no second thought given to the possibility of repayment.[81] With the end of Jamal Bros., Rangoon's foremost Muslim merchant not only disappeared from the scene but also the firm's monthly subscriptions to many Anglo-Indian and Islamic institutions in Burma and India ended. In time, Memon commercial and religious entrepreneurs in Calcutta, Karachi, and Rangoon would take up the slack. Yet their vision of Muslim politics conformed to the communitarian paradigms of the interwar period and differed markedly from the imperial loyalism of Jamal.

Though a spate of Khoja entrepreneurs, Ismaili and Twelver, found modest success in the mercurial economic conditions of the 1920s, the most critical development in Khoja business during this time was the failure of the leading firm, Currimbhoy. The firm had been a pillar of the Ismaili Khoja *jamaat*—and of Indian business life from Bombay to Shanghai—since the 1870s, as chapter 4 has shown. In the early 1920s, a scion of the firm's founder Fazlbhai Karimbhai had participated in various sessions of the League of Nations as a representative for British India, anticipating the Agha Khan III's own tenure as head of that organization.[82] The litany of public distinctions did much to obscure the disaster that befell the Karimbhais' economic empire.

The implosion of the Currimbhoy business empire reverberated throughout business circles on the subcontinent, not least because leading Jewish, Muslim, and Parsi businessmen were on its board of directors.[83] Two years before the firm went into administration, a report on the mill industry in Bombay suggested that Currimbhoy specifically—and Muslim mill ownership more generally—was thriving. The report listed Currimbhoy's holdings as twelve mills, over 500,000 spindles, and nearly ten thousand looms, making the firm second only to the Bombay-based Baghdadi Jewish firm of David Sassoon.[84] Currimbhoy's 1928 calendar confidently depicted the *navaratna* (the nine gems) of Emperor Akbar's court.[85] Evidently the firm imagined that their position at the apex of India's mill industry was as sacrosanct and untouchable as the leading lights of Akbar's inner circle.

Their balance sheets told another story. Throughout the early 1920s, these betrayed wide fluctuations in Currimbhoy's debts and profits. By 1924 the firm had taken on substantial losses.[86] Soon enough it had to be bailed out by a timely loan from the Nizam of Hyderabad. The money, however, was quickly exhausted in the process of fulfilling existing liabilities. When another loan was required in 1933, the Nizam unexpectedly refused to rescue the "premier Moslem business house in India" a second time. But amid the liquidation of the firm, the Currimbhoy group mortgaged its managing agency commission to the Nizam, who appointed a committee to decide the mill's future.

A portion of the Currimbhoy concern, the Osman Shahi Mills, were in turn hypothecated to the Hyderabad government. The mills had been headquartered in the princely state since 1922, after Currimbhoy signed an agreement with the Nizam's government. In 1934, however, the mills were signed over to the trustees of the Industrial Trust Fund of Hyderabad State.[87] Created in 1930 to provide state aid to local industries, including women's home industries, this body was part of a broad-based financial strategy intended to supply Hyderabad State's economy with a road map to industrialization.[88] Although the Industrial Trust Fund salvaged the wreck, Currimbhoy's failure after a decade of very public decline and six decades of successful operations was a worrying portent for Indian business. Financial markets also took notice: the firm's collapse in 1933 caused panic on the Bombay Stock Exchange, and runs on the branches of Bank of India, the Central Bank of India, and the National City Bank of New York.[89] By that year, some of the top Indian Muslim firms—Crescent, Currimbhoy, and Premier, all Ismaili Khoja concerns—had gone bust. Part of the Currimbhoy interest in Bombay was bought up by the city's Marwari industrialists.[90] Even so, the firm's failure was a warning that the Great Depression threatened to wipe out decades of Indian industrial progress.

In reality, Currimbhoy's downfall cast a long shadow over Indian industry. With greater assertiveness, Indian industrialists now demanded that the colonial state erect additional protectionist measures, and tariff barriers were ratcheted up. But calls for more robust government support dovetailed with ambitions to make Indian industry autarkic. The decline of the cotton mill industry was so stark by 1930 that Hussainbhai Lalji, leader of the Twelver Khoja *jamaat* in Bombay, confronted it head-on during his inaugural address as president of the Indian Merchants' Chamber. There he called for a "vigorous scheme of industrialisation" that he hoped would make India self-sufficient.[91] For the next two decades, Lalji would be a stalwart defender of Indian industrial interests while staunchly opposing the program of the All-India Muslim League, sometimes seen by critics as nothing more than the party of Muslim capitalists. In actuality, Lalji presented a sharp contrast with Memon magnates like Adamji Haji Daud, part of a new generation of Gujarati Muslim capitalists who married identarian business interests with loyalty to the Muslim League.

The Rise of a New Generation: A "Sectarian" Business Culture?

At one of the numerous interwar All-India Memon Conferences, hosted in Rajkot in 1933, a participant struck an all-too-common tone of Indian Muslim discourse in the late colonial period. Groaning, "For one hundred years Muslims have been destitute and backward. Muslim means a pauper, pauper means a Muslim," he further inveighed against Hindu mahajans and the Indian National Congress, thereby indulging the strident voice of Muslim economic resentment against Hindus.[92] Of course, many other Indian Muslim communities had made this charge, particularly in Punjab, where the image of the Hindu moneylender had been a bogeyman of the Indian Muslim press and colonial officials for decades. Yet the author of the tract showed no hesitation in declaring that the conditions of Punjab's Muslims now extended to the entirety of Indian Muslims.[93]

It was surprising to hear this from a member of the Gujarati Muslim commercial castes, all of whom had had comfortable associations with Hindu and other non-Muslim merchants across the Indian Ocean region. Statements such as this reflect Memon anxieties about sustaining community wealth in the interwar period. After all, many of the delegates at the conference lamented high interest rates as a roadblock for poor Memons attempting to start businesses and suggested cooperative credit as a partial solution to this problem.[94] And with high interest rates said to be the work of greedy Hindu mahajans throughout the subcontinent, the communal undertones of these diatribes were unmistakable.

Other dynamics spurred on the partial communalization of business. As was noted in the previous section, from the First World War to the onset of the Great Depression, many of the leading Indian Muslim firms had failed. This cleared the way for the rise of a fourth colonial generation of Gujarati Muslim entrepreneurs. Foremost among them was the Memon entrepreneur Adamji Haji Daud, whose commercial dominance ensured that he was the preeminent figure in the Memon *jamaats* of Calcutta and Rangoon from the early 1930s onward—and among the top three most influential Memons in the entire diaspora. His position likewise ensured that he was able to pursue one of the leading ambitions of Muslim nationalists in the 1930s: the creation of a Muslim chamber of commerce. Earlier Muslim business magnates, such as the Ismaili Khoja Karimbhai Ibrahim and the Memon Abd al-Karim Jamal, had advocated the creation of various mercantile associations that transcended religion (even as they sponsored sundry Muslim institutions). Adamji and his Twelver Shiʿi counterpart M. A. Hassan Ispahani, however, were the most instrumental factors in the creation of the Muslim Chamber of Commerce. An initial branch in Calcutta opened in 1933 was soon followed by subbranches throughout the country.[95]

The birth of the Muslim Chamber of Commerce caused palpable disquiet in the Indian financial press. In 1933 a correspondent for *Indian Finance* made this anxiety plain:

> At first sight, it might look like having brought communalism into a region [i.e., business] in which it is even more indefensible than in politics. It is true that if there are no separate Muslim interests in business, the Chamber has no raison d'etre and if there are, the Chamber would only aggravate the discord. But the community is the best judge of its needs. For the average man all that matters is that the Muslim Chamber does not transfer to the sphere of economics the separatism and opposition to the national viewpoint which has characterised Muslim politics.

Even so, Adamji's inaugural speech allayed the correspondent's suspicions: "We are second to none in standing shoulder to shoulder with our countrymen in fighting for the rights and privileges of India, for it would but be repeating an axiom that 'the part is contained in the whole' and is bound to benefit within the benefit of the whole."[96] The speech went on to advocate for protection of Indian industries.

From this point, the Muslim Chamber of Commerce found it hard to shake the "communal" label, despite Adamji's declarations to the contrary. Even in the 1930s, commentators in the Indian press accused the Muslim Chamber of Commerce of playing fast and loose with the facts and figures of several Muslim companies to increase the proportion of Muslim representation on the Bengal Provincial Advisory Committee. For example, in one instance the Muslim Chamber of Commerce submitted a memorandum to the committee on the capital of Dost Mohammed & Co., Ltd., and The Muslim Press & Publication, Ltd., reported as Rs. 750,000 and Rs. 150,000 respectively. But on investigating further, a committee member discovered that Dost Mohammed & Co.'s Rs. 750,000 was only its authorized capital—none of which had been paid up. The Muslim Press & Publication figure, meanwhile, was a complete fiction.[97] Such shady accounting practices hardly encouraged public confidence in the Muslim Chamber of Commerce.

In the late 1930s the connection between these separate Muslim chambers and the All-India Muslim League exacerbated impressions of a Hindu-Muslim communal divide in business. At that time, the Indian National Congress was advancing its Muslim Mass Contact Campaign in a bid to stir up support among Muslim constituencies. The reaction from some prominent Memons was to align themselves more fulsomely with Muhammad Ali Jinnah and the Muslim League. In 1938 one influential group of Memons wrote, "We assure you, that we shall obediently follow you to the extent of laying down our lives in carrying out your commands. Mussalmans in every corner of the country have accepted you as their one and only leader and as their field-marshal. They have fullest confidence in you and your activities in as much as they know that your aim is the welfare of nine [*sic*] million Mussalmans of India. Therefore, please believe us that you have our fullest support and we shall go to any length at your behest so that we may live as free Muslims in free India." Echoing this, the Memon magnate Seth Haji Abd Allah Harun noted that if Muslims "wanted to pursue their trade peacefully, they must take part in politics." Muslim economic improvement was, Harun continued, essential if Muslims hoped to earn the respect of other communities.[98]

Equality and cooperation between communities was certainly a program espoused by many Gujarati Muslim nationalists. But there was also a consistent refrain that Hindu and Muslim interests were fundamentally irreconcilable. Surprisingly, the Agha Khan III, otherwise a figure devoted to Hindu-Muslim reconciliation, had promoted aspects of this program from the early 1930s onward. He came in for some sharp criticism on this score from none other than Jawaharlal Nehru, the leader of the Indian National Congress. Nehru was adamant that the Ismaili imam and other Muslim elites acted as props for British authority by stressing the fundamental incongruity of Hindu-Muslim interests. On one occasion in the mid-1930s Nehru lambasted the Agha Khan III as "the head of a wealthy religious group, who continues in himself, most remarkably, the feudal order and the politics and habits of the British ruling class, with which he has been intimately associated for many years."[99]

Nehru's attacks on the Agha Khan III induced a telling counterattack from the famous Indian Muslim writer Muhammad Iqbal. Critical though he was of the Ismaili vision of the imamate, Iqbal nonetheless defended the Agha Khan III's status as an authentic representative of Muslim India.[100] Elsewhere, he reminded Nehru that the Agha Khan III had pledged to Gandhi that "the Muslim minority" would be happy to serve as "camp-followers of the majority community [Hindus] in the country's political struggle."[101] To Iqbal's mind, Hindu-Muslim interests were compatible, but requisite safeguards had to be put in place by Hindus to ensure the protection of Muslims in an independent India. That both Iqbal and Nehru, whatever their differences, saw the Agha Khan III and his community as either an asset or a liability to their political programs demonstrates yet again that Indian nationalism elevated the *jamaats* to a fraught position in the public sphere. Yet again Gujarati Muslim middle power was placing the Bohras, Khojas, and Memons in the spotlight.

Though Iqbal accented Hindu-Muslim complementarity, among certain members of the Indian Muslim business and political elite, and especially those associated with the All-India Muslim League, the conviction remained that Hindu magnanimity to Muslims was never going to be forthcoming. As ever, the messy world of events disrupted any diagnosis that saw in a bifurcated, communalized business a cause of Muslim economic infirmities. And once outside of Bombay business affairs looked decidedly more variegated. Though in certain Muslim intellectual circles Hindus shouldered the burden for high interest rates and thus for Muslim penury, Indian Muslim politicians did sometimes lump Bohras and Khojas into this same category. Thus, in 1936 Shaukat Ali—a leading member of the Central Khilafat Committee—wrote a damning indictment of the Bohra and Khoja "usurers" he observed in Zanzibar, a diatribe that stirred up a sweeping rebuttal from a Bohra newspaper editor on the island.[102] In a climate where moneylending assumed a communal framing, Bohra and Khoja lending practices threatened to put them outside the Muslim camp in the eyes of the Muslim nationalist.

* * *

The generation from the Balkan Wars to the early years of the Great Depression witnessed the outright politicization of business in colonial India and the British Empire. No longer were the Gujarati Muslim commercial castes, or other Indian corporate bodies, able to remain comfortably apolitical. While the interwar years did see tangible commercial successes, the world of free trade and relatively open borders did not survive 1914. The shocks of deglobalization, protectionism, and mass nationalism guaranteed that the structures of Indian business enterprise were completely remade in the final three decades of colonial rule. In a narrower sense, these three developments also led to a legitimacy crisis for the model of corporate Islam exemplified by the Bohras, Khojas, and Memons. Increasingly, it was unacceptable in the eyes of Indian Muslim public opinion for such tiny communities to line the metaphorical pockets of their *jamaats* while depriving the wider Muslim community from accessing their disproportionate wealth reserves.

In their turn, members of the *jamaats* also grew sensitive on this front and contemplated means by which *jamaat* property could be guaranteed and defended. Yet if one predicament of the interwar period concerned the *jamaats*' character as corporate institutions vis-à-vis other Muslim constituencies, then the parallel dilemma they all faced, albeit in dissimilar ways, was how to manage the internal disputes concerning community trusts that threatened the corporate integrity of the *jamaats*. From the early 1920s onward these disputes became more, not less, ungovernable as texts and actors from outside the *jamaats* progressively tread on their jurisdictional turf.

6

The Battle over *Jamaat* Trusts

1923–1935

FROM AROUND THE TIME of the First World War, Indian Muslims increasingly argued that inadequate access to fluid capital was the prime cause of Muslim economic backwardness. Some attributed this to the dearth of Muslim-owned banks on the subcontinent, which was indeed a conspicuous attribute of Muslim economic life in colonial India. While the number of Muslim community-based thrifts expanded dramatically in the interwar period, banks run by Indian Muslims remained numerically insignificant. In the eyes of most activists, reforming the administration of Muslim pious endowments (*awqāf*) and compulsory religious tax in Islam (*zakat*) was a precondition for increasing the share of Muslim banks. They pinpointed these reforms, along with the creation of a general *bait al-mal* (treasury) modeled on the administration of the first four caliphs, as the way to liberate the "inert" capital sequestered in thousands of pious endowments across the subcontinent—and to redirect that capital toward charitable and profitable enterprises for the economic benefit of all Muslims.

According to the logic of this campaign, Bohra, Khoja, and Memon endowments—hitherto seen as unassailable private property vested in the *jamaats* (corporate caste institutions), a status maintained both by colonial and Islamic legal tenets—became susceptible to external inspection and gatecrashing. As such, the model of corporate Islam embodied by the Gujarati Muslim commercial castes clashed with a new brand of Indian Muslim nationalism propounded by a legion of novel political organizations. These organizations were eager to harness Muslim capital for the good of the imagined Muslim community and to utilize the largesse of the *jamaats* for their own ends. The saga of Seth Chotani covered in chapter 5 had revealed the dangers not only of mixing business and anticolonial politics but also of exposing the *jamaats* to grasping Muslim political activists. The campaign for *awqāf* reform intensified this development.

Interwar attempts to infringe upon the corporate privileges of the Gujarati Muslim *jamaats* marked a sharp transition away from prewar conditions. For example, the Wakf Validating Act of 1913, spearheaded by Muhammad Ali Jinnah and his colleagues in the All-India Muslim League, had attempted to "restore" the legitimacy of family *awqāf* and recognize the rights of heirs to hold these endowments in perpetuity. This was a sea change in the entire legal discourse surrounding sharia in colonial India, as historian Gregory Kozlowski brilliantly argued almost thirty years ago.[1] Consequently, the act was not simply another development in an intra-Muslim struggle over the management of trusts. It had far greater Pan-Indian implications for the next three decades.[2]

Before passage of the Wakf Act, Karimbhai Ibrahim, the Ismaili Khoja industrialist, remarked, "The Bill, when passed into law, will have far-reaching effects on the fortunes of the Islamic community of India. . . . While declaring the true law, that is, the law laid down by the Founder of Islam, it provides adequate safeguards against fraud. It recognises a principle which is of supreme importance to the Musulmans as it will prevent the impoverishment by the transfer of their estates into other's hands."[3] The support of leading figures associated with the Muslim League gave the Wakf Act special significance, suggesting the start of a new era of Indian Muslim legal culture. Jinnah and other leading members of the league involved in the case regarded the protection of family endowments as the best means to safeguard landed families from the depredations of moneylenders—invariably regarded as Hindus—who ran a brisk business in "hunting down" family-run *awqāf*. Despite the bill's unanimous victory in the legislature, it had no practical effect because it never explicitly stated that it protected endowments created before 1913.[4]

But if the 1913 legislation perpetuated—instead of undermining—the long-standing problem of tying up capital in pious endowments, then the subsequent 1923 and 1931 Wakf Acts sought to liberate that capital through the creation of an external and (though the supporters of the act repeatedly denied this charge) interventionist administration. The attempt to dilute the *jamaats*' hold on individual endowments assumed many different forms, running the gamut from small-scale reform to outright seizure. The attempt to integrate the Bohra *jamaats*' endowments under the purview of the Wakf Acts of 1923 and 1931 saw Bohra dissidents, working in cooperation with the Muslim League, attempt to wrest control of the *jamaats*' endowments from the recent and hard-won custodianship of the *dai al-mutlaq* (chief cleric). Though contests over Memon trusts did not assume the same political valence as the Bohras, there nonetheless was much handwringing over how Memon trusts ought to better serve the needs of Memon *jamaats* or, alternatively, their Sunni Muslim brethren.

As for the Khojas, the welter of antithetical ideas about *jamaat* governance ensured that trusts became an apple of discord. For the Twelver Khojas, the expansion of trusts became a way of reorienting *jamaat* religious life away from the embodied authority of the Agha Khan III. On the other hand, given the Agha Khan III's stature in Indian Muslim nationalist causes, Ismaili Khojas became leading proponents of Indian Muslim campaigns to mobilize Islamic charitable trusts as a means of combatting a perceived Muslim economic backwardness.

The Protracted Fight over Bohra Endowments

In 1928 a certain Nathu Khan Ajam Khan Chuvhan composed one of the more remarkable, not to say eccentric, Sunni evaluations of Shiʿi Islam ever written. His Gujarati work—titled *Śīāonā dharmagurūonā darajo juvo ane sunnīonā dharmagurūonā darajo juvo* (Look at the Shiʿi religious teachers and the Sunni religious teachers)—was no heresiography.[5] Rather, it was a clarion call to fellow Sunnis to wake up and look afresh at the achievements of the Bohras and Khojas. For Chuvhan, these two communities of Shiʿi Muslims had much to teach their Sunni brethren about how to craft a viable religious brotherhood. While the sorry status of Sunni pirs and murids was supposedly plain for all to see, Chuvhan groaned, the Agha Khan III and the *dai al-mutlaq* (the chief cleric, who, in the manner of the time Chuvhan called "Mullaji Sahib") were considered among India's foremost religious leaders. For Sunnis like Chuvhan, the apex cleric model had much to recommend it. Though he bid his readers to open their eyes,

Chuvhan's own eyed remained closed to the many internal frictions within the Bohra and Khoja *jamaats*.

As was briefly covered in chapter 5, the two decades after 1914 were a remarkably turbulent period in the history of the Bohra *jamaats*. The excommunication and defection of many leading Bohra merchant families was a shock to the integrity of the *jamaats*. Yet the social stigma that these families subsequently faced demonstrates once again the integral place of the *jamaats* in community social and commercial life. Moreover, the barriers that Bohra breakaway factions faced in articulating a vision of a viable, acephalous Bohra *jamaat* undermined their project in the minds of contemporaries. In the end, a Bohra *jamaat* with no *dai al-mutlaq* was a notion that even Parsis and Twelver Shiʿis mocked as a contradiction in terms. Indeed, in the town of Jabalpur several Gujarati and Urdu texts appeared in support of the *dai*, which were endorsed by Twelver Shiʿi scholars, among others.[6] In this reading, obedience to the *dai* was an essential precondition for membership in the Bohra *jamaat*.

From 1917 onward, contests over control of Bohra trusts became a source of never-ending friction between the Bohra mainline and the nascent dissident *jamaats*. The latter attempted to mobilize their contacts with non-*jamaat* Indian Muslim institutions like the Muslim League, who increasingly envisioned the centralized oversight of *awqāf* as the key to unlocking Muslim capital long pocketed, so they assumed, by corrupt *mutawallis* and Muslim families. Yet in the end, interwar efforts to acquire greater control of *awqāf*, or to subject them to wider administrative oversight, did little to change Muslim economic fortunes and did not free up the capital as the framers hoped.

The famous Chandabhai Gulla Case, adjudicated in Bombay from 1917 to 1921, marked the opening salvo in a protracted Bohra war over trusts in the interwar period. In this case, A. M. Jivanji (a prominent Bohra merchant who managed a firm out of Mauritius from 1890), Sharaf Ali Mamuji, and the sons of Adamji Pirbhai filed a claim in the Bombay high court against Tahir Saif al-Din. The plaintiffs maintained that the *dai* had appropriated the funds of the Chandabhai *gulla* in Bombay and sought to arrogate several other community trusts to his own person. A *gulla* (or *galla*) is an alms box at a shrine or mosque, and the *gulla* in question was housed at the Chandabhai mosque, named for a famous Bohra saint. In addition to the *gulla*, the case adjudicated the ownership of a mosque, four immovable properties, and

Badri Mahall, the *dai*'s residence in Bombay.[7] Four years elapsed from the filing of the original suit to the final judgment, an indication of the case's complexity.

The details of the court case need not slow down the narrative here, but two facts are worth stressing because they marked watersheds in the history of the *jamaat*. The first is that the plaintiff (a Bohra dissident) disputed the succession of Abd al-Qadir Najm al-Din to the *dai*-ship back in 1840—a matter covered in chapters 1 and 3—and further submitted a document written by the *dai* Burhan al-Din in 1891 testifying to the faulty succession. From this moment, the illegitimacy of the 1840 succession and all subsequent *dais* became a cornerstone of the dissidents' program. The second point that needs highlighting is that the trial saw the summoning of Tahir Saif al-Din to the witness stand, a reversal of the privileges enjoyed by Bohra *dais* for some seven decades. The testimony, in which the *dai* effectively stressed that he was above the law and unaccountable to his followers, did the *dai* little credit and was to be used against him by the Bohra dissidents.

The court's final ruling stipulated that the *dai* was not held liable to share any financial information with members of his *jamaats* and appointed him as sole trustee of the Chandabhai gulla, which was designated a religious trust constructed for "public" purposes.[8] Nonetheless, the judge in the case, J. Marten, ruled that the *dai* was accountable as a trustee, whatever his religious station, and that Bohras were subject to the colonial state's version of Shiʿi *waqf* law. Nevertheless, such law in colonial India was based entirely on Twelver Shiʿi statutes, not Ismaili ones. To impose such a body of laws "foreign" to the Bohras' Mustali Ismaili Shiʿi legal culture was potentially detrimental to the corporate privileges of the Bohra *jamaat*, which, in conformity with the model of legal exceptionalism, had more or less followed its own community usages until this point. Indeed, though the evidence is circumstantial, it appears that Bohras had hitherto tried to avoid using the British judicial system because the colonial understanding of Shiʿi law was based solely on Twelver texts. On the other hand, from this point onward, dissident Bohras increasingly resorted to the British courts to make the *dai* accountable to his followers.[9]

Historians of the Bohras have rightfully devoted a good deal of attention to the Chandabhai Gulla Case. However, the rich vernacular sources produced during the court proceedings have been overlooked. These show not only how the case was perceived within the Bohra *jamaats* but also how

Indian public opinion was divided by the proceedings in unpredictable ways, rallying alternatively to the *dai* or the dissidents. They include a nearly six-hundred-page Gujarati translation of the English court transcript, published by Munshi Fateh Khan Ahmad Khan.[10] A Bohra newspaper editor from Ahmedabad, Ahmad Khan went by the pen name Dilkash. He was one of the *dai*'s most prolific defenders in these years, and even seems to have worked with Tahir Saif al-Din's tacit support. In his account to the proceedings, he stressed that many Bohras had read about the case in the newspapers, and though troubled by the attacks on their religion, community, and *dai*, had not yet obtained a record of the whole case.[11] The publication of a Gujarati version of the court transcript signaled that the slow expansion of the Bohra interpretive community over the previous four decades now in theory encompassed the entire *jamaat* rather than just the religious hierarchy.

Just as Khoja authors repeatedly cited the rulings of Justice Joseph Arnould from the Agha Khan Case of 1866 in their own spats, Dilkash and critics of the *dai* hoped to leverage Marten's ruling in their own polemics. Marten's ruling also inspired extended commentary from Muslims outside the *jamaat*. From the Chandabhai Gulla Case onward, the Bohra dissident movement labored to paint its cause as a righteous campaign of individual conscience against religious autocracy. Yet not all other Indian Muslims and non-Muslims saw matters in this light. The evidence suggests that many, in fact, saw the dissidents as the guilty party. In the Parsi newspaper *Kaiser-i Hind* (Emperor of India), a Parsi writer derisively attacked the Bohra dissidents as "the so called reformers." After upbraiding other Indian-owned newspapers for permitting Bohra authors to publish invective against Tahir Saif al-Din, he lamented that the Parsi community had no leaders approaching the stature of Mullaji Sahib.[12] Other Indian newspapers soon condemned *Kaiser-i Hind* for getting caught up in the Bohra dispute, but this ignored how nearly every "internal" dispute involving Gujarati Muslims in this period swept up noncommunity actors as it vaulted the walls of the *jamaats* and moved into the public sphere.

From 1923 onward, the controversies intrinsic to the Chandabhai Galla Case began to transcend the Bohra *jamaats* and subjected the community's wealth to the critical gaze of all-India Muslim political organizations. The catalyst was the revised Wakf Act of that year, which was advanced by a lawyer associated with the Muslim League, Abd al-Qasim. His motive was not to interfere with the rights of *mutawallis* or trustees but rather to compile a register of *awqāf* and supply accounts of expenditure.[13] The process of assembling accounts was elaborate: the provisions of the bill demanded that *mutawallis* furnish evidence of the endowment's annual income and expenditure, as well as the revenue it paid to the government and the salary of the *mutawalli*. In areas where the Wakf Act was enforced, such as the United Provinces, it was said that Muslims had been able to obtain some Rs. 4 million in one year "for the educational and economic advancement of the community."[14] This figure was certainly spurious, but its enormity likely assured many Indian Muslim activists that greater control of *awqāf* would result in mass Muslim economic prosperity.

Unsurprisingly, the mainline Bohra *jamaats* saw the Wakf Act as an explicit violation of their community privileges and fiercely resisted this attempt to interfere with privately administered endowments. The ensuing struggle for proprietary control of *jamaat* property guaranteed renewed conflict between the *dai* and the dissidents. This was signaled toward the conclusion of negotiations over the Wakf Act, when Shafaat Ahmad Khan, a delegate of the Muslim League, called upon the provincial governments to enforce the act. The Sulaimani Bohra Faiz Tayyibji seconded it, but a certain Daudi Bohra named Akbar Ali Muhsin argued that his own community of Bohras objected to the act. As a rejoinder, several other delegates maintained that the Bohras, as Muslims, must be included.[15] They knew that the bill would lack any force if individual Muslim communities were able to opt out—and that an enormous amount of capital would be forfeited if a community as commercially successful as the Bohras did not comply. Notwithstanding these objections, the bill was signed into law with the opt-out clause included.

Almost immediately, the dissident Bohra *jamaat* argued that the entire "Bohra community" had greeted the bill with enthusiasm but that the government had been strong-armed into inserting the exemption clause by certain factors from the mainline *jamaat*.[16] The dissidents even sent a petition to the governor of Bombay, arguing that when the league passed its resolution unanimously there were some 150 Bohras in the room, none of whom objected.[17] They then laid the blame firmly on the *dai*, claiming that in recent decades he had acquired more than six hundred mosques and sixty *gullas*. From 1918 onward, they added, he had also acquired numerous charitable properties and institutions belonging to individuals in the community through coercive means. Moreover, in 1924, the *dai* acquired trusteeship of the Faiż-i Ḥussainī, the institution that managed Bohra pilgrimage to the shrine cities of Iraq—which also happened to be one of the largest Muslim trusts on the subcontinent.[18] Beyond this the *dai* received sizable contributions from the faithful. One report enumerated just how many taxes the eighty to eight-five thousand Bohras were expected to pay to the *jamaat: silah* (reserved for the imam alone), *fiṭra* (a kind of poll tax levied per head every year), *ḥaqq al-nafs* (a death duty), *sabīl* (annual tax on business at rate of ¼ to 1 percent), and *zakat* (compulsory Islamic charitable tax). Moreover, the various Bohra *gullas* in the shrines of Western India were community treasuries, with the *gulla* of Shahid Faqir al-Din at Galya Kote in Dongarpore receiving an annual contribution of Rs. 150,000.[19]

Amid the agitation over the Wakf Act, another dispute called the Burhanpur Dargah Case—in which the affiliates of a dissident Bohra school founded in Burhanpur were excommunicated by the *dai*—made it into the colonial courts in 1925.[20] The dissident *jamaat* members in Burhanpur were vocal advocates for the application of the Wakf Act to Bohra endowments.[21] In a pamphlet published in Burhanpur, the dissenters attempted to justify their program. They noted that the government of Bombay had initially applied the Mussalman Wakf Act of 1923 to the entire presidency and Sindh. However, as the dissidents continued, the Bohras were held exempt from the act "for a period of three years or pending further orders." This was done out of deference to what the government called the "Bohra intelligentsia." The dissenters lampooned the application of this term to the mainline *jamaat,* for in their mind the mainline position was endorsed only by the "mullaji" (the *dai*), who had compelled his followers to oppose the Wakf Act by threatening them with excommunication.

The dissenters then noted the same irony that Justice Marten had acknowledged in the Chandabhai Gulla Case: it was impossible to test the Bohra community's views given the *dai*'s power of excommunication. In pursuing their program, the dissenters added, they also exposed themselves to the possibility of murder. Their fears were corroborated by contemporary attacks by a few mainline Bohras on the Bohra dissidents Ibrahim Pirbhai and Seth Tayyibbhai Thanawalla, as well as the disinterment of Mrs. Alibhai, the widow of Sir Adamji Pirbhai.[22] There is no evidence the *dai* ordered these attacks, but they were in keeping with assaults made by Ismaili Khojas in earlier decades against dissident Khojas, which led to much finger-pointing against the Agha Khans.

Even in exempting the Bohra community from the Wakf Act of 1923, the Bombay government tried to guarantee a settlement wherein the *dai* was still accountable in his capacity as trustee and the rights of community members protected. To the dissenters this was hardly sufficient, and they maintained that the government threatened to harm future generations of Bohras and all beneficiaries of the fruits of *awqāf*, leaving them "on a worse footing than [their] other brother Mohammaden beneficiaries."[23] The dissenters also weaponized their knowledge of Bohra law against the Legislative Council's contention that the Wakf Act violated "the Bohra religion." This, they asserted, was a gross violation of the *awqāf* rules laid out the most hallowed Bohra legal texts, the *Dā'īm al-Islām* and the *Sharh al-Akhbār*, both written by the tenth-century Ismaili jurist Qadi al-Numan, the most hallowed scholar in the Bohra juridical tradition. According to the dissidents, both works contained a *waqf* deed from Ali Abu Talib which contradicted the legislative council's assertions. "There is not a word in the whole Waqf Deed to say that it should be under the management of the religious Head," the dissenters exclaimed, "or that the Trustee should not render accounts or should dispose of the income at his discretion."[24]

According to the dissidents, the act thus fully conformed with the prevailing laws of *awqāf* propounded by the leading medieval Ismaili jurists. The *dai*'s smoke-and-mirrors game was so successful because he had managed to snuff out "religious educational activity in the community," notably by closing Bohra-run religious schools in Surat. This permitted him to advance religious tenets without any precedent in the community. Moreover, recent *waqf* deeds executed in the community showed that the *dai* continued to violate the rulings in the Chandabhai Gulla Case: first, he asserted that he was beholden to no person in the community, and second, that any person requesting to see accounts of any *awqāf* was committing a sin.[25] The dissenters thus accused the *dai* of violating colonial law, classical Ismaili law, and Anglo-Muhammadan personal law all in one fell swoop.

Even if the Bohra dissidents garnered the sympathies of many Indian Muslim activists in their attempts to subordinate Bohra *awqāf* to all-India Muslim legislative enactments and supervisory institutions, not all Indian Muslims rallied to their cause. In truth, the *dai* had no shortage of defenders. An Urdu treatise, *Bohra Qaum aur Waqf Akṭ* (The Bohra Community and the Wakf Act) defended the mainline Bohra *jamaat*'s exclusive proprietary title over all community endowments against the proponents of the

Wakf Act. In the foreword to the text, the author—who cryptically identified himself as "a fair Muslim"—asserted that the proper organization of *awqāf* was among the most pressing current issues facing Muslims. Pulling from various rulings propounded by both Shiʿi and Sunni scholars concerning *awqāf*, the author maintained that it was high time for the Bohras to do their religious duty and use their endowments for the benefit of all Muslims. Two arguments in the text were of special importance. First, the author admitted that the Bohras had the best-organized *awqāf* in India. Second, the author—and the various vernacular newspaper articles he cited—stressed that the Indian government's actions represented a risk to Muslim proprietorship over all *awqāf*. This was perhaps intended as a warning to those Muslims who saw the subordination of *awqāf* to administrative oversight as a panacea for Muslim economic woes. Outlining his own position, he admitted that the Bohra *jamaat* possessed many beliefs that he rejected but nonetheless acknowledged that they were faithful upholders of Islamic law.[26]

The Urdu poet Allama Simab Akbarabadi also turned his attention to the Bohras and the Wakf Act. Akbarabadi had observed Bohra communities across India and was convinced that their "progress and rise" was no accident. "I have seen," he wrote, "that this *jamaat* has taken a line of action in education, religion, lifestyle, and politics. And having put it in view, all of them live according to it. And this is the cause of their progress."[27] Throughout the treatise, Akbarabadi maintained that among all the Muslims of India, the best-managed *awqāf* belonged to the Bohras, who purportedly used their revenues only for education, the construction of mosques, and the conservation of graveyards. He even went so far as to impugn those dissident Bohras who sought to involve the government in managing Bohra *awqāf*.

For Akbarabadi, the Bohra example offered a mirror for evaluating *awqāf* management among other Muslims. Akbarabadi admitted most *awqāf* in India were in an "unspeakable" state and mutawallis mistakenly understood *awqāf* assets to be their own. Such *awqāf* would benefit from government supervision, even if that meant a new kind of colonial interference in Muslim affairs. However, he argued, extending this interference to well-managed Bohra endowments was unacceptable. Perhaps anticipating the accusation that he had shown bias in favor of any one *jamaat*, he shot back, "Today the condition of the Muslims of India is destitute on account of manifold conflicts and hypocrisy. . . . The Bohra community, whose economic, moral, religious, and secular progress stands above and beyond all other Muslims of India today, have been caught up in the tumult and division of the same kind by the hands of animus and personal gain and their greatness will endure a loss."[28] In closing, Akbarabadi bid the government to avoid a course that was so patently against the interests of the majority of the Bohras.

The government obliged, exempting the Bohras from the Wakf Acts until the end of the Raj. Even so, the struggle over endowments did not always play out in favor of the Bohra *dai*. In the case of Karachi's Hasani Academy, or Madressa Hassani Association, a formerly Bohra *jamaat* institution fended off the *dai*'s attempt to sequester it. It instead became an independent nondenominational entity, with its own students, teachers, and board of directors—the latter made up of Bohra dissidents and diverse Muslim and non-Muslim members of Karachi's elite circles. The Hasani Academy's origins lay in the 1890s, when it was founded as a Bohra madrasa by a leading Bohra merchant of Karachi named Alibhai Karimji. Over the next decades it was devoted to Bohra educational progress, opening a separate school for girls with a modest endowment. Another educational institution, the Karachi Academy Society, was incorporated under its auspices in 1926.[29]

In spite, or perhaps because of, their associations with the Bohra dissident movement, the two institutions boasted a cosmopolitan crowd, including Memon students from Calcutta and Parsi presidents. Into the 1930s, the academies became bastions of nonsectarian Sindhi nationalism but also were feted by a host of observers, from colonial educational inspectors to a delegation from Egypt's preeminent Sunni madrasa, Al-Azhar.[30] Beyond this, the two academies' alignment with Sindhi nationalism owed in large measure to the influence of Hatim Alavi, leader of the Bohra dissident *jamaat* and a onetime mayor of Karachi in the 1930s. Alavi was indefatigable in his campaign against the *dai* and what he and his movement branded, in Protestant echoes, as the Bohra "priestly class." From the Hasani Academy his Gujarati newspaper, *Āge Kadama* (Step Forward) pored invective on the mainline Bohra *jamaat*. The paper also became a leading advocate for the reform of women's rights in the Bohra *jamaat*. The growing subscribers to *Āge Kadama* signaled that the Bohra dissident *jamaat* was not about to fall into obscurity like the Mahdi Baghwalas. For although the vast majority of Bohras remained loyal to the *dai* after the Chandabhai Galla Case, the Hasani Academy found no shortage of funding from Bohra merchant princes who had seceded—whether voluntarily or by virtue of excommunication—from the mainline *jamaat*. Donations tabulated in academy literature catalog contributions from Bohras in Kenya, La Réunion, Mauritius, Madagascar, South Africa, Tanganyika, Uganda, and Zanzibar.[31]

Few matched the donations dispatched by the Bohra merchant magnate of Mauritius, Jivanji Karimji Jivanji Mauricewala. Jivanji's business, Currimjee, founded in 1890, still exists today. He himself served on the academy's board of trustees for several years. Academy literature from the 1930s featured full-page photo spreads of Jivanji, as well as images of other Bohra merchants whose capital sustained the two institutions.[32] The academies were lucky to have the support of Bohra merchant princes because the *dai*, Tahir Saif al-Din, led an active campaign to boycott them. In 1931 the *dai* even filed a court case in a bid to wrest the Hasani Academy and Karachi Academy Society away from the dissidents.[33] Though it was dismissed at costs, local mainline Bohras continued to agitate against these institutions well into the 1940s, when the showdown between the *dai* and the Bohra dissidents grew still more intense. As for the Hasani Academy, its prominence in late colonial Karachi only presaged the influence that Gujarati Muslim–affiliated institutions would exert over the city in the postcolonial period.

For all the criticisms, the *dai*'s extended pilgrimage in the Middle East in the mid-1930s marked something of a victory tour for Tahir Saif al-Din and his *jamaat*, despite the tribulations of the past decade. Above all, the pilgrimage signaled the successful transposition of the Bohra *jamaat*'s corporate institutions into the leading cities of Shiʿi and Sunni Islam, and a triumphant return of the *dais* to the Middle East after their permanent departure from Yemen in the sixteenth century. A spate of Bohra texts in Gujarati commemorating the journey had substantial propaganda value in publicizing this fact,[34] as did the photographs of Tahir Saif al-Din's meetings with Muslim luminaries such as Hajj Amin al-Hussaini, the controversial Palestinian mufti (see figure 6.1). These underscored that, for all the litigation endured by the *dai* in the interwar period, *jamaat* trusts had dramatically increased the infrastructural capacity of the *jamaat* and securely fastened the *dai*'s place at the apex of it. They had also made him into one of the most prominent interwar Muslim religious figures in the Middle East and South Asia. The capacity of internal rivalries to both dissipate and strengthen community cohesion—and the reliance on outsiders to solidify competing claims to authority—was one of the key paradoxes of corporate Islam.

FIGURE 6.1 An image of the Bohra *dai*, Tahir Saif al-Din (bespectacled at center) during his mid-1930s pilgrimage in the Middle East. Standing to his left is Hajj Amin al-Hussaini, the Palestinian mufti, and other members of the Supreme Muslim Council of Palestine. The honor accorded to the *dai* by other Muslims in India and elsewhere contrasted with the internal criticism arising from within his own *jamaat*. Reproduced from *Saif o Burhan* 19, no. 1 (1937), between pages 24 and 25.

Memon Trusts and the Elusive Memon Bank

Memon trusts in the interwar period did not attract the same magnitude of attention as their Bohra equivalents, not least because a Memon dissident movement never materialized. The conciliar structure of the Memon *jamaats,* so much more diffuse than the apex cleric model of the Bohras and Ismaili Khojas, preempted that possibility. That did not mean the community sidestepped a confrontation over their trusts. Among the Memons the concerns were twofold: how to maintain community trusts in settings throughout the diaspora shared with other Sunnis, and how to unlock the capital nested in trusts. Some of these disputes were carryovers from those prewar scuffles covered in chapter 3. As ever, the Memons' deep engagement with rival Sunni movements accelerated the pace of conflict. But the years of the First World War brought a further acceleration of these processes, not least in Mauritius, already a hotbed of Memon religious conflicts from the late nineteenth century onward. The entrance of the Ahmadiyya movement into Mauritius around the time of the First World War only intensified intra-Memon competition for pious endowments and the capital sheltered within it.

The Ahmadiyya movement took its name from Mirza Ghulam Ahmad (d. 1908), a Punjabi Muslim who claimed to be the long-awaited Mahdi, or messiah. With amazing swiftness from the moment he proclaimed himself messiah in 1889, Mirza Ghulam Ahmad gained a devout following among Punjabi Muslims of all classes. Judging from the pages of the Ahmadi newspaper *Al-Ḥākam* (The Judge) the identities of these donors to the Ahmadiyya cause included accountants, merchants, court inspectors, headmasters, and post office workers—in other words, middle-class Muslim professionals who had benefited from Punjab's growth over the previous decades.[35] They donated money to construct Ahmadi primary schools, and eventually set up funds for an Ahmadi college, helping to transform the movement into a group with a *jamaat*-based structure similar to the Gujarati Muslim commercial castes. Even if Mirza Ghulam Ahmad gained legions of followers, his claims elicited caustic polemics from Shiʿi and Sunni religious scholars, not least because the Ahmadiyya movement rejected much of the Islamic legal tradition, including the four Sunni *madhahib* (legal schools).[36] Rejection of the legal tradition was not singular to the Ahmadiyya movement, but what really provoked opposition to it were the messianic claims of Mirza

Ghulam Ahmad, which challenged not only the foundations of Islamic eschatology but also the finality of Muhammad's prophethood.

As such, when Ahmadiyya missionaries began traveling throughout the Indian Ocean and winning converts to the cause, there was bound to be controversy in local Muslim communities. Long beset by conflicts colored by the rivalries of the Sunni *masālik* (orientations), the entrance of the Ahmadiyya into intra-Memon disputes added fuel to the fire. The members of one Memon commercial firm, Atchia Brothers & Co., which adopted Ahmadi Islam during the years of the First World War, even had a suit brought against it by other Indian Hanafis over the right of an Ahmadi imam to lead prayers in the Rose Hill Mosque.[37] The Atchia Brothers & Co. held several commercial concerns at Rose Hill, including the Mauritius Hydro Electric Co., which powered several areas of the island. In addition to this, they also owned the New Mill Aloe Fibre Factory.[38] As he described in the case, Ahmad Ibrahim Atchia (who went by the name Major) had, along with his father, plowed a large amount of his own money into the mosque at Rose Hill. Like the other Ahmadis on the island, he had embraced what he called the Ahmadiyya *silsilah* (lineage) after reading Ahmadi works that had been sent to Mauritius, and then invited a certain Ghulam Muhammad to the island to spread the faith.[39]

The Ahmadiyya's entry soon caused conflict at the Rose Hill Mosque, and when conflicts among local Memons found no resolution, matters reached the local court. Dozens of local Muslim merchants were quizzed about the case, and their answers to the lawyers' line of questioning are revealing of the tensions between rival Sunni religious institutions and the Memon commercial factors who underwrote them. Once again, accounting was at the center of the case, and Atchia employed several European firms to make a valuation of the mosque's premises, and handed over his own accounts of the mosque for the court's perusal. The land upon which the mosque was built was valued at Rs 20,000, of which Rs 5,000 was collected by subscription, with the remaining balance coming from the partners of the Atchia firm. According to the court report, the Hanafi plaintiffs had contributed nothing to the purchase of the land nor to the construction of buildings on the site, but they protested in turn that the original mosque had been constructed in 1863 by one Ismail Jiva with collections made among the Muslim community. The Hanafis had further argued that, on account of Mirza Ghulam Ahmad's claims, the Ahmadiyya were not proper Muslims.

In reply, the Ahmadi Memon defendants argued that they were "members of the Ahmadi Movement (*Silsilah*) of the Hanafi school of thought (*Mazhab*) of the Sunni sect (*Firkah*) of the Muhammadan religion (*Din*)," and thus had every right to use the mosque. The attempt to portray the Ahmadiyya as a Sufi order and part of the Hanafi *madhhab* was an interesting interpretation. Initially, the Hanafis, in order to avoid fighting with the Ahmadiyya, had constructed a *jamaat* of their own for prayers, but eventually fatwas came from India declaring the Ahmadis as non-Muslims, prompting an effort by the Hanafis of Rose Hill to reclaim the mosque.[40] After a protracted case that saw extensive hand-wringing among the judges over whether Ahmadi Islam constituted "orthodox" Islam, the local Hanafi Memons were accorded ownership of the mosque. Regardless of their defeat, the Ahmadiyya movement set down deep roots in Mauritius, with capital from sympathetic members of Memon *jamaats* ensuring its expansion into a significant force in the island's religious economy to this day.

The Rose Hill Case in Mauritius signaled a broader showdown between Memons and other Sunni communities throughout the Indian Ocean region over the management of trusts. An excellent illustration comes from the writings of the Indian Muslim nationalist and journalist Maulana Abu al-Kalam Azad, one of the towering intellectual figures of South Asian Islam in the twentieth century, a complex and at times contradictory man.[41] He rejected the sectarian politics of the All-India Muslim League, staying in India after 1947. There, he became minister of education and worked diligently for Hindu-Muslim reconciliation. In the pages of his Urdu newspapers—*Al-Hilāl* (The Crescent) and later *Al-Balāgh* (The Message)—he pioneered an assertive, politically conscious form of Muslim vernacular journalism. In 1920 he published a full-length Urdu treatise titled *Faiṣla-i muqaddama-i Jāmaʿ Masjid Kalkata* (Decision in the Case of the Jama Masjid, Calcutta). It is not only unique among his collective writings but also a singular document in the context of the contemporary Indian Muslim debate over *awqāf*.[42]

A bastion of Memon influence from the mid-nineteenth century onward, the mosque and its accessory institutions became the source of two simultaneous legal spats in the 1910s. The first was between various Memon trustees, the second between Memon and non-Memon members of the congregation. In his treatise, Azad aimed to separate the management and financial resources of the mosque from the Memon *jamaat* without violating the sacred legal principles underpinning *awqāf:* according to nearly all interpretations of Islamic law, the proprietary rights of *awqāf* were inalienable and immemorial.

More specifically, Azad's treatise highlights the knotty issues involved in divorcing the accounts of Memon *jamaats* from religious institutions in which Memons had assumed an ownership stake and which provided services to Memons and non-Memons alike. But it also highlights the difficulties contemporary Indian Muslims faced in their bid to reform *awqāf* administration. How, for example, could one reform the management of *awqāf* without riding roughshod over the proprietary privileges of the trustees? If privately held *awqāf* had long been exemplars of Islamic notions of private property, figures like Azad were hard-pressed to find a compromise between that hallowed status and what they regarded as the justified demands of other Muslims to the economic resources contained within these institutions. Expropriation was not an option for those conscious of the Islamic intellectual tradition's sensitivity to the inviolability of property rights when it came to pious endowments.

Calcutta's Jama Masjid was located on an expansive site in the north of Calcutta; it was variably called Big Masjid or Nakhoda Masjid, the latter referring to the many Memon shipping captains (*nakhodas*) who used to ply their trade out of Bombay. Before 1856, two separate mosques had occupied the site, with an open space between them. The land was owned by a Hindu. The northern side was constructed by one Roshan Hakak, the southern by Munshi Hasan Ali. Roshan Hakak decided to appoint a five-member trust to administer the mosque he constructed, while Munshi Hasan Ali held the title to his own during his lifetime. On Roshan Hakak's death, trusteeship over the mosque passed to his daughter, Shams al-Nissa Begum.[43]

In 1856, Shams al-Nissa Begum aimed to acquire both the mosque at the north end and the intervening land to build a congregational mosque. She applied and was granted trusteeship over both mosques, which were now subordinated to a single trust. A colonial court drew up an official title deed, the oldest document pertaining to the mosque. The stipulations in the deed, among other points, clarified that if one of the four trustees of the new mosque changed religion or was absent from Calcutta for more than a year they would be deposed and a new person elected by popular acclaim. Azad interpreted these stipulations to mean that the trusteeship of the site had passed out of the hands of Shams al-Nissa into those of the trust.[44] Construction on the new mosque began in 1856, and the land between the two mosques was also purchased.

It was at this point that a Memon magnate, Haji Zakariya, entered the picture. He seems to have come to Calcutta from Bombay, though references in Azad's text also suggest that he and his business partner may have come from Medina. Since Haji Zakariya was also a leading member of the local Kachchhi Memon *jamaat* in Medina, he was ensured an interest in the *jamaat* and the mosque from 1856. The Memons, being the wealthiest Muslims in the northern part of the city, acquired an unmatched stake in the mosque. The name of Haji Zakariya became so tied up with the mosque that locals began calling it Masjid Zakariya. In this part of his narrative, and in his discussion of Memon *jamaat* practices, Azad seems less than enthusiastic about what he saw as the Kachchhi Memon *jamaat*'s tendency to close itself off from other Muslims in everything from marriages to burials.[45]

In 1873 Haji Zakariya died, and his son, Haji Nur Muhammad, was appointed as his successor. Unfortunately, Haji Zakariya's firm went belly up shortly after his death. Haji Nur Muhammad's financial status declined as a result. Yet, thanks to the expansion of the Memon Jamaat Fund in this period, which had substantial immovable and movable property in its coffers, he was able to offset his own personal losses while bringing the mosque to rack and ruin. To Azad, the Jama Masjid in Calcutta thus came to resemble all the other *awqāf* of India in its poor management and shoddy accounting. Under Haji Nur Muhammad, the de facto amalgamation of the mosque and the Memon Jamaat Fund, which had begun under Haki Zakaria's watch, was fully consummated.[46]

When senior members of the Kachchhi Memon *jamaat* discovered this unholy mixture of accounts from the mosque and the fund, they demanded that Haji Nur Muhammad share the account books with them. He refused on the pretext that the *jamaat* had no right to make such a request.[47] The *jamaat* filed a case against Haji Nur Muhammad in the High Court in 1907. Unfortunately, Azad does not explain whether the plaintiffs' objection extended to Haji Nur Muhammad's fusion of the Memon Jamaat Fund and the mosque—which seems unlikely—or was limited to his refusal to share the accounts. Such refusals had sparked many Memon court cases in the past, as earlier chapters have shown.

The 1907 case made clear that Haji Nur Muhammad had driven the Memon Jamaat Fund and the mosque into the ground. In turn, the court ordered an inspection of the accounts. But, according to Azad, since the plaintiffs in the case were not aware of the full history of the mosque and the trust, their case was deficient. Because their claims did not discuss the trust of Shams al-Nissa Begum, but only mentioned the Memon *jamaat* trust, Haji Nur Muhammad glimpsed an opportunity to invalidate the entire case. For that reason, the court ruled that the trustees of the mosque would only be appointed from the family of Haji Zakariya.[48] Though Haji Nur Muhammad had died in 1915, the trust had operated on this basis from 1907 until 1918, when the matter made it to the court yet again.

The catalyst of the 1918 case was a conflict between the trustees and the imam of the mosque. Azad first heard about the case when he returned to Calcutta in January 1920. There he was informed that both parties believed it to be against Islamic principles for a non-Muslim court to adjudicate a dispute pertaining to an Islamic legal issue. Thus, Azad was given the chance to hear the dispute himself, and to write a studied judgment of it in accordance with Islamic legal rulings.[49] This bypassing of the colonial courts was undoubtedly informed by the contemporary Khilafat and noncooperation movements. Nonetheless, the Memon trustees agreed to it—irrespective of the fact that private Muslim legal arbitration was more likely to threaten Memon corporate privileges than a colonial court system that had consistently upheld them.

In the end, Azad's ruling was highly nuanced, demonstrating his desire to protect the inviolability of *waqf*. For one, he concluded that the identity of the existing mosque trust was in accordance with Islamic law. However, he qualified this point by asserting that the defendants were misled in their belief that the mosque was built only by and for the Kachchhi Memon *jamaat*. Legally, the trustees could be from outside the *jamaat*. The defendants' declarations to this effect flatly contradicted the original title deed of Shams al-Nissa Begum, which stated that a trustee could be any member of the mosque's congregation, not merely an individual from a single *jamaat*.[50] He argued further that the plaintiffs were incorrect to have trustees chosen by vote of the general Muslim population, just as the 1907 case involving Haji Nur Muhammad was mistaken in its assertion that the trustee was to be chosen by Calcutta's Kachchhi Memon *jamaat*. Rather, the original document said simply that only the existing board of trustees had the capacity to elect a new trustee.

Even if he acknowledged that the Memon monopoly over the mosque had always been less than ideal, Azad recognized that Haji Nur Muhammad had performed many services on behalf of the wider congregation in accordance with Islamic legal principles of *maṣlaḥa* (the common good). Therefore, Azad saw no legal means upon which to break up the trust or to make the trustees non-Memons. Seemingly contradicting his portrait of Haji Nur Muhammad's ungainly management, Azad maintained that, by contrast with so many shabbily administered mosques, funds, and trusts in India, Calcutta's Jama Masjid had progressed substantially over the past fifty years under the oversight of the Memon *jamaat*.[51]

When compared to the dissident Bohra *jamaat*'s agitation against the *dai*, Azad's sophisticated handling of the Jama Masjid case was not matched by most other Indian Muslim activists who attempted *awqāf* reform in this period. In one stroke he had sought to uphold Islamic laws of trusteeship, protect Memon corporate privileges, and keep the colonial state out of Muslim internal affairs. The Bohra dissidents had exemplified a contrary model, in which the champions of all-India Muslim *awqāf* reform invoked colonial intervention and outright expropriation of malfeasant trustees. While members of Calcutta's Memon *jamaat* deliberately eschewed the colonial courts in the Jama Masjid dispute, other Memon *jamaats* continued to prioritize the colonial state in their campaigns for legal reform—none more so than Bombay's Kachchhi Memon *jamaat*. Although they declared that they had the unanimous support of the *jamaat*, advocates for the Kachchhi Memons' reclassification as full Muslims before the law ran into difficulties: many Memon constituents, it turned out, clung to the venerable formulas of custom and law. That story will be examined in chapter 7.

In the meantime, as Memon trusts became politicized in the years after the war, Memon communities explored how to combine the economic resources of Memon *jamaat* trusts in a manner conducive to alleviating unemployment and poverty. This dilemma constituted a refrain at a series of annual all-India Memon conferences in the mid-1930s. Diverse proposals were suggested, including a treasury fund modeled on the *bait al-mal* of classical Islam. Although delegates occasionally advocated for the creation of a Memon bank, much more enthusiasm was exhibited toward suggestions for other thrift institutions. In that sense, the continued growth of thrifts sheltered within the *jamaat* compounded the problem of Muslim underrepresentation in banking. Another potential hand brake on the development of Memon-owned banks was the documented practice among some Memons of depositing *awqāf*-based capital in European exchange banks in the port cities of the subcontinent. Interlinking Memon *awqāf* with exchange banks perhaps made *awqāf* capital more liquid and easier to employ for community welfare and business interests. Yet given the widespread disapproval among Islamic legal authorities, the practice was also fraught with risk. Nevertheless, it was one of the many strategies that Memons employed to transform the *awqāf*'s nominally "inert" capital into productive, self-reproducing capital.

Throughout the 1920s and 1930s, numerous Indian Muslims sought alternative means of integrating Muslims into the banking business than *zakat* or *awqāf* reform. Tufail Ahmad, the editor of the newspaper *Sūdmand* (Profitable), had bitterly complained for years about the sorry economic condition of Muslims. According to Ahmad, the only real option was for Muslims to embrace interest banking. Like Dilwar Hussain, the Bengali Islamic modernist discussed in chapter 2, Ahmad was principally concerned about a perceived Hindu-Muslim wealth gap. Like those surveyed earlier in this chapter, he partially blamed this on the poor management of Muslim institutions.[52] But his broader goal—engineering a banking revolution among Muslims—pointed to what he saw as the dual culprits of Muslim penury: Muslim aversion toward accepting financial interest, and the usurious interest rates charged by Hindu moneylenders.

Seth Harun Jafar, a prominent Memon lawyer, was among those who sought to give Ahmad's defense of Muslim interest transactions added legitimacy.[53] As recounted in *Sūdmand,* Jafar had submitted a petition to the government of India's council of state in March 1925 asking that interest collected from government savings bank accounts be dispatched to Aligarh Muslim University for the benefit of Muslim students. Jafar's recommendation was endorsed by the scholars associated with the Jamāʿat-i ʿUlamāʾ-i Hind (JUH; Society of Indian Muslim Religious Scholars), whose official newspaper originally printed the piece that appeared in *Sūdmand.* They deemed the motion to be in complete conformity with sharia, despite acknowledging that most scholars in India regarded bank interest as haram. In issue upon issue of his newspaper, Ahmed criticized the opinions of most ulama toward bank interest. Yet here he enthusiastically reprinted the decision of the JUH, further stressing that the funds from Muslim *awqāf* and schools should be invested in government promissory notes.

Other strategies existed to circumvent the paucity of Muslim-owned banks. The transfer of *awqāf* capital into the coffers of banks was one way to turn inert trust capital into interest-bearing capital. Since the practice of setting up a bank account for a fund trustee was common practice among the Gujarati Muslim commercial castes, the practice had assumed an aura of legitimacy. In time, however, depositing *awqāf* and mosque assets into banks engendered significant unease among many Muslim populations. Moral reservations alone did not inspire this hesitation; the frequency of bank failures in contemporary India, and indeed the world over, played a part as well.

Doubts concerning the moral legitimacy of such actions are best glimpsed in the many requests for legal clarification sent by Memons and other Muslims to Muslim religious scholars in the interwar period. In 1924, for example, Muhammad Kifayat Allah—a graduate of the Darul Uloom Deoband seminary and president of JUH from 1919 to 1942—received a question from the trustees of the Surti Memon mosque in Rangoon. They wished to know whether it was legally acceptable to deposit mosque funds in a bank and accept interest on the principal. The Surti Memons of Burma had cultivated a close relationship with Deobandi scholars in the years before the First World War, and one of their interwar appeals to Kifayat Allah reflects this trend:

> As it is believed among Muslims that assuming the safekeeping [of funds] was strenuous, the rupees of Surti Masjid Rangoon are stored in a government bank (with the intention of safeguarding it, not to obtain interest). By such means, in spite of growing to around 1 lakh [100,000] rupees, according to the bank's own rules, the fixed interest that must be paid to the masjid each year totals 3[,000] to 4,000 rupees per month. However, the trustees of the mosque, detecting the interest, never like to take the rupees. Still, the government bank always spends it in carrying out its own intention and designs. Therefore, the question is this: while it is certain that non-Muslims spend this relinquished money on purposes contrary to the principles of Islam, and although these people call this money by the name of interest [*sūd*], the trustees of the masjid, however, do not believe this to be interest, rather imagining it to fall under the purview of permissible gifts. They collect it and the servants and notables of the aforementioned mosque and so forth spend [it] on every labor and activity.

> Is this permitted according to the law or not? Again, the request is that which was made plain in the question submitted above; that is to say, the issue is not whether the assumption of safekeeping funds is arduous. Rather [the issues concerns] the aforementioned affair of the mosque, [and compliance with] the government decree: are the trustees of the masjid forced to collect the interest at the bank in excess of 1,000 rupees?

This was Kifayat Allah's answer to the quandary:

> Obtaining such large profit by means of trusting the government bank and taking in excess of the value of the money is not permissible. It is incumbent for Muslims to not have government connections of this type, thus let them not obtain more than the assistance and benefit. However, if there is any compulsion (such as was made clear at the end of the question) then they must strive completely to deny this coercion and, until the cessation of it, that money they obtain, and which the bank takes interest on, the leaders of the mosque must spend this on poor and needy Muslims according to need and with circumspection.[54]

As with any fatwa, this was merely a suggestion, bereft of coercive power. Given their commercial prominence in Rangoon until the Second World War, it is likely that the overseers of the Surti Memon masjid kept their account at the local bank open, concluding that it was better to use the interest funds accrued for the benefits of charity rather than to forfeit them entirely. It also bears emphasizing that Kifayat Allah's position here differed from that of JUH in the case of Seth Harun Jafar, when they had endorsed his appeal to the council of state to forward interest funds on savings bank accounts to Aligarh Muslim University.

Perhaps due to the insufficient legitimacy of Muslim-owned banks, Memon conferences in the 1930s sought to mitigate the economic difficulties of the *jamaats* by bolstering community thrifts—such as the Memon Relief Fund and the Memon Welfare Society—and reforming *awqāf.* In one telling instance, Seth Haji Abd Allah Harun, Karachi's Memon magnate, lamented that the trading position of the Kachchhi Memons especially had fallen into decline. Their place had been partially filled by small contingents of Halai Memons, but this was cold comfort. To arrest the decline, Harun advocated that members of the Memon *jamaats* establish limited companies, a preferable alternative to the humbler proprietary firms operated by most Memon entrepreneurs. Yet Harun also spoke at length about the management of *jamaat* pious endowments, which he, in keeping with the times, regarded as an untapped source of Muslim capital. Remarking on his monthlong stay in Bombay as a member of the Hajj Inquiry Committee in 1929, Harun reckoned that property valued at Rs. 20 million was dispersed throughout ninety-seven Kachchhi Memon trusts. Factoring in the trusts owned by Halai Memons in Calcutta, Karachi, Kathiawar, and Madras, Harun estimated that Rs. 30 million of capital was submerged in Memon trusts.[55]

With so much capital at their disposal, Harun asked, "why has it proven so difficult to travel on the path of community betterment?" These numbers cannot be verified, and undoubtedly were exaggerated. Yet Harun's comments reflect a persistent unease about the institutional weaknesses of *awqāf* and the dormant capital they contained. While Harun believed that *awqāf* required better management, he also recognized that the Memon *jamaat* had largely lost the power to manage its own trusts, presumably to the supervisory authorities designated in the various Wakf Acts, "for the benefit of our community and all Muslims."[56] Despite the acts, into the 1930s individual sites in the Memon diaspora showed wide inconsistencies in *awqāf* administration.

While Harun had failed to organize a committee in Bombay for the management of *awqāf*, members of the Memon *jamaat* in Karachi established a registered association that combined the income of multiple trusts and deducted their costs from a common fund. Harun suggested that other *jamaats* follow the example of the Memon trusts in Karachi. But he also compared the general Memon situation to that of the Parsis in Bombay, who, although fewer in number than the Memons, had trusts that were excellently managed. "Taking the example of our Parsi brothers," he continued, "the Memon community would be better off if it tried to operate our own trusts for the benefit of the collective." Doing so required compiling an exhaustive list of Memon *awqāf*, which Harun hoped to see published for wider consumption. The Memon *jamaat* in Karachi had already compiled such a work, he noted, complete with annual expenditure. Perhaps unmindful of how divisive bookkeeping had proven to be in the Memon diaspora in previous decades, Harun encouraged those who wished to consult the work to travel to the residence of a Memon *sethia* on Karachi's Napier Road for a glimpse.[57]

Harun was a minority voice at the conference in one regard: his declaration that Memons had to establish more banks. A few years earlier, he had participated in the Banking Inquiry Commission, where he lamented both the poor representation of Indians in the country's banking sector and the eccentricities of credit allocation.[58] At one session of the conference, Harun declared that institutions like banks and insurance companies were "inevitable" and a pillar in the world of trade. Expressing the disquietude over the exodus of Muslim capital out of the community, Harun declared, "How much convenience would be saved by us; moreover, how much labor it takes to produce new merchants in the community [when] lakhs of rupees of the community keep falling away hither and thither! Because the money of hundreds of brothers and widows is thrown away in all sorts of places, year by year they fall into loss, or [the money] is misappropriated; how much would be saved!" Harun added that, if there was a Memon bank, members of the community would never again have to watch helplessly as their capital was eroded by high rates of interest. But in the end, few heeded his pleas for a Memon bank.[59] Apart from Pakistan's Muslim Commercial Bank established in 1947 by the Memon industrialist Adamji Haji Daud, a Memon-owned bank was not founded until 1965 in Bombay.[60]

Discrepancies in the Management of Khoja Trusts

In line with the broader history charted in Part II of this book, Ismaili and Twelver contests over trusts were inflected by those wider dilemmas which beset corporate Islam in this period, principally the push and pull between Bohra, Khoja, and Memon allegiance to the colonial government and to Indian Muslim nationalist movements, and the attempt to clarify the place of Gujarati Muslim corporate groups in the larger Indian Muslim political nation. Underpinning this was a constant juxtaposition of Khoja reforms with those made by other Muslims. An excerpt from a 1931 report drawn up by the Mussalman Wakf Committee relayed this dynamic well:

> The Wakfs of the Sunni and Isna Ashari [Twelver] Khojas are also well managed but the same cannot be said with regard to the Wakfs of the Ismaili Khojas who, though not exempted from the Mussalman Wakf Act, do not render their accounts to the Small Causes Court. This is the reason why many trusts amongst the Ismaili Khojas are not even known to the general public. From the evidence of a Khoja gentleman, it appears that several big trusts were created by Ismaili Khoja donors for the benefit of their Jamat but now there is no trace of such trusts nor of their accounts. He cited the instance of a Wakf

> which was intended for the benefit of the poor widows of the Ismaili Khoja Jamat. There is no trace of that fund, since the Mussalman Wakf Act came into force.[61]

The two *Hindi Punch* cartoons bemoaning the state of Khoja trusts (see chapter 4) had revealed that from the late nineteenth century onward, Khojas and other commentators were conscious of the inert capital tied up in community thrifts. But if the excerpt from the report above is any indication, then matters had improved little over the subsequent three decades. Although many Ismaili Khojas were champions of the Wakf Acts, those same figures presided over various trusts that they were reluctant to subject to outside inspection. In truth, the 1920s and 1930s witnessed extensive internal battles among the Ismaili Khojas over the character of wealth in their communities. For the Twelver Khojas in particular, the active expansion of community trusts became a way of securing their *jamaats*' future. But even the Ismaili Khojas witnessed their fair share of disputes over trusts, often pitting the newly ascendant Ismaili Councils against excommunicated dissidents.

More than happy to renounce the Agha Khan III as apex cleric, from the First World War onward the leaders of the Twelver Khoja *jamaats* attempted with special aplomb to reorient their community's sacred authority and political compass away from the embodied authority of the Ismaili imam. The continued excommunication of entire cohorts of Ismaili Khojas, many possessed of sizable fortunes, considerably aided these efforts. So did the profusion of Twelver Khoja publications and institutions across the Indian Ocean region. One consequence was the ascent of a cohort of Twelver Khoja merchants-cum-politicians in Bombay and Karachi, who became bedrocks of conciliar authority in the Twelver Khoja *jamaats* at the turn of the twentieth century. These men founded various caste-centric institutions and published prolifically, helping to knit together widely dispersed Twelver Khoja *jamaats*. Nonetheless, the diffuse character of the conciliar model ensured that Twelver Khoja *jamaats* did not coalesce around monolithic formulations of law and custom, remaining polyvalent in outline with no center of authority.

Having said that, the sacred sites of Shiʿi Islam in the Middle East supplied a fixed geographic point for the centering of widely scattered Twelver Khoja *jamaats*. The foundation of the Anjuman-i Faiż-i Panjatanī, which shepherded Twelver Khojas during their pilgrimage to the shrine cities of Iraq and Iran, was a momentous development in these years. The term *Panjatanī* invoked the five figures from the *ahl al-bayt* (the family of the Prophet Muhammad) revered by Shiʿis: the Prophet Muhammad, Ali, Fatima, Hassan, and Hussain. Founded in Bombay in 1912, this institution—in keeping with Twelver Khoja communal life generally—was managed by leading Twelver Khoja merchants in Basra, Bombay, and Karachi from its inception. Operating from its headquarters on Samuel Street in Bombay, it was registered as a trust in 1932 and expanded its services to the Hijaz, Iran, and Iraq.[62] The trust relied heavily on the support of Twelver Khoja business magnates such as E. A. Karim and Ismail Abd al-Karim Panju (senior partner of the firm Husein Abdulkarim Panju). Although a native son of Zanzibar, Panju migrated to Bombay during the First World War, where he built a diverse business portfolio. He later served as treasurer of the Anjuman-i Faiż-i Panjatanī in addition to being a director of Habib Bank Ltd., founded in 1941 by the Twelver Khoja Muhammad Habib, which later became the cornerstone of Pakistan's early commercial banking sector and was active in the Persian Gulf region from the 1950s onward.[63]

As for the Ismaili Khojas, *jamaat* trusts became sources of increasing infighting in these years. From 1918 onward these disputes dovetailed with a wave of agitation over the purported excesses of the Agha Khan III or, more typically, his officers. This recrimination against the living Ismaili imam reflected the deep dissatisfaction with the apex cleric model of religious authority in the Ismaili Khoja *jamaats* by the 1920s. The Agha Khan III's decision to stay in Europe for most of the interwar period did little to protect his image, producing a paradox in which the individual said to be the living, manifest imam was absent for long stretches. As a result, authority devolved de facto to *jamaat* council members in the diaspora—an expansion of the Agha Khans' long-standing policies of assigning powers of attorney to *jamaat* officials.[64] The Ismaili Khoja *jamaat* in Zanzibar had had a council from the late nineteenth century, but what existed now throughout the Ismaili Khoja diaspora was a much more generalized entity possessed of substantial powers at the local level.

The multiplication of these officers fostered a peculiar dynamic in the Ismaili Khoja *jamaats*. As the officers acquired authority, *jamaats* linked together by fealty to a nominal apex cleric now increasingly assumed a conciliar character. Assertive officers in the *jamaat* had the potential to foment cases of schism, just as new converts were being gained. One objection was that the officers of the Ismaili Khoja *jamaat* councils were improperly administering marriage rituals and inheritance rights. When the petitions of one *jamaat* member—who demanded his brother's property be transferred to him after the *jamaat* council took it into their custody—were repeatedly ignored, the aggrieved constituent published his correspondence with the *mukhi* (chief) and *kamadia* (accountant), which cast the two officers in a very unfavorable light.[65] Some Ismaili Khoja critics took matters one step further in the 1920s, openly condemning the Agha Khan III's exacting monetary demands on his followers and directly attacking his *jamaat* officers by name.

Devolution of authority to these council members ensured that Ismaili Khoja discontent was voiced with greater assertiveness than ever before. With the imam absent, it was easy to maintain, in a variation of the medieval trope about the king and his ministers, that the Agha Khan's officers were in fact to blame for corruption in the *jamaat*. This comes through clearly in the many polemics written by one Rahmat Allah Trijoriwala, who vehemently opposed what he saw as the regular fleecing of the Khoja community by grasping *mukhis*. He maintained that these *mukhis* had enacted a bid for power throughout the tenure of Agha Khan III, taking advantage of his youthful ascent to the imamate and his frequent sojourns to Britain. He deemed them serial harassers and bringers of ruin who had exploited the faithful from their leadership positions on various councils within the *jamaat*. It was his sad duty, Trijoriwala confessed, to bring their "self-serving work" to light. While undertaking these labors, he was ever careful to avoid impugning the name of the Agha Khan III, repeatedly declaring the imam's innocence.[66]

Although Trijoriwala cast aspersions on the members of Khoja *jamaats* as far afield as Kathiawar, Kenya, and Zanzibar, his scornful gaze fell most severely upon Varas Dahyabhai Velji, one of the leaders of the Ismaili Khoja *jamaat* in Poona. Born in 1870 in Kathiawar, Velji migrated to the western Indian city of Ahmednagar in 1888. Twenty years later he established a leather factory which had considerable success. In addition to serving on the local municipal council, he was appointed by the Agha Khan as a vizier for the southern districts and granted the title of *varas* (representative). Velji constructed several boarding houses in the area, but more infamously, he also published a rule book for Poona's Ismaili Khoja *jamaat* that drew the animus of Trijoriwala. Velji indeed had shown considerable boldness with the 1913 publication, which included some rather harsh statutes.[67] Trijoriwala did his utmost to censure the attempts by officials like Velji to promulgate local *jamaat* statutes without the direct consent of the Agha Khan III: "The religion of our community is one. Our leader is also just one. Then why are sundry Ismaili laws being worked out by Ismaili officers in this place or that for the ruination and harassment of the community?"[68]

Some Ismaili Khojas took on the Agha Khan III directly. Representative was a case heard between 1928 and 1929 in Karachi in which one Fakir Muhammad Nanji and his colleagues brought a suit against the Agha Khan III and the local members of the Ismaili *jamaat* council. The plaintiffs, who had recently been excommunicated, argued that a multitude of Khoja immovable properties in Karachi were "the subject of a trust created for public purposes of a charitable and religious nature in favour of the members of the Khoja community of Karachi" and the plaintiffs were unjustly barred from them. They further added that the Ismaili Council that had been created without the sanction of the community and its jurisdiction was therefore nonviable. The defendants countered with the tried-and-true line that all *jamaat* properties were vested in the Agha Khan III. The judge saw much merit in the plaintiffs' case, going as far as to argue that the case was not merely about remedying "a particular infringement of an individual right." Rather, it concerned the larger question of whether access to these properties was a "public right." In the end, the judge dismissed the case on a technicality (the case was not registered properly with the local collector). Even so, the case was crucial for two reasons. First, it established that the court had a right to interfere in *jamaat* excommunications provided the act of banishment violated "ordinary principles of justice."[69] Second, other portions of the judgment also maintained that the Agha Khan Case of 1866, which only concerned properties in Bombay, had no bearing on Khoja *jamaat* trusts in Sindh.

In turn, it was from Sindh that a disaffected group of dissident Ismaili Khojas (rather than breakaway Twelvers) emerged, constituting the kernel for the Khoja Reformers' Society. Karim Ghulam Ali, their head, published a series of polemics and an open letter to the imam himself around this time. Like the Bohra dissidents, the Khoja reformers repeatedly juxtaposed the Agha Khan III's life of splendor in Europe with the impoverished state of his followers. They credited the Agha Khan III with one achievement—the establishment of *jamaat* councils—but argued that these were simply a means for him to tighten his grip on the community. Like Trijoriwala, earlier in the decade, the signatories demanded to know who had the right to compose these rules. But unlike their excommunicated forebears, they held the Agha Khan III wholly responsible, citing various statutes from existing rule books to confirm his involvement in the legislation. Curiously, what the group resented was the Agha Khan III's wholesale seizure of the *jamaat*'s powers to remove council members. Predictably, they thus also condemned the hierarchy of accountants and collectors in the Khoja *jamaats*. Still more seriously, they accused the *jamaat* councils of "depriving heirs and dependants [*sic*] of their rightful inheritance" by ensuring that any property left to the Agha Khan in a will was speedily transferred to the imam.[70]

At a time when Indian Muslims were sponsoring various projects of *zakat* collection, Ghulam Ali contrasted *zakat*'s low 2.5 percent levy on voluntary contributions with the mandatory 50 percent purportedly paid by Ismaili Khojas in cash and kind to the imam. And while Indian nationalists since the late nineteenth century had been lamenting Britain's drain of wealth from India, Ghulam Ali spoke of the "heavy and continuous drain of wealth from the community" that was inimical to Khoja progress. Elsewhere the reformers demanded that the "commercial Jamait-khanas" be converted into mosques and that the Agha Khan III forfeit all pecuniary awards. While colonial legal commentators had maintained that the Ismaili Khoja *jamaat* was inseparable from the sovereignty of the Agha Khan, the *sarkar-sahib* (supreme leader), the reformers were adamant that rulemaking was "the indefensible right of the community as an autonomous body which alone is competant [*sic*] to govern itself and manage its own affairs; it being Ultra Vires of your highness to do so."[71] This vision of the *jamaats* as little republics acting as bulwarks against arbitrary executive power was a myth, but a potent one in the minds of self-designated reformers with a liberal education.

Despite the splash made by the Ismaili Khoja dissidents' open letter in English, their attacks on the Agha Khan III and the "missionaries" of the *jamaat* were far more strident in Gujarati. From Rajkot in Gujarat they published a remarkable journal titled *Khoja Jāgrati*, (Khoja Vigilance), the cartoons of which contrasted the high living of the Agha Khan III and the destitution of his followers (see, for example, figure 6.2).[72] Besides lampooning the leaders of the *jamaats* and highlighting the contrast between the poverty of the average Khoja and the Agha Khan III, they also used the journal as a

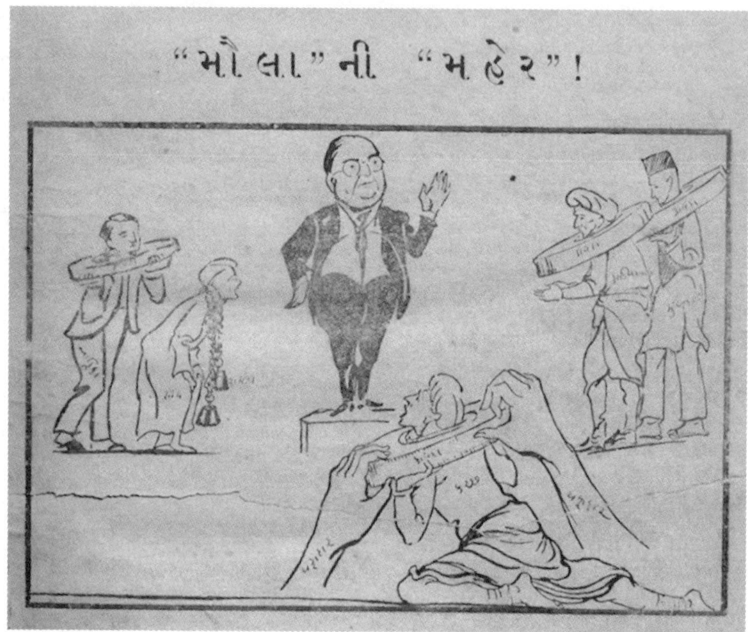

FIGURE 6.2 A cartoon from the Ismaili Khoja dissident newspaper *Khoja Jāgrati* (Khoja Vigilance). The image—the top caption of which reads “The mark of the Maula”—stresses the subjugation of Khoja *jamaats* in Africa, Bombay, Kachchh, Kathiawar, and Sindh by the Agha Khan III. Such polemical depictions elicited counter-salvos from mainline Ismaili Khoja authors. Reproduced from *Khoja Jāgrati*, 22 May 1934.

platform to engage the support of leading Khoja politicians, not least Jinnah and Rahim Allah.[73] Unsurprisingly, the reformers’ attack did not go unchallenged. A briskly delivered countersalvo came from one Nur Muhammad J. Mahatma. In order to respond to the accusations against the Agha Khan III, however, he first had to have Ghulam Ali’s open letter translated from English into Gujarati. (Only a small minority of Gujarati Muslim *jamaats* kept records in English—yet another reminder of the importance of integrating Gujarati sources into narratives of *jamaat* life.) Purportedly writing at the invitation of the Agha Khan III, Nur Muhammad ably defended the living imam, especially the monetary donations due to him by right. Like many mainline Bohras of this period, Nur Muhammad castigated the pretensions of the reformers to set up rival councils in the *jamaat*, maligning their lack of legal knowledge with great relish.[74] With capital and religion equally at stake, the discourse and practices surrounding "reform" was a key bone of contention in the wider struggle over corporate Islam in this period.

Notwithstanding these salvos against the Agha Khan III, non-Khoja Muslims occasionally put forward his name as a candidate for administering all-India Muslim *awqāf*. In one case he was suggested to head up the Muslim Mission Foundation, a trust with a prospective capital of Rs. 1 million whose object was the conversion of those Gandhi called Harijans (Dalits).[75] Perhaps for this reason, various Ismaili Khoja officers loyal to the Agha Khan III voiced support for the foundation of Muslim *zakat* and *bait al-mal* institutions.[76] Throughout the 1930s these schemes served as a vehicle for advancing a discourse of Islamic economics that was consciously anticapitalist, and even statist, in orientation, injecting another criteria in the Indian Muslim political landscape for weighing the merits and defects of corporate Islam.

* * *

The last decade and a half of colonial rule in South Asia supplied ample cause for the renegotiation of the Gujarati Muslim commercial castes' middle power vis-à-vis Hindus, other Muslims, and the colonial state. This was apparent both in the realm of business and law. In many respects, Gujarati Muslim business was pulled in opposite directions, between sectarian and cosmopolitan nationalism, between cooperation with international firms and a resort to imperial protectionism. Despite this, very little is known about the role of Indian Muslim business in Indian politics during the Raj's twilight years. While historians have made an illuminating initial foray into the subject, no study of interwar Indian Muslim business exists on a scale equivalent to the pioneering work on business and the Indian National Congress.[77]

Although the all-India Muslim League did not immediately garner the support of many leading Muslim merchants, the growth of Muslim-specific institutions such as banks, chambers of commerce, and cooperatives from the early 1930s onward supplied a forum for the articulation of Muslim-specific economic goals. In turn, these institutions transformed the diffuse idea of a Hindu-Muslim wealth gap into an explicit program. In an age in which Muslim economic actors had to negotiate the currents of confrontational nationalism, economic protectionism, and legislative homogenization, there were bound to be lasting implications for Indian business. And with Muslim businesses forced to declare for one political ideology or another, the Gujarati Muslim commercial castes were also increasingly hemmed in by the demands of new all-India Muslim religious and political institutions.

Just as the rules of the game governing business were rewritten thanks to the rise of a new breed of Muslim politics, Islamic law in the British Empire saw its own recasting. The primary force propelling the transformation of the legal underpinnings was a bid by Muslim activists of various stripes to reduce the remit of legal exceptionalism and to create a universal law code for all Muslims in British India. In theory, what this entailed was the dissolution of Bohra, Khoja, and Memon peculiarities—of corporate Islam in the round—into a larger Muslim melting pot. In the end, no melting pot materialized, but the cauldron of internal discord in the *jamaats* certainly was stirred, with explosive consequences in the final years of empire.

The *Jamaats* and the End of the Raj

1933–1947

SPEAKING BEFORE THE MEMON Chamber of Commerce in 1943, the president of the All-India Muslim League, Muhammad Ali Jinnah—a nominal Twelver Khoja himself—intoned that "he desired not a Memon, Khoja or Bohra Chamber of Commerce but a Muslim Chamber of Commerce."[1] Two months later, the Federation of Muslim Chambers of Commerce was founded in Delhi. Its establishment surprised Sir Sultan Chinoy, an Ismaili Khoja entrepreneur and president of the preexisting All-India Muslim Chamber of Commerce and Industry.[2] The de-Anglicized, Gujarati version of Chinoy's name was Cinai (Chinese), a measure of where his Khoja ancestors made their fortune. He was representative of the long-standing Ismaili Khoja prominence in Bombay's elite circles. He and three of his brothers individually had become directors of the Central Bank of India, the Imperial Bank of India, and the Reserve Bank of India, a fact that serves as a notable contrast with the paucity of privately owned Khoja banks.[3]

Yet by 1944 Chinoy had fallen out with the leader of the Bombay branch of the All-India Muslim Chamber of Commerce. Instead, he threw his weight behind the Bombay Muslim Chamber of Commerce. Chinoy thus became party to the schemes of the Muslim League, which hoped to get the Twelver Khoja banker Muhammad Habib—founder of an eponymous bank and one of Jinnah's closest collaborators—elected as president of the Bombay Muslim Chamber of Commerce. When Habib was subsequently elected, in part thanks to Chinoy's registration as a voting representative, one prominent member of the Muslim League wrote joyously to a colleague that "the grace of *Allah* and the support of the Memon, Khoja and Bohra communities and the Muslim League" had made it all possible.[4] Chinoy's defection revealed the divisiveness of the Muslim League program, which fueled endless personal spats and political maneuverings among elites of the Gujarati Muslim commercial castes. Yet it also reflected the surprisingly outsized role of the Bohras, Khojas, and Memons in supporting the Muslim League during the late 1940s.

While Gujarati Muslim links to the league were never all-encompassing, its program from the mid-1930s onward marked a crucial turning point in the Bohra, Khoja, and Memon experience. As the leading Indian Muslim capitalists, they had no choice but to grapple with the constant overtures from the Muslim League to bring them onside. Nevertheless, the jealous demands of the league's program—above all, its claim that all Indian Muslims were a unified "nation" independent of caste, regional, and doctrinal particularities—presented a direct challenge to the corporate Islam of the Gujarati Muslim commercial castes and the middle power they had long enjoyed in the colonial system.

All the same, scholars disagree on the precise role that the Gujarati Muslim mercantile castes played in the movement for the creation of a separate Muslim homeland in South Asia. One Marxist developmental economist, Hamza Alavi, rejected the claims by Indian and Soviet scholars that Muslim businessmen from Western India had any definitive role in the Pakistan movement before 1947.[5] Alavi was himself a Bohra who obtained a master's degree in economics from Aligarh Muslim University and worked for the State Bank of Pakistan until 1952.[6] According to Alavi, the key supporters of the movement were actually the class of bourgeois Muslim professionals and the "salariat," which he defined as those Muslim bureaucratic and legal functionaries who had worked for the colonial state. He argued that the salariat served the special interests of its own members and the economically dominant classes. In Pakistan, their ranks were later dominated by Punjabis but also contained substantial numbers of Muslims from Bihar and the pre-Partition United Provinces who had migrated to Pakistan.[7] Yet even if Alavi was right that only select members of the Gujarati Muslim mercantile castes aligned with the Muslim League, the historian Mushirul Hasan has hypothesized that the salariat and the trading communities each possessed their own spheres of influence in the Pakistan movement. Hasan also rightly emphasizes that the association between the Gujarati Muslim commercial castes and the brand of Muslim nationalism espoused by the Muslim League was a late one.[8]

Some Bohras, Khojas, and Memons throughout the diaspora also embraced the league's program, confirming one scholar's claim that Pakistan's chief proponents did not envision a country based on European romantic ideas of "blood and soil." Instead, their vision owed more to utopian, Enlightenment ideas of a nation untied to any particular geographic territory.[9] Fittingly for communities that abided no easy communal divide, the actions of individual *jamaats* (corporate caste institutions) show not only support for the Indian National Congress or the Muslim League but also collaboration with African nationalists, the Japanese Imperial Army during the Second World War, and regional movements (such as the Sindhi movement) in the decade and a half before the end of the Raj. The promiscuity of Bohra, Khoja, and Memon nationalism should therefore give pause to any communalist account of their political activities and instead strive to catalog the hard political choices made at the level of individual *jamaats*. Many of those choices were not theirs alone to make, but thrust upon them by circumstance.

The Bid to End Legal Exceptionalism

In a 1938 speech Bhulabhai J. Desai, a Gujarati Hindu lawyer and Indian National Congress activist, used the Gujarati Muslim commercial castes to illustrate how the subcontinent's Muslims had "Indianized" themselves over the centuries:

> If you want instances, I would point to my friends of the Khoja community and I will point to my friends of the Bohra community, and will point to my friends of the Memon community who only adopted Islam not more than two hundred years ago, and yet they are to-day a part of the Islamic population of India. It is not a secret, it is found in the first volumes of the Indian Law Reports that so far as the Khojas are concerned, they are but a part of the same trading population known as Bhatias of whom they are the counterparts in energy and business habits, in fact even their name and appellation. But for the dress one cannot say whether one is a Khoja or a Bhatia. And the same thing I can say of another community which forms a part of the Islamic community

> of India to-day, and that is the Memon community, who are perhaps a little more assertive and who have spread themselves in every part of India in quest of trade, and yet it is difficult to distinguish them from their Lohana brothers who are equally adventurous and who are also to be found in all parts of India, Burma and in many parts of Eastern and Southern Africa. That is how you find two branches, two descendants of the great common ancestors, one professing the Hindu Faith and the other professing Islam, but who are in culture and in understanding the same as my own brother in every sense of the term.[10]

This was a supreme compliment in the eyes of Desai, but their portrayal as indistinguishable from Hindus was certainly not how many Bohras, Khojas, or Memons preferred to view themselves. This honorary Hindu title was not granted to the Gujarati Muslim commercial castes by Vinayak Damodar Savarkar, regarded by many as the ideological progenitor of Hindutva. Savarkar, though admitting their Hindu "blood" and adherence to Hindu customs, ultimately excluded the Bohras, Khojas, and Memons from the political nation of Hindutva on account of their following of Islam.[11] Such were the intellectual somersaults the *jamaats* inspired.

A telling contrast with Desai's and Savarkar's depictions emerged from the writings of a Maulana Mufti Ismail Bismillah, a scholar trained at the Darul Uloom Deoband seminary. Originally from Surat, Ismail completed his course work at Deoband and then shuffled between South Africa and Burma. He spent his final years in Gujarat. Throughout his scholarly career, his fatwas were published in *Muslim Gujarat,* a Gujarati weekly from Surat, and he was a particular favorite of many Memons.[12] Many of Mufti Ismail's opinions concern the permissibility of sundry *jamaat* practices, from the legality of fines to fees for circumcision, marriage, and divorce services.[13] The scholar deplored them all. When a petitioner asked if a *jamaat* could rightly fine members who divorced, he even condemned the entire practice of establishing *jamaats:* "Muslim *jamaats* should abandon such practices and their own *jamaat* standards, and revert to Islamic, sharia rules and regulations."[14] Mufti Ismail was to be sorely disappointed, for *jamaats* continued to function as primary arbiters of Bohra, Khoja, and Memon legal life even in the face of such attacks.

Despite the continued accent on legal exceptionalism, three dramatic legislative reforms affecting the Bohras, Khojas, and Memons occurred in the period covered in this section: the two Cutchi Memons Acts of 1920 and 1938, the Muslim Personal Law (Shariat) Application Act of 1937, and the Dissolution of Muslim Marriages Act of 1939. The Cutchi Memons Acts, the outcome of four decades of Kachchhi Memon agitation, guaranteed that henceforth a member of the *jamaat* was considered a full Muslim in the eyes of colonial law. The 1937 Shariat Act safeguarded the inheritance rights of Khoja and Memon women by subjecting all Indian Muslim inheritance and succession rules to Islamic law, regardless of caste custom.[15] In the words of a prominent late colonial and postcolonial survey of Islamic law, the act was said to abrogate Muslim customs that were contrary to sharia. By doing so, the act aspired to compel Muslims like the Khojas and Memons, among others, "to give up rights contrary to Muhammadan law, to merge into the general Islamic community, and to be governed exclusively by the laws of the *shariat*."[16] For its part, the Dissolution of Muslim Marriages Act of 1939 nullified caste-specific customs governing divorce and erected a simplified, universal process governing all Indian Muslim divorces.

Though these acts marked a shift in the legal history of British India, one must be careful to not extend their effects too far; there is no doubt that Bohra, Khoja, and Memon particularism persisted in the face of these legislative actions. These laws only applied in the colonial courts, and while they were championed by select members of the *jamaats*, they did not become *jamaat* orthodoxy.[17] What is more, rather than receiving universal endorsement from the *jamaats*, these acts fostered new divisions over custom and law. As ever, affairs played out differently in each community. For the Kachchhi Memons, the shifting parameters of law and custom were wellsprings of debate. The long-awaited passage of the Cutchi Memon Acts by no means ensured that all Kachchhi Memons wished to be categorized as full Muslims. The architects of the acts seriously underestimated the preference many community members harbored for long-standing customs of organizing inheritance and succession. In some sense, expunging the stain of "Hindu" custom was an aim that most Memons could support. But more divisive was the issue of whether all vestiges of Memon caste particularism had to be done away with, even to the point that "half-caste" sons produced by mixed marriages could become full voting members of the *jamaat*. That quandary in turn dredged up all manner of questions about whether Memon caste boundaries were commensurate with the normative Sunni legal tradition.

These scuffles were part of a wider Memon effort to reconceptualize their identity as both "new Muslims" (late medieval converts to Islam) and Sunni

Muslims of diverse affiliations. While most other Indian Muslims had impugned the Memons' status as full Muslims, these assertive takes on the Memon past were evocative of Memon struggles to situate themselves in an imaginary, albeit increasingly socially concrete, Muslim collective. Contemporary exercises in Memon history writing revealed the tensions inherent in these conceptions. The first full-length Gujarati history of the Memons, published in 1921 by Memon Abd Allah Ismail of Amreli, revealed how little material existed on the community's history.[18] Ismail spent ten years laboring on his nearly four-hundred-page account, relying for material in part on his business partner, the Twelver Khoja polemicist Edalji Dhanji Kaba.[19] The main stumbling block was that Ismail and his colleague, Ibrahim Daud, had spent nearly a decade unsuccessfully attempting to marshal a source base for their project. Swimming against the tide of interwar communal assertions and seeking to combat a prejudiced account of the Memons composed by an earlier Indian Muslim historian, Ismail's narrative framed the Memons as high-caste Hindus who enthusiastically accepted Islam and were the social equals of not merely elite Hindu traders but also warriors.

Ismail's history appeared around the same time as the passage of the first Cutchi Memons Act, which in its effort to do away with Hindu inheritance practices among Kachchhi Memons revealed a far more anxious attitude among Memons toward their Hindu lineage. Several colonial legal precedents facilitated the act's appearance before the Imperial Legislative Council. In 1915 the Privy Council ruled that Kachchhi Memons who had migrated to Mombasa were, by default, governed by Islamic law. It further stipulated that any Memon emigrant to Kenya had to individually establish the existence of a special custom in matters of inheritance and succession and prove that they had transferred this custom from India. Crucially, colonial officials concluded that if a Memon died without a will (intestacy), then those rules of inheritance and succession governing the case were merely "analogous" to Hindu law and concepts of the joint family taken from Anglo-Hindu law had no bearing on them.[20]

Members of Bombay's Kachchhi Memon *jamaat* who advanced the Cutchi Memons Act had the sympathetic ear of the odd colonial official, though for every supporter there were other colonial officials contemptuous of the bill. One of the bill's supporters, C. A. Kincaid, acknowledged the plight faced by Bombay's Kachchhi Memons. In contrast to both the Halai Memons and

Kachchhi Memons who emigrated to Sindh and East Africa, the Kachchhi Memons in Bombay had "become the sport of Hindu and Hinduising lawyers. One High Court decision after another had tied them up more and more securely in the meshes of Hindu law. At last it was laid down that in matters of inheritance and succession a Cutchi Memon's estate was indistinguishable from a Hindu's. The wags of the Bar library commented on this by saying that a Cutchi Musulman was a live Musulman, but a dead Hindu." Kincaid faulted British and Hindu lawyers alike for this legacy, memorably writing that they "hovered like vultures over the state of a dead Cutchi Memon, and derived endless and unholy profit from the bewildered and helpless struggles of the lawful heirs."[21]

According to Kincaid, this pitiful situation continued until one Sir Frank Beaman passed a series of judgments on the eve of the First World War. His rulings called into question decades of colonial legal judgements pertaining to the Kachchhi Memon *jamaat*.[22] Indeed, these rulings supplied the means for the Kachchhi Memon Sir Ibrahim H. Jaffer to put forward the Cutchi Memons Act. Even so, despite his fastidious adherence to colonial legislative procedural norms, Jaffer encountered the animus of several colonial legal officials, one of whom dismissed him as "the representative of some obscure Musulman sect. . . . An infernal bore and nuisance."[23] In the face of such opposition, Jaffer's motion seemed about to meet the same fate as previous Memon bids at reform over the past four decades. Yet, in Kincaid's telling, his own magnanimous support of the bill overcame the cynicism of his British colleagues.

Although the bill was narrowly passed, the real work of popularizing it within Bombay's Kachchhi Memon *jamaat* remained. Kincaid boasted that now Kachchhi Memons "have taken full advantage of the enabling Act, and anyone assailed by a blackmailing relative has only to declare himself bound by Islamic law to get rid of his enemy."[24] Despite his self-congratulations, the Cutchi Memons Act of 1920 was not universally applied to Bombay's Kachchhi Memon *jamaat*, as a subsequent Cutchi Memons Act in 1938 clarified. On the contrary, individual Memons had to officially register their adoption of Islamic laws of inheritance and succession for themselves and their heirs.[25] Colonial records indicate that in 1921–1922 some 735 Memons elected to do so—not a modest number, but certainly not the entire male population of the *jamaat*.[26] Even if Jaffer and other Memon architects of the bill spoke of Kachchhi Memon unanimity,[27] the clause demanding personal assent betrayed the fact that many in the *jamaat* opposed it.

The 1938 Cutchi Memons Act betrayed how a looming Hindu-Muslim communal politics spurred on Memon concerns about their legal exceptionalism. During the debate over the bill, its prime mover, H. A. Sathar H. Ishak Sait, stated, "It has always been admitted on all hands that the Cutchi Memons are good Muslims and pious Muslims. I hope we continue to deserve these appellations but it was held by the High Courts that it is the Hindu Law of inheritance and succession that should apply to them with its pernicious provision of depriving women from any right of property."[28] According to the transcript from the debate, however, an undisclosed member of the house, most likely a Hindu, objected to the word "pernicious." Sait then withdrew the adjective from the record, though he remained adamant that it was a grave injustice for Kachchhi Memons to be considered Muslims when alive but Hindus upon their death.

Employing the same language of *jamaat* unanimity as his Memon predecessors from the 1880s onward, Sait also stressed that Kachchhi Memon *jamaats* in Bombay, Calcutta, Karachi, and other cities "have expressed their whole-hearted support" for the bill. The *jamaats* were, he clarified, "fully autonomous bodies as regards the communal affairs of Cutchi Memons. Every adult Cutchi Memon is a member of the body in his own right and has the right to vote." Yet that statement was difficult to reconcile with Sait's subsequent claim that, due to the election clause, in certain instances a Memon male was governed by Islamic law while his brother, father, or son fell under the jurisdiction of Hindu law. In seeking to apply Islamic inheritance laws to the entire community, Sait's goal was not only to address this anomaly but also to grant "our mothers, sisters, and widows what Islam gave to them fourteen hundred years ago, but what our men, because of their selfishness, withheld from them for such long years—the privilege to own and inherit property in their own right." With the assistance of such high-flown rhetoric, the bill passed.[29]

Subsequent court rulings show that the 1938 act was applied retroactively to Memon wills composed before that year. For example, the will of one Ismail Ahmed—drawn up in 1933—stipulated that he wanted to leave a bequest of more than one-third of his net estate to an appointed heir. When Ahmed died in 1941, one Bayabhai (presumably his daughter) argued that the will violated Islamic inheritance law—which it surely did.[30] Notwithstanding such episodes, the passage of the 1938 Cutchi Memons Act and the 1937 Shariat Act (which undid Bohra, Khoja, and Memon legal exceptionalism in one fell swoop) might give the false impression that Islamic law's victory over Memon *jamaat* custom was total or, at the very least, that the kind of Islamic law embraced by the Memon *jamaats* was foreign to their long-standing internal culture of customary law. But, as chapter three stressed, *jamaat* custom and the ever-expanding corpus of Sunni law were continually locked in dialogue. Nevertheless, the compulsion felt by several influential Memons to implement Islamic inheritance law over and above any form of community custom reflected pervasive interwar concerns about the status of the *jamaats* as *Muslim* corporate institutions commensurate with the imagined Indian Muslim "nation."

Besides inheritance and succession, marriage was also a subject of intense squabbling in Memon *jamaats* in these years. Marriage outside of one's caste was (and is) exceedingly rare among the Bohras, Khojas, and Memons. The exception that proves the rule was captured in a 1938 photograph published in *Life* magazine, showing the marriage ceremony of the son of the Memon magnate Seth Haji Abd Allah Harun to the niece of the Agha Khan III.[31] Such arrangements were possible only among the highest elites or, alternatively, in the far corners of the Memon diaspora where *jamaat* power was weak. After all, the Agha Khan III had long forbidden his followers from marrying non-Khojas, including Memons.[32] Despite some signs of wavering, Memon *jamaats* doubled down on endogamous marriage in the 1930s. Because Memon men tended to emigrate alone to places like Burma or Mombasa before returning to Greater Gujarat to marry, questions of *jamaat* membership had vexed Memon congregations for generations. Were the "half-caste" sons produced by the marriage of a Memon father and non-Memon mother full members of the *jamaat*, able to acquire voting rights? What did centuries of Memon *jamaat* custom and the Islamic legal and historiographical tradition have to say about the validity of such mixed marriages?

These were the questions confronted by Saleh Muhammad Haji Harun Kabli in his *Śud'dha ke aśud'dha ane Memaṇa tavārīkha* (Pure or impure, and Memon history), a 1931 Gujarati text that captures many of the fraught conversations around Memon corporate identity in the interwar period.[33] Kabli owned textile and debt collection companies and was one of the many Gujarati Muslim capitalists who had a literary side hustle. His brief survey of Memon history in the first section of the book, aimed largely at Memon teenagers, offered the standard fare of all Memon chronicles: slim empirical data and bountiful conjecture. But the book's second half, featuring a fictitious debate among members of a Memon *jamaat* over the rights of half-caste sons, was a singular contribution to contemporary intracaste debates over Memon corporate privileges. The disputation was more than thirty-three pages long. Although it frequently sank into the picaresque, the text conveyed in quite stirring ways how diaspora and regular intercommunal contact defied the ability of Memon *jamaats* to maintain a hold over their constituents. Yet it also drove home that the administrative elites of the *jamaats* sought to maintain caste boundaries against attempts to relax them.

Perhaps the most fascinating section from the text concerned the introduction of fatwas into the debate. With so much of the debate hinging on questions of immemorial Memon custom, this was a curious ploy to push the dispute in other directions. It also betrayed how remarkably divided *jamaat* members were over what sharia ordained in episodes of cross-community marriage—and how sharia-based rules stood in relation to what was perceived as centuries of unbroken caste custom. Before the opponents of the bid to introduce half-caste sons could begin reading the fatwa to the *jamaat*, the motion's architect tried to preempt them by citing an example of cross-community marriage from the very first Muslim community. He appealed to the example of Zayd bin Hasham, a former slave and adopted son of the Prophet Muhammad, and Bibi Zainab, who were married for a period despite not being from the same clan. Ibrahim asked his audience, "If the Quraish did not see the high or the low in such a family, then what? Have Memons become greater than the Quraish?" According to this understanding, the story of Zayd bin Hasham and Bibi Zainab was framed as an effort by the Prophet Muhammad to nullify the stigma against slaves in the first Muslim community and to encourage equality among Muslims. Yet there was more to this story, for the subsequent dissolution of the union between Zayd bin Hasham and Bibi Zainab complicated matters.[34] The details are complex, but after divorcing Zayd, Bibi Zainab married the Prophet Muhammad. As Bibi Zainab and the Prophet were both from the Quraish tribe, the divorce was cited as proof during the debate that cross-community marriage did not adhere to the prophetic exemplar.

The argument against cross-caste marriage was clinched by an extended Urdu *istiftā*ʾ (request for legal clarification) and fatwas presented by the Memon opponents of the motion. The *istiftā*ʾ asked whether it was permissible for a *jamaat* council to bar marriage between caste members and those outside it. The scholar consulted on the matter ruled that such a ban was "correct and permissible" in the name of preserving *kafāʾāt* (equality of lineage between the husband and wife), the "limitation of corruption," and the "betterment of the community."[35] To buttress his conclusion, the scholar included two extracts from Burhan al-Din al-Marghinani's twelfth-century *al-Hidāya* and ʿAla al-Din al-Haskafi's seventeenth-century *Durr al-Mukhtār*. In their own ways, these rulings confirmed "that marriage should not be consummated unless from the same clan" and that considerations of "lineage must be met by both the man and wife." In the end, the Memon opponents of mixed marriage used both rulings to justify the assertion that "five hundred years" of *jamaat* custom was commensurate with sharia.[36] Though it was a close-run thing, the motion ultimately failed and with it any attempt to extend the boundaries of the Memon *jamaat*.

Clashes over law and custom were no less intense among the Khojas, both Ismaili and Twelver. Whereas Twelver Khoja elites labored to popularize Twelver Shiʿi legal norms within their communities, their Ismaili Khoja counterparts did not attempt to jettison "Hindu" customs as such but to articulate a vision of their *jamaat* (and the Agha Khan III) as the synthesis of Hinduism and Islam. This was partially a consequence of being squeezed by Hindu and Muslim activists who were intent on bringing the Khojas—whom they saw as a "liminal" group between the two religions—on side. Still, some matters were nonetheless out of the Khoja *jamaats*' control—especially the inheritance rights of Khoja women. The 1937 Shariat Act helped a small stratum of Khoja women to secure property for themselves. Perhaps unsurprisingly, the *jamaats* continued to subject these properties to their own administrative oversight, curtailing the autonomy of new property owners.

The previous two decades had seen much intra-Khoja wrangling over questions of law. Notwithstanding the dramatic changes in the demographics of the Ismaili Khoja *jamaats*, throughout the 1920s the calls for reform of Khoja law became more intense. In a 1921 Gujarati text titled *Khojā komane eka apīl* (An appeal to the Khoja community), a pseudonymous Twelver Khoja author condemned his fellow Twelver Khojas, and particularly those in Bombay, who clung tenaciously to "Hindu" law. By the author's reckoning, these individuals had not only invalidated the prayers of the *jamaat* through their adherence to "Hindu" ways but also rendered illegitimate the wealth of the whole community. They had done so because property acquired by means of Hindu law was regarded as "usurped" by the standards of sharia. Hindu law, the author went on, also served to usurp the economic rights of Khoja daughters. There had been a time when the *jamaat* had labored to nullify the grip of Hindu law in this regard, but now the reform of Khoja legal status had been confined merely to the realm of rumination, not action.[37]

While the author coded Khoja custom as "Hindu," using the same language that colonial jurists had used to describe them since the 1840s, European and Indian legal experts in the Anglosphere undertook their own reevaluations of Khoja custom and law. In an important development, their analysis of Khoja law departed from the standard Hindu-Muslim communal framing. In a work on Khoja and Memon law published in 1924, S. R. Dongkery, an Indian judge in the Bombay High Court, declared that Khojas and Kachchhi Memons who died without a will were subjected to "rules analogous to those of Hindu law." Yet in all other matters—from marriage to divorce, gifts, and pious endowments—Islamic law applied. But in a rereading of Khoja legal cases over the previous seventy-odd years, Dongkery maintained that the customary practices recognized by the court and Khojas alike, which excluded daughters from inheritance, had only been analogous to Hindu law. "It would be unsafe," Dongkery emphasized, "to carry the analogy further and to treat the Khojas as having adopted or retained the Hindu law of joint family property with all its implications."[38]

In Dongkery's telling, many of the cases involving Khoja women in this period had diverged from strict Hindu law and conformed instead to a shifting formulas of Khoja custom. To Dongkery, four overarching facts could be deduced from the Khoja judicial record over the decades. First, Khojas were governed by Islamic law according to general presumption. Second, where customs of inheritance and succession analogous to those of Hindus existed, then rules of Hindu law applied to the Khojas. Third, these first two declarations could be voided by the existence of a contrary custom among the Khojas. And fourth, it was wrong to presume that the entire Hindu law of the joint family applied to Khojas, even if the managers of joint Khoja family property could "bind the other members [of the family] by a transaction made by him in his representative capacity and for the benefit of the joint family."[39]

The rules governing that last remark would change with the 1937 Shariat Act, imposed over the heads of the Khoja *jamaats*. The act singlehandedly reinforced the tenuous advent of propertied Khoja women. This is an easily missed development because Khoja women's hold over such property in the interwar period was precarious and often temporary. As earlier chapters have shown, due to Sir Erskine Perry's 1847 decision, Khoja women were typically dispossessed of any share of inheritance. Now, however, some began to secure a small nest egg. To be sure, Khoja women continued to be largely peripheral to the world of business, but they did inherit property from wealthy husbands in select instances where no male issue existed. For these women, passing that property on to their next of kin was another matter entirely. Predictably, contestations over the inheritance of these women became especially fraught in the wake of their deaths, as male members of the *jamaats* sought to wrest control of their assets. In their sparring matches, these men advanced competing theses regarding the correspondence among Hindu law, Islamic law, and Khoja custom.

For Khoja women, the most relevant point was that Muslim women who received property upon the death of a male relative became full legal heirs according to Islamic law. According to standard Khoja legal precedents of the previous century, this property would have reverted to the "heirs of the last male owner."[40] Nevertheless, there were two potential snags for Khoja women, even after the 1937 Shariat Act. For one, the act extended only throughout the provinces of India, leaving open the question of its application to other parts of the British Empire. Second, the opt-in clause likely made it overly burdensome and expensive for Khoja women to ensure full legal recognition for their newly acquired rights outside of the *jamaats*.

Confirmation of this comes from a court case adjudicated in Zanzibar in 1939–1940. There the Agha Khan III, through his local attorney, sued a male member of the *jamaat* who had been appointed a trustee by one Bai Bilgimbai Binti Ismail Jetha.[41] Bilgimbai's last testament, dictated orally in 1927, had nominated two men as trustees and managers of her property. These men would supervise her burial according to Shiʿi Imami Ismaili practices and remit proceeds from the sale of her jewelry to the *mukhi* (chief) and *kamadia* (accountant) of the local Ismaili *jamaat*. Monetary donations would also be made to the Ismaili Council for the benefit of the Agha Khan and one of his daughters.

Such arrangements were probably typical in the wills of wealthy Khojas. What was specifically contested in the case were two houses formerly owned by Bilgimbai. In her will, Bilgimbai had declared that the appointed trustees would manage the sites and, after deducting expenses and taxes, would pay Bilgimbai's daughters the balance as maintenance. Though the daughters possessed no rights to the property other than the income from the rent, Bilgimbai declared that if she died before her daughters married, then the houses would provide collateral for the debts incurred. Despite this generosity, Bilgimbai made no concessions to any of her daughters' potential offspring. Instead, as the translation of her statement relayed, after her daughters passed away, "no other party has any sort of right over these houses except my religious father Hazar Imam to whom both these houses should be given as religious gifts for the happiness of my soul and that my trustees should make out for him the proper deeds according to laws."[42]

Unfortunately, nothing is known about the circumstances of Bilgimbai's death. Sadder still, her youngest daughter, Kulsumbai, passed away at a presumably untimely age in 1938. Yet, in violation of the precise terms of the will, the Agha Khan III's representatives and one of Bilgimbai's trustees sought to attain control over Bilgimbai's erstwhile property, notwithstanding the fact that Bilgimbai's older daughter, Khatijabai, was still living. Apparently the two contestants found a window of opportunity in Bilgimbai's assertion that her daughters could claim nothing but monetary maintenance from the properties. In a fascinating twist, each party attempted to argue that Khoja custom adhered to, alternatively, Hindu or Islamic law. While the Agha Khan III's attorney pointed to the fact that the *jamaat* had always followed Hindu law, Abd al-Rasul Fazl Pirani, one of the trustees, strove to block the transfer of the properties to the Ismaili imam. Pirani even attempted to acquire one of the properties for himself by arguing that Bilgimbai's will was governed by "Mohammedan law and, alternatively, that the gift in favour of the plaintiff could only come into existence and be operative after the death of Khatijabai." As the summary of the presiding judge elaborated, Pirani acknowledged that the law of simple inheritance and succession applied to the estate of a Khoja was Hindu law. However, he argued that Ismaili Khoja wills fell within the remit of Islamic law. Pirani's advocate further maintained that the courts of Zanzibar had "assumed without evidence" that Ismaili Khoja wills were subjected to Hindu laws of inheritance simply by conflating Khoja customary practice with Hindu usages.[43]

The judge in Zanzibar rejected the lawyer's assertion. And, in a crucial qualification, the judge admitted that Indian courts had entertained Khoja dissent on the subject over the past generation. He added, however, that "while entitled to respect, [decisions of the Indian courts] are not necessarily binding on this court and caution is to be observed in following them in circumstances in which their application to the customs of Zanzibar may be inapt." He also could not resist revisiting a famous line from a colonial court case of the 1880s, "The living Mahomedan [meaning a Kachchhi Memon or a Khoja] by operation of law becomes a dead Hindu." In the Zanzibar judge's latter-day version, when a Khoja Muslim struck up a will, "the dead Hindu" was the testator and not the "living Mohammedan."[44]

The judge went still further, condescending to explain Bilgimbai's unspoken intentions. He was skeptical that Bilgimbai intended to postpone her self-proclaimed religious obligations to the Agha Khan III by granting her elder daughter "an income greater than that which she considered adequate." Khatijabai thus was obstructed from securing a larger share in her mother's bequest. Pirani—himself no friend to Khatijabhai's cause, as he aspired to acquire control over the house—was ordered to deliver the property to the Agha Khan III.[45] As ever, women's hold over property was tenuous, at best, within the Ismaili Khoja *jamaat,* not least because the Agha Khan III's legal team adeptly deflected the attempts of select *jamaat* members to gain control over property earmarked for the imam. For all the challenges from within the Ismaili Khoja *jamaats,* the power of the *sarkar-sahib* (supreme leader) over his congregations proved unshakable thanks to the solidity of colonial judicial precedents in the final years of the Raj.

By contrast, the Bohra *dai* was subjected to a deluge of pressure from his own constituents and the Bohra dissidents. A cudgel was handed to the dissidents in the form of the Dissolution of Muslim Marriages Act of 1939, which streamlined the process by which Indian Muslim women could dissolve their marriages and put additional pressure on the mainline Bohra *jamaats* to clarify and reform their own marriage laws. Despite this pressure, the *dai,* Tahir Saif al-Din, was intent during these years to inculcate his view of proper marriage practices in the community. But in one of the many twists that remind one of the *jamaats'* status as hotbeds of religious debate, attempts to introduce these measures were resisted by members of the community as un-Islamic. The Bohra dissident movement then took full advantage of this discontent—and the subsequent 1939 act—and weaponized it in its campaign against the *dai.* Yet the dueling Bohra movements also engaged in a process of what has been called competitive modernization in which Bohra women on both sides of the mainline and dissident divide were active agents in the acquisition of greater rights as members of the *jamaats.*

Writing from Surat in 1944, one Bohra author lambasted the recent trend of young Bohras choosing their marriage partners without parental guidance: "The great disaster of encouraging love-marriages is that it leads to inter-communal marriages. When once the youngsters are allowed to select their own partners, without the sanction of their parents they may soon begin to cast their glances towards other communities. Besides, our girls, with their false sense of freedom and education, will fall sooner into this trap than the Parsi girls who have already fallen into it."[46] (And this in a journal that otherwise spoke freely of the merits of male-female platonic friendship, of conjugal sex, and freemasonry). Over the previous decade and a half, marriage had indeed been a divisive issue in the Bohra *jamaats,* yet another contest in the tug-of-war between the mainline and dissident *jamaats.*

In a move that echoed his attempts to control the trusts dispersed throughout the *jamaats,* the *dai,* Tahir Saif al-Din, sought greater control over marriages in the community, at least according to his critics. This was supposedly done to restrain "modernist" tendencies within the *jamaat.* This seems doubtful given the intellectual breadth of contemporary mainline Bohra publications like Surat's *Ummīd,* but one point of division was the proclivity of Bohra young men to shave, with the *dai* seeing fit to bar any beardless Bohra groom from marriage. In one instance a certain Shaikhsiraj Vasi was forced to deposit seven hundred rupees with the *dai,* pledge that he would grow a beard within one year, and swear off contact with his dissident brothers in order to get his marriage approved. Indeed, many photographs of Bohra professionals dating from this period show beardless men (see figure 7.1), a sharp contrast with both earlier and later twentieth-century Bohra norms.[47]

Several Bohra women, however, were having none of this. In one episode, two aspiring brides, Asmabai Basrai and Zubeda Bai Vasi, presented themselves at the *dai*'s residence in Bombay and "called upon Mullaji to respond to their call according to the holy commands of Shariat and perform the "Nikah" ceremony himself or cause it to be performed through his agent." After some foot-dragging by the *dai,* the brides strong-armed their guardians and the *dai*'s representative, an *amil* (officer) named Numanbhai Sahib, into performing a marriage ceremony for them and their beardless bridegrooms. In reply, the *dai* published a notice in the papers reiterating

FIGURE 7.1 A photograph of beardless Bohra professionals in the 1940s. Beardless men were a source of controversy in the mainline Bohra *jamaat* in this period, especially in the context of marriage. Author's personal collection.

that all Bohra marriages must be approved by him. But as the *Bombay Chronicle* noted, "How far this rule is in consonance with Islamic jurisprudence the intelligent Bohras are to consider well."[48]

This was precisely the issue at stake: To what extent were Bohra marriage practices consonant with currents of Islamic law? Certainly Bohra marriage customs followed a mixture of the Islamic foundational sources, the instructions of Fatimid-era Ismaili scholars like Qadi al-Numan, and *jamaat* custom.[49] But, as was seen in earlier chapters, most Indian Muslims remained remarkably ignorant of the details of Bohra law. What is more, a greater urgency was lent to these questions by the tendency of the Bohra dissidents to use the courts to their advantage. This tactic had, in the words of a Bohra mainline author, "necessitate[d] that special features of the law [of marriage] applicable to the Dawoodi Bohras should be stated as based on their authoritative texts."[50] Bohra marriage laws had hitherto been, in his words, a "sealed book," closed off to both the colonial courts and the wider Muslim public. Now the revolving door of Bohras in the courtroom demanded that the archives of Bohra jurisprudence be opened to the prying eyes of colonial judges.

To be sure, some Bohra-specific practices—especially the general adherence to monogamy and an allowance for widow remarriage[51]—permitted the Bohra *jamaats* to sidestep some of the other pressing nuptial issues that troubled other Indian Muslims in these years. Still, the 1939 Dissolution of Muslim Marriages Act was seen, in the words of one contemporary Bohra legal commentator, as "an ill-conceived law. It has not been passed with due regard to other provisions of the [Muslim] Personal Law in the matter." For one, the act had rendered inapplicable all manner of Bohra rules pertaining to *iddat* (the period in which a wife was forced to wait before remarrying if she had divorced or if her husband had died or otherwise disappeared), a real concern for a diasporic community.[52]

Whereas the leaders of the mainline *jamaat* saw the act as an infringement on venerable corporate rights to make community law as they saw fit, many disaffected Bohras, and even those in the mainline *jamaat*, saw it as an opportunity. Perturbed by the strict marriage procedures and the imposition of heavy monetary dues, a sizable number of young Bohras in the later 1930s attempted to circumvent *jamaat* marriage rules. Initially, Bohra women such as Karachi's Shirin Tayyibali Mandviwalla—whose marriage was blocked by the *dai*, first on account of a speech she had given opposing purdah (which she refused to retract), and subsequently because of her association with the Bohra dissidents—had tried to circumvent the *dai*'s restrictions by enlisting her brother as officiant.[53] Mandviwalla then turned to the Anglophone press to offer a rejoinder to the *dai*'s attempt to deprive Bohra women of the right, promised to them by the "law of Islam," to choose their own partners. In her version of events, the *dai*'s firman forbidding beardless young men from marrying was itself an attempt to supersede what Islam had ordained. Mandviwalla also condemned the monetary demands that unemployed youths were forced to pay to the *dai* during the Great Depression.[54]

In the face of such intractability, several Bohras, fed up with the inertia of the *jamaats*, also registered their marriages with non-Bohra *qazis* (Muslim judges).[55] A watershed in this respect were the sister suits launched by one Abd-i Ali Fatima and her husband, Amir al-Din. Abd-i Ali Fatima was the daughter of Seth Abd-i Ali Chibavalla, a wealthy merchant from Surat who had supposedly expended a great deal of capital in service of the *dai*.[56] Chibavalla eventually had a falling out with the *dai*, Tahir Saif al-Din, but this was only one cause of his daughter's marriage being blocked. According to a Bohra dissident historian, the other was the fact that the father of the groom had campaigned against the exclusion of the Bohras from the 1923 Wakf Act.[57] Despite protests from the couple, the *dai* was unmoved, and so Abd-i Ali Fatima approached a *qazi* to get a "sharia" marriage performed. The ensuing marriage was then voided by the *dai*'s lieutenants, who excommunicated Abd-i Ali Fatima and her husband. In turn, the couple sued the *dai* for defamation.

Nevertheless, when the case made it to the court, the *dai* was handed a resounding defeat.[58] By 1942 the *dai* lost yet another suit concerning marriage and was reproached by the presiding judge, who stated, "No text from any religious book nor any authority from any of the recognised text books on Mahomedan Law was cited to me in support of the defendant's extreme claim that his permission was necessary or obligatory as a 'sine qua non' for the validity of the marriage of a Dawoodi Bohra under the Mahomedan Law."[59] Again, this reproach of the Daudi Bohra leadership would have been unthinkable in the prewar era of nominal colonial nonintervention in community religious affairs. It owed entirely to the nullification of Bohra legal exceptionalism and the application to the community of an interpretation of Islamic law unbothered by considerations of caste particularism.

The Bohra dissident who published the pamphlet on the case made much of the "slavery" in which Tahir Saif al-Din had fettered the mainline *jamaat*.[60] It would be a mistake, however, to assume that Bohra women successfully emancipated themselves only in the Bohra dissident *jamaat*. What developed, in turn, was the process of "competitive modernization," in which the mainstream and dissident Bohra *jamaats* sought to outdo one another in advocating progressive attitudes toward women in public life.[61] Women of the mainstream Bohra *jamaat* penned articles in the newspaper *Ummīd* decrying full-scale purdah with a boldness undetectable in prewar Bohra literature. In that same paper, other Bohra women asserted the values of the values of female exercise and modern education. It is plain, therefore, that the mantle of "reform" was itself up for grabs between the mainline and dissident *jamaats*.

As to be expected, there were still plenty of Bohra mainline authors who pointed to changing gender norms, marriage practices, and women's education as a sign of a decline in the *jamaats*' religious and economic standing.[62] Yet, as will be seen in the next section, the circumstances of the Second World War and Partition accelerated processes of emancipation for Bohra women in India's main urban centers, one of the many ways in which these years irrevocably shaped the silhouette of corporate Islam.

Many Muslim Nationalisms: The Years of the Second World War

The primary effect of the Second World War was to hasten Gujarati Muslim participation in politics and to foreshadow the violence and dislocation that many India-based *jamaats* experienced during the years 1945–1947. Nonetheless, the war proved how fungible Gujarati Muslim political participation truly was: a *jamaat*-level analysis shows that the options presented to Bohra, Khoja, and Memon activists were not singular and their actions conformed to that menu of choices. All the same, the war intensified anxieties about the fate of Muslims in a foreseeable postcolonial future and it foreclosed certain political possibilities open to Indian nationalists before 1939, especially since the war gave the Muslim League an unprecedented opportunity to pursue its agenda. And when viewed against events of the early postcolonial period, the period 1945–1947 marked the initial stages in the unraveling of the geopolitical conditions that had fostered Gujarati Muslim commercial success over the past century.

Between 1941 and 1945, Gujarati Muslim *jamaats* in East, Southeast, and South Asia faced the horrors of modern war—from firebombing to enemy occupation to devastating famine. The city of Kobe, where a mix of Memons, Sunni Bohras, and Tatars had financed the construction of Japan's first mosque in the early 1930s, was so heavily bombed by American forces that the mosque was seemingly the only structure left standing at war's end in August 1945.[63] Meanwhile, Gujarati Muslim capital flight was virtually impossible in those parts of the British Empire conquered by the Japanese between December 1941 and May 1942: Hong Kong, Malaya, Singapore, and large swaths of Burma were all encircled by the Japanese Imperial Army in short order, with escape only possible from Burma. Gujarati Muslim entrepreneurs were among the waves of Indian refugees who left their homes in Burma, abandoned by their erstwhile colonial overlords.

Those who did make it to India tended to resettle in the environs of Calcutta, where there were long-standing Bohra, Khoja, and Memon *jamaats*. While firms like that of Adamji Haji Daud managed to relocate, not all Gujarati Muslim entrepreneurs had the means to leave Japanese imperial territory. Adamji spent the war years shuttling between his birthplace in Jetpur and the new center of his business in Calcutta, all the while benefiting from extensive colonial government contracts. By 1947 he was the single largest exporter of jute goods from India.[64] Unlike Adamji, many members of Rangoon's Memon *jamaat* stayed in the city. During the First World War, the city's Memon *jamaat* had produced a few outright opponents of British rule, including in the form of the Ottoman honorary consul. A generation later, the Second World War produced more of the same. With the British absent from the city from 1942 to early 1945, several Memons became involved with the breakaway Indian nationalist movement that collaborated with the Japanese.

One of these individuals was Memon Abd al-Habib, a figure who yet again attests to the dramatic political pivots the war encouraged among Gujarati Muslim capitalists scattered across Asia and Africa. Information about Habib's prewar business is elusive, but in 1944 he distinguished himself by donating his entire fortune to Subhas Chandra Bose. Bose, formerly a member of the Indian National Congress, had fled to Nazi Germany in 1941. A year later, he was in Japan helping to organize the Indian National Army (INA), a collaborationist outfit made up of former members of the Indian Army who had surrendered to the Japanese in Burma, Hong Kong, Malaya, and Singapore. Two years later, as the tide began to turn against the Japanese, Bose solicited funds from Indian communities living under Japanese rule.

If the accounts of the INA can be credited, Habib donated some Rs. 10 million to Bose's cause.[65] According to the testimony of an INA officer, given during the famous trial of INA ringleaders held in Delhi at the Red Fort, Habib served as chairman of the board.[66] The sheer scale of Habib's contribution suggests that Japan's wartime economy in Southeast Asia was a boon for some Gujarati Muslim entrepreneurs, despite the overwhelmingly disastrous macroeconomic consequences of Japanese occupation.[67] Even Bose recognized the gravity of Habib's intervention, hoping to replicate it as he retreated with Japanese armies out of Burma in 1944–1945. An inset printed in Singapore's *Azad Hind* (Free India) newspaper in 1945 contained the title, "Who Will Be the First Habeeb Here? Netaji's Challenge to Indians in Malai [Malaya]."[68] Several weeks earlier, Bose had lamented, as one paper put it, that "no millionaire Indian in Malai [*sic*] had come forward and offered his millions for the liberation of the motherland. He reminded them of the great example set by Habib and hoped that at least a few Indians in Malai would emulate his example."[69]

Not all Gujarati Muslim capitalists living under Japanese occupation—even those who resided in Japan—were willing to do so. When the Azad

Hind government pressed Japanese authorities to levy a forcible loan on Indians resident in Japan—totaling 40 percent of all their assets—there was an outcry in the Indian community against it. According to a report by the Swiss consul, who served as intermediary between British and Japanese officials, many Indians claimed that they "consider themselves to be British subjects, but they fear that if they refuse, all their personal property as well as the property of their firms will be confiscated."[70] Meanwhile, Japanese officials in Rangoon actively discouraged the operation of the Azad Hind Bank. Though his patrons took umbrage at his insubordination, Bose was adamant—much like Jinnah—that a central bank was a sine qua non of national sovereignty. In the teeth of such opposition Bose eventually carried the day and his bank was greenlighted by the Japanese.[71]

Like Bose, Jinnah was aided during the war by another Habib in his aspiration for a national bank: the Twelver Khoja Muhammad Ali Habib, whose eponymous bank was the most important Muslim-owned bank of late colonial India and early Pakistan. Habib moved his bank's headquarters to Karachi in 1947. Before India handed over Pakistani-owned assets, Habib reputedly gave Jinnah a blank check, to which some Rs. 80 million was added.[72] Such nationalist myths are a dime a dozen, but they do speak to Habib's contribution to the All-India Muslim League in the twilight years of colonial rule. Habib's drift into the league's camp was surprising; he is not easily pigeonholed as a figure espousing a separate Muslim homeland given that he possessed deep links with non-Muslim bankers in Bombay.

Yet it bears remembering that the Gujarati Muslim embrace of the Muslim League did not entail a repudiation of relationships across the communal divide, a wholly unrealistic option considering the intimate social and economic links between the Bohras, Khojas, and Memons and their non-Muslim cognate communities. Even two of Habib Bank Ltd.'s managing directors were nominal Hindus. The Muslim directors included Abd al-Karim Panju, a Twelver Khoja with leadership positions in several enterprises and *jamaat* trusts—among them the Kaiser-i-Hind Insurance Co. Ltd. He was also a chief benefactor of the Anjuman-i Faiż-i Panjatanī, the Twelver Khoja institution with offices in Bombay and Karachi that served pilgrims going to the Shiʿi shrine cities in Iraq. This association suggests that other Twelver Khoja thrifts, such as the Hidayat Fund, played supporting roles in the operation of Habib Bank. At the very least, for the Twelver Khoja directors, the bank and *jamaat* thrifts were an interlinked institutional portfolio. It was appropriate, then, that Habib Bank adopted as its emblem the lion-and-sun effigy, the so-called *sher-i khudā* (lion of God) long used by Twelvers as a representation of Imam Ali.[73]

Habib Bank was an institution that reaped the rewards of the wartime production boom in India—and most likely the rampant speculation that boom engendered. Its balance sheets show a consistently successful performance of a kind mostly unmatched by Indian-owned banks of the 1920s and 1930s. Those entities had to endure seismic shifts in the financial landscape, including mercurial banking legislation and the fallout from the Great Depression. Habib Bank had the good fortune of being founded during the war, when the colonial state had a heavy hand in industrial production. Its success, however, was not entirely due to government intervention. In fact, concerns over the stability of the empire led millions of Indians to withdraw money from banks and post office savings accounts between 1942 and 1944.[74] Even in the teeth of these obstacles, Habib Bank recorded a profit of Rs. 600,000 in 1943 and maintained a high proportion of liquid assets compared to liabilities.[75] Its six-year progress report, published in March 1947, showed a near 600 percent increase in deposits and a 400 percent increase in net profit.[76]

Habib Bank's success, singular as it was, only heightened Jinnah's constant lament at the lack of Muslim-owned banks. The Muslim League's leader was nonplussed, as many Muslim nationalists were, by a perception that Muslim capital was being devoured by and subjected to the machinations of "Hindu" moneylenders. As one of his confidants recalled in later years, Jinnah had once said, "We claim that we are a nation one hundred million strong and yet have just one bank (the Habib Bank) out of the scores which operate in India."[77] For this reason, the league was heavily dependent on Habib Bank in the run-up to Partition. Jinnah's collected correspondence is littered with references to the institution, as its branches in Bombay, Delhi, and Calcutta performed the crucial work of remittance transfers among the dispersed agents of the Muslim League.[78] The dependence only grew in the midst of Partition and its aftermath: when Habib Bank agreed to move its headquarters from Bombay to Karachi (now Pakistan's principal economic center) in 1947, the new state acquired its first commercial bank. The Muslim Commercial Bank, the brainchild of the Memon industrialist Adamji Haji Daud, followed soon after. The actions of Habib and Adamji unambiguously indicated that the wartime economy fostered the Muslim

League's program, not least because some of the main Gujarati Muslim beneficiaries of the wartime trade boom were throwing in their lot with the party.

The war was also a windfall for the Bohra *jamaats* in India, both mainstream and dissident, each of which declared support for the Muslim League at war's end. Like the Khojas and Memons, the Bohras had long associated with Japanese firms, leading some Bohra companies to be blacklisted in 1942 for enemy trading.[79] But Bohra loyalty was dependable enough by 1941 that British authorities received a petition to send a Bohra delegation to Vichy North Africa to stir up anti-Axis feeling among Algerian and Tunisian Muslims.[80] Leaving aside the *dai*'s would-be role as Muslim defender of Allied interests, the onset of war in 1939 actually prompted a modest democratization of rules governing public life within the mainline Bohra *jamaat*. Indeed, a salient aspect of the Bohra wartime experience was the movement of Bohra women into war work, part of the global trend of unprecedented female labor conscription.

That fact necessarily entailed the decline of purdah in the community.[81] The abolition of purdah had been a main demand of Bohra dissidents since the 1920s, but now surprisingly the mainstream *jamaat* advocated it as well. What one historian has called "competitive modernization"—in which dissident and mainline Bohra jamaats competed for the mantle of "reform"—thus gained steam as never before. Confirmation of this came with the war of words that broke out in the wake of the Dawoodi Bohra Conference held in Bombay in 1944. The four-day event was engineered by Hatim Alavi, a onetime mayor of Karachi and one of the city's foremost public voices. In remarks given on the occasion, Alavi stressed the imperative of redressing the injustices of the Chandabhai Gulla Case from a quarter century earlier and demanded that the *dai* do right by his followers.[82]

Members of the mainstream Bohra *jamaat* vocally resisted this message. One lambasted the conference organizers' attempts to pitch themselves as monopolists of reform: "What indeed has prompted me to write these few words is the misuse of the word REFORMIST with which the conveners and supporters of that unhealthy conference style themselves. TO REFORM in the real sense i.e. the meaning we have learnt from the dictionary is 'to abandon evil and to return good' or 'to amend one's behaviour.'" The author further praised the progress of the Bohra *jamaat* under Tahir Saif al-Din's leadership and encouraged the dissidents to "come forward and seek the cooperation of our community."[83] When the war ended in 1945 and Britain's exit from India became a geopolitical inevitability as a result, there was little hope of a reconciliation between the two dueling Bohra *jamaats*, even if their leaders both rallied to Jinnah's Muslim League on the eve of Partition.

Partition and the Fragmentation of Middle Power

The end of the Second World War in 1945 accelerated Britain's exit from its Indian empire and heightened the showdown between the two principal political parties, the Indian National Congress and the All-India Muslim League. In its bid to attract Muslim capital, from the early 1940s, the league positively encouraged many Muslim firms to institutionally separate themselves from non-Muslims. This is evident from a 1944 letter to Jinnah by Haji Abd al-Karim, president of the Memon Merchants Association, who noted that Hindu and Muslim merchants throughout Berar and the Central Provinces had created "combined" mercantile associations in the big cities and small towns that would act as lobbying bodies for merchants' interests. Nevertheless,

> As these associations consist of an overwhelming majority of Hindus, some of the Muslim general merchants who fear that Muslim business interests will suffer in the long run by joining these associations have kept themselves aloof from them. Now we approach you with the request of honouring us with your opinion in the matter. If you think that joining these associations is harmful for Muslim merchants and that they should form separate associations for protecting their rights please advise us so that armed with your valuable opinion we may persuade those Muslim merchants who have joined the above named association to sever their connections with them and form their own local, as well as provincial, association for safeguarding their own interests.[84]

In reply, Jinnah advised Abd al-Karim to form a distinct Muslim Chamber of Commerce and affiliate it with the Federation of Muslim Chambers of Commerce and Industry. Jinnah supported the latter as a counterweight to the Federation of Indian Chambers of Commerce and Industry, which had linked itself to the Indian National Congress. The federation subsumed a series of Muslim commercial concerns under its administrative umbrella.[85]

By 1944–1945 many Muslim merchants in greater Bombay and Punjab were forming independent Muslim mercantile associations, following the lead of those in Berar and the Central Provinces. Even so, as noted at the beginning of this chapter, internal Muslim rivalries often spurred the formation of such associations. In the case of the Chinoy family of Bombay, their decision to leave the All-India Muslim Chamber of Commerce and form the separate Bombay Muslim Chamber of Commerce was fueled by rivalries with the Muslim commercial magnates at the head of the former organization.[86] The creation of these Muslim-centric institutions was thus not a response to communal conflict as such but rather resulted from more immediate commercial or personal rivalries. In time, however, they produced Hindu-Muslim communal tensions of their own.[87] Yet they also acted as a convenient smokescreen for the papered-over divisions among Indian Muslim political activists.

While Memon support for the Muslim League from 1938 to 1946 appears most consistent, the Bohra and Khoja (both Ismaili and Twelver) *jamaats* offer a study in contrasts.[88] The latter, especially the Ismaili *jamaat*, were far more divided over Pakistan. Ironically, that was perhaps because the Agha Khan III had been politically active for the previous half century, both at the subcontinental and global levels. Both his personal friendships and judicious method of political activism meant that he was supportive of both the Indian National Congress and the Muslim League throughout the 1930s and 1940s (notwithstanding the criticism he had attracted from Jawaharlal Nehru and other Indian National Congress officials on occasion; see chapter 5).

The Agha Khan III had spent most of the war in Britain, but his return to India in 1945 was an occasion of some fanfare, not least because the council of the "Aga Khan Legion" in Bombay was anxious to organize the celebrations for his Diamond Jubilee.[89] The festivities were held in Bombay's Brabourne Stadium in 1946. A photograph from the event shows attendees from not only Ismaili *jamaats* in East Africa and Madagascar but also Lebanon and Syria, both of which gained independence from France that very year.[90] The event was also noteworthy for the special paper currency drawn up for the occasion. Bearing the visage of the Agha Khan III, these notes promised the bearer "One-Thousand Good Wishes" and were said to be issued by "The Bank of Goodluck" (see figure 7.2). At a time when Muslim representation in banking was paltry—except for the Twelver Khoja-run Habib Bank—it was a standout addition to a ceremony already distinct for its flashy materiality.

In a way, the images of transimperial Ismaili unity projected by the media obscured some of the divisions within the Ismaili Khoja *jamaat*. These di-

FIGURE 7.2 The "1,000 Good Wishes" from the "Bank of Goodluck" circulated at the Agha Khan III's Diamond Jubilee, held in Bombay in 1946. Author's personal collection.

visions were not a threat to the integrity of the *jamaat* but are revealing of the difficulties the Pakistan option presented to diasporic communities like the Ismaili Khojas. Take the example of Muhammadbhai Rowji, both a vizier to the Agha Khan III and a president of Bombay's Ismaili Khoja *jamaat* council. Rowji was a devoted opponent of the Muslim League. In 1946 he demanded that Bohras and Khojas boycott the league after Bombay's Provincial Muslim League Parliamentary Board attempted to exclude Bohras and Khojas from running for posts in the Bombay Provincial Assembly or Council. He said on that occasion, "I have frequently warned all Shias not to have any confidence in the Muslim League which is really a Sunni body and misleads to represent all Mussalmans with a view to exploit Shia. If Shias want to safeguard their very existence, there is no alternative for them but to defy the Muslim League and put their own candidates to contest the elections in the Assembly and the Council and convince the league that Shias are not meant for exploitation."[91] Yet, balancing out Rowji was Ghulam Ali Allana, a future mayor of Karachi and head of the Federation of Pakistan Chambers of Commerce and Industry.[92] The leaders of the Ismaili Khoja *jamaat* were thus divided among themselves over the Pakistan option.

Leading figures in the Twelver Khoja *jamaat* in India were also deeply divided over Pakistan. Because another Twelver Khoja, Hussainbhai Lalji, openly resisted the Muslim League's bid for Pakistan, it was hardly predetermined that Habib Bank became the cornerstone of Pakistan's nascent commercial banking sector. Indeed, at a meeting of the Council of Action of the All Parties Shia Conference held in Poona in December 1945, Lalji presided over a meeting that passed a resolution: "The Council decided to work for the independence of India shoulder to shoulder with other organisations. The Council feared that the establishment of Pakistan would ostensibly result in the establishment of the Hanafi Shariur [*sic:* sharia] in that area, a Shariat, which was fundamentally different from the Shariat Jaffri' or Imamia Law which was followed by the Shias."[93] Other motions passed at the All Parties Shia Conference were less tame in their attack on the Muslim League.[94] No doubt the attempt to frame Pakistan as the handiwork of Sunnis was a something of a stretch given that Jinnah was (nominally) a Twelver Khoja and several prominent Shiʿis supported the party. Nonetheless, the charge does speak to the perception among many Shiʿis, including some Bohras and Khojas, that the league was in the pocket of Muslim landlords from the Sunni heartland of North India. Throughout 1946 the inter-Shiʿi contest over India's postcolonial future grew more intense in Bombay.

That contest was most divisive among the mainstream Bohra *jamaat* and the dissidents, which was surprising because the leadership of both groups supported Jinnah. In one of the many paradoxes common to Partition, this was despite the fact that both were supporters of the Muslim League. Hatim Alavi, the Bohra dissident, maintained an extensive correspondence with Jinnah and other leaders of the league. In one letter he complained bitterly about "Mullaji's adherents" for blocking his candidature and spoke of the *dai*'s two-timing of the league, asserting that the latter had "tried to ingratiate himself with the Congress and secure a promise that they will exempt him from the operation of the Wakf Act, a legislative measures [*sic*] which the Mullajee has dreaded the most. Only when the Congress refused to give this undertaking that he swung over to us."[95] Elsewhere he wrote to Liaquat Ali Khan, "We have fought the almost devilish forces of the Priests so that our community may fall into step with the broad currents of the Islamic life and begin to consider itself as a part and parcel of the *Millat* [nation]." Purportedly, the *dai* had used Alavi's biography of the Prophet Muhammad to, in the Bohra dissident's words, "instigate the Muslim mass against me."[96]

The irony of it all was that the mainstream and dissident Bohra *jamaats* had a common friend in Jinnah. For all the bad blood over the Wakf Act in the 1930s, the *dai* became a key supporter of Jinnah and the Muslim League in the 1940s. To be sure, the *dai* seems to have appealed to both the Indian National Congress and the All-India Muslim League: in a May 1946 issue of the illustrated Urdu weekly *Tegh* (Dagger), Tahir Saif al-Din was depicted alongside both Jinnah and Nehru.[97] Despite the impression of evenhandedness, the fatwa issued by Tahir Saif al-Din to the Bohra *jamaat* demanding that its members vote for Jinnah in the Central Assembly election and not his rival, the Twelver Khoja Lalji, ensured that the Muslim League leader was swept into power in 1946.[98] The *dai* also gave considerable donations to the league, at one point remitting Jinnah some Rs. 15,000.[99]

During these years, the Bohra dissidents also backed Jinnah, with Z. A. Banduk Wala pledging his support and condemning the "obscurantist" hold of "mullaji" (a derogatory name for the *dai*, meaning the mullah) over the vast majority of Bohras.[100] Two rival Bohra *jamaats*, which had previously been divided over the Muslim League's legislation for the administration of pious endowments, thus came to see their community's future as inextricably bound up with the idea of Pakistan. Although the leader of the mainstream faction, the *dai*, refused to relinquish control of his own community trusts, the paradox was that he was more than happy to use community funds to support the creation of a separate Muslim homeland, even if that meant that the two cities with the largest Bohra populations, Bombay and Karachi, were separated by a border.

Bohra women, now buffeted by the emancipation they had gained during the war years, were in the thick of the struggle. In one instance, one Mrs. Daudpota, running on the Muslim League ticket in the 1946 general election, faced opposition from other members of the league. Initially she had the support of the *dai*, who instructed local Bohras to support her candidacy.[101] However, she was eventually compelled to withdraw her candidacy as a member of the league, despite her long-standing affiliation with the organization, and ran as an independent, losing by a significant margin. The election led to some dissatisfaction with the league within the mainstream Bohra *jamaat*. In a bid to smooth matters over, an article in the Bohra newspaper *Ummid* remarked that while the seat had traditionally gone to a Bohra candidate, it was for the greater cause of Muslim solidarity that the seat was forfeited to a non-Bohra Muslim supporter of the Muslim League.[102] The Bohra *jamaat*'s forthright support for the league was to be a source of considerable suffering for Bohras in India in the years immediately following Partition.

In the months before Partition, Sir Chimanlal Setalvad—a Hindu barrister of Brahmakshatriya extraction who had participated in innumerable court cases involving the Gujarati Muslim commercial castes—articulated the fate awaiting diasporic groups like the Bohras, Khojas, and Memons: "Where are the Muslims in the Bombay presidency to be transferred and what is to become of their business and commercial interests in this presidency? Where are the Mullaji Saheb and his *borah* [*sic*] followers to be transferred? Where are the Aga Khans and his *khoja* followers to be sent away? Will the Chinoys, Habibs, Munjees, Rahimtoolas, the Yusuf and Killedars agree to leave this presidency and go to what are styled as the homelands of the Muslims in the Punjab?"[103] Setalvad spoke only of Gujarati Muslim constituencies in the Bombay Presidency. But there also remained the question of whether Bohras, Khojas, and Memons in Colombo, Johannesburg, Mombasa, Rangoon, Shanghai, and numerous other sites along the Indian Ocean would settle in India, in Pakistan, or stay put.

The decision was not theirs alone to make, as violence in several parts of India befell these groups, not least in Greater Gujarat. On August 15, 1947—the day the Indian republic awoke, in the words of Prime Minister Jawaharlal Nehru, "to life and freedom"—a public notice was signed by the leading Hindus and Muslims of Dhoraji. Dhoraji was the birthplace of several of the Gujarati Muslim commercial magnates discussed throughout this book, including the Bohra magnate Adamji Pirbhai, the Memon world traveler Haji Sulaiman Shah Muhammad, and the grandfather of Muhammad Ali Jinnah. Bemoaning the undoing of Hindu-Muslim brotherhood in Dhoraji and underscoring the need for mutual reconciliation between the communities, the document expressed the signatories' shock at the tragic killing of many innocent people in the town. The Dhoraji City Peace Committee was hurriedly established at the behest of the signatories, part of a venerable local tradition of intercommunal collaboration and arbitration, a tradition in which the *sethias* (caste leaders) of the Gujarati Muslim *jamaats* had figured prominently.[104]

Tragically, despite the courageous effort at compromise in Dhoraji, none of these gestures ensured that the town was a site of Hindu-Muslim harmony in the early years of the Republic of India. In the 1930s Dhoraji, and the larger Princely State of Junagadh of which it was a part, had been a fertile ground for a disgruntled strand of Hindu nationalism. The support of Memon *jamaats* in Gujarat for the program of the Muslim League, and Jinnah's occasional visits to surrounding towns like Rajkot, exacerbated this tension. But existing alongside these strains of communalism were the continued links among the Muslim *jamaats*, the non-Muslim corporate associations, and the princely house that ruled Junagadh. The Dhoraji City Peace Committee was a reminder that such legacies could and did persist amid the maelstrom of communal violence.

Sadly, in the face of the violence that flared up in the region in the years after 1947, these gestures proved unable to stem the outward flow of the Gujarati Muslim commercial castes. Although a Bohra, Khoja, and Memon presence persists in Dhoraji to this day, many Muslim inhabitants left in the late 1940s and early 1950s for other parts of India, Africa, and Pakistan. Two branches of Dhoraji's Memon *jamaat* survive in Karachi and Surat. The Karachi branch, the Dhoraji Memon Association, became one of a handful of Memon institutions that transformed the city after 1947. Even in the wake of migration, many Memons sought to maintain their links to their original homes in Greater Gujarat. On one occasion, Memon *jamaats* in Burma and Ceylon, whose members hailed originally from Kutiyana, desperately petitioned the Indian government to return property owned by them in Junagadh. This had been confiscated by the government on the grounds that it was "evacuee property."[105]

Such petitions were replicated, in one form or another, across the Gujarati Muslim diaspora over the next two decades as empire in Asia and Africa came to its ignominious and bloody end. A representative episode occurred in December 1947 when the president of Indore's Bohra *jamaat* wrote a telegram to Gandhi praying for immediate action to protect "lives and properties of minorities" after several Bohras were killed and wounded in communal violence.[106] Collectively these petitions convey that decolonization, and the rise of new nation-states, ushered in a new paradigm of minority citizenship for the Bohra, Khoja, and Memon *jamaats*. But even as the corporate status of the *jamaats* became more fraught in the postcolonial period, the Gujarati Muslim commercial castes continued to experience spectacular economic success for the first two decades after India and Pakistan gained independence in 1947.

* * *

Decolonization had dramatic repercussions for the Gujarati Muslim commercial castes in Africa and Asia. Their migration to Pakistan, the self-proclaimed homeland for South Asia's Muslims, was gradual, and often impelled by violence or threats thereof. Those who sought to return to India after short stints in East or West Pakistan found their path blocked by bureaucratic red tape and hostility. *Jamaats* in India splintered or disappeared wholesale. From the 1960s onward, similarly tragic episodes occurred in Burma, East Africa, and numerous other sites in the Indian Ocean region. Still, the Gujarati Muslim commercial presence persisted, and even found new productive avenues of expansion. But whereas in countries outside of Pakistan the Gujarati Muslims were suspect for their "Indian" or "Asian" identity, only in Pakistan did their devotion to Islam and their credentials as Muslims come under suspicion. Arguably, this suspicion owed more than anything to the intra-Muslim stratification wrought by a century and a half of capitalist stratification, as well as to the erroneous impression that the *jamaats* were a world unto themselves.

Indeed, from 1800 to 1947 the *jamaats* were enmeshed in the world of transregional empire, which had facilitated the circulation of Gujarati Muslims across the Indian Ocean. Their movement within that world was hamstrung by racialized politics of migration and capital constraints. After 1947 the demands of the nation-state presented novel challenges to the model of corporate Islam, throwing up unprecedented barriers to Gujarati Muslim attempts to maintain links with geographically disparate *jamaats*. As chapters 5–7 have demonstrated, the period from the beginning of the First World War to the end of the Second World War had reshaped the character of Gujarati Muslim middle power. However, by no means did these decades displace the Bohra, Khoja, and Memon prominence in the public spheres and economic circuits of the Indian Ocean region. All the same, middle power had become a source of reputational damage for these groups in the eyes of other Indians and Africans. With the end of empire, the special rights bestowed upon these groups by the colonial government were anathema to the programs of political equality and economic leveling preached by postcolonial nationalists of various stripes from Nairobi to Rangoon.

If the Gujarati Muslims had been counted among the Muslim "minority" in colonial India—an ideological construct, but a persistent one, at that—in postcolonial contexts they were often spoken of as "minorities." Minorities' rights, of course, implied that they were at a perpetual demographic deficit with the so-called majority—which, of course, meant different things in individual countries in Africa and Asia. Minority status was often a headache for those who were labeled as such, but being seen as hangovers from colonialism was far worse. Whether in East Africa or South Asia, the taint of colonial collaboration dogged the Gujarati Muslim commercial castes, as did the perceptions of runaway wealth and legal exceptionalism that were also regarded by critics as legacies of colonial rule. As chapter 8 demonstrates, the period between 1947 and 1975 saw a wave of state expropriation and violence crash upon the Gujarati Muslim commercial castes, undermining the corporate status of the *jamaats* in its wake, albeit only temporarily.

8

Decolonization and Postcolonial Dilemmas

1947–1975

WRITING IN THE MID-1960S and early 1970s Sergey Levin, the Soviet South Asian scholar, published a fascinating series of studies in English and Russian and on the Bohras, Khojas, and Memons. One of these was a 1965 Russian-language piece entitled "Ob ėvoli͡utsii musul′manskikh torgovykh kast v svi͡azi s razvitiem kapitalizma (na primere bokhra, memanov i khodzha)" (concerning the development of the Muslim merchant castes in capitalist society [in particular, the Bohras, Memons, and Khojas]). Levin's thesis was that the Gujarati Muslim commercial castes had developed into a unified, if competing, bourgeoisie in Pakistan. Unlike many scholars who have written on these communities, Levin did not regard their emergence as "trading castes" as the elaboration of a premodern occupational status existing from time immemorial. Instead he saw that process of identity formation as part and parcel of the development of modern capitalism on the subcontinent. In turn, Levin supplied probably the most empirically sophisticated academic account of all three groups to that time.[1] But during the ensuing decade his work and that of many other American and Pakistani social scientists contributed to the myth of the so-called twenty-two families of Pakistan.

Communists, Islamists, separatists, and technocrats seldom agree on what is wrong with an economy. Yet this is precisely what happened in Pakistan in the late 1960s and early 1970s. While critics of American economic inequality since 2008 have referred to the stratum of highest earners by the pithy shorthand of "the 1 percent," the number bandied about in Pakistan was twenty-two, a reference to the twenty-two families regarded as the owners of Pakistan's economy. Zulfiqar Ali Bhutto, the future (though ultimately doomed) prime minister of Pakistan, did more than anyone else to popularize the notion of the twenty-two families, making it a mainstay of his years in the opposition. In a 1968 speech he lamented Pakistan's extreme inequality: "May I know which other country in the world has such a system? Even in America, the centre of capitalism, such a wretched system does not exist. They don't have 22 families controlling the entire capital of the land. This system of ours has no parallel in the world."[2]

The fixation on the twenty-two families among Pakistan's establishment bureaucrats and oppositionists alike was evocative of the strained relationship between economic planning and private enterprise in the country. The perception that these twin pillars of the economy had only enriched a small coterie of oligarchs was sufficient to discredit both developmental strategies. Were this not enough, both were increasingly held up against emerging notions of an Islamic economy—envisioned as a just economic order that conformed to Islamic ethics and in which the fruits of labor were shared with the common Muslim multitudes—and found wanting. A member of Pakistan's National Assembly said as much when, in response to a buoyant speech by Pakistan's finance minister on the conclusion of the Second Five-Year Plan, he shot back in reply: "Sir, Pakistan was not achieved to make 21 or 22 families its masters, but it came into existence for the common man. It was millions of Muslims of undivided India who laid down their lives not to create cartels and monopolies at the cost of the interest of the common man."[3]

Pakistani officialdom's inability to see the twenty-two families as true people of the soil but merely as foreign carpetbaggers encapsulated the inter-Muslim tensions that have been a hallmark of Pakistan's identity from its inception. Uniquely, the controversy over the economic status of the Bohras, Khojas, and Memons was a case in which both Islam and capitalism were intertwined sources of conflict. It entailed, therefore, a larger battle over the legitimacy of corporate Islam as a model of modern Muslim economic and religious organization. It further demanded a wholesale rejection of the middle power that had underwritten Gujarati Muslim business success since roughly 1800.

Because many Muslim political activists in early Pakistan believed that the pre-Partition stratum of Muslim capitalists was slight, and associated capitalism with just a few tiny communities, the intra-Muslim wealth disparities of late colonial India were earmarked as an issue to be rectified. Though grumbles were voiced, such imbalances in economic outcomes were tolerated for two decades after 1947, so long as Pakistan's developmental schemes gained traction and shifted with the winds of Cold War politics. However, the secession of East Pakistan and the creation of Bangladesh in 1971, and the crisis of Islamic identity it stirred up in a now truncated Pakistan, ensured that drastic action was eventually taken against the twenty-two families. Since a central justification for the foundation of Pakistan was that the Muslims of pre-Partition India had been deprived of economic advancement by British and Hindu machinations, Pakistan's failure to raise millions of Muslims out of poverty needed a scapegoat. No better scapegoat existed than the top commercial firms owned and operated by the same Gujarati Muslim castes who had, so the thinking went, monopolized business opportunities in British India and held back the ordinary Muslim laborer or clerk, just like the Hindu or the British capitalist had done.

Justified on the grounds that Islam enjoined equitable distribution of wealth and that the government had to do more to protect the common man, the Economic Reforms Order of 1972 not only endorsed state seizure of private companies but also gave Pakistan's government the powers to nominate the board of directors for leading companies, a measure that ensured the demographic dilution of firms that had community or family-centered management. Pakistan thus joined a group of predatory governments—from Apartheid South Africa to Burma, Tanzania, and Uganda—that subjected Gujarati capitalists to acts of dispossession, harassment, and nationalization. The cataclysms the Bohras, Khojas, and Memons experienced between 1965 and 1975 were multifarious in their causes, inflected by the domestic dynamics of individual countries. What united all of them was a general attack on private property and minority groups, a program engendered by a widespread crisis in the postcolonial developmental state, across Africa and Asia in the late 1960s and early 1970s. The greatest paradox of all, however, was that the Gujarati Muslim commercial castes were seen as a foreign presence (tantamount to a "Hindu" one) in Pakistan, the purported homeland for South Asia's Muslims. When the assets of Pakistan's leading firms were nationalized, though it was a temporary setback, it marked the abrupt termination of an epoch of South Asian Muslim capitalism that had persisted for nearly a century and a half.

Expulsion, Migration, and Surveillance between India and Pakistan, 1947–1950

The Bohras, Khojas, and Memons were among the dozens of diasporic communities who attracted the ire of state authorities in both India and Pakistan between 1947 and 1950. Even though individuals from these groups were devoted citizens of each state, geopolitical rivalry guaranteed that the attempts by the Gujarati Muslim commercial castes to remit funds or travel across borders was closely monitored. Bureaucrats on both sides of the border sought to confine Gujarati Muslim capital within the territories demarcated in the summer of 1947. Competition between the two countries for the loyalties of Gujarati Muslim communities, including those in East Africa, continued for two decades. At the same time, resentment grew over the prominence of the Bohras, Khojas, and Memons in the economy of both countries, though in India it was Gujarati trading communities as a unit, rather than Muslims specifically, that rankled contemporary government ministers.

Though possessing very different political economies, both India and Pakistan confronted a problem common to postcolonial countries: how to encourage domestic enterprise while mitigating enormous disparities in wealth. Should the partition of the Reserve Bank of India serve as any indication, segregating Hindu and Muslim financial life was an unmanageable affair precisely because there was no clear-cut institutional separation in the economic life of late colonial India.[4] Thousands of similar divisions of assets likely occurred throughout South Asia as partnerships and firms comprising Muslim and non-Muslim personnel were dissolved. Additionally, the shortfall arising from the departure of leading Hindu, Parsi, and Sikh merchants from the territories of East and West Pakistan could never be made up by the migrating commercial firms coming from as far afield as Burma and East Africa.[5]

In the minds of political elites in Karachi and New Delhi, Muslim and non-Muslim Gujarati commercial groups were eidolons of comprador capitalism, the unmistakable beneficiaries of colonial collaboration. Anti-Gujarati sentiment was low-hanging fruit for Indian and Pakistani politicians, for the belief was rampant that the various Gujarati trading communities had been in cahoots with colonial capital from the eighteenth century onward. Erroneously, their very success was attributed to colonial patronage. It found sympathy in many unexpected quarters. Even a personality as sensitive to the politics of defamation as B. R. Ambedkar, the champion of the Dalits against high-caste Hindu chauvinists, had this to say about the Gujarati commercial castes, Muslim and non-Muslim, during debates about whether Bombay should be considered part of Maharashtra:

> Are the Gujarathis natives of Bombay? If they are not, how did they come to Bombay? What is the source of their wealth? No Gujarathi would claim that the Gujarathis are the natives of Bombay. If they are not the natives of Bombay, how did they come to Bombay? Like the Portuguese, the French, the Dutch and the English on adventures to fight their way through and willing to take any risks? The answers which history gives to these questions are quite clear. The Gujarathis did not come to Bombay voluntarily. They were brought to Bombay by the officers of the East India Company to serve as commercial Adatias or go-betweens. They were brought because the East India Company's officers who had their first factory in Surat had got used to Surti Banias as their go-betweens in carrying on their trade. This explains the entry of Gujarathis in Bombay. Secondly, the Gujarathis did not come to Bombay to trade on the basis of free and equal competition with other traders. They came as privileged persons with certain trading rights given to them exclusively by the East India Company. It may be granted that the Gujarathis have a monopoly of trade. But, as has already been pointed out, this monopoly, they have been able to establish because of the profits they were able to make which were the result of the privileges given to them by the East India Company on their settlement in Bombay. Who built up the trade and industry of Bombay is a matter for which no very great research is necessary. There is no foundation in fact for the statement that the trade and industry of Bombay was built up by Gujarathis. It was built up by Europeans and not by Gujarathis.[6]

Ambedkar's view that the Gujaratis were nothing more than Indian imitations of colonial capitalists was commensurate with the statist and populist economic ideas popular among Indian nationalists. This was bad history, but it was a view with wide appeal among those figures in Asia and Africa concerned with economic growth in the postcolonial state. Even so, Ambedkar's formulation did not go unchallenged. Pushing back against Ambedkar's remarks, M. L. Dantwalla, whom Ambedkar had criticized for deeming Bombay a city bequeathed to India by Gujarati business acumen, asserted that he made no special claims "on behalf of the Gujeratis [to Bombay]. What we have done is to emphasise Bombay City's cosmopolitan character not only today but during the entire history of its building up. We have praised the contribution of the Parsis, Khojas, Memons, and even the Marathas. Dr. Ambedkar distorts our statements and attempts to give them a Gujerati colour."[7]

The exchange between Ambedkar and Dantwalla was evocative of the persistent controversies over the exceptionalism of all the Gujarati commercial castes, Hindu, Jain, Muslim, and Parsi. It was not an isolated controversy, and it revealed how the politics of language joined the politics of religion—both ultimately a numbers game—in isolating conspicuous economic actors like the Gujarati Muslim commercial castes. Whereas Ambedkar attempted to chalk up Gujarati success to colonial patronage, other Indian politicians were adamant about depriving Gujaratis of their special legal rights in matters of personal law. These were held to be not only a nefarious legacy of colonial rule, but also a roadblock in efforts to implement a uniform civil code in India. In fact, K. M. Munshi, one of the advocates for such a uniform civil code, cited the example of the Khojas and Memons to attack the notion, introduced under British rule, "that personal law is part of religion." However, Munshi also used the foisting of the Muslim Personal Law (Shariat) Application Act of 1937 upon the Khojas and Memons by the Central Legislature as proof that "minority rights" must never impede the enactment of a uniform civil code.[8] In one of the many parallels of early Indian and Pakistani legal history, on the other side of the border, the conundrum for Pakistani legislators was whether "Hindu law" continued to apply to groups like the Kachchhi Memons and the Khojas in a nominally Muslim state.[9]

If depriving the Gujarati Muslim commercial castes of legal exceptionalism was one strategy to subject them to the new realities of national sovereignty, then another was the attempt to impose strict capital controls on them. A representative letter sent in 1949 to Dr. John Matthai, the finance minister for the government of India, stated,

> For sometime [*sic*] past, here in Bombay City, we are getting confidential news of the large transfer of funds that took place to Pakistan specially by the Bantwa Memons and Khoja merchants soon after the Partition. As a result of this, a large amount of Indian capital which was of a doubtful character had flown away to Pakistan and sought refuge there. From enquiries and reports, it appears that by an executive order, the Pakistani Government has accorded shelter to such funds by issuing directives to Income-tax officers not to enquire about the source of such capital that may be declared by the various assessees in respect of capitals accumulated before 1948. In other words, the black money which is flown away from India has been given a legal sanction and no penalty has been imposed. Of course this capital has been most useful not only for the trade and commerce of the new sister dominion but also to build up some industries there. During the past few months, it is also reported that some of this capital has been loaned out by the sister firms in Pakistan to concerns in India. By this process, the black money has been converted into white so far as India is concerned on the top of it, the loan interest paid on this money is a sort of a profit to the Pakistan firm and is deducted as interest charges paid out of profits by the Indian organisation. Of course you may have been apprised of this or similar methods. I have thought it fit however to draw your attention to this specially, as I understand Government is likely to consider shortly ways and means by which the hidden capital may be brought up and put to some useful purpose.[10]

This incident was suggestive of the continued viability of cross-border business relationships among Gujarati Muslim entrepreneurs in the years immediately following Partition. Though money laundering and tax evasion were justifiable concerns for government authorities, the overarching anxiety was whether communities with residents on either side of the India-Pakistan border could be counted upon to be loyal citizens.

Notwithstanding the Khojas and Memons singled out in the above quote, for a time the suspicion of both the Indian and Pakistani states was most intense in regard to the Bohra *jamaat* (corporate caste institution). Few high-level Indian bureaucrats had forgotten the support the *dai al-mutlaq* (chief cleric of the sect) had given Muhammad Ali Jinnah and the All-India Muslim League in 1946–1947, and it appears he was monitored by Indian government officials in the years after Partition. In December 1949 the Bombay Police Department forwarded to the government of Bombay a letter from one Muhammad Ali Allah Bakhsh detailing a series of transactions carried out by the Bohra *dai* and his family. The reports outlined how they had purchased a range of properties in Karachi, as well as ginning and pressing factories, rolling mills, and printing presses. These were all organized under the banner of the Saifee Development Corporation, Ltd. Other relatives were said to have decamped to East Africa, where they intended to reside permanently or as a temporary measure pending eventual relocation to Pakistan.

The correspondence eventually made its way to Morarji Desai—a future prime minister of India—and thence to Vallabhbhai Jhaverbhai Patel and Jawaharlal Nehru. Desai was most insistent on taking action against the *dai* in accord with the Evacuee Property Ordinance of 1949. He wrote to Patel that there was "sufficient material to declare the Mullaji Saheb and his two sons as intending evacuees." As such, Desai continued, the government should move against the Bohra leader. Before doing so, Desai intended to contact the *dai*, Tahir Saif al-Din, and "to advise him to desist from such disloyal conduct and to ask him to recall his son and other relatives to India." Desai would also demand that the *dai* and his family renounce all claims to properties purchased in Pakistan and elsewhere. As he told Patel, Desai's concern was to prevent "the flight of capital from India and the possible use of a part of it for purposes of anti-Indian propaganda."[11]

Patel, for his part, did not wish to intervene in the *dai*'s affairs, writing to Nehru that it was best to let the law of evacuee property run its course.[12] In his secret letter to Patel, Nehru noted that while he harbored "no sympathy for the Mullaji" he was uncertain of how the government could "come in the way of a person sending money to Africa or opening business there." All the same, Nehru wondered whether sending money to Karachi, then Pakistan's capital, was an entirely different matter.[13] Subsequently, Patel instructed Desai to contact the *dai*, warn him about the potential violations of the Evacuee Properties Ordinance, and encourage him to repatriate both his capital and family from Pakistan to India.[14] By no means was this the last encounter between the *dai* and the institutions of the new Indian state. In the 1950s the *dai* and the Bohra dissidents faced off in Indian court rooms on several occasions. The legality of excommunication from the *jamaat* was the issue at stake. Each side mobilized competing interpretations of the Indian Constitution, particularly those clauses respecting freedom of religion. Yet again the Bohras were serving as a test case for a fast-evolving state legal apparatus, and the matter of excommunication exercised the minds of many preeminent Indian judges. After an initial suit in which the *dai* was deprived of his power to excommunicate dissidents, that authority was restored to him by the Supreme Court of India in 1958.[15] In so doing, the Supreme Court perpetuated a right that the late colonial state had gradually taken away from the *dai*.

Meanwhile, on the other side of the border in Pakistan, Gujarati Muslim *jamaats* (and the companies owned by their constituents) in Pakistan were filling many of the "institutional voids" that the nascent state could not.[16] In colonial India the institutional voids filled by the *jamaats* had been predominantly, though not exclusively, geared toward the needs of the community. Now, in absence of strong state institutions, Pakistan's government relied on the infrastructural capacities of the *jamaats*. In 1951 the Pakistani government requisitioned Karachi's Bohra Gymkhana, presumably for the purposes of refugee relief. The building was still not restored to Karachi's Bohra *jamaat* by April 1954.[17]

Jamaat-based charities also assisted in the resettlement of refugees from India into the 1950s. Ahmad E. H. Jaffer, a Memon from Sindh, noted before the Pakistani Constituent Assembly that the Memon Committee was assisting large numbers of refugees arriving from India. Jaffer lamented that little, if anything, was being done by the Pakistani government to assist the refugees.[18] Suitably, that same year also saw the foundation of the first dispensary by Abd al-Sattar Edhi, a Memon originally from Bantva who migrated to Karachi in 1947. Edhi's charities later became internationally renowned, though his decision to offer services to individuals free of religious or caste affiliation perturbed many, including the Bantva Memon *jamaat*, recently shifted to Pakistan. The subsequent birth of the Edhi Foundation represented a clean break with the Memon *jamaat* and allowed the institution to offer a far greater range of services than if it had remained a *jamaat*-centric entity.[19]

The ability of Gujarati Muslim commercial castes to transplant and reconstitute the *jamaat* in Pakistan was a logistical feat that left them well positioned to exploit the enormous economic opportunities Pakistan presented to those with business know-how and contacts. The economic power accrued by the Gujarati Muslim commercial castes in postcolonial Pakistan would prove more controversial from the early 1960s onward. But before discussing this development, it is crucial to investigate the fate of Bohra, Khoja, and Memons *jamaats* in Africa and Asia from 1947 to 1965. At multiple sites the *jamaats* were at once participants and victims of nationalist movements, easy prey for those unsavory political entrepreneurs who, like their contemporaries in India and Pakistan, saw the Gujarati Muslim commercial castes, along with other Indians, as the unwanted patrimony of colonial rule.

Years of Uncertainty: Africa and Asia, 1947–1965

The emergence of India and Pakistan in 1947 posed awkward questions of national identity to Bohra, Khoja, and Memon *jamaats* in the Indian Ocean region. Despite the shifting political sands, Gujarati Muslims rarely felt the need to declare for one country or another. For one, *jamaats* navigated the early postcolonial period in manifold ways, sometimes seeking to have their pie and eat it too. By way of an illustration, in the mid-1950s, Khojas in Burma were keen to apply for Burmese citizenship "if they could be assured that ownership of their property in India will not be disturbed." They sent this request for clarification after learning that the evacuee property law was applicable only to Indians and Pakistanis.[20] Meanwhile, in 1954, the Memon Association of Ceylon sent a memorandum to the Pakistani prime minister detailing the difficulties Memons faced in acquiring citizenship in Ceylon. The issue was broached in the Pakistani Constituent Assembly.[21] For all the uncertainty, migration to select territories from South Asia continued apace after 1947, with the numbers of Memons in Ceylon increasing from that year onward. Beginning in the late 1950s, Bohras and Memons alike had their own state-appointed *qazis* (Muslim judges) in the country, which gained its independence in 1948.[22]

In Africa the picture was variegated. The onset of apartheid in South Africa in 1948 ensured that the economic life of Indian communities was riven by a systematic color barrier. Those barriers had certainly existed South Africa from the late nineteenth century (as seen in chapter 4), but they now assumed grotesque proportions. Nevertheless, as Thomas Blom Hansen has argued, owing to their deep integration into the Afrikaner farming economy in the Transvaal, Memons were spared the worst economic ravages of apartheid.[23] Yet by the 1970s many South African Muslims of Indian descent,. including the Memons, found their voice in the anti-Apartheid struggle and began to mobilize against it.[24]

By contrast, East Africa, still largely under colonial rule until the mid-1960s, persisted as a fertile ground for Gujarati Muslim entrepreneurship. This did not stem from any special dedication to colonial authorities. There were many Gujarati Muslims, including Harun Ahmed, a Bohra journalist, who were prolific critics of colonial rule and imprisoned for their trouble.[25] Instead their success stemmed from their pursuit of the economic opportunities furnished by the postwar order. Perhaps the best indicator of this are the directories produced by Bohra, Khoja, and Memon *jamaats* in the 1960s and 1970s.[26] In Anglophone and Francophone East Africa alone, these show ever-increasing numbers of Gujarati Muslim-owned businesses in operation. As ever, the capital of these entrepreneurs was joined to the *jamaat*, where it underwrote educational and religious programs of great variety.

Processes of intra-*jamaat* religious rivalry persisted, among the Ismaili and Twelver Khojas most of all, but the tone of polemic appears comparatively more restrained. For example, when an anti-Ismaili polemic was printed in Zanzibar in 1947, members of the local Ismaili *jamaat* predictably penned a fierce rebuttal. Even so, the editors of a Twelver Khoja newspaper in Zanzibar, *Inquilab* (Revolution), dispatched a telegram to the Agha Khan III, then in Marseilles, denouncing the action and asking him to restrain those in the Ismaili *jamaat* eager to exact reprisals. As their telegram stated, "Taking reprisal through press may result regrettable feelings between two communities amidst good foundation of brotherhood laid by your highness during [your] Diamond Jubilee."[27] Even if the long-standing debates among Ismaili and Twelver Khojas over the question of the imamate proved irresolvable, at the very least a modus vivendi of a sort had been reached in East Africa.

The Agha Khan III and local Ismaili Khoja *jamaats* had busied themselves since the 1950s with the matter of East African economic and educational developments. Their ambitions were strengthened by two processes. First, beginning in the 1930s, the leaders of the Ismailia Provincial Council in Tanganyika had diversified from trade into modest industrial production.[28] Second, in a move advocated at the global level by the Agha Khan III and his successor from 1957, the Agha Khan IV, Ismaili Khojas attempted to acquire a greater share in the ownership of industrial enterprises in Africa in the early 1950s.[29] Likewise, Ismaili Khoja *jamaat* councils became ever more ambitious in their corporate and public activities, and in 1962 a Constitution of the East African Nizaris was promulgated by the Agha Khan IV which established a clear-cut hierarchy of *jamaat* judicial authorities and provincial bodies across the region, and dramatically overhauled Khoja personal law.[30]

Although for the Bohras, Khojas, and Memons alike the old problems of *jamaat* administration never disappeared, there was a demonstrable turn in 1950s East Africa toward philanthropic projects of a more resolutely public nature in the sense that non-*jamaat* Muslims were targeted as beneficiaries.[31] Bohra and Khoja capital was sometimes pooled, along with the Colonial Development Fund, to fund Muslim educational establishments in East Africa. Private Bohra capital also continued to endow *jamaats* and public institutions. In the case of the Karimjee Group in Zanzibar in 1963, £256,000 went to institutions as various as the town hall in Dar es Salaam, a Bohra school in Mombasa, and the Sports Gymkhana in Tanga, among other entities. Though the question of the extent to which Africans were the beneficiaries of these projects is still a subject of controversy, it must be remembered that *jamaat*-centered institutions excluded Africans and Indians alike. What is more, several educational institutions founded by Indians included African students, though their numbers were admittedly modest. One distinct approach in the matter of African-Indian rapprochement was presented by the Twelver Khojas, who had been more forthright than other Indian Muslim groups about interacting with and converting local Africans from an early period.[32] The Bilal Muslim Mission, set up by Twelver Khojas in 1964, marked an ambitious new phase in that endeavor. The organization survives to this day, responsible for converting a sizable share of African families to Twelver Shiʿism.[33]

Although Indians occasionally worked alongside African nationalists, African anticolonial politics left the Indian communities of the region in an awkward position. As was mentioned above, even in India and Pakistan, Gujaratis were framed as colonial stooges by state bureaucrats. The leap was all the easier in East Africa since the arrival of Indians in large numbers—leaving aside the longstanding pre-colonial presence—was enabled by colonial policy. Anti-Indian sentiment took many forms. Though Kenya, independent as of 1963, never expelled or forcibly expropriated the assets of its Indian populations as Tanganyika and Uganda did in the ensuing decade, the wealth possessed by some Indian families and institutions was controversial. Jomo Kenyatta, for one, voiced frequent disquiet about economic disparities between Africans and Indians, and made no effort to disrupt the outward migration of Indians from Kenya from 1968.[34]

Kenyatta's measured stance did not prevent others in the Kenyan government from making aggressive gestures toward the Gujarati Muslim commercial castes, including the Agha Khan IV himself, who had in 1966 declared his Kenyan followers' loyalty to Kenyatta.[35] A year before, in 1965, one delegate crowed that the country's economic enemies were formerly British imperialists, "but now, Mr. Speaker, Sir, we must defeat and liquidate our economic enemies, and these people are the Indian community." In a remark that could be considered humorous if it was not so deadly earnest, he deemed the Agha Khan IV "the head of these exploiters." (Earlier that year the Agha Khan IV's fortune had been attributed to his "bloodsucking" of Kenya.) For all his bluster, the delegate also voiced concern that Khoja accounts would be impossible to read, as they were composed in Gujarati.[36] Saber-rattling of this sort could only mean catastrophe for the corporate privileges of the Gujarati Muslim commercial castes.

Similar sentiments were voiced over the better part of the ensuing decade by state actors in numerous settings where the Gujarati Muslim commercial castes called home. Pogroms, expulsions, and expropriation were the logical outcome. Pakistan, a country that proclaimed itself the safe haven for South Asian Muslims, was to prove one of the many transgressors, a reminder that the economic disparities among South Asian Muslims that the Bohras, Khojas, and Memons exemplified distinguished these groups in Pakistan as much as African-Indian, Burmese-Indian, and Sinhalese-Indian disparities did in other parts of the diaspora. Before turning to those events, the question of Gujarati Muslim economic capture in early Pakistan must be grappled with.

Pakistan, the *Jamaats*, and Economic Capture, 1947–1965

Beginning in the 1970s, American and Soviet academics noticed that Pakistan's economic sector was inordinately dominated by a small cluster of firms, many of whose proprietors hailed from the Gujarati Muslim commercial castes. The question remains to what degree the runaway success of the Gujarati Muslim commercial castes and other leading firms operating in early Pakistan was dependent upon direct associations with the salariat. In the 1960s commentators within Pakistan, not least the economist Mahbub ul Haq, regarded the fortunes of the leading Pakistani companies as a direct outgrowth of their governmental contacts. In the minds of many Bangladeshi nationalists and India-based Pakistan watchers, too, the economic oligopoly of the Bohras, Khojas, Memons (and Chiniotis) was inextricably tied to the political dominance of the Pathans and Punjabis in the bureaucracy and army from the time of Ayub Khan especially.[37] Meanwhile, contemporary Soviet specialists, like the aforementioned Sergey Levin, saw the Memons as the most powerful group among the upper bourgeoisie of Pakistan, a "self-contained" caste that kept aloof from others and duked it out with other industrial bourgeoisie for preferential market opportunities.[38]

There is some evidence that the Pakistani civil bureaucracy did look to the "nascent industrial bourgeoisie to help off-set the influence of indigenous landowning and tribal groups," an alliance cemented partially by the nonlocal origins of both the bureaucrats and industrialists, their urban background, and their shared commitment to projects of Islamic "reform."[39] All the same, the process of co-optation took a decade and a half to germinate and was by no means total. More convincing is the analysis of Hanna Papanek, who has described the structure of the so-called "big houses" (the leading Pakistani commercial firms) at length and argued that the political prominence of firms was a second-generation phenomenon.[40] This move by many of Pakistan's early commercial firms was conditioned by the transformation of their economic portfolios from 1947 and the growing conviction among second-generation managers that they had a stake in the Pakistani political system.

One factor facilitated this movement above all: nearly all the pre-independence commercial firms that migrated to Pakistan had shifted their primary occupation from trade to industry in the years after 1947. As Papanek has described it, "Most of the twelve industrial-commercial combines . . . are relative newcomers to large-scale industrial activity, even though the scope of commercial activity in which some of them engaged . . . was very large in the Indian context." Their pronounced access to liquid capital explained why, despite migrating in large numbers from outside the territories of East and West Pakistan, they made an inordinate investment in early Pakistani industrial enterprise, albeit disproportionately in the west wing.[41]

The boom time in West Pakistan was bound up with the meteoric rise of Karachi after 1947. Earlier chapters have demonstrated Karachi's importance in the economic lives of the Muslim mercantile castes. From the 1920s onward the Harun family, who had earlier headed the Karachi branches of the

Red Crescent and Khilafat Committee, invested heavily in the district of Lyari, where they built orphanages, madrasas, colleges, and mosques. When Mahmud, the son of Seth Haji Abd Allah Harun, became mayor of Karachi in the 1950s, he allocated sizable funds to Lyari's development.[42] It is worth noting, however, that migration from Burma, East Africa, and Western India to Karachi peaked in the late 1950s and early 1960s, a time when Muslim firms were encouraged by the better business climate—and less regulation—to leave India for Pakistan.[43]

As a consequence of this, the early 1950s in Pakistan was a period where private enterprise soared, far more than in independent India, where import and exports were subjected to intense regulation from the late 1940s onward, well before the "license Raj" soon took effect.[44] This early period of liberalization is something that appears to have been missed in comparative studies of the political economy of India and Pakistan, which tend to assume that the Pakistani Army's role in the economy was substantial from the start.[45] Although many of the same firms studied here became part of Pakistan's small business elite, there were plenty of entities that had not existed before 1947 who hit the jackpot in the speculative economy encouraged by the "vacuum" of Partition.[46]

In Karachi the arrivals of Bohra, Khoja, and Memon constituencies set up new religious enterprises in the city—assisted no doubt by the building boom then transforming the urban topography of the city and the vacancies of non-Muslim properties—complete with charitable and educational subsidiaries that continued to fill the "institutional voids" in Pakistan's weak social services sector. As never before, Gujarati Muslim businessmen in Karachi became enthusiastic proponents of education, acknowledging its human capital benefits and setting up educational and industrial institutions to support them.[47] Many of these preserved the "sectarian" *jamaat*-centric character they had possessed in the colonial period, reflecting the sustained links between religious and commercial firms that survived the double dislocations of Partition and migration.

Immediately, numerous Memon-funded schools were constructed that, though secular, predominantly served the members of select *jamaats,* giving the first generation of Pakistan-born Memon commercial entrepreneurs a distinct educational advantage.[48] Memon capital also underwrote various educational schemes for Memon women, who rank among the most successful female entrepreneurs in Pakistan today.[49] The Kutiyana Memon *jamaat*, transplanted from Kutiyana in Gujarat to Karachi in the early 1950s, was one of many examples. Over the subsequent decades this *jamaat* founded a host of hospitals, schools, sports teams, business, and residential complexes for the exclusive use of Kutiyana Memons.

Parallel exertions were undertaken by the Bohras and Khojas. The Sunni Khoja *jamaat* set up its own base in Karachi, where it has maintained its distinct identity from other Pakistani Sunnis while retaining links with its counterpart *jamaat* in Bombay.[50] It was eclipsed by the many *jamaats* and *anjumans* (societies) constructed by Twelver Khojas, who have made Karachi their foremost base in Pakistan. The Anjuman-i Khuddām al-Qurʾān (Society for the Protection of the Quran) was one of many Twelver Khoja entities dedicated to religious education and strengthening links between Twelver Shiʿi ulama and the laity.[51] Like their Sunni counterparts, they also retained links with brethren in Bombay, where the *jamaat* has founded several trusts that supply loans and other welfare services to its members.[52] Bohra institutions in Karachi—such as the Hasani Academy, covered in detail in chapter 6—preserved the Bohra footprint in Karachi, though in a compelling development, many of the Bohra dissidents of the interwar period rejoined the mainline Bohra *jamaat* in the early 1950s, including Hatim Alavi, formerly the self-designated head of the dissidents. Rumors had it that he had done so at the insistence of the Pakistani prime minister, Liaquat Ali Khan, who, as a condition for Alavi's entrance into Pakistani politics demanded the Bohra bring a bloc of Bohra votes with him.[53] As it had been in the late colonial era, the *jamaat* was a force to be reckoned with in politics.

Unsurprisingly, the influx of Gujarati Muslim capital caused animosity with other Pakistani merchant groups. Even from an early period some of this was predicated on the notion that the Gujarati Muslim commercial castes were foreign interlopers. Such a charge was low-hanging fruit, as these groups did not hail from the five territories that made up Pakistan: Baluchistan, Kashmir, Khyber Pakhtunwala, Punjab, or Sindh (although, as noted in chapter 1, a sizable number of Khojas and Memons were of Sindhi extraction). An internal memo produced by the Indian government related that "There is considerable jealousy and illfeeling [*sic*] between the Memons and Khojas on the one hand and the other traders from Western Pakistan on the other. The Memons and Khojas are strongly entrenched in Karachi but have not been able to find a footing upcountry."[54] Even so, it would be a mistake to think the Gujarati Muslim commercial castes carried all before them. If another confidential Indian government memo sent from Karachi on October 15, 1948, is to be credited, the late Adamji Haji Daud's son stated that Muslim merchants were disappointed in the lack of opportunities in Karachi and returning to Bombay and Kathiawar.[55]

In retrospect, these appear to have been temporary setbacks. Assisted by long-accumulated merchant capital and bolstered by *jamaat* support, Memon migrants carved out a cavernous niche in Karachi. Ismaili Khojas also made Karachi their main bastion, given a boost by not only the international activism of the Agha Khan IV but also the decision of the commercial magnate Amir Ali Fancy, who had close ties to the Ismaili imam, to migrate from East Africa to Karachi in 1947. Shortly after his arrival, Fancy was appointed head of the Ismailia Supreme Council for West Pakistan and summoned the council to encourage research into economic opportunities for Ismaili Khojas. By the 1960s Fancy was chairman of Industrial Managements Ltd., as well as head of the Platinum Jubilee Finance and Investment Corporation, managed by the *jamaat*. The Agha Khan IV and his family also plowed capital into two jute mills in East Pakistan: Crescent Jute Mill and the People's Jute Mill.[56] Like no other religious firm, the Ismaili Khoja *jamaat* has supplied its constituents in Pakistan from the 1950s with ready access to cooperative credit societies, bountiful education opportunities, and healthcare.

The underdevelopment of the banking sector was a core feature of the economy in early Pakistan. Still, access to the cheap liquid credit supplied by state or state-adjacent banking institutions supplied substantial advantages to top Gujarati Muslim commercial firms. Though the exact relationship between the leading commercial firms and the state may be debated at length, what is indisputable is that, as Lawrence Wright argued almost fifty years ago, the high concentration of banking power in the hands of select commercial firms translated easily into political power. While the initial springboard for the growth of the early banking sector in Pakistan was the capital supplied by leading industrial families, including the Adamjis, Habibs, and Saigols, once the financial system became robust enough, some firms began utilizing their position to channel large shares of capital into their own accounts. The weak character of state-owned banks in Pakistan only exacerbated this.[57] The inevitable by-product was the emergence of a cartel comprising leading industrial consortia that had monopolized the country's blank slate of a finance sector.

Once again, the coalescence of this cartel can be attributed in no small measure to the Muslim underrepresentation in banking before 1947. As was discussed in chapter 7, on the eve of Pakistan's creation Jinnah gained the loyalty of one of India's only Muslim-owned banks, Habib Bank Ltd., founded in Bombay in 1941 by Muhammad Habib, a Twelver Khoja. Habib moved his bank's headquarters to Karachi in 1947. Before India handed over Pakistani-owned assets, Habib reputedly gave Jinnah a blank check, to which was added some Rs. 80 million.[58] At Partition, Habib Bank had a paid-up capital of Rs. 5 million, which had grown within a decade to Rs. 15 million. Over the course of the same period, its reserve funds had increased from Rs. 2.5 million to Rs. 15 million. It also expanded its branches from two in the area of West Pakistan to sixty-seven by the end of 1955, with an additional one in India. It also set up offices in Colombo, Mombasa, and Rangoon through a subsidiary. By 1958 the bank's deposit liabilities were equivalent to approximately one-fourth of all the bank deposits within Pakistan.[59]

While Habib Bank pursued the large profits to be had in the commercial field, the State Bank of Pakistan turned its initial attention to fleshing out the state sector. The State Bank's first president was Zahid Hussain, an economics graduate from Aligarh Muslim University who had worked first as an accountant in the colonial bureaucracy, then as minister of finance for Hyderabad State, and finally on the All-India Muslim League's Planning Commission in 1944. In its initial stages, the State Bank of Pakistan under Hussain was praised by international observers as a model government financial institution in the developing world.

In the early 1950s Hussain also oversaw the beginning of Pakistan's First Five-Year Plans. If one analysis of development regimes in postcolonial Asia has posited that three strategies—a land reform program that breaks up large farms in favor of family plots, export-oriented manufacturing, and tight financial control—make the difference between economic success and stagnation, then Pakistan's early planners have to be considered alongside their counterparts in Southeast Asia who pursued almost none of these policies.[60] The failure of land reform in Pakistan is well known, and it can be safely argued that without the capacity to generate the agricultural surpluses that are a prerequisite for the expansion of a developing country's financial and manufacturing base, Pakistan's development schemes were fatally undermined from the start. Moreover, without a strong handle on central finance—and, besides this, lacking a bureaucracy willing to discipline industry and subordinate it to national purposes—the economy of early Pakistan was susceptible to rent-seeking behaviors of the most egregious kind.

Whereas the state bank in most countries with advanced capital and financial markets concerns itself with government monetary policy, in light of Pakistan's weak commercial banking scene, the State Bank of Pakistan had to assume the burden for the growth of this sector too. The creation of the National Bank of Pakistan in 1948, as a commercial subsidiary of the State Bank, was intended to do just this, but over the next two and a half decades the bank's performance left much to be desired. A work completed on Pakistan's economy in the 1950s made plain just how difficult the State Bank's plight was: "At the outset, the State Bank was faced with the formidable task of organizing normal central banking services within a very short period and simultaneously undertaking certain other duties of an altogether exceptional nature. The dearth of trained and experienced personnel rendered its task difficult. It had a skeleton staff of only a few experienced officers who had opted for service in Pakistan from the personnel of the Reserve Bank of India."[61]

The case that best illustrates how the leading industrial families operated something akin to a cartel in the financial sector was the Pakistan Industrial Credit and Investment Corporation Ltd. (PICIC). Created in 1957, the PICIC was set up to supply loans and equity investment to new enterprises.[62] If the National Bank of Pakistan failed to live up to its potential as a lender to enterprises outside the leading merchant families, but at least preserved the fiction of independence, then the PICIC serves as an example of a banking institution that was made subservient to the whims of the leading industrialists. In 1966 its board of directors included executives from Amin, Adamjee, Crescent, Dawood, Fancy, and Valika.[63] According to one estimate, between 1958 and 1970, thirty-seven monopoly houses acquired 65 percent of the loans supplied by PICIC, with thirteen of those thirty-seven earning 70 percent of that number.[64] This was a textbook definition of state capture.

As will be shown in the next two sections, the controversy over economic capture in Pakistan by the twenty-two families came to a head in the 1970s, but it was preceded by a wave of attacks across Africa and Asia against the Gujarati Muslim commercial castes and other Indian merchant communities.

TABLE 8.1 A list of top twelve Pakistani firms in the late 1960s and early 1970s.

Name	*Community*	*Family Origin*	*Business HQ, before 1947*
Dawood	Memon	Kathiawar (Bantva)	Bombay
Habib	Twelver Khoja	Bombay	Bombay
Adamjee	Memon	Kathiawar (Jetpur)	Calcutta
Crescent	Punjabi Sheikh	Western Punjab (Chiniot)	Delhi
Saigol	Punjabi Sheikh	Western Punjab (Chakwal)	Calcutta
Valika	Daudi Bohra	Bombay	Bombay
Hyesons	N / A	Madras	Madras
Bawany	Memon	Kathiawar (Jetpur)	Rangoon
Amin	Punjabi Sheikh	Western Punjab	Calcutta
Wazir Ali	N / A, Sayyid	Western Punjab (Lahore)	Lahore
Fancy	Ismaili Khoja	Kathiawar	East Africa
Colony	Punjabi Sheikh	Western Punjab (Chiniot)	Lahore

The high proportion of Punjabi Chinioti-owned enterprises is a reminder that Gujarati Muslim firms did not singlehandedly dominate the economy. Yet the table as a whole reflects the fact that the same four communities who held sway over Muslim business in late colonial north and western India were able to recreate their influence in early Pakistan.

Reformatted, with the permission of the University of Chicago Press, from Hanna Papanek, "Pakistan's Big Businessmen: Muslim Separatism, Entrepreneurship, and Partial Modernization," *Economic Development and Cultural Change* 21, no. 1 (1972): table 1.

State Violence in Tanganyika, Iraq, Uganda, and East Pakistan, 1965–1973

The wave of state-sanctioned violence that crashed upon the Gujarati Muslim commercial castes in the eight years from 1965 to 1973 was a remarkable, albeit tragic, historical conjecture. Even though these episodes were discrete phenomena, they happened with surprising frequency and followed one after another in short order. The persecution of Gujarati Muslim populations represented the high water mark of the early postcolonial period's turn against capitalism and minority rights and ensured that the lofty discourse of third world solidarity advanced over the previous decade rang hollow. Throughout the diaspora there was resentment against the particularism of Gujarati Muslim *jamaats*, making them soft targets for economic expropriation. Many of these pogroms against Indians have been well covered by historians of Africa. The case of East Pakistan—and the subsequent birth of Bangladesh—supplies a lesser-known example, one that foreshadowed the eventual crackdown in Pakistan after 1971, covered later in the chapter.[65]

Socialism was not always and everywhere inimical to the Gujarati Muslim commercial castes. During the period of *ujamaa* (state socialism) in Tanzania in 1961 the Agha Khan IV encouraged his followers to respect it, but also remain dedicated to individual enterprise.[66] But in environments of extreme inequality it took no great leap of the imagination to see socialism as a battering ram against the forces of capital. With the Zanzibar Revolution of 1964 the turn against Arab and Indian communities became a matter of official policy.[67] Over the next decade the persecution of the Khoja population was particularly nefarious. Between 1970 and 1973 the prospect that Khoja girls would be subjected to "forced marriages"—a very real possibility given that four young Iranian women were compelled to do just that—prompted an exodus of Khoja families from the island.[68] With their flight disappeared one of the most affluent, if hotly contested, sites in the diasporas of both the Ismaili and Twelver Khojas.

Yet another "socialist" revolution—that launched by the Baʿathists in Iraq in 1968—also brought tragedy to the Twelver Khoja population in the country. The most notorious incident was the dispossession of the Gokal Co., one of the leading Gujarati Muslim businesses in Iraq and a stalwart in regional shipping. That year the firm's longtime proprietor, renowned among local Iraqi Shiʿis for his charitable work, was executed by the Baʿathists on the ridiculous charge of spying for Israel.[69] His nephews fled Iraq, and over the next decade the company expanded to unprecedented limits.[70] The nephews benefited handsomely from government contracts awarded by Pakistan's military dictatorship, and within a few years they would be leading underwriters of the al-Khoei Foundation, an important transnational Twelver Shiʿi organization. In that guise they carried on a brisk business with Iran during its war with Iraq in the 1980s, even supplying arms to the regime of Ayatollah Ruhollah Khomeini.[71] Only after 2003 did the Twelver Khoja *jamaat* reestablish its pilgrimage infrastructures in Iraq's shrine cities.[72]

Though no friend of the Baʿathists, the Bohras appear to have avoided the genocidal violence that regime exacted on its Shiʿi populations over the next three and a half decades, and the *dai* was able to perform pilgrimage to the shrine cities throughout the reign of Saddam Hussein. However, the same year of the Iraqi revolution saw the Bohra *dai* summarily expelled from Tanzania. Having assumed the mantle of *dai* in 1965 with the death of Tahir Saif al-Din, Muhammad Burhan al-Din carried on his predecessor's habit of visiting *jamaats* throughout the diaspora. His ouster in 1968 by the Tanzanian government was a serious rebuff, but the nature of events in Tanzania are rather controversial.[73] A report published in 1979 by the Citizens of Democracy—a body commissioned to investigate the persecution of Bohra dissidents in India by the mainline faction—regarded it as just desserts for poor treatment of dissidents.[74]

Whatever the case, the *dai*'s expulsion from Tanzania said much about the precarious position of the Bohras in postcolonial East Africa. Still, it was a nonevent when compared to the well-known sufferings endured by Asians in Uganda in 1972–1973 after Idi Amin's infamous expulsion decree. In an example of how traditions of corporate Islam were attacked in the country at this time, Radio Uganda reported in February 1973 that the army's head of religious affairs was handing over property abandoned by Indian communities to the state's chief qadi. Forthwith properties once owned by the Bohra, Ismaili Khoja, Twelver Khoja, and Sunni *jamaats* were "the property . . . of all Muslims in Uganda."[75] That odious link between military and state-run religious authority, and the license it gave to the appropriation of private assets, was soon to be replicated in Pakistan.

As the chaos in Uganda reached fever pitch, events in East Pakistan were no less dramatic. The Pakistani Army's genocide casts a long shadow over much scholarship on the history of East Pakistan in the two and a half decades after Partition, and rightly so. Having said that, the trope of a West Pakistani dominance in the economy of East Pakistan should perhaps be treated with greater caution than has previously been the case. It was not simply West Pakistani capital: it was capital that had been built upon from Mombasa to Moulmein over many generations. Moreover, the Bengali contribution to the East Pakistani economy was something that commentators recognized, including Sergey Levin, the Soviet scholar mentioned at the beginning of this chapter. One of the largest corporate conglomerates was run by A. K. Khan, a Chittagong native, who set up A. K. Khan Co. Ltd. in 1945. Before becoming head of East Pakistan's industrial policy in 1958, he had founded several factories, mills, plants, and shipping concerns.[76] Still, as the head of Pakistan's Five-Year Plans later admitted, for all the economic growth of the 1960s, "unemployment increased, real wages in the industrial sector declined by one-third, per capita income disparity between East and West Pakistan, and concentrations of industrial wealth became an explosive economic and political issue."[77] In the mind of this commentator, the growing chasm between East and West Pakistan was an unambiguous sign of development gone terribly wrong.

To what extent the actions of the Gujarati Muslim commercial firms can be blamed for this inequality is hard to gauge. First, there is the problem of long-term regional and demographic-based inequalities stemming from the colonial period that continued to affect postcolonial economic endowments into the 1970s. Second, to say that industrialists were merely working at the behest of the state is to seriously overrate the coherence of Pakistan's planning policies and to underrate the self-interest of these economic firms. East Pakistan–based political actors also benefited from the largesse of commercial firms, including Shaikh Mujibur Rahman, who was not only employed by the Haroon consortium (the legacy of Seth Haji Abd Allah Harun) for a time, but whose election campaigns on the Awami League ticket were supported financially by Dawood and Haroon alike, both Memon commercial firms.[78] Rather than an exploitative elite cornering the market with the help of state authorities, many of the Pakistani industrialists operating in East Pakistan in these decades simply were taking advantage of the new commercial vacuum made available by the departure of leading non-Muslims.

One example of this was the Bawany Group, a Memon entity whose original proprietor, Ahmad Ibrahim Bawani, had started operations in Rangoon in 1900, building a successful hosiery and textile business before moving to India during the Second World War.[79] By the 1950s the firm had several enormous mill operations in Dhaka and Karachi. Successive yearbooks of the Karachi Stock Exchange make its prominence unambiguously clear. In East Pakistan its operations included Ahmed Bawany Textile Mills Ltd., Latif Bawany Jute Mills Ltd., and Eastern Tubes Ltd. (all in Dhaka), and Eastern Chemical Industries Ltd. and R. R. Textile Mills Ltd. (both in Chittagong).[80] Some of the firm's East Pakistan concerns held associations with Japanese firms, not least Eastern Tubes Ltd., a joint venture with Toshiba for the manufacture of fluorescent tube lights.[81] The firm's capital made a permanent imprint on the religious economy of Dhaka through the funding it supplied for the construction of the sprawling Bait al-Mukarram National Mosque, a complex with an attached bazaar containing a veritable beehive of warehouses and shops and a capacity of some thirty thousand worshippers.[82] As they had in the colonial period, Gujarati Muslim commercial entrepreneurs continued to give several varieties of Islam in Pakistan a robust physical expression.

Having said that, tensions in East Pakistan—between, on the one hand, local labor and, on the other, non-Bengali labor and capitalists—could be explosive. This is best illustrated through the case of the Adamjee Jute Mills. Before his death in 1948, Sir Adamji Haji Daud established the Muslim Commercial Bank Ltd. and Orient Airways Ltd. in West Pakistan but maintained extensive holdings in what was pre-Partition Bengal. One year after Adamji's demise, his sons put before the government of Pakistan the scheme for the expansion of their father's already enormous jute mill complex at Dhaka to Narayanganj, making it the world's largest jute operation.[83] Tariq Omar Ali argues that the Adamjee Jute Mills marked a "successful partnership between the state and favored capitalists."[84] The second generation of Adamjis did indeed cultivate links with army general (and, later, president) Ayub Khan from the late 1950s onward, with the general heralding the Adamjee Science College as a model institution mixing charitable outreach with educational and economic development.[85] Cozying up to the state was a sine qua non of survival for many top commercial firms in postcolonial developmental regimes, part of an elastic strategy that simultaneously kept the state at arm's length and in one's pocket. Over time, however, the risk became that the state asserted its full authority over the firm.

The cordial relations between the Adamji family and Ayub Khan masked deeper unrest on the company's factory floors. Even before Ayub Khan came to power, Adamjee Mills was the locus for intense feuds between local Bengali workers and transplanted Urdu speakers from Bihar that descended into a bout of deadly rioting in 1954.[86] From then on, the management of Adamjee Jute Mills was seen by many local Bengalis as a primary expression of a West Pakistani monopoly over East Pakistan's economy.[87] Henceforth the mill's Bengali workers were organized in a union led by Darul Uloom Deoband seminary graduate Maulana Bhashani, the famous "Red Maulana" who became a key advocate first for the growth of Bengali-owned industry and later for an independent Bangladesh.[88] Bhashani was a religious and political entrepreneur whose blending of Islamic activism and socialism was of a piece with broader currents in contemporary Pakistan. Amid the war for Bangladesh's independence, he was later to exhort the workers, "Don't burn the Adamjee Jute Mills, burn Adamjee!"[89] Similar pronouncements were to rear their head in West Pakistan a few months later, as they had in Burma and East Africa earlier.

"Islamic Socialism" and the Attack on Corporate Islam in Pakistan, 1970–1973

The advent of a geographically truncated and ideologically fitful Pakistan in the 1970s laid the framework for three developments: first, for the articulation of an Islamic form of socialism under Prime Minister Zulfiqar Ali Bhutto; second, for the nationalization of key industries, the decline of leading Muslim firms, and the integration of cowed businessmen into the state; and, third, for a reaction among an alliance of religious firms, landlords, and business leaders against the "un-Islamic" socialist policies pursued by Bhutto. In turn, this instigated the coup orchestrated by Zia al-Haqq, who sought to integrate the Islamists and business leaders into a dramatically reshaped state structure that made the Islamization of Pakistani society its end goal. These decades rewrote the institutional framework governing the political and religious economies of Pakistan, with implications for the birth of Islamic finance as a global phenomenon.

As one historian has argued, although the 1950s had seen the onset of unresolved constitutional debates about the Pakistani state and Islam, it was only in the 1960s under the economic development programs implemented by Ayub Khan "that the spotlight turned on the economic and social complexion of a state that professed to be founded on Islam." At the same time, certain actors within the All-India Muslim League in Bengal and Punjab championed land reform did so on the pretext that this was what an Islamic economic system ordained, with the "Red Maulana," Bhashani, one among many who drew this link. But after a decade in which the fruits of Ayub Khan's development schemes failed to reach a broader demographic base, in part because of an inadequate focus on social welfare sectors, Muslim business was caught in the middle ground between the Muslim socialists demanding economic programs they deemed commensurate with Islam and the proponents of an Islamic economy among the Islamists and the ulama.[90] Even if Ayub Khan's rule was characterized by his special patronage of Pashtun entrepreneurs, the links between him and some Memon businessmen, like Sadiq Daud, were substantive. Even Memon firms, including the Haroon Corporation, which had never supported the general, were seen as beneficiaries of their relationship with the government and were eventually subjected to nationalization under Bhutto as a result.[91]

Ideas of "Islamic socialism" certainly did not originate in 1960s Pakistan, but had their origins in late colonial India and Egypt.[92] Several interwar Muslim commentators conflated some of the goals of socialism and Islam, although many of the same figures were keen to preserve at least an element of free enterprise. Yet the accent was placed on an "Islamic" variety of free enterprise, in which room was left for state control. Thus, in the early 1950s, the nascent Pakistani state turned its attention to fostering the creation of an Islamic economic zone stretching into the Middle East, with Pakistan at its head. This took many forms. For one, Liaquat Ali Khan, Pakistan's prime minister, called for the extension of US president Harry Truman's aid plan to the Middle East, and the fostering of economic cooperation between the Arab states and Pakistan for the "realization of Islamic values, democracy, and social justice."[93] In another case, Muhammad Hamid Allah (a transplant from Hyderabad) would advocate, as early as 1949, the creation of an Islamic currency zone incorporating Muslim countries in the Middle East and South Asia.[94]

From the late 1950s onward, amid the drive for economic modernization, these ideas gained added urgency. According to Fazlur Rahman, Ayub Khan had invoked the term "Islamic socialism" in his "Introduction to the Guidelines of the Third Five-Year Plan," but it was eventually expunged in the plan's printed reports after objections from Muslim businessmen, the Islamist organization Jamāʿat-i Islāmī, and the ulama.[95] The objection of the Jamāʿat-i Islāmī—founded in Punjab in 1941 by the prolific commentator Sayyid Abu al-Aʿla Mawdudi—is noteworthy. With its protest, the organization signaled that its Islamist program had a staunch economic dimension that diverged from that of the Pakistani state. Two decades later that economic program would gain official backing under military dictatorship. At the time, however, Ayub Khan brushed aside this opposition, invoking the phrase "Islamic socialism" in a speech to the National Economic Council, as the mouthpiece of the Karachi-based World Muslim Congress noted with approval.[96] The Council Muslim League had in turn adopted a resolution in 1968 calling for "the establishment of Islamic social and economic justice for all the people of Pakistan" by means of the creation of state monopolies in industry, energy, trade, and agriculture.[97] Surprisingly, even a business magnate like Ispahani told the Pakistan Soviet Cultural Society in December 1969 that Muhammad Ali Jinnah "was a believer in Islamic socialism," words that came in for criticism in the *Pakistan Review,* which held that Islam had no need for a socialist "crutch."[98]

In a curious mix of commercial entrepreneurship and Sunni religious activism, Ahmad Ibrahim Bawani, a prolific Muslim proselytizer and member of the great Memon industrial family, wrote his *Revolutionary Strategy for National Development* in 1970, where he railed against the "curse of interest" and the imperative for an Islamic economy built on socialist principles.[99] Therefore, among an uneasy constellation of business and religious firms there was a vague sense that what the moment demanded was a reconciliation of the ideals of Islam and socialism. Mawdudi's Jamāʿat-i Islāmī serves as an interesting case study of how these ideas of Islamic economics and socialism coalesced, albeit awkwardly, in the program advanced by a religious firm. Mawdudi had earlier criticized ideas of Islamic socialism, which he saw as a contradiction in terms and an overextension of the state's role in economic affairs. By the end of the 1960s, however, his economic program came to share many of the statist ideas espoused by the Pakistan People's Party, including the nationalization of industries.[100] In time, Mawdudi's *jamaat,* a stalwart advocate for the creation of an "Islamic economy," would supplant the Gujarati and Punjabi firms as the ultimate benchmark of Muslim economic enterprise in Pakistan.

When dovetailing with ideas of Islamic socialism, this mobilization around crystallizing ideas of an Islamic economy in Pakistan ensured that, by the end of the decade, the resentment felt toward the leading commercial firms reached a boiling point. Kalim Siddiqui, a political Islamist who merged socialist and Islamic economic ideas, spoke for many prominent Pakistanis when he argued that the "arrival of these wealthy quasi-caste Muslims can be described as an economic invasion of Pakistan. By virtue of their successful occupation of Pakistan's economy at the outset they now claim the right to be included among the 'saviours' of Pakistan."[101] For Siddiqui, the oligopoly of these "quasi-caste Muslims" was a violation of Pakistan's founding ideology and a roadblock to the attainment of an Islamic economic order where the fruits of commerce were shared equally.

The chief consequence of Islamist and socialist mobilization around the idea of an Islamic socialism was an attack on the leading Muslim commercial firms. Paradoxically, the valorization of the twenty-two families into a polemical set piece owed not to the protests of socialists or Islamists but to a developmental economist trained at Cambridge and Yale Universities, Mahbub ul Haq, who became chief economist of the National Planning Commission under Ayub Khan. At a speech given in Karachi in April 1968, Haq inveighed against the concentration of "two thirds of the industrial assets, 80 percent of banking, and 70 percent of insurance" in the hands of these twenty-two families. He further argued that this pattern of development had exacerbated disparities between East and West Pakistan and a spectacular decline in the real wages of industrial workers.[102] For their own contrary purposes, the Awami League in East Pakistan had also mobilized these numbers to stir up support among the Bengali-speaking masses.[103]

Although Haq's primary aim was to reform the economic program of Ayub Khan, his speech turned out to be a miscalculation, as he himself later acknowledged, writing that "the debate on twenty-two family groups in Pakistan got completely out of control."[104] Other Western economists writing at the time, such as Lawrence Wright, disputed Haq's assessment, maintaining that he was right to argue that wealth concentration in Pakistan was high but that he had inflated the actual figures.[105] Once the genie was out of the bottle it could not be contained. Even if Haq's speech was intended to jump-start institutional reforms that would strengthen capitalism by spreading the benefits of development more widely and bringing an end to what he called "economic feudalism" of the bureaucrats, landlords, and industrialists, it morphed into a call for dispossession of the leading Muslim commercial firms.[106] As a lone dissenting voice put it at the time, the number twenty-two had taken on "mysterious currency" in Pakistan, rather like the Trinity or the Seven Deadly Sins.[107] Subsequent commentators have corroborated this, pointing out that the notion of twenty-two families was nothing but a pernicious myth, with the *Pakistani Economist* in 1972 unable to mask its surprise that certain leading industrial families were excluded from this most unwelcome of lists.[108]

Upon acceding to power in 1971, Bhutto began maneuvering against the twenty-two families. But before examining the effects of nationalization it is worth asking: Who exactly were these twenty-two families? Few Pakistani politicians save Bhutto dared to speak their name outright. They hardly needed to anyway, for most of the Pakistani public knew them well—Adamji, Bawani, Fancy, and Habib, to list a few. Though there were a sizable number of Punjabis in their ranks, these firms were disproportionately drawn from the Bohras, Khojas, and Memons. None of their nationalist credentials immunized these firms from the growing public resentment in mid-1960s Pakistan. The resentment made much of the fact that the Gujarati commercial castes did not hail from the core territories of Pakistan but were recent immigrants from the port cities of the Indian Ocean. In truth, the extraterritorial dimension of the Gujarati Muslim diaspora was seen as nothing less than malignant. Thus, a delegate in Pakistan's National Assembly representing East Pakistan condemned those who, "not belonging to this country and coming from Burma and East Africa, have had control over its economy by making the administration and the politicians dishonest and corrupt and by taking the advantage of the inexperience of the people of this country."[109]

Such remarks were revealing of the expansive geography in which the Bohras, Khojas, and Memons had made their wealth—a geography of economic activity that was in rapid, albeit temporary, contraction during the early decades of postcolonial independence in Africa and Asia. The Gujarati Muslim commercial castes' settlement within Pakistan after Partition, where before 1947 they were confined largely to Karachi and parts of Sindh, was confirmation that the world in which they struck their fortune was shrinking beneath their feet. Nevertheless, their critics were not interested in treating them as a godsend to a capital-starved Pakistan or condemning the country to serve as a haven for greedy capitalists.

The controversy over the twenty-two families came to a head shortly after Bhutto's election as prime minister when he nationalized the assets of the leading firms with the passage of the Economic Reforms Order of 1972. The opening articles give a glimpse of the strange fusion of socialism and Islamic economic ideas then en vogue in Bhutto's administration:

> Whereas the benefits of economic development and industrialization have remained confined to the privileged few to the detriment of the common man;
>
> And whereas Islam enjoins equitable distribution of wealth and economic power and abhors their concentration in a few hands;
>
> And whereas it is the duty of Government to ensure that the wealth and economic resources of the country are exploited to the maximum advantage of the common man;

> And whereas those who control the means of production are accountable to the people through their chosen representatives;
> And whereas it is necessary to safeguard the interest of the small investor;
> And whereas it is necessary for that purpose to provide for redeeming the promises made to the people in that behalf from the time to time since the creation of Pakistan.[110]

The act gave Pakistan's federal government the powers to nominate the board of directors for companies, a measure that ensured the demographic dilution of firms that had community or family-centered management.[111]

Long-standing Gujarati Muslim commercial concerns were not spared Bhutto's nationalization, including the Muslim Commercial Bank, which had been founded by Adamji Haji Daud in 1947, and Habib Bank, Pakistan's only commercial bank at independence. The resistance launched by some business leaders was largely futile, even when appeals were made to unassailable arithmetic: at a conference of business leaders held at Karachi in 1973 it was argued by one attendee, Razak Adamji, "that the total wealth of the so-called twenty two families is not even one tenth of the assets of [the] TATA family."[112] (The Tatas were a Parsi merchant family whose founder was famous for establishing India's first native-owned industrial enterprise in the late 1860s. In independent India they were the country's preeminent firm, with a global reach.)[113] Perhaps unknown to Adamji was that portions of the Tata family's business empire in India had been nationalized in the intervening decades—not least their airline company in the early 1950s, but they narrowly escaped Indira Gandhi's nationalization of the steel industry in 1972.[114]

With Bangladesh lost and the leading entrepreneurs quickly extracting their capital from the country, Pakistan's economy experienced an enormous contraction under Bhutto, with growth declining from its peak 6 percent under Ayub Khan to 4 percent under Bhutto's Pakistan People's Party.[115] By several accounts, Bhutto's cabinet did not possess a single economist. With many of the best Pakistani economists working for the International Monetary Fund, World Bank, or in Saudi Arabia, or linked to the preeminent commercial firms, this proved to be a severe disadvantage. According to a *New York Times* piece written at the time of Bhutto's ascendancy to office, when World Bank president Robert S. McNamara met with him and his officials in Islamabad, a significant portion of the time was spent explaining basic banking terminology to the group. This severe dearth of trained economists meant that Bhutto had to go cap in hand to the very families he had dispossessed in the nationalization drive, but many refused to play his game.[116]

Ultimately the prime consequence of Bhutto's nationalization was the obstruction of progress in capital-intensive industries, the decline of leading business houses, and a reform deadlock in the corporate, industrial, and state sectors.[117] If anything, nationalization only benefited the bureaucracy and the army, as the economic gains (unsurprisingly) failed to trickle down to the masses.[118] At the same time, Bhutto's regime tried to instrumentalize the popular discourse of Islamic economics for its own purposes. It was under his watch that the famous Lahore Summit was held in 1974, where ideas were debated for the creation of an international Islamic bank.[119]

These efforts sat at odds, however, with other economic policies of a more outright socialist bent that Bhutto implemented—especially land reform. These were deemed "un-Islamic" by a broad range of actors, who formed the nucleus for an opposition movement called Nizām-i Muṣtafa, which took shape by 1975. This movement instigated a deeper reaction against socialism. Over time, the leftward swerve under Bhutto led to a massive capital infusion from a range of the lower middle class, landed elites, *muhajirs* (migrants from the territories of pre-Partition India), and even Saudi Arabia into groups like the Jamāʿat-i Islāmī. The Saudis, in particular, deposited substantial sums into the coffers of the Jamāʿat-i Islāmī, and deeper ties were made between Saudi ulama and Jamāʿat-i Islāmī activists.[120] It was these forces that toppled Bhutto in 1977, with the Jamāʿat-i Islāmī having the biggest hand.[121]

Pakistan's nationalization drive—carried out in part on the pretext that such a move was what Islamic socialism demanded—eviscerated the leading commercial firms. Subsequently, the state co-opted personnel from the leading commercial firms and used them as a vehicle of social engineering and economic development. If the period from 1947 to 1972 had been one in which the top commercial firms engaged in state capture, from 1972 to 1977 their assets were captured by the state. Many of these entrepreneurs who reconciled themselves to the state, however, did so out of necessity rather than conviction. None were willing to go to the wall for Bhutto's regime, and they quickly transferred their loyalties to the new military regime of Muhammad Zia al-Haqq in 1978, who was regarded as more sympathetic to business and keen to recruit the support of capitalists and Islamists alike.

Although the new regime in Pakistan was happy to recruit business support, it was by no means interested in restoring the commercial firms to prominence. From this point the Pakistani military expanded vigorously into the business sector, coming to control huge portions of the economy, to the lasting detriment of the country as a whole.[122] As intimated by the example of the Muslim Commercial Bank, founded by the Memon industrialist Adamji Haji Daud in 1947, many erstwhile Gujarati enterprises were sold off to the government's crony capitalists once privatization was reintroduced.[123] By such means the regime consolidated its grip over the economy and began openly advocating for the turn to an "Islamic" financial system. Over the next decades the contours of that emerging industry would be hashed out between Islamabad and Jeddah, where several Pakistani economists had been employed to modernize the Saudi financial system since the late 1950s.[124]

* * *

As this chapter has shown, the general crisis faced by postcolonial states from the mid-1960s to the early 1970s—fundamentally a crisis of the developmental state that found its expression in attacks on minorities and counterproductive waves of nationalization—proved a disaster for the Gujarati Muslim commercial castes at several levels. Though often neglected, the crisis was especially acute in Pakistan, where the Gujarati Muslim commercial castes faced unique pressures as distinguished Muslim capitalists. Over the ensuing decades, the economic fortunes of the Bohras, Khojas, and Memons revived, not least because of the return of more liberal migratory regimes and capital flows with the installation of a neoliberal economic system from the period immediately after Bhutto's economic order of 1972. In fact, Pakistan's nationalization drive amounted to something of a hiccup, even if some Gujarati Muslim commercial firms left Pakistan for friendlier shores as a consequence.

Nonetheless, in hindsight, the Pakistani government's nationalization of the commercial enterprises owned by the Gujarati Muslim commercial castes, when combined with attacks elsewhere in Asia and Africa, marked the abrupt termination of an epoch of South Asian Muslim capitalism that had persisted for more than a century and a half. Since 1800 the lives of the Bohras, Khojas, and Memons had been interwoven with a world of empires, migration, and entrepreneurship, all of which were in low demand in the statist economies of the early postcolonial world. In the later 1970s, a new commitment to erect an "Islamic economy" followed in the vacuum between the failure of nationalization and the ascent of neoliberalism in parts of the Middle East and Pakistan, and this further helped to delegitimize corporate Islam. The notion of an Islamic economy—which has placed a strong accent on economic equality among Muslims—has not left the Bohras, Khojas, and Memons untouched. In truth, these communities have acclimated themselves to that nebulous paradigm and even fashioned them into tangible social realities, both through the reform of communal economic practices and the formation of transnational financial and commercial enterprises.

In their own ways, the Bohra *dais* and the Agha Khan IV made quite similar pronouncements about the need to Islamize the economy and introduced reforms to this end within their communities.[125] An unambiguous measure of the assimilation by Bohras, Khojas, and Memons of the norms and assumptions of Islamic finance is the prevalence from the 1970s onward of interest-free loan schemes in the three *jamaats*.[126] Though this is not acknowledged typically, these schemes should also be regarded as part of an effort to combat the underbanked or unbanked status of many *jamaat* congregants. Moreover, financial services offered by the *jamaats* have dovetailed with various microfinance and governmental schemes, as exemplified best by the Aga Khan Agency for Microfinance, part of the enormous transnational umbrella entity of the Aga Khan Development Network headquartered in Geneva.[127] On the other hand, Memon bureaucrats and entrepreneurs have been the most energetic of all Gujarati Muslims in making Islamic finance a viable enterprise at the global level. The overseas Memon diaspora has been central to this, especially those Memons associated with the Saudi Arabian Monetary Authority from the mid-1970s onward.[128]

The valorization of *interest-free banking* as a byword of Islamic economics, and the refashioning of the latest financial instruments in the guise of medieval Islamic profit-and-loss instruments (*mudaraba*) by "sharia boards" employed by multinational banking conglomerates, has been criticized by many Muslim commentators as nothing less than a euphemism that fails to supply a substantial financial alternative to conventional banking institutions. Euphemism or not, analysts and proponents of Islamic economics have proven susceptible to historical amnesia. Their overt emphasis on the interest-free *mudaraba* as the only authentically Islamic institutional form ignores successful models of Muslim capitalism from the past two centuries. One would do well to reckon with that messy—institutionally indiscriminate, though no less authentically Islamic—world of capitalist and religious exchange encompassed by Gujarati Muslim corporate Islam.

Conclusion

The Past and the Future of Corporate Islam

IN HIS *Mahāgujarātanā Musalamāno* (The Muslims of Greater Gujarat), first published in 1936, the pioneering Ismaili Khoja historian Karim Muhammad Mastar defined the Bohras, Khojas, and Memons as the "three main trading communities of Muslims."[1] His portrait of these groups and other Gujarati Muslims, though partially reliant on material sent to him by community factors, supplied little not found in earlier colonial gazetteers.[2] Despite this, Mastar's account was representative of a centuries' old tradition of intimacy and interconnection, however guarded, among these three castes. By studying them in dialogue with one another, Mastar captured the dialectic of particularism and pluralism that has been a hallmark of their collective history.

Standing on the shoulders of figures like Mastar, this book has done its utmost to fill in the blanks in the modern history of these three groups by marshaling a heterogeneous array of sources in several languages. First, it has made the case for the utility of "paraeconomic" resources in the writing of histories of capitalism, sources without an overt economic content, but that nonetheless illuminate the worlds of merchant activity like no other. Second, it has attended to the diverse ways in which non-market, pre-colonial institutions like the *jamaat* have been grafted onto capitalist institutions in the modern period and in turn facilitated the market transactions of their constituents. Third, it has looked at the advantages and disadvantages of these same institutional arrangements, stressing in turn the distributional conflicts that have arisen from the inequality and wealth disparities they fostered. Fourth, it has endeavored to "people" the history of capitalism—an aspect often missed in recent global histories[3]—by taking stock of an array of actors who moved in and out of the *jamaats.*

With all this said, a deeper appreciation of the lifeworlds of corporate Islam remains in its infancy. After all, the *jamaats* (corporate caste institutions) are ideal candidates for the writing of "infinite histories," of which this book can only furnish a sample.[4] In telling the story of the rise, consolidation, and partial eclipse of corporate Islam, the aim here has been to provide a narrative of modern Islam and capitalism that is symbiotic rather than antagonistic. Of course, corporate Islam as it existed among the Bohras, Khojas, and Memons was not a mode of Muslim enterprise universally endorsed by other Muslims, and the key challenge, especially in the postcolonial period, has been to disaggregate community-based enterprise and scale it up to be more inclusive of those who are not members of castes. Even so, the preceding chapters have demonstrated that Muslim constituencies married capitalist institutions and Islamic ethical concerns long before what some commentators have called Meccanomics, the period from the 1970s until today when sizable Muslim middle classes began to emerge.[5]

Throughout the nearly two centuries covered in this book, *jamaats* acted as underwriters for a persistent form of Muslim corporate capitalism, the parameters and behaviors of which were no doubt transformed by the structures of the colonial and global economy but which remained tethered to Islamic ethical concerns and embedded within an economy of religious obligation. So even as the geographic loci of Gujarati Muslim capital moved with the tide of colonial conquest between the Bay of Bengal, East Africa, and the South China Sea, there was always an institutional core in the form of *jamaats* underwriting the entire enterprise. Amid the dissemination of corporate Islam, no particular form of Islam was a prerequisite for economic success, and especially not that of the "reformist" or "modernist" type. All this serves to confirm the elliptical formulation, as Stephen Kotkin notes, that "modernity was not a sociological but a geopolitical process."[6] In other words, modernity was never a matter of shedding tradition but of developing institutions conducive to success in an all-too-hardheaded world. The *jamaats* were among those institutions contributing to the making of capitalist and political modernity in Africa and Asia, and historians of capitalism would do well to accord greater attention to the survival and interaction of these institutions with "Western" institutional forms.[7]

As many actors surveyed in this book can attest, in no way are the *jamaats* always benign institutions. Like all corporations, they take a carrot-and-stick approach to their constituents, crushing dissent and demanding conformity. And, as is the case in modern business corporations, women have been the first victims of many of their policies. At the same time, one cannot ignore the many instances in which individuals from within the *jamaats* campaigned to make them more just and equitable and obliged these institutions to live up to the Islamic ideals they were meant to embody. Their appeals variably sought to reform, undermine, or strengthen the corporate character of the *jamaat*. They remind the historian that no institution is ever free of distributional conflicts, governed at all times by a seamless culture of trust and kinship that binds all members together. As this book has maintained, shared kinship and sect were never a barrier to discord, and the very intimacy of shared identity frequently exacerbated, rather than mollified, antagonism. The familiar juxtaposition between Muslim and non-Muslim endemic to Greater Gujarat often provided more fertile grounds for commercial cooperation than the intimacies of community.

This book has also underscored the potential windfall of bringing economic and religious history into conversation. For all this, there remains a certain reluctance in the social sciences to mix the study of religion and the history of capitalism. But even if modern historians tend to blush when the two are blurred, as Peter Brown reminds us, "Perhaps it is we who are strange. Why is that [modern persons] have such inhibitions in approaching the subject of the joining of God and gold?"[8] This book has harbored no reservations on this front, for a key contention in the foregoing pages has been that the corporate Islam of the Gujarati Muslim commercial castes and the history of modern global capitalism have been coconstitutive.

Unfortunately, in Islamic studies there has been a persistent historiographical line that regards capitalism as a "universalizing" juggernaut that Muslims responded to by retreating behind the protective walls of an Islamic "moral economy" that purportedly supplied them with the capacity to resist the "logics of capitalism."[9] Such narratives are impervious to empirical qualification and perpetuate the vaguest caricatures of capitalism. Scholars would do well to pay heed to that great historian of religion and capitalism, R. H. Tawney, who, in his inimitable style, put the matter in these terms:

"The philosophy which would keep economic interests and ethical idealism safely locked up in their separate compartments finds that each of the prisoners is increasingly restive."[10]

This mutual imbrication has been underappreciated because most existing accounts of modern Muslim economic history tend to obscure institutional variation from within the Islamic tradition and overlook intra-Muslim economic divergences. As one moves from a normative model of religion to case studies—as is done here with the Bohras, Khojas, and Memons—it is clear that Islamic law, and Islamic religious institutions generally, possessed a variety of economic functions within Muslim constituencies that belies any universal pattern of institutional stagnation. The narrative of Islam and modern capitalism becomes more variegated when historians take endogenous Islamic institutions seriously in the study of modern economic history. Discrepancies among Islamic institutions must be parsed and scrutinized. And any narrative must remember that, for all the uptake in institutions exogenous to Islamic traditions, Islamic institutions have persisted in the portfolios of the most successful Muslim entrepreneurial groups.

The example of the Bohras, Khojas, and Memons offers numerous instances in which the lexicons of market activity and Islam were intertwined. Analogies between religion and economics were second nature, with authors from these groups regularly analyzing religious matters in terms of profit and loss. It is disputable how much these ethical considerations inflected the character of business: for one, was the stark underrepresentation of these groups in formal banking a consequence of Islamic disapproval of lending at interest / usury? Arguably, concerns about financial interest / usury only became sensitive subjects among the Gujarati Muslim commercial castes in the interwar period and probably owed more to the perceptions of a Hindu-Muslim wealth gap than to Islamic legal norms.

Whatever the chain of causation, it would be wrong to say that Islamic institutions (whether the *jamaats* in the round or their subsidiary trusts) were always conducive to positive economic outcomes, as the Gujarati Muslim commercial castes and other Muslim commentators studied in these pages recognized. In fact, while one can take umbrage at the forcefulness of narratives that posit Islamic law as a contributing factor to economic divergence,[11] that scholarship must also be situated within a longer endogenous Muslim autocritique of Islamic economic institutions. This book has aspired to do just that. With that said, it is telling that while many Indian Muslim commentators examined in this book inveighed against Islamic law, the inviolability of *awqāf* (pious endowment), and attitudes to interest as factors contributing to Muslim penury, they also saw the *jamaats* as cornerstones of Gujarati Muslim success. Still, as the empirical record of the Bohras, Khojas, and Memons suggests, Islamic institutions were best able to survive and contribute to economic gains when they were fastened onto other institutions such as the business corporation and the bank.

In the end one must remember that the institutional worlds inhabited by the Bohras, Khojas, and Memons were multiplex, and the *jamaats* both a point of ingress into and egress out of other institutions. The assumption that legal exceptionalism—the notion that they stood apart from other Indian Muslims by virtue of their place in the colonial legal system or their apathy toward Islamic law—has been a hallmark of their collective histories has masked that reality. If from the vantage point of the colonial courts these groups were reduced to "Hindus" in all but name, that image falls apart upon inspection of the litany of sources they produced as members of *jamaats*. These relate that the *jamaats* operated as intermediary, *corporate* institutions straddling the realms of colonial law and the jurisprudential worlds of the ulama. The resulting legal formulas they arrived at were multiplex, differing from one *jamaat* to the next. Their engagement with Islamic legal norms were constantly modulated by the shifting yardsticks of law and custom as variably determined by the caste corporation, the colonial civic order, and wider Muslim organizations.

The traditions of corporate Islam surveyed in this book are most under threat in their place of origin: Gujarat. The tragic economic reality of India's Muslim communities is best evoked by the violence exacted against the Muslims of Gujarat during the 2002 pogroms. Constituting an economic elite of sorts in the state, Bohras, Khojas, and Memons were brutally attacked in many rural and urban areas of Gujarat.[12] That property damage to the tune of hundreds of millions of rupees occurred was inexcusable enough. It was overshadowed by the irreparable human losses experienced by the three communities, who ranked among the thousands of Muslims butchered in the ensuing violence. Gujarat in 2002 was only the latest round in a heritage of illiberal state power—whether in the form of precolonial rulers, the colonial state, or postcolonial authoritarian regimes—that has exacted its arbitrary whims upon successful corporate communities like the Gujarati Muslim commercial castes.

Even as these commercial castes face extreme pressures in their historical heartland, they, and the corporate Islam they have personified for the past two centuries, have found success over the past five decades in the corners of the globe where racial animus and capital asymmetries once kept them at bay—namely in Britain's former "outer" empire: Australia, Britain, Canada, and New Zealand, as well as in the United States. So even as traditions of corporate Islam hold on tenaciously in Amreli, Bhavnagar, and Surat against the tide of communal hate, new roots are planted as far afield as Auckland, Balham, and Detroit. Whether in South Asia or the global diaspora, internal *jamaat* debates over reform—especially in regard to women's economic and bodily rights[13]—continue apace, with the state an active participant in adjudicating these disagreements.

Since the late eighteenth century the *jamaats* have had a complex relationship with various iterations of state authority. State authorities supplied infrastructures of law, protected community capital, and fostered migration, three variables crucial in the sustenance of middle power. It also supplied the *jamaats* with a body of privileges that transformed them into de jure and de facto corporations, with exclusive rights and protections, that could be mobilized across borders. Yet state power has also brought frequently unwanted outside meddling and arbitration into the *jamaats,* ensuring that, as institutions, they are not merely the property of their members. These contradictory impulses in the forms of state power applied to the *jamaats* are also present in the capitalism and Islam practiced by their members. Both make and unmake community and both encourage interaction with the outside world and to keep it at a distance.

It was this Bohra, Khoja, and Memon ability to integrate state patronage, conspicuous wealth, and religious community in the space of the *jamaats* that so fascinated the Tatar Muslim traveler, Abd al-Reşid Ibrahim, when he passed through the ports of the northern Indian Ocean around 1909.[14] At turns Ibrahim simultaneously appreciated and criticized this formula. In this Ibrahim was of a piece with other Tatar Muslims on the eve of the First World War who searched between Cairo and Singapore for a living paradigm of Muslim capitalism they could hold up as an archetype to their audience.[15] In the Gujarati Muslim commercial castes Ibrahim found one such model. Not all modern Muslim commentators have shared his viewpoint, but even critics can scarcely deny that the Bohras, Khojas, and Memons have embodied, as few others have, the rich interplay between assorted forms of modern Islam and capitalism.

Abbreviations

BL	British Library, London
	India Office Records (IOR)
BOA	Başbakanlık Osmanlı Arşivi (Ottoman Archives of the Prime Minister's Office), Istanbul
	Bab-ı Ali Evrak Odası (BEO)
	Dahiliye Nezareti Mektubi (DH.MKT)
	Haritalar (HR.TH)
	İrade, Dahiliye (İ.DH)
	Yıldız Perakende Elçilik ve Şehbenderlikler Tahriratı (Y.PRK.EŞA)
	Yıldız Sadaret Resmi Maruzat Evrakı (Y.A.RES)
	Yıldız Mütenevvi Maruzat Evrakı (Y.MTV)
DU	Durham University
	Abbas Hilmi II Papers (HIL)
IIS	Institute of Ismaili Studies, London
NAI	National Archives of India, New Delhi
QDL	Qatar Digital Library (https://www.qdl.qa/en), Qatar National Library, Al Rayyan
SBI	State Bank of India, Calcutta
TRC	Kızılay (Turkish Red Crescent), Ankara
ZLR	Zanzibar Law Reports
ZNA	Zanzibar National Archives, Zanzibar, Tanzania
	HC 2: High Court: Insolvency, 1887–1962

Notes

Introduction

1. Abd al-Reşid Ibrahim, *ʿĀlem-i İslām ve Jāponyāda intiṣār-ı İslāmīyet*, vol. 2 (Istanbul: Ḳadr Maṭbaʿası, 1911), 9.

2. Ibrahim, *ʿĀlem-i İslām*, 2:15, 35.

3. Ibrahim, *ʿĀlem-i İslām*, 2:65.

4. Ulrich Brandenburg, "The Multiple Publics of a Transnational Activist: Abdürreşid İbrahim, Pan-Asianism, and the Creation of Islam in Japan," *Die Welt des Islams* 58 (2018): 148–149.

5. "Law and Police. In H.B.M.'s Court at Kanagawa," *Japan Mail*, 24 October 1878, 544–548.

6. "Mr. A. M. Essabhoy," *Straits Times*, 5 November 1897, 2; "Departure of a Bombay Merchant," *Mid-day Herald and Daily*, 4 November 1897, 3.

7. "Messrs. A. M. Essabhoy," *Straits Times*, 4 August 1911, 3.

8. See the notice in *Islamic Fraternity* 1, no. 10 (1911): 4. Many thanks to Ulrich Brandenburg for sharing this source with me.

9. Hubert Bonin, *French Banking and Entrepreneurialism in China and Hong Kong: From the 1850s to 1980s* (Abingdon, UK: Routledge, 2020), 111, 116.

10. "Annulment under Section 97," and "(42) A.M. Essabhoy (No. 189 of 1914)," *Annual Departmental Reports of the Straits Settlements for the year 1914* (Singapore: Government Printing Office, 1915), 386, 396.

11. "Alleged Breach of Contract," *Japan Weekly Chronicle*, 23 September 1915, 512–513.

12. Historians are accustomed to speaking of Gujarat as a distinct territory, but this is only a shorthand for a broader region. "Greater Gujarat" is a better substitute

for the range of territories inhabited by the Bohras, Khojas, and Memons, which included Gujarat, Kachchh, Kathiawar, Rajasthan, and Lower Sindh.

13. Chhaya Goswami, *Globalization Before its Time: The Gujarati Merchants from Kachchh* (Gurgaon, India: Penguin Books India, 2016), 15–16. All the same, there has been extensive debate about the accuracy of these claims. To cite but one example, see Syed Abu Zafar Nadvi, "The Origin of the Bohras," *Islamic Culture: The Hyderabad Quarterly Review* (October 1935): 638–644.

14. By one count from 1891, their collective numbers in Bombay were roughly 277,000, a number that obviously did not include Greater Gujarat and the diaspora. Khan Bahadur Fazalullah Lutfullah, "Gujarat Muslims: Earliest Settlement in A.D. 634 to the Present Period (A.D. 1898)," *Gazetteer Of The Bombay Presidency*, vol. IX, part II (Bombay: Government Central Press, 1899) 1. I have added up the separate entries for Bohras, Khojas, and Memons to reach this figure.

15. Sir Herbert Risley, *The People of India* (Calcutta: Thacker, Spink, 1908), 328.

16. Mirza Muhammad Kazim Birlas Moradabadi, *Tārīkh-i Kachchh o Makrān, ma'ahu hālāt-i qaum-i maimanān* (Moradabad, India: Maṭbū' al-hind pres, 1905); Reprinted in Abd al-Rahman Asir, ed., *Asās-i Meman qaum* (Karachi: Meman Yūth Ārganā'izeshan, 1978), 31–32.

17. For an analysis of one such text see Michael O'Sullivan, "'Indian Money', Intra-Shī'ī Polemics, and the Bohra and Khoja Pilgrimage Infrastructure in Iraq's Shrine Cities, 1897–1932," *Journal of the Royal Asiatic Society* 32, 1 (2022): 213–250.

18. Najm al-Ghani Khan, *Silk al-javāhir fī aḥvāl al-bavāhir, ya'nī davudīyya buhrunkī tārīkh* (Morababad, India: Maṭba Maṭla' al-'ulūm, 1914), 65–66.

19. Khvaja Hassan Nizami, *Fāṭimī da'vat-i Islām: banī Fāṭimah ki tablīgh-i Islām kī mufaṣṣal tārīkh* (Delhi: Khvājah Ḍipo, 1943).

20. Ansari Ali Sher Ali, *A Short Sketch, Historical and Traditional, of the Musalman Races Found in Sind, Baluchistan and Afghanistan, Their Genealogical Sub-divisions and Septs, Together with an Ethnological and Ethnographical Account* (Karachi: Commissioner's Press, 1901), 64–70.

21. A recent BBC article contains the following opening: "The Memon predisposition towards frugality is iconic within Pakistan, but they celebrate their stereotyping as an achievement; a tribute to their enduring prosperity and resilience." Aysha Imtiaz, "Pakistan's Centuries-Old Zero-Waste Movement," *BBC News*, 9 December 2019, http://www.bbc.com/travel/story/20191208-pakistans-centuries-old-zero-waste-movement.

22. Hanna Papanek, "Pakistan's Big Businessmen: Muslim Separatism, Entrepreneurship, and Partial Modernization," *Economic Development and Cultural Change* 21, no. 1 (1972): 1–32; Sergey Levin, "The Upper Bourgeoisie from the Muslim Commercial Community of Memons in Pakistan, 1947 to 1971," *Asian Survey* 14, no. 3

(1974): 231–243; Harish Damodaran, *India's New Capitalists: Caste, Business, and Industry in a Modern Nation* (Basingstoke, UK: Palgrave Macmillan, 2008), 297; Shobha Bondre, *Dhandha: How Gujaratis Do Business* (Noida, India: Random House India, 2013); Timur Kuran and Anantdeep Singh, "Economic Modernization in Late British India: Hindu-Muslim Differences," ERID Working Paper 53, Economic Research Initiatives at Duke, Duke University, July 2010; Anantdeep Singh, "The Divergence of the Economic Fortunes of Hindus and Muslims in British India: A Comparative Institutional Analysis" (PhD diss., University of Southern California, 2008).

23. Ashgar Ali Engineer, *The Muslim Communities of Gujarat: An Exploratory Study of Bohras, Khojas, and Memons* (New Delhi: Ajanta, 1989); Iqbal Akhtar, *The Khōjā of Tanzania: Discontinuities of a Postcolonial Religious Identity* (Leiden, Netherlands: Brill, 2016); Olly Akkerman, *A Neo-Fatimid Treasury of Books: Arabic Manuscripts among the Alavi Bohras of South Asia* (Edinburgh: Edinburgh University Press, 2022), 15–16; Jonah Blank, *Mullahs on the Mainframe: Islam and Modernity among the Daudi Bohras* (Chicago: University of Chicago Press, 2001); Denis Gay, *Les Bohra de Madagascar: Religion, commerce et échanges transnationaux dans la construction de l'identité ethnique* (Berlin: Lit Verlag, 2009).

24. Tirthankar Roy, *A Business History of India: Enterprise and the Emergence of Capitalism from 1700* (Cambridge: Cambridge University Press, 2018), 7–9.

25. "Mission of Sir Bartle Frere to the East Coast of Africa," *The Church Missionary Intelligencer, A Monthly Journal of Missionary Information*, vol. IX, (London: Church Missionary House, 1879), 339.

26. Adapa Satyanarayana, "'Birds of Passage': Migration of South Indian Laborers to Southeast Asia," *Critical Asian Studies* 34.1 (March 2002), 89–115.

27. "Mr Burke's Speech . . . on Mr. Fox's East India Bill," *The Works of the Right Honourable Edmund Burke*, vol. 2 (Boston: West and Greenleaf, 1807), 297.

28. A curious distinction came in a 1986 work on Sri Lankan Muslims in which M.A.M. Shukri contrasted the Bohras and Memons who "had made this island their home," with the "Coast Moors" who supposedly remained "birds of passage, with no abiding interest in this land and her people." M.A.M. Shukri, "Introduction," in M.A.M. Shukri ed., *Muslims of Sri Lanka: Avenues to Antiquity* (Beruwala, Sri Lanka: Jamiah Naleemia Inst., 1986), 56.

29. A. A. Esmail, "Satpanth Ismailism and modern changes within it with special reference to East Africa," (PhD Diss., University of Edinburgh, 1972), 222.

30. Henry S. Turner, *The Corporate Commonwealth: Pluralism and Political Fictions in England, 1516–1651* (Chicago: University of Chicago Press, 2016), xii.

31. Ritu Birla, *Stages of Capital: Law, Culture, and Market Governance in Late Colonial India* (Durham, NC: Duke University Press, 2009), 25.

32. Timur Kuran, "The Absence of the Corporation in Islamic Law: Origins and Persistence," *American Journal of Comparative Law* 53, no. 4 (2005): 785–834;

Avner Greif, *Institutions and the Path to the Modern Economy: Lessons from Medieval Trade* (Cambridge: Cambridge University Press, 2006), 396–397; Ron Harris, *Going the Distance: Eurasian Trade and the Rise of the Business Corporation, 1400–1700* (Princeton, NJ: Princeton University Press, 2020), 342.

33. On the transfer of the dai-ship to India, see the Arabic history written by the Bohra historian Sulaimanji Burhanpuri, Muntazaʿ al-akhbār fī akhbār al-duʿāh al-akhyār, ed. Samir Faruq Tarablusi (Beirut: Dār al-Gharb al-Islāmī, 1999).

33. Jairus Banaji, *A Brief History of Commercial Capitalism* (Chicago: Haymarket Books, 2020), 132.

34. C. A. Bayly, *Imperial Meridian: The British Empire and the World, 1780–1830* (London: Longman, 1989), 21, 73–74, 253–254; Banaji, *A Brief History*, chaps. 3–4, appendix.

35. André Raymond, *Artisans et commerçants au Caire au XVIIIe siècle*, vol. 1 (Damascus: Presses de l'Ifpo, 1973), 243–305; Satish C. Misra, *Muslim Communities of Gujarat: Preliminary Studies in Their History and Social Organization* (Bombay: Asia Publishing House, 1964), 143.

36. Ashin Das Gupta, *Indian Merchants and the Decline of Surat, c. 1700–1750* (Wiesbaden, West Germany: Franz Steiner Verlag, 1979, reprinted in Ashin Das Gupta, *India and the Indian Ocean World: Trade and Politics* (New Delhi: Oxford University Press, 2004), 105n148.

37. Ashin Das Gupta, "The Maritime Merchant of India, c. 1500–1800," in *The World of the Indian Ocean Merchant, 1500–1800*, ed. Uma Das Gupta (New Delhi: Oxford University Press, 2001), 99.

38. Timothy Guinnane, Ron Harris, Naomi R. Lamoreaux, and Jean-Laurent Rosenthal, "Putting the Corporation in Its Place," *Enterprise and Society* 8, no. 3 (2007): 687–729; Philip J. Stern, "'Bundles of Hyphens': Corporations as Legal Communities in the Early Modern British Empire," in *Legal Pluralism and Empires, 1500–1850*, ed. Lauren Benton and Richard J. Ross (New York: New York University Press, 2013), 21–48.

39. Michael Aldous, "Avoiding Negligence and Profusion: The Failure of the Joint-Stock Form in the Anglo-Indian Tea Trade, 1840–1870," *Enterprise and Society* 16, no. 3 (2015): 648–685.

40. Harris, *Going the Distance*, 352–354. A classic article that attempted to disaggregate the history of Indian family firms over the long term is Thomas A. Timberg, "Three Types of the Marwari Firm," *The Indian Economic & Social History Review*, 10, no. 1 (1973): 3–36.

41. "(4)—Caste-Account Books—Rights of Members to Inspect Them Fully and Freely," *All India Digest, 1811–1911*, sec. 2, *Civil*, vol. 2 (Madras: T.A. Venkasawmy Row and T.S. Krishnasawmy Row, 1912), 772.

42. L. T. Kikani, *Caste in Courts, or Rights and Powers of Castes in Social and Religions Matters as Recognised by Indian Courts* (Rajkot, India: Gantra Printing Works, 1912), 126.

43. Kikani, *Caste in Courts*, 126.

44. Elisée Reclus, *The Earth and Its Inhabitants: Asia*, vol. 3, *India and Indo-China* (New York: D. Appleton, 1895), 284.

45. Sadasukh Lal, *An Anglo Urdu Dictionary in the English & Persian Characters* (Allahabad, India: Nurulabsar, 1873), 90; John T. Platts, *A Dictionary of Urdū, Classical Hindī, and English* (London: Sampson Low, Marston, 1884), 388.

46. Taisu Zhang, *The Laws and Economics of Confucianism: Kinship and Property in Preindustrial China and Europe* (Cambridge: Cambridge University Press, 2017), 2–9.

47. *Middle power* is a term with its origins in international relations. I adapt it for use here because it conveys well the constraints in which the Gujarati Muslim commercial castes were compelled to act.

48. Misra, *Muslim Communities*, 139–149; Douglas Haynes, *Small Town Capitalism in Western India: Artisans, Merchants, and the Making of the Informal Economy, 1870–1960* (Cambridge: Cambridge University Press, 2012), 87–88.

49. Jean-Claude Penrad, "The Ismaili Presence in East Africa: A Note on Its Commercial History and Community Organisation," in *Asian Merchants and Businessmen in the Indian Ocean and the China Sea*, ed. Denys Lombard and Jean Aubin (New Delhi: Oxford University Press, 2000), 233.

50. Anas Malik, *Polycentricity, Islam, and Development: Potentials and Challenges in Pakistan* (Lanham, MD: Lexington Books 2018), 237.

51. Edward Simpson, *Muslim Society and the Western Indian Ocean: The Seafarers of Kachchh* (London: Routledge, 2004), 92–94.

52. Nile Green, *Bombay Islam: The Religious Economy of the Western Indian Ocean* (Cambridge: Cambridge University Press, 2011), 16.

53. Nile Green, *Terrains of Exchange: Religious Economies of Global Islam* (Oxford: Oxford University Press, 2015), 13.

54. Tony Judt, *Postwar: A History of Europe since 1945* (New York: Penguin, 2006), 9.

55. Teena Purohit, *The Aga Khan Case: Religion and Identity in Colonial India* (Cambridge, MA: Harvard University Press, 2012), 23–24.

56. David Washbrook, "The Cambridge History of Capitalism: India," in *Capitalisms: Towards a Global History*, ed. Kaveh Yazdani and Dilip M. Menon (Oxford: Oxford University Press, 2020), 136.

57. Norbert Peabody, "Knowledge Formation in Colonial India," in *India and the British Empire*, ed. Douglas M. Peers and Nandini Gooptu (Oxford: Oxford University Press, 2012), 75–99.

58. Kuran and Singh, "Economic Modernization."

59. "Bombay High Court. The Advocate General—Plaintiff versus Jimbabai and Others—Defendants," in *Indian Cases Containing Full Reports of Decisions . . .*, vol. 31, ed. S. D. Chaudhri (Lahore: Law Publishing House, 1915), 106–152.

60. Sir Roland Knyvet Wilson, *Anglo-Muhammadan Law: A Digest Preceded by a Historical and Descriptive Introduction* (London: Thacker, 1903), 56–57.

61. Werner Plumpe, *German Economic and Business History in the 19th and 20th Centuries* (London: Palgrave Macmillan, 2016), 4.

62. Sebouh Aslanian, *From the Indian Ocean to the Mediterranean: The Global Trade Networks of Armenian Merchants from New Julfa* (Berkeley: University of California Press, 2011), 15.

63. Heiko Schrader, "Chettiar Finance in Colonial Asia," *Zeitschrift für Ethnologie / Journal of Social and Cultural Anthropology* 121, no. 1 (1996): 101–126; David West Rudner, *Caste and Capitalism in Colonial India: The Nattukottai Chettiars* (Berkeley: University of California Press, 1994); Thomas Timberg, "Three Types of the Marwari Firm," *Indian Economic and Social History Review* 10, no. 1 (1973): 3–36; Karen I. Leonard, "Family Firms in Hyderabad: Gujarati, Goswami, and Marwari Patterns of Adoption, Marriage, and Inheritance," *Comparative Studies in Society and History* 53, no. 4 (2011): 827–854; Claude Markovits, "Indian Merchant Networks outside India in the Nineteenth and Twentieth Centuries: A Preliminary Survey," *Modern Asian Studies* 33, no. 4 (1999): 883–911.

64. Rudner, *Caste and Capitalism in Colonial India.*

65. Claude Markovits, *The Global World of Indian Merchants, 1750–1947: Traders of Sind from Bukhara to Panama* (Cambridge: Cambridge University Press, 2000), 256–257.

66. Markus Friedrich, "Government and Information-Management in Early Modern Europe: The Case of the Society of Jesus (1540–1773)," *Journal of Early Modern History* 12, no. 6 (2008): 539–563.

67. Steven J. Harris, "Confession-Building, Long-Distance Networks, and the Organization of Jesuit Science," *Early Science and Medicine* 1, no. 3 (1996): 287–318.

68. Francesca Trivellato, *The Familiarity of Strangers: The Sephardic Diaspora, Livorno, and Cross-cultural Trade in the Early Modern Period* (New Haven, CT: Yale University Press, 2009), 151–152.

69. Sheilagh Ogilvie, *The European Guilds: An Economic Analysis* (Princeton, NJ: Princeton University Press, 2019), 577.

70. Ha-Joon Chang, *Economics: The User's Guide* (London: Pelican Books, 2014), 154–156.

71. Paul D. McLean, *The Art of the Network: Strategic Interaction and Patronage in Renaissance Florence* (Durham, NC: Duke University Press, 2007), 7.

72. McLean, *The Art of the Network*, 16.

73. Faisal Devji, *Muslim Zion: Pakistan as a Political Idea* (London: Hurst, 2013), 65.

74. "The Gujarati Way; Going Global: Secrets of the World's Best Business-people," *Economist*, 19 December 2015, 105–107; Shobha Bondre, *Dhandha: How Gujaratis Do Business* (Noida, India: Random House India, 2013).

75. Gagan Sood, *India and the Islamic Heartlands: An Eighteenth-Century World of Circulation and Exchange* (Cambridge: Cambridge University Press, 2016), 32.

76. Timur Kuran, *The Long Divergence: How Islamic Law Held Back the Middle East* (Princeton, NJ: Princeton University Press, 2012).

77. David Landes, *The Wealth and Poverty of Nations: Why Some Are So Rich and Some So Poor* (New York: W. W. Norton, 1998), 392–421; Charles Tripp, *Islam and the Moral Economy: The Challenge of Capitalism* (Cambridge: Cambridge University Press, 2006); Robert J Barro and Rachel M. McCleary, *The Wealth of Religions: The Political Economy of Believing and Belonging* (Princeton, NJ: Princeton University Press, 2019), 67–88.

78. Vali Nasr, *Meccanomics: The March of the New Muslim Middle Class* (Oxford: One World, 2010).

79. Omar Khalidi, *Muslims in the Indian Economy* (Gurgaon, India: Three Essays Collective, 2006); Sriya Iyer, *The Economics of Religion in India* (Cambridge, MA: Harvard University Press, 2018).

80. Ibrahim, *ʿĀlem-i İslām*, 2:32, 43.

81. Though originally written in 1870, the text was only printed in 1883. Muhammad Abbas Rafaat Shirvani, *Qalāyid al-javāhir fī aḥvāl al-bavāhir dar aḥvāl-i ṭāʾifa-i maẕhab-i Ismāʿīlīyya, mulaqqab bi ʿumdat al-akhbār* ([Bombay]: n.p., 1883), 4.

1. The Making of Gujarati Muslim Middle Power circa 1800–1850

1. His Holiness the Moolajeesaheb, Syedna Moulana Abdool Hossain Hoosamooddin, *Eulogy in Praise of Her Most Gracious Majesty: The Queen-Empress*, 2nd ed. (Bombay: Gujerat Standard Press, 1890; repr. 1910), 3.

2. Hoosamooddin, *Eulogy*, 7.

3. Maulana Sayyid Abu Zafar Nadvi, *ʿIqd al-javāhir fī aḥvāl al-bavāhir* (Ahmedabad: Khāksār Muʿizz Miyān, 1975 [?]), 259–264 contains an Urdu translation of the Persian history. Nadvi's text was originally published in 1936.

4. Pedro Machado, *South Asian Merchants, Africa and the Indian Ocean, c.1750–1850* (Cambridge: Cambridge University Press, 2014), 4.

5. Howard Spodek, "Rulers, Merchants and Other Groups in the City-States of Saurashtra, India, around 1800," *Comparative Studies in Society and History* 16, no. 4 (1974): 448–470.

6. Muzaffar Alam, *The Crisis of Empire in Mughal North India*, 2nd ed. (New Delhi: Oxford University Press, 2013); C. A. Bayly, *Rulers, Townsmen and Bazaars: North Indian Society in the Age of British Expansion, 1770–1870* (Cambridge: Cambridge University Press, 1983).

7. Bayly, *Rulers, Townsmen and Bazaars*, 110–115.

8. Farhat Hasan, *State and Locality in Mughal India: Power Relations in Western India, c. 1572–1730* (Cambridge: Cambridge University Press, 2004), 121–122.

9. P. J. Marshall, introduction to *Indian Merchants and the Decline of Surat, c. 1700–1750*, by Ashin Das Gupta (Wiesbaden, West Germany: Franz Steiner Verlag, 1979), xv.

10. Sanjay Subrahmanyam and C. A. Bayly, "Portfolio Capitalists and the Political Economy of Early Modern India," *Indian Economic and Social History Review* 25, no. 4 (1988): 401–424.

11. Subrahmanyam and Bayly, "Portfolio Capitalists"; Samira Sheikh, "Jibhabhu's Rights to Ghee: Land Control and Vernacular Capitalism in Gujarat, circa 1803–10," *Modern Asian Studies* 51, no. 2 (2017): 350–374.

12. Ghulam A. Nadri, *Eighteenth-Century Gujarat: The Dynamics of Its Political Economy, 1750–1800* (Leiden, Netherlands: Brill, 2009); Kaveh Yazdani, *India, Modernity and the Great Divergence: Mysore and Gujarat (17th to 19th C.)* (Leiden, Netherlands: Brill, 2017).

13. Das Gupta, *Indian Merchants*, 17; Lakshmi Subramanian, *Indigenous Capital and Imperial Expansion: Bombay, Surat and the West Coast* (Delhi: Oxford University Press, 1996).

14. Giorgio Riello, *Cotton: The Fabric That Made the Modern World* (Cambridge: Cambridge University Press, 2013), 285.

15. "Dress, ca. 1880 (Made)," Victoria and Albert Museum, South and South East Asia Collection, IS.2327-1883, 1 August 2008, https://collections.vam.ac.uk/item/O164893/dress-unknown/.

16. Mirza Muhammad Kazim, preface to *A Dictionary, Goojratee and English*, comp. Mirza Mahomed Cauzim of Cambay, corrected and rev. Nowrozjee Furdoonjee (Bombay: Courier Press, 1846), unpaginated.

17. Jyoti Gulati Balachandran, *Narrative Pasts: The Making of a Muslim Community in Gujarat, c. 1400–1650* (New Delhi: Oxford University Press, 2020), 7–8.

18. Habib Lakhani, *Memaṇa itihāsanī rūparekhā* (Karachi: Lākhāṇī Pablīkeśaṃsa, 1983), 27.

19. Das Gupta, *Indian Merchants*. The older narrative of an absolute decline in Indian shipping during the eighteenth century has been replaced by one that emphasizes those routes where Indian shipping continued to thrive, Machado, *Ocean of Trade*, 76.

20. For the Bohra case see Abd al-Tayyib bin Haidar Ali Divan, *Hādīqah al-Tārīkh: Risāla al-mutaḍammina akhbār al-sadāh āl Bhārmal-jī al-qādah* (Bombay: Metro Printing and Lithograph, 1949), 42–43.

21. Samira Sheikh, "A Gujarati Map and Pilot Book of the Indian Ocean, c. 1750," *Imago Mundi* 61, no. 1 (2009): 67–83.

22. R. J. Barendese, *Arabian Seas 1700–1763*, vol. 1, *The Western Indian Ocean in the Eighteenth Century* (Leiden, Netherlands: Brill, 2009), 500, 1241.

23. Saleh Muhammad Haji Harun Kabli, *Śuddha ke aśuddha ane Memaṇa tavārīkha* (n.p., 1931), 4–17.

24. Lakhani, *Memaṇa itihāsanī rūparekhā*, 47; for a partial English-language account, see Dhoraji Association Karachi, "History of Dhoraji Memons," accessed 5 September 2021, https://dhorajiassociation.org/history.

25. Claude Markovits, *The Global World of Indian Merchants, 1750–1947: Traders of Sind from Bukhara to Panama* (Cambridge: Cambridge University Press, 2000), 35.

26. Sarah F. D. Ansari, *Sufi Saints and State Power: The Pirs of Sind, 1843–1947* (Cambridge: Cambridge University Press, 1992), 50.

27. J. C. Masselos, "The Khojas of Bombay: The Defining of Formal Membership Criteria during the Nineteenth Century," in *Caste and Social Stratification among Muslims in India*, ed. Imtiaz Ahmad (Delhi: Manohar, 1978), 97–116; Teena Purohit, *The Aga Khan Case: Religion and Identity in Colonial India* (Cambridge, MA: Harvard University Press, 2012).

28. Zahir Bhalloo and Iqbal Akhtar, "Les manuscrits du sud de la vallée de l'Indus en écriture khojkī sindhī: État des lieux et perspectives," *Asiatische Studien-Études Asiatiques* 72, no. 2 (2018): 319–338.

29. Ali Muhammad Jan Muhammad Chunara, *Nūram mubīna: Athava Allāhanī pavitrā rassī*, 4th ed. (Bombay: n.p. [Khoja Sindhi Printing Press], 1961), 386, 387.

30. Chunara, *Nūram mubīna*, 387–388.

31. Chunara, *Nūram mubīna*, 428.

32. "Ismail Gangji Varas," Mumtaz Ali Tajddin Sadik Ali, *101 Ismaili Heroes: (Late 19th Century to Present Age)*, (Karachi: Islamic Book Publisher, 2008), 207–212.

33. Farhad Daftary, *The Isma'ilis: Their History and Doctrines*, 2nd ed. (Cambridge: Cambridge University Press, 2007), 279–280; On the transfer of the *dai*-ship to India, see the Arabic history written by the Bohra historian Sulaimanji Burhanpuri, *Muntaza' al-akhbār fī akhbār al-du'āh al-akhyār*, ed. Samir Faruq Tarablusi (Beirut: Dār al-Gharb al-Islāmī, 1999).

34. Haidar Ali Divan, *Hādīqah al-Tārīkh*, 46; Hoosamooddin, *Eulogy*, 3–4.

35. Haidar Ali Divan, *Hādīqah al-Tārīkh*, 46; Hoosamooddin, *Eulogy*, 4.

36. Satish Misra, *Muslim Communities of Gujarat: Preliminary Studies in Their History and Social Organization* (Bombay: Asia Publishing House, 1964), 32–34.

37. M. F. Lokhandwala ed., *Mirat-i-Ahmadi: A Persian History of Gujarat* (Baroda: Oriental Institute, 1965), 317.

38. Jivabhai, *Mawsim-i bahār*, 528.

39. For a discussion of some of these manuscripts, see Ismaili Poonawala, *Biobibliography of Ismaili Literature* (Malibu, CA: Undena, 1977); Delia Cortese, *Arabic Ismaili Manuscripts: The Zāhid ʿAlī Collection in the Library of the Institute of Ismaili Studies* (London: I. B. Tauris / Institute of Ismaili Studies, 2003); François de Blois, *Arabic, Persian and Gujarati Manuscripts: The Hamdani Collection in the Library of the Institute of Ismaili Studies* (London: I. B. Tauris / Institute of Ismaili Studies, 2011).

40. Muhammad Ali ibn al-Javid Jivabhai, *Mawsim-i bahār fī akhbār al-ṭāhirīn al-akhyār*, (Bombay: Maṭbaʿ Ḥaidarī Ṣafadrī, 1882), 528, 753–755.

41. Nadvi, *ʿIqd al-javāhir*, 227–233.

42. Ghulam Ali Azad Bilgrami, *Subḥat al-marjān fī athār Hindustān* (Bombay: M. S. Maḥmūd, 1884), f. 66b.

43. Alibhai Sharaf Ali ed., *Ṣaḥīfat al-ṣalāh* (Bombay: ʿAlī Bhāʾī wa Sharaf ʿAlī, 1933), 343–345.

44. For more on these disputes see Jonah Blank, *Mullahs on the Mainframe: Islam and Modernity among the Daudi Bohras* (Chicago: University of Chicago Press, 2001), 41–43.

45. Ismail K. Poonawala, "Majduʿ, Esmāʿil," in *Encyclopædia Iranica*, online edition, last updated 22 September 2015, http://www.iranicaonline.org/articles/majdu-esmail.

46. S. M. Edwardes, *The Rise of Bombay*, Vol. 10 (Bombay: Times of India Press, 1902), 194.

47. Hugh David Sandeman, ed., *Selections from Calcutta Gazettes of the Years 1816–1823 Inclusive, Showing the Political & Social Condition of the English in India, Fifty Years Ago*, vol. 5 (Calcutta: Calcutta Central Press, 1869), 235.

48. Saifiyah Qutbuddin, "History of the Daʾudi Bohra Tayyibis in Modern Times; The Daiʿs, the Daʿwat, and the Community," in *A Modern History of the Ismailis: Continuity and Change in a Muslim Community*, ed. Farhad Daftary (London: I. B. Tauris, 2010), 309.

49. Jivabhai, *Mawsim-i bahār*, 684, 692.

50. Jivabhai, *Mawsim-i bahār*, 537–538.

51. Hoosamooddin, *Eulogy*, 6.

52. Jivabhai, *Mawsim-i bahār*, 680–681.

53. Jonah Blank, "The Dāʾūdī Bohras (Mustaʿlī Ismāʿīlī Shīʿa): Using Modernity to Institutionalise a Fāṭimid Tradition," in *Handbook of Islamic Sects and Movements*, ed. Muhammad Afzal Upal and Carole M. Cusack (Leiden, Netherlands: Brill, 2021), 261; Qutbuddin, "History of the Daʾudi Bohra Tayyibis," 309.

54. C. A. Bayly, *Indian Society and the Making of the British Empire* (Cambridge: Cambridge University Press, 1990), 5, 18; Ian J. Barrow and Douglas E. Haynes,

"The Colonial Transition: South Asia, 1780–1840," *Modern Asian Studies* 38, no. 3 (2004): 469–478; Norbert Peabody, "Knowledge Formation in Colonial India," in *India and the British Empire*, ed. Douglas M. Peers and Nandini Gooptu (Oxford: Oxford University Press, 2012), 75–99.

55. Bayly, *Indian Society*, 63, 104.

56. James Burnes, *Narrative of a Visit to the Court of Sinde: A Sketch of the History of Cutch, from its First Connexion with the British Government in India till the Conclusion of the Treaty of 1819; and Some Remarks on the Medical Topography of Bhooj* (Bombay: Summachar, 1831), 228.

57. James Rivett Carnac, "Some Account of the Famine in Guzerat in the Years 1812 and 1813," *Transactions of the Literary Society of Bombay*, vol. 1 (Bombay: Bombay Education Society's Press, 1819), 302.

58. George C. D. Adamson, "Institutional and Community Adaptation from the Archives: A study of Drought in Western India, 1790–1860," *Geoforum* 55 (2014): 110–119.

59. Jivabhai, *Mawsim-i bahār*, 585, 633.

60. Abd al-Hamid Tayyib Suriya, *Sham'-i 'ilm: tārīkh va khidmāt: Okhā'ī Meman Yūth Sarvisaz* (Karachi: Okhā'ī Meman Yūth Sarvisaz, 2009), 29–31.

61. "Zanzibar," *Bombay Gazette*, 22 January 1874, 3.

62. Rustomji Pestonji Masani, *Evolution of Local Self-Government in Bombay* (London: Oxford University Press, 1929), 140.

63. "No. II. State of the Mussulman Population of the Island of Bombay, from a Survey by Kazee Shabodeen Mohuree," in *Transactions of the Literary Society of Bombay*, vol. 1 (London: Longman, Hurst, Rees, 1819), xxxv.

64. John Taylor, *Reports on the Epidemic Cholera Which Has Raged throughout Hindostan and the Peninsula of India since August 1817* (Bombay: Jos Fran de Jesus, 1819), 196.

65. Anonymous, *Jān-i Bamba'ī* (Calcutta: n.p., n.d [ca. 1820]), 35.

66. Lakhani, *Memaṇa itihāsanī rūparekhā*, 46.

67. Muhammad Vizir Ali, *Risāla-i sirāj al-hujjāj*, Punjab Archives, Lahore, MS. 571, Acc. no. 3594, ff. 8a–13b. Thanks to Sohaib Baig for sharing this exceptional manuscript with me.

68. Ali, *Risāla-i sirāj al-hujjāj*, f. 9b.

69. Haji Zakariyya, whose eponymous mosque was constructed in the 1830s at Khadak, was renowned for his generosity. One anecdote records him, his real identity obscured by a dirty sheet, tenderly shampooing a drowsy maulvi who had taken shelter in the mosque. Lulled to sleep by the gesture, the maulvi awoke the next morning to find a twenty-rupee note under his pillow. When the affair was repeated the next evening, the maulvi seized the mysterious shampooer by the arm and in the tussle that followed the figure of Haji Zakariyya was revealed, sheepishly

holding a one-hundred-rupee note, upon which was written, "A tribute of respect for learning. Pray for the forgiveness of this humble instrument of Allah's will." *Gazetteer of the Province of Gujarat: Population Musalmans and Parsis,* vol. 9, pt. 2 (Bombay: Government Central Press, 1899), 52–53n4.

70. "The Native Poor of Bombay," *Bombay Quarterly Review* 4 (1856): 264.

71. Ali, *Risāla-i Sirāj al-Hujjāj,* ff. 11b–12b; On Gujarati Vaniya capital as facilitator of exchange across the Indian Ocean, see Machado, *Ocean of Trade,* 63.

72. "Khoja Merchant Prince Dead: Mr. Abdoolabhoy Laljee Passes Away at Age of 101," *Bombay Chronicle,* 26 December 1934, 7.

73. Abdul Sattar Dalvi, *Pūne ke Musalmān: tārīkhī, tahzībī aur adabī muṭāla'ah* (Poona, India: Ḥājī Ghulām Muḥammad A'ẓam Ejūkeshan Ṭrasṭ, 2001), 20.

74. Abu al-Kalam Azad, *Faiṣla-i muqaddama-i Jāma' Masjid Kalkata* (Calcutta: Ḥaidarī, n.d. [1920?]), 1, 5.

75. "Extract Bombay Judicial Consultations, 25 January 1832—From the Acting Session Judge of Surat to Mr. Secretary Bax (2 January 1832)," in *Copies or Abstracts of All Correspondence between the Directors of the East India Company and the Company's Government in India, since the 1st day of June 1827, on the Subject of Slavery . . .,* vol. 16 (London: House of Commons, 1838), 470–471.

76. William Gervase Clarence-Smith, *Islam and the Abolition of Slavery* (Oxford: Oxford University Press, 2006), 132.

77. "Surat 24th January 1798," 71. Surat: Diary and Consultations, 1 Jan to 31 Dec [1798], Available through: Adam Matthew, Marlborough, East India Company, accessed 12 November 2021, http://www.eastindiacompany.amdigital.co.uk.eui.idm.oclc.org/Documents/Details/BL_IOR_G_36_77.

78. Amiya Kumar Bagchi, *Colonialism and Indian Economy* (New Delhi: Oxford University Press, 2010), 31–32.

79. Mohamad Tavakoli-Targhi, *Refashioning Iran: Orientalism, Occidentalism, and Historiography* (London: Palgrave Macmillan, 2001), 18–31.

80. Robert Travers, *Ideology and Empire in Eighteenth-Century India: The British in Bengal* (Cambridge: Cambridge University Press, 2007), 15–16.

81. Alexander Tilloch, ed., "Intelligence and Miscellaneous Articles," *The Philosophical Magazine Comprehending the Various Branches of Science, the Liberal and Fine Arts, Geology, Agriculture, Manufactures and Commerce,* vol. 8 (London: Davis, Taylor, and Wilks, 1800), 85.

82. Nadvi, *'Iqd al-javāhir,* 241, 243, 249, 261.

83. Mountstuart Elphinstone, *Report on the Territories, Conquered from the Paishwa* (Calcutta: Government Gazette Press, 1821).

84. Benjamin Hopkins, *The Making of Modern Afghanistan* (New York: Palgrave Macmillan, 2008).

85. Purohit, *The Aga Khan Case,* 29.

86. Sir T. E. Colebrooke, *Life of Hon. Mountstuart Elphinstone*, vol. 2 (London: John Stuart, 1884), 114–115.

87. G. W. Forrest, ed., *Selections from the Minutes and Other Official Writings of the Honourable Mountstuart Elphinstone, Governor of Bombay* (London: Richard Bentley and Son, 1884).

88. James Jaffe, *The Ironies of Colonial Governance: Law, Custom, and Justice in Colonial India* (Cambridge: Cambridge University Press, 2015), 103.

89. Jaffe, *The Ironies of Colonial Governance*, 4–5.

90. William Milburn, *Oriental Commerce: Containing a Geographical Description of the Principal Places in the East Indies, China, and Japan, with Their Produce, Manufactures, and Trade*, vol. 1 (London: Black, Parry, 1813), 171; Edward Moor, ed., *Hindu Infanticide: An Account of the Measures Adopted for Suppressing the Practice of the Systematic Murder by Their Parents of Female Infants* (London: J. Johnson, 1811), 168.

91. Henry George Briggs, *The Cities of Gujaráshtra: Their Topography and History Illustrated in the Journal of a Recent Tour, with Accompanying Documents* (Bombay: Times' Press, 1849), 141–154.

92. Nile Green, *Bombay Islam: The Religious Economy of the Western Indian Ocean* (Cambridge: Cambridge University Press, 2011), 175. Y. S. Taherali, "The Origin of Bohras," *Ummīd* (February 1943): 25–31.

93. Briggs, *The Cities of Gujaráshtra*, 154.

94. Azimusshan Haider, *Economic History of the Region Constituting Pakistan, from 1825 to 1974: An Analytical Study of Mainstreams* (Karachi: Haider, 1975), 26.

95. Lakhani, *Memaṇa itihāsanī rūparekhā*, 34–35.

96. Mitra Sharafi, *Law and Identity in Colonial South Asia: Parsi Legal Culture, 1772–1947* (Cambridge: Cambridge University Press, 2014), 88–89.

97. "From the Managing Committee of the Parsee Community at Bombay to the Governor and President in Council of Bombay dated 9th March 1861," in *Report of Her Majesty's Commissioners Appointed to Prepare a Body of Substantive Law for India, &c* (London: Eyre and Spottiswoode, 1863), 136–144.

98. "From the Managing Committee," 138.

99. Sharafi, *Law and Identity*, 79.

100. Lieutenant Edward Conolly, "II.—Observations upon the Past and Present Condition of Oujein or Ujjayani," *Journal of the Asiatic Society of Bengal* 6, pt. 2 (1837): 813–856.

101. Faiz Badruddin Tyabji, *Muhammadan Law: The Personal Law of Muslims* (Bombay: N. M. Tripathi, 1940), 62.

102. *Vol. 3: Persian Gulf—Effects of a British Subject Who Died at Muscat, Taken Possession of, by the Resident in the—and Made Over to the Heirs*, BL, IOR / F/ 4/ 1929 / 82845.

103. More likely, "Austrian Crowns," otherwise known as Maria Theresa thalers, a metallic currency in common use in the Indian Ocean region into the twentieth century.

104. Jivabhai, *Mawsim-i bahār*, 703–705.

105. Jivabhai, *Mawsim-i bahār*, 705.

106. Jivabhai, *Mawsim-i bahār*, 713.

107. Sir Roland Knyvet Wilson, *Anglo-Muhammadan Law: A Digest Preceded by a Historical and Descriptive Introduction of the Special Rules Now Applicable to Muhammadans as Such by the Civil Courts of British India: With Full References to Modern and Ancient Authorities*, 2nd ed. (London: W. Thacker, 1903), 42.

108. An excellent survey of these debates is Daniel Beben, "Introduction," *The First Aga Khan: Memoirs of the 46th Ismaili Imam: A Persian Edition and English Translation of Muḥammad Ḥasan al-Ḥusaynī's ʿIbrat-afẓā*, eds., Daniel Beben and Daryoush Mohammad Poor (London: I.B. Tauris and the Institute of Ismaili Studies, 2018), 1–70; Compare with Hamid Algar, "The Revolt of Aghā Khān Mahallāti and the Transference of the Ismāʿīlī Imāmate to India," *Studia Islamica* 29 (1969): 55–81.

109. William Francis Patrick Napier, *The Conquest of Scinde, with Some Introductory Passages in the Life of Major-General Sir Charles James Napier*, pt. 2 (London: T. and W. Boone, 1845), 369, 372.

110. "The Secret Societies of Asia—The Assassins and the Thugs," *Blackwood's Edinburgh Magazine* 49, no. 304 (1841): 240–241.

111. Beben and Mohammad Poor, *The First Aga Khan*, 118–121.

112. *Case of the Persian Nobleman Agha Khan Mehlatee*, vol. 4, BL, IOR / F / 4 / 2388 / 127595.

113. *Case of the Persian Nobleman*, ff. 35, 175.

114. Amrita Shodhan, "Caste in the Judicial Courts of Gujarat, 1800–60," in *The Idea of Gujarat: History, Ethnography and Text*, ed. Edward Simpson and Aparna Kapania (New Delhi: Orient Blackswan, 2010), 44–45.

115. Erskine Perry, *Cases Illustrative of Oriental Life* (New Delhi: Asian Educational Services, 1988), 124, emphasis added.

116. Edward Steere, "The Religions of the World: Mohammedanism in Zanzibar," *Mission Life; Or Home and Foreign Church Work* (London: Cassell, Petter, and Galpin, 1870), 141.

117. C. J. [Chief Justice] Perry, "Case of the Kojahs: Hirbae and Others vs. Sonabae; Gungbae v. Sonabae / Case of the Memons: Rahimatbae v. Hadji Jussap and Others," in Sir Erskine Perry, *Cases Illustrative of Oriental Life: And the Application of English Law to India, Decided in H. M. Supreme Court at Bombay* (London: S. Sweet, 1853), 120, 121.

118. Perry, "Case of the Kojahs," 129.

119. Sir Richard Burton, *Sindh, and the Races that Inhabit the Valley of the Indus* (London: W. H. Allen, 1851), 248. See also Perry, "Case of the Kojahs," 114.

120. Amrita Shodhan, "Legal Formulation of the Question of Community: Defining the Khoja Collective," *Indian Social Science Review* 1, no. 1 (1999): 144.

121. Erskine Perry, quoted in Shodhan, "Legal Formulation," 144.

2. The Vise of Legal Exceptionalism and Colonial Capitalism, 1850–1880

1. *An Account of the Khoja Sunnat Jamat, Bombay* (Karachi: Oxford Book House, 1969), 34.

2. Michel Boivin, *La rénovation du Shî'isme ismaélien en Inde et au Pakistan: D'après les ecrits et les discours de Sultān Muhammad Shah Aga Khan* (Abingdon, UK: Routledge, 2003), 284; Sorabji Mancherji Desai, *Tavārīkhe Navasārī, nakaśā sāthē* (Navsari, India: Navasārī Āryavijaya Press, 1897), 318.

3. Cambridge University Library, Jardine Matheson Collection, GBR / 0012 / MS JM / BC / 4, Bom. 5637, 7075, 7225.

4. Damodar Ishwardas, *Cīnanī musāpharī* (Bombay: Nowrojee Framjee, 1868). For more information on this account, see Michael O'Sullivan, "Vernacular Capitalism and Intellectual History in a Gujarati Account of China, 1860–68," *Journal of Asian Studies* 80, no. 2 (2021): 267–292.

5. Tirthankar Roy, *A Business History of India: Enterprise and the Emergence of Capitalism from 1700* (Cambridge: Cambridge University Press, 2018), 7–8.

6. Mirza Muhammad Qasim Barlas Muradabadi, *Sayr-i daryā: pahlī mauj Jazīra-i Lankā ke ḥālāt men* (Moradabad, India: Maṭbaʿ Aḥsan al-Maṭābʿ, 1896), 84. Special thanks to Nile Green for sharing this citation with me.

7. Charles Northcote Cooke, *The Rise, Progress, and Present Condition of Banking in India* (Calcutta: Bengal Printing, 1863), 69–70.

8. Maria Graham, *Journal of a Residence in India* (Edinburgh: George Ramsay, 1813), 33, 128–129; J. H. Stocqueler, *The Hand-Book of India: A Guide to the Stranger and the Traveller, and a Companion to the Resident* (London: Wm. H. Allen, 1845), 518–520; Henry Moses, *An Englishman's Life in India: Or, Travel and Adventure in the East* (Bath, UK: Binns and Goodwin, 1853), 308–311.

9. Rajnarayan Chandavarkar, *The Origins of Industrial Capitalism in India: Business Strategies and the Working Classes in Bombay, 1900–1940* (Cambridge: Cambridge University Press, 1994), 56.

10. The classic expositions of the "peddler" thesis are J.C. Van Leur, *Indonesian Trade and Society: Essays in Asian Social and Economic History* (The Hague: W. van Hoeve. 1955); Niels Steensgaard, *The Asian Trade Revolution of the Seventeenth Century: The East India Companies and the Decline of the Caravan Trade*

(Chicago: University of Chicago Press, 1974). The "peddler" thesis has long been rejected by historians, for further discussion Aslanian, *From the Indian Ocean to the Mediterranean*, 99–100.

11. Victor Jacquemont, *État politique et social de l'Inde du Sud en 1832; extraits de son journal de voyage* (Paris: Société de l'Histoire des Colonies Françaises / E. Leroux, 1934), 76–77.

12. Jacquemont, *État politique*, 77.

13. Jacquemont, *État politique*, 77.

14. S. T. Lokhandwalla, "Islamic Law and Ismaili Communities (Khojas and Bohras)," *Indian Economic and Social History Review* 4, no. 2 (1967): 175.

15. Mushiru-l-Haqq, "Indian Muslim Attitude to the British in the Early Nineteenth Century: A Case Study of Shāh ʿAbd al-ʿAzīz," (M.A. Thesis, McGill University, 1964), 39–40.

16. Jacquemont, *État politique*, 77.

17. Stewart Gordon, "Burhanpur: Entrepot and Hinterland, 1650–1750," *Marathas, Marauders, and State Formation in Eighteenth-Century India* (New Delhi: Oxford University Press, 1994), 174–175.

18. Jacquemont, *État politique*, 77, 85.

19. *Facts for Factories: Being Letters on Practical Subjects, Suggested by Experiences in Bombay*. (Bombay: Education Society's Press, 1857), 36.

20. Marianne Young, *The Moslem Noble: His Land and People, with Some Notices of the Parsees, or Ancient Persians* (London: Saunders and Otley, 1857), 71–87.

21. Narayan Dinanathji, "XIV. The Present State of the Guzarathis and the Marathas Compared" (n.p. [Bombay?]: n.d., ca. mid-nineteeth century), 98.

22. Dinanathji, "The Present State," 98, 99.

23. Claude Markovits, "Merchant Circulation in South Asia (Eighteenth to Twentieth Centuries): The Rise of Pan-Indian Merchant Networks," in *Society and Circulation: Mobile People and Itinerant Cultures in South Asia, 1750–1950*, ed. Claude Markovits, Jacques Pouchepadass, and Sanjay Subrahmanyam (New York: Anthem, 2006), 149.

24. *38 Paintings Bound into a Volume Depicting Castes and Trades in Bombay. By a Western Indian Artist, Perhaps at Belgaum, c. 1856*, BL, Add. Or.1584–1621, f. 18.

25. See the relevant photographs at the Library of Southern Methodist University Library, "Photographs of Western India, circa 1855–1862: A Guide to the Collection," accessed 10 September 2021, https://txarchives.org/smu/finding_aids/00237.xml.

26. "Khoja Merchant Prince Dead: Mr. Abdoolabhoy Laljee Passes Away at Age of 101," *Bombay Chronicle*, 26 December 1934, 7.

27. Bomanjee Byramjee Patell, *The Parsee Patells of Bombay: Their Services to the British Government* (Bombay: English and Gujarati Job Printing Press, 1876), 21.

28. Cowasjee Sorabjee Cowasjee Patel, *Account of China: Comprising a View of the Topography, History, Manners, Customs, Languages, Literature, Arts, Manufactures, Commerce, Religion, Jurisprudence, Etc. Etc. of the Chinese Empire, Together with a General Sketch of the Late British Expedition in China*, 2 vols. [in Gujarati] (Bombay: Courier, 1844).

29. "Preface," in Patel, *Account of China*, n.p.

30. H. K. Dhabar, *Cīn Deś; Chin Desh, containing a succinct view of the moral and social character, manners, customs, language and religion of its inhabitants* [in Gujarati] (Bombay: Union, 1894), 8.

31. Caroline Plüss, "Globalizing Ethnicity with Multi-local Identifications: The Parsee, Indian Muslim and Sephardic Trade Diasporas in Hong Kong," in *Diaspora Entrepreneurial Networks: Four Centuries of History*, ed. Ina Baghdiantz McCabe, Gelina Harlaftis, and Ioanna Pepelasis Minoglou (Oxford: Berg, 2005), 254.

32. Claude Markovits, "Indian Communities in China, c. 1842–1919," in *New Frontiers: Imperialism's New Communities in East Asia, 1842–1953*, ed. Robert Bickers and Christian Henriot (Manchester, UK: Manchester University Press, 2000), 66.

33. Barbara Sue-White, *Turbans and Traders: Hong Kong's Indian Communities* (Hong Kong: Oxford University Press, 1994), 60.

34. Haji Sulaiman Shah Muhammad, *Pr̥athvīnī pradakshiṇā* (Bombay: Daphatara Āśakārā Ôīl Press, 1895), 125.

35. Current proprietor of Abdoolally Ebrahim & Co., zoom interview with the author in Hong Kong, 29 September 2021.

36. Ishwardas, *Cīnanī musāpharī*.

37. Rajnarayan Chandavarkar, *The Origins of Industrial Capitalism in India: Business Strategies and the Working Classes in Bombay, 1900–1940* (Cambridge: Cambridge University Press, 1990), 60.

38. *Bombay Riots of 1874* (Bombay: Bombay Gazette Steam Press, 1874), 3, 49.

39. *Gaḍhaḍa masajīda gajaba kes* (Ahmedabad: Politikal Bhomiyo, n.d. [1906?]).

40. Raman, *Dhana rokāna yāne sherbājarano sāthī* (Bombay: Vasanjī Paramaṇd, 1920).

41. Ek Parsi, *Mumabaīnā śera saṭānī tavārīkha: tenuṃ cahaḍavuṃ tathā paḍavuṃ ane tenāṃ śevaṭanāṃ parīṇāmo* (Bombay: Jāba Printing, 1867).

42. D. E. Wacha, *A Financial Chapter in the History of Bombay City*, 2nd ed. (Bombay: A. J. Combridge, 1910), 224.

43. "Memon Company," *Allen's Indian Mail*, 6 October 1860, 736.

44. Ek Parsi, *Mumabaīnā śera saṭānī tavārīkha*, 39–41, 45–49, 52, 151, 205.

45. Murali Ranganathan, ed., *Govind Narayan's Mumbai: An Urban Biography from 1863* (London: Anthem, 2009), 139.

46. "India and Continental Financial Assosiation [*sic*] (Limited.)," in Ek Parsi, *Mumabaīnā śera saṭānī tavārīkha*, 223.

47. Cooke, *The Rise, Progress, and Present Condition of Banking*, 363.

48. "Oriental Financial Association (Limited)," in Ek Parsi, *Mumabaīnā śera saṭānī tavārīkha*, 230–231.

49. Ek Parsi, *Mumabaīnā śera saṭānī tavārīkha*, 224.

50. Wacha, *A Financial Chapter*, 181.

51. Ek Parsi, *Mumabaīnā śera saṭānī tavārīkha*, 213.

52. Wacha, *A Financial Chapter*, 181.

53. Ek Parsi, *Mumabaīnā śera saṭānī tavārīkha*, 210.

54. Wacha, *A Financial Chapter*, 182.

55. Wacha, *A Financial Chapter*, 63.

56. Sorabji M. Rutnagur, *Bombay Industries: The Cotton Mill; A Review of the Progress of the Textile Industry in Bombay from 1850 to 1926 and the Present Constitution, Management and Financial Position of the Spinning and Weaving Factories* (Bombay: Indian Textile Journal, 1927), 27.

57. Ek Parsi, *Mumabaīnā śera saṭānī tavārīkha*, 152, 153, 213, 309.

58. "Bombay Bank Commission: Minutes of Evidence Taken in India . . . Charles Edward Chapman," in *Minutes of Evidence Taken in India by the Commissioners, Acting in Execution of Act XVII of 1868 of the Legislative Council of India* (London: George Edward Eyre and William Spottiswoode, 1869), 39.

59. Behramji M. Malabari, *Gujarat and the Gujaratis: Pictures of Men and Manners Taken from Life*, 3rd ed. (Bombay: Fort Printing Press, 1889), 168.

60. "The Ocean Telegraph to India: A Narrative and a Diary, By J. C. Parkinson. (Blackwood & Sons)," *Athenaeum*, 9 July 1870, 45.

61. "24th July 1868. Mahomed Cassim. affirmed" and "24th July 1868. Govindjee Kessowjee. affirmed," in *Minutes of Evidence*, 47.

62. Ek Parsi, *Mumabaīnā śera saṭānī tavārīkha*, 301–302.

63. Delawarr Hosaen Ahamed Meerza, *Muslim Modernism in Bengal: Selected Writings of Delawarr Hosaen Ahamed Meerza, 1840–1913*, ed. Sultan Jahan Salik (Dhaka: Centre for Social Studies, 1980), 67–68.

64. Timur Kuran and Anantdeep Singh, "Economic Modernization in Late British India: Hindu-Muslim Differences," ERID Working Paper 53, Economic Research Initiatives at Duke, Duke University, July 2010.

65. "The Humble Petition of Certain Mahomedan Inhabitants of Bombay," in *First Report from the Select Committee on Indian Territories; Together with the Minutes of Evidence, and Appendix*, vol. 27 (London: House of Commons, 1853), 422.

66. Bijay Kisor Acharyya, *Codification in British India* (Calcutta: S. K. Banerji and Sons, 1914), 88n3.

67. See, for example, a petition of a generation before in which 4000 Bombay "natives" stressed that both the former Recorder's Court and the Supreme Courts that replaced them "have always been *scrupulously observant* of the religious doc-

trines, rites, and observances, and of the manners and usages of the Natives." "Administration of Justice in India," *The Law Magazine or Quarterly Review of Jurisprudence,* vol. 6 (London: Saunders and Benning, July and October 1831), 238. Italics in original.

68. "The Humble Petition," 423.

69. "The Humble Petition," 424.

70. Amrita Shodhan, "Caste in the Judicial Courts of Gujarat, 1800–60," in *The Idea of Gujarat: History, Ethnography and Text,* ed. Edward Simpson and Aparna Kapania (New Delhi: Orient Blackswan, 2010), 35.

71. *A Voice from India. Being an appeal to the British Legislature, by Khojahs of Bombay, against the usurped and oppressive domination of Hussain Hussanee, commonly called and known as "Aga Khan." By a Native of Bombay, etc.* (London: Waterlow and Sons, 1864).

72. J. Barton Scott, "How to Defame a God: Public Selfhood in the Maharaj Libel Case," *South Asia: Journal of South Asian Studies,* 38:3 (2015): 387–402.

73. *Judgment by the Hon'ble Sir Joseph Arnould in the Kojah Case, Otherwise Known as the Aga Khan Case, Heard in the High Court of Bombay, During April and June, 1866* (Bombay: Bombay Gazette Steam Press, 1866), 4.

74. Amrita Shodhan, "Legal Formulation of the Question of Community: Defining the Khoja Collective," *Indian Social Science Review* 1, no. 1 (1999): 137–151.

75. See, for example Edalji Dhanji Kaba ed., *Mahuvā kamīśan kesno rīporṭ* (Amreli, India: Aruṇodaya Printing Press, 1920).

76. Nile Green, *Bombay Islam: The Religious Economy of the Western Indian Ocean* (Cambridge: Cambridge University Press, 2011), 11–12.

77. "Original Jurisdiction. Ecclesiastical Side. In the Goods of Mulbai," *Reports of Cases Decided in the High Court of Bombay, 1864–66,* vol. 2, 2nd ed., ed. Richard Tuohill Reid (Bombay: Education Society's Press, 1868), 292–300.

78. "The Grand Master of the Order of Assassins," *Bombay Guardian,* 9 March 1867, 10.

79. Teena Purohit, *The Aga Khan Case: Religion and Identity in Colonial India* (Cambridge, MA: Harvard University Press, 2012).

80. Soumen Mukherjee, *Ismailism and Islam in Modern South Asia: Community and Identity in the Age of Religious Internationals* (Cambridge: Cambridge University Press, 2017), 40–41.

81. Copy of Letter No. 1643 / 451 of 1872 from Colonel Lewis Pelly, HBM's Political Resident in the Persian Gulf, on Board British India Steam Navigation Company's Steam Ship *India,* to the Secretary to Government, Political Department, Bombay, QDL, [11v] (2 / 8)–[12r] (3 / 8).

82. Copy of Letter No. 1643 / 451, [12v] (4 / 8).

83. Copy of Letter No. 1643 / 451, [13r] (5 / 8).

84. Muscat Affairs 1869–1892, QDL, [51r] (107 / 318).

85. Michel Boivin, "The Isma'ili-Isna 'Ashari Divide among the Khojas," in *The Shi'a in Modern South Asia*, ed. Justin Jones and Ali Usman Qasmi (Cambridge: Cambridge University Press, 2015), 43.

86. Ghulam Ali Ghulam Hussain, ed., *Khojā sunatjamātanā navā kayedā vīrūddha Khojā Abdallā Hājī Alārakhīānā ūrdu copānīāno tarajumo* (Bombay: Kāsīd Mumbaī Press, 1880). Although based on a translation of an Urdu work, I have only been able to locate the Gujarati version.

87. Hussain, ed., *Khojā sunatjamātanā,* 5.

88. This is a point made in full form in Paolo Sartori, "Between Kazan and Kashghar: On the Vernacularization of Islamic Jurisprudence in Central Eurasia," *Die Welt des Islams* 61, no. 2 (2021): 1–31.

89. Maria Misra, *Vishnu's Crowded Temple: India since the Great Rebellion* (New Haven, CT: Yale University Press, 2008), 55–56.

90. Acharyya, *Codification in British India,* 359.

91. Green, *Bombay Islam.*

3. Clarifying and Contesting Religious Authority

1. H. Neville Chittick, *Kilwa: An Islamic Trading City on the East African Coast* (Nairobi: British Institute in East Africa, 1984), 2 vols; Sanjay Subrahmanyam, *The Career and Legend of Vasco Da Gama* (Cambridge: Cambridge University Press, 1997), 105.

2. Edalji Dhanji Kaba, ed., *Kīlavānā savāla javāba yane āftābe hīdāyata* (Amreli, India: Amarasinhajī Printing Press, 1918), 9–10.

3. Kaba, ed., *Kīlavānā savāla,* 10, 11, 14.

4. Kaba, ed., *Kīlavānā savāla,* 14–16, 19, 22–23.

5. Christine Dobbin, *Asian Entrepreneurial Minorities: Conjoint Communities in the Making of the World Economy, 1570–1940* (Abingdon, UK: RoutledgeCurzon, 1996), 117; Abdul Sheriff, *Slaves, Spices, and Ivory in Zanzibar: Integration of an East African Commercial Empire into the World Economy, 1770–1873* (Athens: Ohio University Press, 1987), 107.

6. Soumen Mukherjee, *Ismailism and Islam in Modern South Asia: Community and Identity in the Age of Religious Internationals* (Cambridge: Cambridge University Press, 2017), 50n32.

7. "The Zanzibar Khojas: The Editor of the "Bombay Gazette," *Journal of the Society of Arts* 37, no. 1899 (1889): 502–503.

8. J. A. Saldanha, "Précis on Slave Trade in the Gulf of Oman and the Persian Gulf, 1873–1905 (with a Retrospect into Previous History from 1852)," QDL, [14] (22 / 126), (23 / 126).

9. "Slave-Dealing and Slave-Holding by Kutchees in Zanzibar," QDL, [114v] (17 / 63).

10. Seyyid Saeed Akhtar Rizvi and Noel Q. King, "Some East African Ithna-Asheri Jamaats (1840–1967)," *Journal of Religion in Africa* 5, fasc. 1 (1973): 12–22.

11. Saldanha, "Précis on Slave Trade," QDL [14] (23 / 126).

12. H. B. E. Frere, "The Khojas II: the Disciples of the Old Man of the Mountain," in *Macmillan's Magazine, May 1876 to October 1876*, vol. 34 (Cambridge: Macmillan, 1876), 432.

13. The text is reproduced in Naoroji Maneckji Dumasia, *A Brief History of the Aga Khan with an Account of His Predecessore, the Ismailian Princes or Benefatimite Caliphs of Egypt* (Bombay: Times of India Press, 1903), 166–167.

14. "Bombay: Sir Bartle Frere on the Slave Trade," *Allen's Indian Mail*, 27 May 1873, 485.

15. Zulfikar Hirji and Karen Ruffle, "Diasporas," in *The Shi'i World: Pathways in Tradition and Modernity*, ed. Farhad Daftary, Amyn B. Sajoo, and Shainool Jiwa (London: Bloomsbury, 2015), 337.

16. Nile Green, *Bombay Islam: The Religious Economy of the Western Indian Ocean* (Cambridge: Cambridge University Press, 2011), 155–178.

17. S. A. A. Rizvi and N. Q. King, "Some East African Ithna-Asheri Jamaats (1840–1967)," *Journal of Religion in Africa* 5, no. 1 (1973): 12–22; Shireen Mirza, "Muslims, Media, and Mobility in the Indian Ocean," in *The Shiʿa in Modern South Asia*, ed. Justin Jones and Ali Usman Qasmi (Cambridge: Cambridge University Press, 2015), 142.

18. For records of some of al-Bohri's transactions on behalf of Devji Jamal, see Indian Ocean in World History, "Ocean of Paper," database, accessed 03 March 2021, https://www.indianoceanhistory.org/oceanofpaper/. For example, "Shamba Sale from Al-Tangani to Al-Hindi No. 1512."

19. "Aga Khan II," in *Historical Dictionary of the Ismailis*, ed. Farhad Daftary (Lanham: The Scarecrow Press, Inc, 2012), 9–10.

20. *Memoirs of Mulla Qadir Husain Sahib*, trans. H. Prakash (Karachi: Peermahomed Ebrahim Trust, 1972), 7.

21. *Memoirs of Mulla Qadir Husain*, 46–48.

22. Ayat Allah Zain al-Abidin ibn Muslim Mazandarani, *Zakhīrat al-maʿād* (Bombay: Duttpragad, 1315 [1899]).

23. Iqbal Akhtar, *The Khōjā of Tanzania: Discontinuities of a Postcolonial Religious Identity* (Leiden, Netherlands: Brill, 2016), 96–97; Iqbal Akhtar, "Ismā'il, Gulāmalī (Hājī Nājī)," in *Encyclopedia of Indian Religions*, ed. Arvind Sharma (Dordrecht, Netherlands: Springer, 2019); https://www.hajinaji.com/.

24. Mir Sayyid Ali, *Hidāyatul muslimīna* (Surat, India: Rising Star Printing Press, 1894), 2.

25. Mir Sayyid Ala Kadri, *Majamuā hajāra māsāyela* (n.p.: n.p., n.d.), 2.

26. Mastar Hasham Bogha, *Ismāilī Prakāśa: Ismāilī dharmanā abhyāsa māṭe eka upayōgī pustaka*, vol. 1 (Mumbai: Gujarati Printing Press, 1906), 8–9, 113.

27. Bogha, *Ismāilī Prakāś*, 7–8.

28. Hashim Bogha Mastar, *Aslīyate Khojā* (Bombay: K.N. Selar, 1912); Edalji Dhunji Kaba, *Khojā kōmanī tavārīkha* (Amreli: Dhī Gujarāta ēnḍ Kāṭhīyāvāḍa Printing Works, 1913).

29. Jumabhai Alibhai Suratwala, *Makasade hakīkata* (Bombay: Dhī Khojā Siṇdhī Printing Press, 1913).

30. *Jaffer Fuddoo Defamation Case, Containing Counsel's Addresses to Courts, Reported for the Defence by Mr. H.J. Lilley, and the Connected History of the Assassins* (Karachi: Sind Observer and Mercantile Steam Press, 1924), 29–31.

31. *Khojā Śīā Isnā Aśarī jamātanā kāydā buk* (Bombay: Dhī Isṭarn Printing Press, 1901). On the subject of inheritance, the book notes, "Until now the government [*sarkar*] has not established Islamic rules for the Khojas in matters of inheritance and succession, and to date the *jamaat* could not do anything in this regard" (18). Consequently, members of the *jamaat* were encouraged to draw up a will according to Islamic law, for if they died without one, the *jamaat* was powerless to ensure the estate was distributed in conformity with what normative Islam prescribed.

32. Edalji Dhunji Kaba, ed., *Jāfar Fadu badnakṣī kes*, vol. 1 (Amreli, India: Dhi Aruṇodaya Printing Press, 1924), 3–5.

33. Kaba, ed., *Jāfar Fadu*, 21.

34. *Jaffer Fuddoo Defamation Case*, 6. There were rumors bandied about during the case that two leading Ismaili Khojas of Bombay, Ibrahim Rahmat Allah and Karimbhai Ibrahim, were sympathetic to the Twelvers, but out of fear remained loyal to the Agha Khan III. *Jaffer Fuddoo Defamation Case*, 28.

35. "Allarakhia Nanji vs Lakha Kanji," ZLR HC7 / 799. Sincere thanks to Fahad Bishara for sharing this source with me.

36. *Yādgāre Śarīpha* (n.p.: n.p., n.d.)

37. *Mālagāsī rīpablīka, mōrīśī'asa, sōmālīyā tathā rīyunī'anamāṁ kōmī birādarōnā vasāhatanā itihāsanī rūparēkhā tathā vyavasāya nidrēśikā* (Arusha, Tanzania: Dhī Suprīm Kāunsīl ōph dhī Phēdarēśan ōph Khōjā Śīā Isnāaśarī Jamāts ōph Afrikā, 1960), 149–151.

38. "Allarakhia Nanji vs Lakha Kanji," ZLR HC7 / 799.

39. "Fazal Jahnmahomed, Master vs. Shariff Jiwa (Khoja) of Majunga Madagascar," ZLR, HC7 / 1126. Thanks again to Fahad Bishara for sharing this source with me.

40. Azim Nanji, "Modernization and Change in the Nizari Ismaili Community in East Africa—A Perspective," *Journal of Religion in Africa* 6, no. 2 (1974): 124.

41. Azim Nanji, *The Nizārī Ismā'īlī tradition in the Indo-Pakistan subcontinent* (Delmar, NY: Caravan Books, 1978), 25, 29.

42. Christopher Shackle and Zawahir Moir, *Ismaili Hymns from South Asia: An Introduction to the Ginans* (Abingdon, UK: Routledge, 2000), 9; Mukherjee, *Ismailism and Islam*, 39.

43. "Haji Bibi v. Aga Khan, Bombay High Court, Sept. 1, 1908," *Citator (Civil)*, vol. 3A, nos. 7 to 13 (Madras: India Printing Works, 1908), 668.

44. Govandlal Balaji, *Nāmadār Hījhāinesh Sarsultāna Mahamadshāhā Āgākhāna . . . Hajībībīvāḷo prakhyāta kes peḍhīnāmā sātheno* (Ahmedabad: Pānkornānāke Manahar Printing Press, 1910); Alibhai Lakhani, *Hajībībī v. Āgākhāna Kes* (n.p.: n.p., n.d.)

45. Lakhani, *Hajībībī v. Āgākhāna Kes*, 9.

46. "Haji Bibi v. Aga Khan," 671, 677.

47. Muhammad Zardar Khan, *Safarnāma-i Ḥaramain* (n.p. [Lucknow, India]: Maṭba' Nāmī Munshī Naval Kishor, 1290 [1873]), 17. Sincere thanks to Sohaib Baig for sharing this source with me.

48. S.M. Edwardes, *By-ways of Bombay* (Bombay: D.P. Taraporevala Sons & Co., 1912), 82. The same account also describes Memon women as driving a hard bargain, 84.

49. Muhammad Hadi Husain, *Syed Ahmed Khan: Pioneer of Muslim Resurgence* (Lahore: Institute of Islamic Culture, 1970), 65.

50. Syed Ahmed Khan, *A Voyage to Modernism*, ed. and trans Mushirul Hasan and Nishat Zaidi (Delhi: Primus Books, 2011), 65–66.

51. Sayyid Amir al-Din Nuzhat, *Risāla-i ibrāz al-hāqq* (Bombay: Bandar Zewar, 1873). This work was edited by Memon historians in Karachi in the 1970s who had acquired it from a community leader. As they acknowledged, the text was one of the very few Urdu histories of the Memons to have survived the nineteenth century. See Abd al-Rahman Asir, ed., *Asās-i Meman qaum* (Karachi: Meman Yūth Ārganā'izeshan, 1978).

52. Memon Abd Allah Ismail, *Memaṇa tavārīkha* (Amreli, India: Śrī Nārāyaṇa, 1921).

53. Nuzhat, *Risāla-i ibrāz al-hāqq*, 6.

54. Nuzhat, *Risāla-i ibrāz al-hāqq*, 19.

55. "Kacchī Memanonā vārasā hīssāne māṭe raju thayaluṁ bīl," *Kaiser-i Hind*, 1 November 1885, 1139.

56. Sir Roland Knyvet Wilson, *Anglo-Muhammadan Law: A Digest Preceded by a Historical and Descriptive Introduction* (London: Thacker, 1903), 58.

57. "Cutchee Memons and the Law of Inheritance and Succession," *Times of India*, 1 July 1885, 5.

58. "The Cutchee Memons' Memorial," *Indian Jurist: A Journal and Law Reports* 17 (1893): 141.

59. "The Cutchee Memons' Memorial," 142. *Kaiser-i Hind* continued to voice support for the Kachchhi Memons' protest; see "A Right Protest of the Kutchi Memons" [in Gujarati], *Kaiser-i Hind*, 4 September 1892, 7.

60. "Ayshabai v. Ebrahim Haji Jacob," *Bombay Law Reporter*, vol. 10 (Bombay: Bombay Law Reporter Office, 1908), 117.

61. "Sarabai Amibai vs Mahomed Cassum Haji Jan Mahomed—22 August 1918," Indian Kanoon, accessed 1 April 2021, https://indiankanoon.org/doc/1075949/.

62. "Bombay High Court: Appeal from Original Civil Suit No. 1136 of 1915. September 21, 1918 . . . Mahomed Haji Abu—Appellant versus Khatubai and others—Respondents," *Bombay Law Reporter*, vol. 41 (Bombay: Bombay Law Reporter Office, 1919), 528.

63. Khoja Lavji Jhina Master Benaras, *Kāshīthī Karbalā* (Ahmedabad: Amarsinhjī Press, n.d. [1922?]). See the notice at the back of the text.

64. Khoja Lavji Jhina Master Benaras, *Gausul Ājama hajrata mahoṭā pīranuṁ jīvanacaritra* (Ahmedabad: Amarasinhajī Printing Press, n.d. [1921–1922?], 47–48.

65. "Enclosure: Copy of a note by S. M. Edwards, Esq., Commissioner of Police, Bombay, No. U.O.R., No. 3376 M.—40, dated the 11th September 1914," QDL, IOR / L / PS / 10 / 462, File 3136 / 1914, pt. 1, "German War. Situation in Turkish Arabia & Persian Gulf."

66. BOA, A. MKT. MHM, 460 / 83 / 1-6. Many thanks to Sohaib Baig for sharing this source with me.

67. Goolam Vahed, "'Unhappily Torn by Dissensions and Litigations': Durban's 'Memon' Mosque, 1880–1930," *Journal of Religion in Africa* 36, fasc. 1 (2006): 23–49; Green, *Bombay Islam*, 220.

68. Abdul Cader Kalla, "The Gujarati Merchants in Mauritius, c. 1850–1900," *Journal of Mauritian Studies* 2, no. 1 (1987): 45–65.

69. Maulana Qari Hakim Abd Allah Rashid, *Mawrish aur Islām* (Bombay: Khilāfat, 1342 [1923]), 12–13.

70. R. N. Gassita, "L'Islam a l'ile Maurice," *Revue du monde musulman* 20–21 (1912): 291–313.

71. "Supreme Court . . . Sulliman Hajee Mamode—Plaintiff. Versus The Sonnee Cutchee Maiman's Society—Defendants," in *Decisions of the Supreme Court of Mauritius, 1904*, ed. Arthur Thibaud and Leon Leclezio (Port Louis, Mauritius: Cooperative Establishment, 1906), 89–91.

72. Coates, *The Old "Country Trade" of the East Indies* (London: Imray, Laurie, Norie & Wilson, 1911) 197.

73. Gassita, "L'Islam a l'ile Maurice," 300.

74. "Supreme Court . . . Sulliman Hajee Mamode," 69.

75. "Case of the Mosque, 1906," in *Decisions of the Supreme Court of Mauritius, 1906*, ed. Leon Leclezio and G. E. Nairac (Port Louis, Mauritius: Cooperative Establishment, 1907), 87.

76. "Case of the Mosque, 1906," 87.

77. Amenah Jahangeer-Chojoo, "Islamisation Processes among Mauritian Muslims," *Internationales Asienforum* 33, nos. 1–2 (2002): 120, 121; Patrick Eisenlohr, *Sounding Islam: Voice, Media, and Sonic Atmospheres in an Indian Ocean World* (Berkeley: University of California Press, 2018), 35.

78. Jonah Blank, *Mullahs on the Mainframe: Islam and Modernity among the Daudi Bohras* (Chicago: University of Chicago Press, 2001), 49–51.

79. Muhammad Ali ibn al-Javid Jivabhai, *Mawsim-i bahār fī akhbār al-ṭāhirīn al-akhyār,* (Bombay: Maṭbaʿa Ḥaidarī Ṣafadrī, 1882), 716–717; Blank, *Mullahs on the Mainframe,* 49–50.

80. Jivabhai, *Mawsim-i bahār,* 720.

81. Jivabhai, *Mawsim-i bahār,* 755.

82. Jivabhai, *Mawsim-i bahār,* 749–750; Farhad Daftary, *The Ismāʿīlīs: Their History and Doctrines,* 2nd Edition (Cambridge, Cambridge University Press, 2007), 287.

83. Blank, *Mullahs on the Mainframe,* 302.

84. Abd al-Qadir Najm al-Din, *Risāla al-waḍiyya fī īḍāḥ al-naṣṣ wa-l-wasiyya,* IIS, MS 1563, Hamdani Collection. For a brief description see "Ms.1563," in François de Blois, *Arabic, Persian and Gujarati Manuscripts: The Hamdani Collection in the Library of the Institute of Ismaili Studies* (London: I. B. Tauris / Institute of Ismaili Studies, 2011), 166.

85. Blois, *Arabic, Persian and Gujarati Manuscripts,* xxx.

86. Blank, *Mullahs on the Mainframe,* 236.

87. "Ūpyogī savāla ane javāba," Shaykh Tahirbhai Muhammad Ali Hamdani, *Rīsālatul mumīnīna,* vol. 3 (Bombay: Dhī Mustaphāī Printing Press, 1900), 20–21.

88. Abbas Hamdani, "History of the Hamdani Collection of Manuscripts," Blois, *Arabic, Persian and Gujarati Manuscripts,* xxx.

89. IIS, MS 1670, Hamdani Collection.

90. Shetjee Sahibjee, "A Day with My Indian Cousins, VII—The Bohra," *Vanity Fair: A Weekly Show,* 7 October 1882, 207–208.

91. *Dasturūl amalanō vadhārō: Judā judā kesesnā phāinal jajamenḍs* (Bombay: Dhī Mustaphāī Printing Press, 1899), 7.

92. *Dasturūl amalanō vadhārō,* 7.

93. Ashgar Ali Engineer, *The Bohras* (New Delhi: Vikas Publishing House, 1993), 137–138.

94. *Dasturūl amalanō vadhārō,* 61.

95. *Dasturūl amalanō vadhārō,* 35–36.

96. *Dasturūl amalanō vadhārō,* 35–36.

97. "Phayje Husēnī ṭrasṭ," *Pākistānī Dā'udī Vōhrā Vastī Patrak* (Karachi: Yusuph Alī Abdula Alī Kāj, 1966), 118–119.

98. Sayyid Muslim Riza, *Ruznama-i safar-i ʿiraq-o-iran* (Hyderabad: np., 1920), 18.

99. "Mesopotamia: Oudh Bequest" QDL, IOR / L / PS / 10 / 77, File 1290 / 1905, [56r].

100. *Ōl-Inḍiyā Memaṇa kōnphēransni cothī beṭhaka upara eka dṛsṭi* (n.p. [Karachi?]: np., n.d. [1936?]), 105.

101. For more details, see the interesting study by Yoginder Sikand, "Shiʿism in Contemporary India: The Badri-Vakili Controversy among Indian Ismailis," *Muslim World* 93, no. 1 (2003): 99–115.

102. This was reported in the Gujarati newspaper *Akhbāre Sodāgara,* 13 April 1892, and translated in *Report on Native Newspapers,* published in the Bombay Presidency, for the Week Ending 16th April 1892 (1892): 12–13.

103. Sikand, "Shiʿism in Contemporary India."

104. "Khan Bahadur H. M. Malak (Hijab-e-Moualana Malak), Budruddin Goolam Husein . . . ," in *The Cyclopedia of India,* vol. 3 (Calcutta: Cyclopedia Publishing House, 1909), 457–459.

105. Abbas Hamdani, "History," xxx.

106. Muhammad Ali Hamdani, "Daʾwa (i)bn Jiwa al-Kaparwanji wa-l-radd ʿalayhi in al-mawla Muhammad Ali al-Hamdani" (second manuscript of three), IIS, MS 1569, Hamdani Collection.

107. Hamdani, "Daʾwa (i)bn Jiwa al-Kaparwanji," 12b, 16a, 16b.

108. Yusuf Ali Bakirbhai, *Āgalā pāchalā muddaiyonī tapāsa,* 3rd ed. (Surat, India: Nādir Printing Press, 1915), 16.

109. "In the Court for the Relief of Insolvent Debtors, Bombay: In the Matter of Abdul Husen Jiwabhoy of Bombay . . . ," *Bombay Gazette,* 13 October 1892, 2.

110. Bakirbhai, *Āgalā pāchalā,* 23.

4. Racialized Empire, Thrifting, and Swadeshi, 1880–1912

1. Maulvi Sayyid Lutf Ali, *Lakchar jo Janāb Maulvī Sayyid Lutf ʿAlī Sāḥib . . . tijārat par* (Hyderabad: Maṭbaʿa Burhānīyya, 1894).

2. Maulvi Sayyid Muhammad Ghulam Hayar, "Khulāsa-i Taqrīr . . . ," in Ali, *Lakchar jo Janāb Maulvī Sayyid,* 24.

3. Faisal Devji, *Muslim Zion: Pakistan as a Political Idea* (London: Hurst, 2013), 63–65.

4. Mohsin ul-Mulk, *Causes of the Decline of the Mahomedan Nation* (Bombay: Bombay Gazette, 1891), 78–79.

5. Racial differences between European and Indian businesses hardened still more after 1914, However, European discrimination in the generation before the First World War cleared the ground for interwar demands by many Indian nationalists for the "Indianization" of business. On racial divisions in India in the

interwar period, Maria Misra, *Business, Race, and Politics in British India, c. 1850–1960* (Oxford: Clarendon Press, 1999), 123–141.

6. On Gujarati links to European and American business see Chhaya Goswami, *Globalization Before Its Time: The Gujarati Merchants from Kachchh* (Gurgaon, India: Penguin Books India, 2016), ch. 3.

7. Madhavrai Gigabhai Joshi, *Madrās īlākānuṁ digdarśana*, vol. I (Bhavnagar: Gujarati Punch Press, 1928), 32.

8. Ratansha Rustemji Bhuri, *Sīlônni tavārīkha* (Bombay: Vartamāna, 1908), 89–90.

9. Dinshaw H. Vania, *Jepenījh Shikshaka* (Bombay: Gujāratī Printing Pres, 1905); Edalji Dhanji Kaba, *Kābānī kahānī* ([Amreli?]: n.p., 1918).

10. Iqbal Akhtar, *The Khōjā of Tanzania: Discontinuities of a Postcolonial Religious Identity* (Leiden, Netherlands: Brill, 2016), 50.

11. "Appendix, No. 7 . . . List of Ships Chartered for and Employed in connection with the Abyssinian Expedition," in *Reports from Committees: Abyssinian War; Mail Contracts; Public Accounts; Telegraph Bill*, vol. 6, *10 December 1868–11 August 1869* (London: House of Commons, 1869), 157–161.

12. Takashi Oishi, "Muslim Merchant Capital and the Relief Movement for the Ottoman Empire in India, 1876–1924," *Journal of the Japanese Association for South Asian Studies* 11 (1999): 71–103.

13. Dadabhai Naoroji, "Mr. Shapoorjee Burjorjee Bharoocha," in *Poverty of India*, pt. 3 (London: East India Association, 1877), 88.

14. Dinyar Patel, *Naoroji: Pioneer of Indian Nationalism* (Cambridge, MA: Harvard University Press, 2020), 63.

15. Colonel H. S. Olcott, "The Spirit of the Zoroastrian Religion: Delivered at the Town Hall, Bombay, on the 14th of February, 1882," in *A Collection of Lectures on Theosophy and Archaic Religions, Delivered in India and Ceylon* (Madras: A. Theyaga Rajier, 1883), 160-B.

16. Claude Markovits, "Merchant Circulation in South Asia (Eighteenth to Twentieth Centuries): The Rise of Pan-Indian Merchant Networks," in *Society and Circulation: Mobile People and Itinerant Cultures in South Asia, 1750–1950*, ed. Claude Markovits, Jacques Pouchepadass, and Sanjay Subrahmanyam (New York: Anthem, 2006), 149.

17. Vallabhaji Sundaraji Punjabhai, *Mumbaīnā mahāśayo: Doḍhaso chabīo tathā lagabhaga teṭalañja vṛttānto*, vol. 3 (n.p. [Bombay]: Va. Su. Punjabhāi, 1920), 85.

18. Samuel Spence Parkyn, *Transport in Southern Afghanistan between Sukkur and Quetta, 1878–1880*, 2nd ed. (London: Harrison and Sons, 1882), 34.

19. *The Gazetteer of Bombay City and Island*, vol. 1 (Bombay: Times Press, 1909), 499–500.

20. William Herbert Coates, *The Old "Country Trade" of the East Indies* (London: Imray, Laurie, Norie and Wilson, 1911), 199.

21. Coates, *The Old "Country Trade,"* 202.

22. Saki, *Karīmbhāi* (Bombay: Jī Mahamada, 1925), 54–58.

23. Thomas A. Timberg, *The Marwaris, from traders to industrialists* (New Delhi: Vikas, 1978), 168.

24. "Our Trip to China," *Islamic Fraternity* 1, no. 5-6 (1910): 3. Many thanks to Ulrich Brandenburg for sharing this source with me.

25. "Municipal Properties: Shanghai, October 12, 1910," *Municipal Gazette*, 27 October 1910, 351.

26. *The Charge of Conspiracy against the So-Called Swatow Opium Guild* (Shanghai: Celestial Empire Office, 1879), 15–16.

27. Haji Sulaiman Shah Muhammad, *Pṛathavīnī pradakshiṇā* (Bombay: Daphatara Āśakārā Ôīl Press, 1895), 6. An English version of this the first volume of Haji Sulaiman's travel diary was published that same year. Hajee Sullaiman Shah Mahomed, *Journal of my tours round the world (1886–1887 and 1893–1895), embracing travels in various parts of Africa, Australia, Asia, America and Europe* (Bombay: The Duftur Ashkara Press, 1895).

28. Haji Sulaiman, *Pṛathavīnī pradakshiṇā*, 7, 19.

29. *Summary of Events of the Administration of the Gondal State for the Year 1891–92* (Bombay: Education Society's Press, 1892), 42.

30. Basharat Ahmad, *The Great Reformer: Biography of Hazrat Mirza Ghulam Ahmad of Qadian*, vol. 1, trans. Hamid Rahman (Dublin, OH: Ahmadiyya Anjuman Ishaat Islam, 2007), 223.

31. Webb's travels were funded in other ports, such as Rangoon, by Memon businessmen.

32. Maulvi Hassan Ali, *Risāla-i tāʾīd al-ḥaqq* (Sialkot, India [now Pakistan]: Munshī Ghulām Qādir, 1897), 81–86. This portion of the text is also reproduced in Ahmad, *The Great Reformer*, 221–226.

33. Ahmad, *The Great Reformer*, 221–226.

34. Oishi, "Muslim Merchant Capital," 89–90.

35. BOA, Y.PRK.EŞA, 9.32.

36. BOA, İ.DH, 1140.88979; BOA, DH.MKT, 1786.12.

37. BOA, Y.MTV, 38.145.

38. BOA, Y.A.RES, 30.27; BOA, Y.PRK.EŞA, 8.22.

39. BOA, HR.TH, 168.19. The proposal to operate such a line was once again broached in 1913 by some Ottoman subjects in Bombay. BOA, BEO, 3881.291044.

40. BOA, HR.TH, 201.75.

41. John Slight, *The British Empire and the Hajj: 1865–1956* (Cambridge, MA: Harvard University Press, 2015), 3.

42. Dominique Harre, "The Indian Firm G. M. Mohamedally & Co in Ethiopia (1886–1937) / La firme indienne G. M. Mohamedally & Co en Éthiopie (1886–

1937)," *Annales d'Éthiopie* 30 (2015): 285–311; Denis Gay, *Les Bohra de Madagascar: Religion, commerce et échanges transnationaux dans la construction de l'identité ethnique* (Berlin: Lit Verlag, 2009); Takashi Oishi, "Indian Muslim Merchants in Mozambique and South Africa: Intra-regional Networks in Strategic Association with State Institutions, 1870s–1930s," *Journal of the Economic and Social History of the Orient* 50, nos. 2–3 (2007): 287–324; Luisa Pinto Teixeira, "Partners in Business," *Lusotopie* 15, no. 1 (2008): 39–58; Nicole Khouri and Joana Pereira Leite, eds., *Khojas Ismaïli: Du Mozambique colonial à la globalization* (Paris: Harmattan, 2014).

43. Gaurav Gajanan Desai, *Commerce with the Universe: Africa, India, and the Afrasian Imagination* (New York: Columbia University Press, 2013), 88; "Note," in *Official History of the Operations in Somaliland, 1901–04* (London: Harrison and Sons, 1907), 528.

44. William J. Baumol, Robert E. Litan, and Carl J. Schramm, *Good Capitalism, Bad Capitalism, and the Economics of Growth and Prosperity* (New Haven, CT: Yale University Press, 2007), 3.

45. I am slightly modifying how economic historians use thrifts to include religious institutions as well. For more on the thrift movement in the contemporary US context, see Mehrsa Baradaran, *How the Other Half Banks: Exclusion, Exploitation, and the Threat to Democracy* (Cambridge, MA: Harvard University Press, 2015).

46. Seth Hassan Mian Rahmat Allah, *Masjīda [kes] Halāi Memaṇa mohallānī hīsāba* (Bombay: [Kasīde Mumbaī Press], 1881).

47. To cite a couple of examples see entries for Shah Chanpshi Mulji, Thakkar Madhvaji Premji, and Pardeshi Atmaram Prataplal on page 15.

48. Fahad Bishara, *Sea of Debt: Law and Economic Life in the Western Indian Ocean, 1780–1950* (Cambridge: Cambridge University Press, 2017), ch. 2.

49. "Bill Ledger Extract," SBI, Bank of Bengal Reports, 1742 / BR / Rgoon / Cor / 006.

50. "Calcutta, 30 June 1910, No. 84," SBI, Bank of Bengal Reports, 1742 / BR / Rgoon / Cor / 006.

51. This paragraph is based largely on a reading of the Gujarati and English commercial correspondence contained in "Alidina Visram vs Abdoola Megji & Rehem Lilani," *ZNA*, HC7 / 285.

52. "Case 607 of 1892, Re: Saleh Chatoor, Bankrupt," ZLR, HC7 / 414. I am grateful to Fahad Bishara for sharing this source with me.

53. "Case 2 of 1895, Re: Saleh Chatoor, Bankrupt," ZLR, HC7 / 483.

54. Captain F. M. Hunter, *An Account of the British Settlement of Aden in Arabia* (London: Trübner, 1877), 38.

55. Fazulbhoy Visram, *A Khoja's Tour in Australia* (Bombay: Times of India Steam Press, 1885), v, 1–2.

56. Haji Sulaiman, *Pṛathavīnī pradakshiṇā*, 76–88.

57. Mohamed Hasan Musakhan, *History of Islamism in Australia from 1863–1932* (Perth: n.p., 1932).

58. Claude Markovits, *The Global World of Indian Merchants, 1750–1947: Traders of Sind from Bukhara to Panama* (Cambridge: Cambridge University Press, 2000), 214.

59. Zarina Patel, *Alibhai Mulla Jeevanjee* (Nairobi: East African Publishers, 2002), 4–5.

60. "Mr. Walsh to Government of Bombay," in *Correspondence Respecting the Construction of the Uganda Railway, 1895–1896*, 154, accessed 1 June 2021, through Archives Direct, https://www.archivesdirect.amdigital.co.uk/.

61. Howard Schwartz, *The Rise and Fall of Philanthropy in East Africa: The Asian Contribution* (New Brunswick, NJ: Transaction Publishers, 1992), 52.

62. Johan Mathew, *Margins of the Market: Trafficking and Capitalism across the Arabian Sea* (Berkeley: University of California Press, 2016), 46–47.

63. Patel, *Alibhai Mulla Jeevanjee*, 24; Gijsbert Oonk, *Settled Strangers: Asian Business Elites in East Africa (1800–2000)* (New Delhi: Sage, 2013), 146–147.

64. Patel, *Alibhai Mulla Jeevanjee*, 24.

65. "Indians in British East Africa," *Modern Review*, January 1911, 54.

66. The Hon. Mr. Jeevanjee, "Indians in East Africa," *Indian Review*, May 1912, 383–384.

67. Nile Green, *Bombay Islam: The Religious Economy of the Western Indian Ocean* (Cambridge: Cambridge University Press, 2011), 213.

68. Mahatma Gandhi, "81. Johannesburg Letter," in *The Collected Works of Mahatma Gandhi*, vol. 7, *June–December 1907* (New Delhi: Publications Division, Government of India, 1962), 144.

69. Mahatma Gandhi, "158. Need for Great Caution," in *The Collected Works of Mahatma Gandhi*, 7:200.

70. Mahatma Gandhi, "245. Perversity of Memons," *The Collected Works of Mahatma Gandhi*, 7:236.

71. Mahatma Gandhi, "282. Memons Who Have Escaped," *The Collected Works of Mahatma Gandhi*, 7:363.

72. "Witness No. 348. Mr. Karimbhoy Adamjee Peerbhoy, Partner, Sir Adamjee Peerbhoy and Sons, Bombay. Written Evidence," *Indian Industrial Commission, Minutes of Evidence 1916–18*, vol. 4, *Bombay* (Calcutta: Superintendent Government Printing, 1918), 514–516.

73. David Omissi, "India: Some Perceptions of Race and Empire," in *The Impact of the South African War*, ed. David Omissi and Andrew S. Thompson (New York: Palgrave, 2002), 229n35.

74. Memon Abd Allah Ismail, "786: Arpaṇa patrikā," *Memaṇa tavārīkha* (Surat, India: 1921), n.p.

75. Moshe Yegar, *The Muslims of Burma* (Wiesbaden, West Germany: O. Harrassowitz, 1972), 40.

76. *The Cyclopedia of India: Biographical-Historical-Administrative-Commercial*, vol. 3 (Calcutta: Cyclopedia Publishing Coy., 1909), 444–445.

77. "A Moslem Philanthropist," in *The Moslem World: A Quarterly Review of Current Events, Literature and Thought among Mohammedans and the Progress of Christian Missions in Moslem Lands*, vol. 5, ed. Rev. S. M. Zwemer (London: Nile Mission Press, 1915), 84–85.

78. *The Annual Administration Report of the Limbdi State, for the Year 1915–16* (n.p.: [Limbdi State?], n.d. [1917?]), 30–31.

79. Moulvi Muhammad Aziz Mirza, *Proceedings of the Annual Meeting of the All-India Muslim League, Held at Nagpore on the 28th and the 30th of December 1910* (Allahabad, India: Indian Press, 1910), 45.

80. Shireen Mirza, "Travelling Leaders and Connecting Print Cultures: Two Conceptions of Twelver Shiʿi Reformism in the Indian Ocean," *Journal of the Royal Asiatic Society* 24, no. 3 (2014): 455–475.

81. Ziauddin Ahmad Suleri, *Muhammad Ali Jinnah: The Architect of Pakistan* (Karachi: Royal Book Co., 2000), 164. A fuller discussion of Punjabhai's business activities is found in Sharif Mujahid, *Quaid-i-Azam Jinnah: Studies in Interpretation* (Karachi: Quaid-i-Azam Academy, 1981), 35–37.

82. Suleri, *Muhammad Ali Jinnah*, 78.

83. Rightfully, there is considerable debate about whether Jinnah ever publicly declared for any particular sub-branch of Khoja Islam. Faisal Devji, *Muslim Zion: Pakistan as a Political Idea* (London: Hurst, 2013), 218–220.

84. For a larger discussion of the disparities between trade and agriculture in colonial India, see Tirthankar Roy, *How British Rule Changed India's Economy: The Paradox of the Raj* (Cham, Switzerland: Palgrave Pivot, 2020), chaps. 3–4.

85. Achyut Yagnik, "The Pathology of Gujarat," in *Gujarat: The Making of a Tragedy*, ed. Siddharth Varadarajan (New Delhi: Penguin Books India, 2002), 408.

86. Mike Davis, *Late Victorian Holocausts: El Niño Famines and the Making of the Third World* (London: Verso, 2001), 7.

87. "1317no Hindī dukāḷa mumīṁ bhāīo taraphanī tājavījho anē maddada," *Rīsālatul Mumīnīna* 4 (Bombay: Mustaphāī Printing Press, 1901): 1–6.

88. "1317no Hindī dukāḷa," 2–6.

89. *Report of the Municipal Commissioner on the Plague in Bombay for the Year Ending 31st May 1899* (Bombay: Municipal Commissioner's Press, 1899), 110–112.

90. *Report of the Municipal Commissioner*, 262, 336–337.

91. "Plague in India," *Medical Press*, 4 January 1899, 21.

92. J. C. Masselos, *Towards Nationalism: Group Affiliations and the Politics of Public Associations in Nineteenth Century Western India* (Bombay: Popular Prakashan, 1974), 160–161.

93. "Appendix E: The All-India Moslem League. Presidential Address by Sir Adamjee Peerbhoy," in *Surat Congress and Conferences: A Collection of the Presidential and Inaugural Speeches* . . . (Madras: G. A. Natesan, n.d.), xxxiii, xxxiv–xxxv.

94. This is perhaps because historians tend to extrapolate from the Bengali Muslim experience, concerning which, see Manu Goswami, *Producing India From Colonial Economy to National Space* (Chicago: University of Chicago Press, 2004), 266. However, the Gujarati Muslim experience was distinct.

95. "47. Mr. Mushir Hosain Kidwai, Bar-at-Law," in *The Swadeshi Movement: A Symposium*, 2nd ed. (Madras: G. A. Natesan, n.d.) 289–290.

96. Sorabji M. Rutnagur, *Bombay Industries: The Cotton Mill; A Review of the Progress of the Textile Industry in Bombay from 1850 to 1926 and the Present Constitution, Management and Financial Position of the Spinning and Weaving Factories* (Bombay: Indian Textile Journal, 1927), 27, 75, 274–275.

97. "Indenture for Sale of Jivraj Baloo Mills," in the author's private collection; shared upon request.

98. Rutnagur, *Bombay Industries*, 54.

99. "Match-Making in India," *Indian Industries and Power* 12 (1915): 285.

100. W. T. Morison, *Report: Indian Factory Labour Commission, 1908*, vol. 2, *Evidence* (London: HMSO, 1909), 9–10.

101. Bishnupriya Gupta, Dilip Mookherjee, Kaivan Munshi, and Mario Sanclemente, "Community Origins of Industrial Entrepreneurship in Pre-independence India," CEPR Discussion Paper No. DP14263, Center for Economic Policy and Research, Washington, DC, January 2020, https://ssrn.com/abstract=3518603.

102. "Cassamally Jairajbhai Peerbhai, Plaintiff, v. Sir Currimbhoy Ebrahim, and Others, Defendants," in *The Indian Law Reports*, vol. 36 (Bombay: Government Central Press, 1912), 246.

103. *Amadāvāda Khōja īsnā aśarī hidāyata phaṇḍanā ṭrasṭī* (Ahmedabad: n.p., 1909), 2.

104. *Amadāvāda Khōja*, 1.

105. "Islāmī Bahnk [*sic*] Dār al-Sulṭānat Rūs Maiṉ," *Aligarh Institute Gazette*, 6 May 1908, 5.

106. Michael O'Sullivan, "Interest, Usury, and the Transition from 'Muslim' to 'Isamic' Banks," *International Journal of Middle East Studies* 52, no. 2 (2020): 261–287.

107. *The Bombay Merchants Bank Limited. Directors' Report as on 31st August 1909* (Bombay: Uniform Press, n.d. [1909?]).

108. "Dissolutions," *Bombay Chronicle*, 6 September 1929, 4; S. K. Muranjan, *Modern Banking in India* (Bombay: New Book, 1940), 294.

109. Ali Coşkun Tunçer, *Sovereign Debt and International Financial Control: The Middle East and the Balkans, 1870–1914* (New York: Palgrave Macmillan, 2015), 53–76.

Part II

1. Sana Haroon, *Mosques of Colonial South Asia: A Social and Legal History of Muslim Worship* (London: I. B. Tauris, 2021), 48–49.

2. Faiz Badruddin Tyabji, *Muhammadan Law: The Personal Law of Muslims*, 3rd ed. (Bombay: N.M. Tripathi & Co., 1940), 648. Italics added to *jamaats* are my own.

5. Corporate Crises from the Balkan Wars to the Great Depression, 1912–1933

1. "The Chotani Sawmills," in *The Bombay Presidency, the United Provinces, the Punjab . . .*, ed. Arnold Wright (London: Foreign and Colonial Compiling and Publishing, 1920), 150.

2. P. C. Bamford, *Non-co-operation and Khilafat Movements* (Delhi: Government of India Press, 1925), 143, 176, 182.

3. Faruq Ahmad Chotani, *Nāṣir al-Islām: Miyān Muḥammad Ḥājī Jān Muḥammad Choṭānī* (Bombay: Choṭānī, 1982), 21, 24.

4. Mahatma Gandhi, "19. Notes," in *Collected Works of Mahatma Gandhi*, vol. 21, *August–December 1921* (Ahmedabad: Government of India, Publications Division, 1966), 383.

5. Mahatma Gandhi, "173. Letter to Hakim Ajmal Khan," in *Collected Works of Mahatma Gandhi*, vol. 23, *March 1922–May 1924* (Ahmedabad: Government of India, Publications Division, 1966), 136.

6. Chotani, *Nāṣir al-Islām*, 22–23.

7. Bombay Port Trust, *Administration Report for the Years 1919–20* (Bombay: Bombay Port Trust, 1920), ix.

8. "Extract from the Diary of the Political Resident in Turkish Arabia for the Week Ending 13th February 1905: February 10th," QDL, File 53 / 7 D (D 7) Koweit [Kuwait] Affairs, January 1905—December 1905 [77r] (160 / 366), B.

9. BOA, DH.MKT, 1319 / 28.

10. *Defter-i ʿİāne-i Hindīyye* İstanbul Üniversitesi Kütüphanesi [Istanbul University Library], no. 79834; Azmi Özcan, *Pan-Islamism: Indian Muslims, the Ottomans and Britain* (Leiden: Brill, 1997), 68–69.

11. Takashi Oishi, "Muslim Merchant Capital and the Relief Movement for the Ottoman Empire in India, 1876–1924," *Journal of the Japanese Association for South Asian Studies* 11 (1999): 71–103.

12. "Report on Native Papers: Published in the Bombay Presidency for the Week Ending 3rd March 1888," No. 9, 03-03-1888, 8–9, accessed through the South Asia Open Archives, https://www.jstor.org/stable/saoa.crl.25635699.

13. Abd al-Reşid Ibrahim, *ʿĀlem-i İslām ve Jāponyāda intiṣār-ı İslāmīyet*, vol. 2 (Istanbul: Ḳadr Matbaʿası, 1911), 32, 43.

14. S. M. Tevfik, "Hindistān Mektūpları: Bombay Şehr-i Şehīri," *Sebīl al-Reşād* 10, no. 258 ([1913]), 392–395.

15. In 1899, a Bohra merchant named Yusuf Ali Alibhai was in the running for the post of Ottoman consul in Karachi, but rumors of his nomination (and those of two other Shiʿis) prompted a letter of protest from Sunnis in Karachi. BOA, HR.SFR.3, 480.112.

16. An Ottoman transliteration and English translation of the document is produced in "28—Foreign Minister to the Grand Vizier about the Appointment of Medeni Molla Ahmed Daud Efendi to the Consulate in Rangoon, 1913," in *Ottoman-Southeast Asian Relations*, vol. 1, ed. İsmail Hakkı Kadı and A. C. S. Peacock (Leiden, Netherlands: Brill, 2019), 458–459.

17. One example is BOA, BEO, 4185 / 313820. See also TRC, 33 / 74; and TRC, 33 / 134, 134.1.

18. S. M. Tevfik, "Hindistān Mektūpları: Bombay Şehr-i Şehīri," *Sebīl al-Reşād*, 10, no. 255 ([1913]), 343.

19. TRC, 95 / 189.22; TRC, 95 / 189.10.

20. "VIII," in *The Indian Muslims: The Tripoli and Balkan Wars*, vol. 3, ed. Shan Muhammad (Meerut, India: Meenakshi Prakashan, 1980), 173.

21. TRC, 95 / 58; BOA, H.R.TO, 544, 44 18 / 1913; BOA, BEO, 4147, 310952, 16 / Ra / 1333.

22. "Müslümanlar arasında marifet-i nefs beşâirinden: Rangon'da Ahmad Mulla Davud Efendi'nin taht-ı riyâsetinde münʿakit iâne-i Osmaniye heyʾeti," *Şehbal* 87 (1913), 290.

23. Muhammad ed., *The Indian Muslims*, 166.

24. TRC, 95 / 147; TRC, 95 / 147.1.

25. TRC, 96 / 145.2.

26. H.H. the Agha Khan, G.C.S.I., "The Turkish Treasury Bonds," *Comrade*, 1 March 1913, 182–183.

27. Gail Minault, *Khilafat Movement: Religious Symbolism and Political Mobilization in India* (New York: Columbia University Press, 1982), 49–50.

28. Tim Harper, "Singapore, 1915, and the Birth of the Asian Underground," *Modern Asian Studies* 47, no. 6 (2013): 1782–1811.

29. *Report of Committee Appointed to Investigate Revolutionary Conspiracies in India, with Two Resolutions by the Government of India* (London: HMSO, 1918), 71, 72.

30. *Report of the Chief Inspector of Mines in Mysore, 1918–1919* (Bangalore: Government Press, 1919), 31.

31. Naoroji M. Dumasia, *The Aga Khan and His Ancestors: A Biographical and Historical Sketch* (Bombay: Times of India Press, 1939), 133.

32. "British War Loan," BL, IOR / L / AG / 14 / 17 / 1–2.

33. "Surat Notes: War Loan Investments," *Times of India*, 30 August 1918, 7.

34. "Second War Loan: 15,53 Lakhs Subscribed," *Times of India*, 25 June 1918, 8.

35. Maulvi Sayyid Al-i Ahmad, *Qarẕa-i jang ke muta'lliq ek mufīd mashvirah* (Moradabad: Amroha, 1917).

36. M. Naeem Qureshi, *Pan-Islam in British Indian Politics: A Study of the Khilafat Movement, 1918–1924* (Leiden, Netherlands: Brill, 1999), 342; Sayyid Muhammad Miyan, *The Prisoners of Malta (Asira'n-e-Malta): The Heart-Rending Tale of Muslim Freedom Fighters in British Period* (New Delhi: Jamiat Ulama-i-Hind, 2005), 234.

37. Mian Bhai Mulla Abdul Hussain, *Gulẕare Daudi: A Short Note on Bohras of India*, Reprint Edition (Surat: Progressive Printing Press, 1977), 65–70.

38. Siobhan Lambert-Hurley, *Muslim Women, Reform and Princely Patronage: Nawab Sultan Jahan Begam of Bhopal* (Abingdon, UK: Routledge, 2007) 48–49.

39. Ibrahim Adamji Pirbhai, *Manāẓir alamnāk* (Nagpur: Mushfiq Ṭayyibjī Rishamvālā, 1969).

40. For further discussion, see Michael O'Sullivan, "The Multiple Registers of Arabic in the Daudi Bohra Da'wa and South Asian Public Life, c. 1880–1920," Manuscript, 01 August 2022.

41. "Favouritism in Govt. Contracts: Mr. K. A. Peerbhoy's Allegations," *Bombay Chronicle*, 1 December 1917, 7.

42. "Favouritism in Govt. Contracts," 7.

43. "Notification of Sale of the Adamjee Peerbhoy Mills at Tardeo," *Bombay Chronicle*, 7 August 1919, 3.

44. E. J. Varteji, *Āgākhānī khudāino jhalakāta* (Bombay: Mukhtār Nānjī, 1919).

45. "Pharmāna 207," in *Kalāme īmāme mubīna: yāne, Nūr maulānā hājara īmāma pavitra phāramāno, ī.s. 1911 thī 1951 sudhīnī*, vol. 2 (Bombay: Ismaili Printing Press, 1952), 35.

46. Agha Khan III, quoted in Devji, *Muslim Zion*, 71.

47. "HIL / 88 / 1-139: Appendix 6," DU, HIL / 88 / 31–39.

48. Muhammad Ali Chunara, "Aga Khan and Mesopotamian Throne," in *Īmānanī rōśanī* (Bombay: Yaṅg Ismāilī Vidhāvinōda Kalaba, n.d. [1919?]), 16.

49. Qureshi, *Pan-Islam*, 368–369.

50. Mumtaz Ali Tajddin Sadik, *101 Ismaili Heroes: Late 19th Century to Present Age*, vol. 1 (Karachi: Islamic Book Publisher, 2003), 16.

51. "Pharmān 212," in *Kalāme īmāme mubīna,* 2:42.

52. Michael O'Sullivan, "'Indian Money', Intra-Shī ʿī Polemics, and the Bohra and Khoja Pilgrimage Infrastructure in Iraq's Shrine Cities, 1897–1932," *Journal of the Royal Asiatic Society* 32, 1 (2022): 229–231.

53. Qureshi, *Pan-Islam,* 292.

54. "Situation in Sindh: Loyalty of Aga Khan's Followers," *Pioneer Mail,* May 8, 1919, 24.

55. "Bangalore Mosque Case—High Priest Examined—Khilafat Excommunication," *Pioneer Mail,* 31 December 1920, 22; Qureshi, *Pan-Islam,* 245n82.

56. "News and Notes," *Commerce and Industries* 1, no. 2 (1919): 40.

57. "The Non-Cooperation Agitation," in *The Indian Annual Register,* 2nd ed., ed. H. N. Mitra (Calcutta: Annual Register Office, 1921), 196.

58. Mahatma Gandhi, "Burning in Bombay," in *The Collected Works of Mahatma Gandhi,* vol. 20, *April 15, 1921–August 19, 1921* (Ahmedabad: Navajivan, 1966), 472.

59. R. C. Majumdar, *History of the Freedom Movement,* vol. 3, pt. 1, 410.

60. "Girls' Spinning School: Gift of Mrs. Haji Yousuff Sobani," *Bombay Chronicle,* 16 July 1921, 9.

61. S. Bhattacharya, "Cotton Mills and Spinning Wheels: Swadeshi and the Indian Capitalist Class, 1920–22," *Economic and Political Weekly* 11, no. 47 (1976): 1832.

62. K. K. Chaudhari, *Maharashtra State Gazetteers: Greater Bombay District,* vol. 1 (Bombay: Gazetteers Department, Government of Maharashtra, 1986), 415.

63. "Dange on 'Gandhi vs Lenin,'" in *Documents of the History of the Communist Party,* vol. 1, *1917–1922,* ed. G. Adhikari (New Delhi: People's Publishing House, 1972), 307.

64. Danish Khan, "The Politics of Business: The Congress Ministry and the Muslim League in Bombay, 1937–39," in *Bombay Before Mumbai: Essays in Honour of Jim Masselos, eds.* Prashant Kidambi, Manjiri Kamat, and Rachel Dwyer (New York: Oxford University Press, 2019), 297.

65. Bamford, *Non-co-operation,* 176, 182.

66. Chotani, *Nāṣir al-Islām,* 24.

67. See the article reproduced in a letter by Shaukat Ali and Ismail Basin, head of the Turkish Red Crescent, in Chotani, *Nāṣir al-Islām,* 35.

68. Chotani, *Nāṣir al-Islām,* 207–208.

69. Shaub Qureshi, "Mr. Chotani and the Khilafat Funds," *Comrade,* 9 October 1923, 162–164.

70. Chotani, *Nāṣir al-Islām,* 26.

71. The debate raged in the Indian Muslim press; see Qureshi, "Mr. Chotani and the Khilafat Funds."

72. TRC, 1389 / 92; TRC, 1389 / 92.1.

73. Chotani, *Nāṣir al-Islām,* 31–33.

74. Hüsnü Ada, "The First Ottoman Civil Society Organization in the Service of the Ottoman State: The Case of the Ottoman Red Crescent (Osmanlı Hilal-i Ahmer Cemiyeti)," M.A. thesis, Sabancı University, 2004, 111.

75. R.K. Trivedi, *The Critical Triangle: India, Britain, and Turkey, 1908–1924* (Jaipur: Publication Scheme, 1994), 204, n. 15.

76. Chotani, *Nāṣir al-Islām*, 45.

77. P. Das, "Development of Chemical Industries and Its Necessity," *Calcutta Review*, 3rd ser., 2 (1922): 138.

78. H. E. W. Braund, ed., *Calling to Mind: Being Some Account of the First Hundred Years (1870 to 1970) of Steel Brothers and Company Limited* (Oxford: Pergamon, 1975), 61.

79. *The Legislative Assembly Debates: Official Report of the First Session of the Fifth Legislative Assembly, 1935* (New Delhi: Government of India Press, 1935), 2811.

80. "The Up-Country Paper Mills," in *The Report of The Indian Tariff Board: Paper and Paper Pulp Industries* (Calcutta: Government of India Central Publication Branch, 1925), 4; "Fire Brigade," *Report on the Municipal Administration of the City of Rangoon* (Rangoon: Rangoon Times Press, 1922), 9.

81. Bakhtiar Dadabhoy, *Barons of Banking: Glimpses of Indian Banking History* (Noida, India: Random House India, 2013), 19–28.

82. "Brussels Conference," *Pioneer Mail*, 3 December 1920, 30–31.

83. Sorabji M. Rutnagur, *Bombay Industries: The Cotton Mill; A Review of the Progress of the Textile Industry in Bombay from 1850 to 1926 and the Present Constitution, Management and Financial Position of the Spinning and Weaving Factories* (Bombay: Indian Textile Journal, 1927),158. The famous Parsi and Jewish industrialists, Sir Jamshetjee Jeejebhoy and Sir David Sassoon, respectively, were two of the five.

84. Rutnagur, *Bombay Industries*, 58.

85. In author's personal collection. Image available upon request.

86. Rutnagur, *Bombay Industries*, 158.

87. *Memorandum of Association of the Osman Shahi Mills Limited: With Articles of Association and Managing Agency Agreement Annexed* (Hyderabad: n.p., 1922).

88. *Some Economic Facts and Figures Of H.E.H the Nizam's Dominions: Prepared for the All-India Economic Conference Hyderabad-Deccan* (Hyderabad-Deccan: Government Central Press, 1937), 80–81.

89. P. R. Srinivas and C. S. Rangawsami eds., *Indian Finance* 12, no. 15 (1933): 825–826.

90. Thomas A. Timberg, *The Marwaris, from Traders to Industrialists* (New Delhi: Vikas, 1978), 64.

91. "Re-organization of Industries," *Indian Review* 31 (1930): 133.

92. Muhammad Jamal al-Din Gawsi, *Islāmī hita hakōnā rakṣaṇa kāje* (n.p. [Rajkot, India?]: n.p., n.d. [1933?]), 3.

93. Gawsi, *Islāmī hita*, 4.

94. *Ōl-Inḍiyā Memana kōnphēransni cothī beṭhaka upara eka dṛṣṭi* (n.p. [Karachi?]: n.p., n.d. [1936?]), 102.

95. *Report of the Bengal Jute Enquiry Committee* (Calcutta: Bengal Government Press, 1939), 222.

96. "The Voice of Business," *Indian Finance* 11, no. 11 (1933): 479.

97. Jatindra Mohan Datta, "Bengal Government Proposals on the Delimitation of Constituencies," *Modern Review*, September 1935, 341.

98. "Jinnah's Hit at Congress: Mass Contact Programme, Means to Wreck Award," *Bombay Chronicle*, 6 June 1938, 1, 7.

99. Jawaharlal Nehru, "Hindu and Muslim Communalism," in *Recent Essays and Writings: On the Future of India, Communalism and Other Subjects* (Allahabad: Kitabistan, 1934), 48.

100. Muhammad Iqbal, "Reply to Questions raised by Pandit J.L. Nehru," in *Speeches and Statements of Iqbal*, ed. Shamloo (Lahore: Al-Manar Academy, 1944), 143–144.

101. Muhammad Iqbal, "Statement explaining the attitude of Muslim delegates to the Round Table Conferences, issued on the 6th December 1933," in Shamloo, ed., *Speeches and Statements*, 191.

102. Ibrahim Kassim, "Shaukat Ali and Zanzibar," *The Bombay Chronicle* 27 December 1937, 10.

6. The Battle over Jamaat *Trusts, 1923–1935*

1. Gregory Kozlowski, *Muslim Endowments and Society in British India* (Cambridge: Cambridge University Press, 1985), chap. 6.

2. Tirthankar Roy and Anand V. Swamy, *Law and the Economy in Colonial India* (Chicago: University of Chicago Press, 2016), 102.

3. "The Mussalman Wakf Validating Bill (5 March 1913)," in *Extract from the Proceedings of the Council of the Governor General of India, assembled for the purpose of making Laws and Regulations under the provisions of the Indian Councils Acts, 1861 to 1909 . . .*, BL, IOR / L / PJ/6/1079, File 1261, 3–4.

4. Kozlowski, *Muslim Endowments*, 187–189.

5. Nathu Khan Ajam Khan Chuvhan, *Śīāonā dharmagurūono darajo juvo ane sunnīonā dharmagurūono darajo juvo* (Surat, India: Ambīkā Vijaya Printing Press, 1928).

6. Maulvi Abd al-Rauf Sahib, *Istidlāl* (Jabalpur: Matbaʿ Nadiri, n.d.), 7; Munshi Sayyid Hamid Miyan Dosa Miyan, ed., *Meāyāra* (Jabalpur: Nādirī Press, 1926), 43–54.

7. "Marten, J., Advocate General of Bombay—Plaintiff v. Yusuf Ali Ebrahim and others—Defendants," *All India Reporter*, Bombay Section, 1921 (Nagpur: V. V. Chitaley, 1921), 339.

8. "Marten, J., Advocate General of Bombay—Plaintiff v. Yusuf Ali Ebrahim," 364.

9. Jonah Blank, *Mullahs on the Mainframe: Islam and Modernity among the Daudi Bohras* (Chicago: University of Chicago Press, 2001), 346n38.

10. Dilkash, *Cāṃdābhāinā Gallāno Kes,* vol. 1 (Bombay: Insāfa ane Islāma, 1921).

11. Dilkash, *Cāṃdābhāinā,* 2.

12. "Social Reform among the Borah Community," *Kaiser-i Hind,* 12 August 1917, 27.

13. "Bohras and Waqf Act," *Bombay Chronicle,* 9 January 1925, reprinted in *Bohras and the Waqf Act: Being a Plea for the Application of the Mussalman Waqf Act of 1923 to the Dawoodi Bohra Community in the Bombay Presidency and Elsewhere* (Burhanpur, India: Dawoodi Bohra Education Conference / Hakimia Society, 1928) 3–4.

14. "Bhoras [*sic*] and Waqf Act," *Advocate of India,* 1 January 1925, reprinted in *Bohras and the Waqf Act,* 54.

15. "Bohras and Waqf Act: All-India Muslim League's Resolution Pertaining Application of Waqfs Act of 1923," *Bombay Chronicle,* 5 January 1925, reprinted in *Bohras and the Waqf Act,* 48.

16. *Bohras and the Waqf Act,* 5.

17. "Muslim Waqfs Bill: Support from Dawoodi Bohras," *Bombay Chronicle,* 15 January 1925, reprinted in *Bohras and the Waqf Act,* 52–53.

18. "Bohras and Waqf Act," *Bombay Chronicle,* 15 January 1925, reprinted in *Bohras and the Waqf Act,* 14–15.

19. *Bohras and the Waqf Act,* 16.

20. Saifiyah Qutbuddin, "History of the Da'udi Bohra Tayyibis in Modern Times; The Dai's, the Da'wat, and the Community," in *A Modern History of the Ismailis: Continuity and Change in a Muslim Community,* ed. Farhad Daftary (London: I. B. Tauris, 2010), 315–316.

21. *Bohras and the Waqf Act,* i.

22. *Bohras and the Waqf Act,* i–iii, v–vi.

23. *Bohras and the Waqf Act,* xiii.

24. *Bohras and the Waqf Act,* xii, xiii, vii.

25. *Bohras and the Waqf Act,* viii, ix–x.

26. Ek Musannif Musalman, *Bohra Qaum aur Waqf Akṭ* (Jabalpur, India: Maṭba' Nādirī, n.d. [1932?]), 43.

27. Allama Simab Akbarabadi, *Mushāhidāt, ya'nī Daudī Bohra awqāf ke chashmdīd ḥalāt* (Jabalpur, India: Maṭba' Nādirī, 1933), 2; the page numbers in the copy I consulted were cut off, so I have counted the beginning of the preface as page 1.

28. Akbarabadi, *Mushāhidāt,* 16–17, 63.

29. Tayabali A. Alavi, ed., *The Hasani Academy Society: Origins and Progress, 1895–1935* (Karachi: Hasani Academy Society, 1936).

30. *Hasani Academy Society: Muriswala School Building Number with Report for 1936–1937* (Karachi: Civil and Military Press, 1937), 10.

31. Alavi, ed., *The Hasani Academy Society*, 81–88.

32. *Hasani Academy Society: Muriswala School Building*, photospread, unnumbered page.

33. For details of the legal proceedings, see Alavi, ed., *The Hasani Academy Society*, 44–56.

34. Arz-i pak Karbala main huzur-i ali ki tashrif avari . . .," *Saif-o-Burhan* 19, no. 1 (September 1937); Shaikhbhai Yusufbhaivala, *Manazere Neamata* (Poona, India: Haidari Printing Press, 1937).

35. As an example see the donors listed in early twentieth-century Ahmadiyya newspapers. "Resīd-i zār-i amādanī-i madrasa," *Al-Ḥākam*, 10 February 1905, 2.

36. Adil Hussain Khan, *From Sufism to Ahmadiyya: A Muslim Minority Movement in South Asia* (Bloomington: Indiana University Press, 2015), 5.

37. *Record of Proceedings: No. 32,452, Mamode Issackjee and Ors. versus A.I. Atchia and Ors.* (Rose Hill, Mauritius: Indo-Mauritian Printing Establishment, 1921).

38. "ATCHIA BROS.," Allister Macmillan ed., *Mauritius Illustrated* (New Delhi and Madras: Asian Educational Services, 2000), 424.

39. *Record of Proceedings*, 232.

40. *Record of Proceedings*, 233–238.

41. John M. Willis, "Azad's Mecca: On the Limits of Indian Ocean Cosmopolitanism," *Comparative Studies of South Asia, Africa and the Middle East* 34, no. 3 (2014): 574–581.

42. Abu al-Kalam Azad, *Faiṣla-i muqaddama-i Jāmaʿ Masjid Kalkata* (Calcutta: Ḥaidarī Press, n.d. [1920?]).

43. Azad, *Faiṣla-i muqaddama-i Jāmaʿ Masjid*, 1–2.

44. Azad, *Faiṣla-i muqaddama-i Jāmaʿ Masjid*, 2–4.

45. Azad, *Faiṣla-i muqaddama-i Jāmaʿ Masjid*, 1, 5.

46. Azad, *Faiṣla-i muqaddama-i Jāmaʿ Masjid*, 7–8.

47. Azad, *Faiṣla-i muqaddama-i Jāmaʿ Masjid*, 8.

48. Azad, *Faiṣla-i muqaddama-i Jāmaʿ Masjid*, 9, 11.

49. Azad, *Faiṣla-i muqaddama-i Jāmaʿ Masjid*, 11–12.

50. Azad, *Faiṣla-i muqaddama-i Jāmaʿ Masjid*, 47.

51. Azad, *Faiṣla-i muqaddama-i Jāmaʿ Masjid*, 48.

52. "Amānat main khiyānat," in *Maẓamīn-i Sūdmand*, vol. 1 (Badayun, India: Nizami, 1936), 68–76.

53. "Bank se sūd wuṣūl karnā hadam arkān-i sharīʿat hai," in *Maẓamīn-i Sūdmand*, 1:52–55.

54. Muhammad Kifayat Allah, *Kifāyat al-muftī*, vol. 8 (Karachi: Dar al-ishāʿat, 2001), 66.

55. *Ōl-Inḍiyā Memaṇa kōnphēransni cothī beṭhaka upara eka dṛṣṭi* (n.p. [Karachi?]: np., n.d. [1936?]), 111–112.

56. *Ōl-Inḍiyā Memaṇa*, 102.

57. *Ōl-Inḍiyā Memaṇa*, 102–104.

58. *The Indian Central Banking Enquiry Committee, 1931, vol. IV, Discussion with Foreign Experts* (Calcutta: Government of India, 1932), 306–307.

59. *Ōl-Inḍiyā Memaṇa*, 112.

60. Parekh Mahmood, Habib Lakhani, and United Memon Jamat of Pakistan, eds., *The Memon: Commemorative Publication of the First Ever Memon Alami Milan at Karachi, Pakistan, from 18th to 20th September, 1986* (Karachi: United Memon Jamat of Pakistan, 1986), 83.

61. *Report of the Mussalman Wakf Committee, Bombay* (Bombay: Government of Bombay, 1931), 12.

62. "Anjuman-i-Faize-Panjetani (Pilgrim Institution)," in *The Times of India Directory of Bombay (City and Province), including Karachi and Hyderabad State* (Bombay: The Times of India), 1940), 210.

63. "Esmail Abdulkarim Panju," in *The Indian Year Book*, vol. 33, ed. Sir Stanley Reed (Bombay: Bennett, Coleman, 1947), 1087.

64. Soumen Mukherjee, *Ismailism and Islam in Modern South Asia: Community and Identity in the Age of Religious Internationals* (Cambridge: Cambridge University Press, 2017), 119.

65. Muhammad Ali Daya Gondalwala, *Ismāilī Āgākhāna Khojā Mukhī Mēghajībhāī* (Bombay: Sarasvatī Press, 1919 [?]).

66. Rahmet Allah Ismail Trijoriwala, *Varasa Ḍāhyāe Ahamēdnagarnī kōrṭanī . . . tēnō hevāla* (Bombay: Sarasvatī Press, n.d.), 21–22.

67. Maulana Sarkar, *The Khoja Shia Imāmi Ismaili Council (Poona): Rules and Regulations* (Poona, India: Khoja Shia Imāmi Ismaili Council, 1913).

68. Trijoriwala, *Varasa Ḍāhyāe*, 24.

69. "A.I.R. 1930 Sind 204 . . . Fakir Mahomed Nanji and Others—Plaintiffs. v. Agha Khan and Others—Defendants," *All India Reporter*, 1930—Sind Section, Containing Full Reports of All Reportable Judgments of the Sind Judicial Commissioner's Court (Nagpur: V.V. Chitaley, 1930), 204–205, 208.

70. Karim Goolamali, *An Open Letter to His Highness the Aga Khan, G.C.S.I., etc.* (Karachi: Kohinoor Printing Works, 1927), 11–15, 20.

71. Goolamali, *An Open Letter*, 5–6, 26–27.

72. My sincere thanks to the staff of McGill University Library, who went to great lengths to digitize this newspaper for me.

73. "Sar Ibrahīm Rahematullāh . . . āgevān sabhyone khullo patra," *Khojā Jāgrati*, 15 May 1934, 21.

74. *Hasadakhorone hadīyo, yāne khullā patrano radīyo* (Bombay: Nurmahamada J. Mahātmā, 1928), 12–13, 18–21.

75. "'Islamisation' of Harijans," *Bombay Chronicle*, 6 January 1936, 1.

76. Al-Haj Qassim Ali Jairazbhoy, *Zakat (Poor Rate) in Islam* (Bombay: M. T. Modi, 1933), 3.

77. See Claude Markovits, *Merchants, Traders, Entrepreneurs: Indian Business in the Colonial Era* (Basingstoke, UK: Palgrave Macmillan, 2008).

7. The Jamaats *and the End of the Raj, 1933–1947*

1. Muhammad Ali Jinnah, quoted in A Barrister-at-Law [Akbar A. Peerbhoy], *Jinnah Faces an Assassin* (Bombay: Thacker, 1943), 123–124.

2. K. B. Krishna, *Plan for Economic Development of India: A Critical and Historical Survey* (Bombay: Padma, n.d. [1945]), 77.

3. Sultan Chinoy, *Pioneering in Indian Business* (New York: Asia Publishing House, n.d. [1962]), 118.

4. "Enclosure 1 to No. 275, Sikander Dehlavi to M.A. Hassan Ispahani, SHC, Bengal III / 55," in *Quaid-i-Azam: Mohammad Ali Jinnah Papers*, vol. 10, *Quest for Political Settlement in India, 1 October 1943–31 July 1944*, ed. Z. H. Zaidi (Islamabad: National Archives of Pakistan, 1993), 292, emphasis in the original.

5. Hamza Alavi, "Pakistan and Islam: Ethnicity and Ideology," in *State and Ideology in the Middle East and Pakistan*, ed. Fred Halliday and Hamza Alavi (London: Macmillan Education, 1988), 65.

6. Arif Azad, "Hamza Alavi," *Guardian*, 18 December 2003, https://www.theguardian.com/news/2003/dec/19/guardianobituaries.race

7. Alavi, "Pakistan and Islam," 65, 69, 72.

8. Mushirul Hasan, *Legacy of a Divided Nation: India's Muslims since Independence* (London: Hurst, 1997), 73.

9. Faisal Devji, *Muslim Zion: Pakistan as a Political Idea* (London: Hurst, 2013).

10. Bhulabhai J. Desai, "We can never be divided: Nagpur, 1934," in *Speeches of Bhulabhai J. Desai, 1934–1938* (New Delhi: Hindustan Times Press, 1938), 73.

11. Faisal Devji, "Fatal Love: Intimacy and Interest in Indian Political Thought," in *Negotiating Democracy and Religious Pluralism: India, Pakistan, and Turkey*, ed. Karen Barkey, Sudipta Kaviraj, and Vatsal Naresh (New York: Oxford University Press, 2021), 82–83.

12. Sayyib Mahboob Rizvi, *History of the Dar al-Ulum Deoband*, vol. 2 (Ahmedabad, India: Sahitya Mudranalaya, 1981), 94–95.

13. "2211: Jamātī lagā nājāyajh chē . . . ," in *"Muslima-Gujarāta" fatāvā-saṅgraha*, vol. 3 (Surat, India: Halal Buk Haus, 1955), 950; "2207: Jamāt islahi daṇḍa kevi rite kari sake?," in *"Muslima-Gujarāta" fatāvā-saṅgraha*, 3:947.

14. "2210: Talāk āpavā badala jamātī daṇḍa," *"Muslima-Gujarāta" fatāvā-saṅgraha*, 3:949–950.

15. Carissa Hickling, "Disinheriting Daughters: Applying Hindu Laws of Inheritance to the Khoja Muslim Community in Western India, 1847–1937," (MA thesis, University of Manitoba, 1998), 197.

16. Asaf Ali Ashgar Fyzee, *Outlines of Muhammadan Law* (London: Oxford University Press, 1964), 57.

17. S. T. Lokhandwalla, "Islamic Law and Ismaili Communities (Khojas and Bohras)," *Indian Economic and Social History Review* 4, no. 2 (1967): 174–175.

18. Memon Abd Allah Ismail, *Memaṇa tavārīkha* (Surat, India: Śrī Nārāyaṇa, 1921).

19. Zawahir Moir, "Historical and Religious Debates amongst Indian Ismailis 1840–1920," in *The Banyan Tree: Essays in Early Literature in New Indo-Aryan Languages*, vol. 1, ed. Mariola Offredi (New Delhi: Manohar, 2001), 136–142.

20. "Abdurahim Haji Ismail Mithu . . . Appellant and Halimabai . . . Respondent: On Appeal from the Court of Appeal for Eastern Africa (1)," in *The Law Reports . . . Indian Appeals: Being Cases in the Privy Council on Appeal from the East Indies . . .*, vol. 43, 1915–1916, ed. Sir Frederick Pollock (London: Council at 10, 1916), 35–42.

21. C. A. Kincaid, *Forty-Four Years a Public Servant* (Edinburgh: William Blackwood and Sons, 1934), 226, 227.

22. For more on Beaman's judgments see, Rachel Sturman, *The Government of Social Life in Colonial India: Liberalism, Religious Law, and Women's Rights* (Cambridge: Cambridge University Press, 2012), 208–209.

23. Kincaid, *Forty-Four Years*, 227.

24. Kincaid, *Forty-Four Years*, 228.

25. "The Cutchi Memons Bill—Passed," *The Legislative Assembly Debates*. Official Report, vol. 3, 1938 (Simla: Government of India Press, 1938), 2454–2458.

26. *Bombay 1921–1922: A Review of the Administration of the Presidency* (Bombay: Government of India, 1923), 47.

27. "The Cutchi Memons Bill," 2454.

28. "The Cutchi Memons Bill," 2454.

29. "The Cutchi Memons Bill," 2455–2458.

30. "Law Governing Cutchi Memons: Important Ruling," *Bombay Chronicle*, 13 August 1942, 4.

31. "The Aga Khan of the Ismaili Moslems Marries His Niece at Bombay," *Life*, 31 January 1938, 53.

32. Iqbal Akhtar, *The Khōjā of Tanzania: Discontinuities of a Postcolonial Religious Identity* (Leiden, Netherlands: Brill, 2016), 39–42.

33. Saleh Muhammad Haji Harun Kabli, *Śuddha ke aśuddha ane Memaṇa tavārīkha* (n.p. [Bombay?]: n.p., 1931).

34. Kabli, *Śuddha ke aśuddha*, 39, 42–43.

35. For more on the role of *kafā'āt* in regimes of social differentiation in Gujarat, see Edward Simpson, *Muslim Society and the Western Indian Ocean: The Seafarers of Kachchh* (London: Routledge, 2007), 92.

36. Kabli, *Śuddha ke aśuddha*, 47–48, 50.

37. Madrah [pseud.], *Khojā komane eka apīl* (Bombay: Navrang, 1921), 7–9.

38. S. R. Dongkery, *The Law Applicable to Khojas and Cutchi Memons* (Bombay: Satya Mitra Press, 1929), 5, 8, 10.

39. Dongkery, *The Law*, 15–16.

40. Dongkery, *The Law*, 56.

41. "A: Translation of the Will: Bilgimbai Ismail Jetha," in "HH Sit Sultan Mahomed Shah Aga Khan . . . vs. Abdulrasul Fazel Peerani, trustee of estate of Bilgimbai . . . ," ZLR, HC3 / 3750.

42. "A: Translation of the Will."

43. "A: Translation of the Will."

44. "A: Translation of the Will."

45. "A: Translation of the Will."

46. Mr. Taibjee M. Vasi, "Believe It or Not," *Ummīd*, September 1944, 31–32.

47. Jonah Blank, *Mullahs on the Mainframe: Islam and Modernity among the Daudi Bohras* (Chicago: University of Chicago Press, 2001), 190–195.

48. "Beard Essential for Bridegrooms: Mullaji's Dictum; Set at Naught by Brides," *Bombay Chronicle*, February 6, 1930, 10.

49. Mian Bhai Mulla Abdul Hussain, *Gulzare Daudi: A Short Note on Bohras of India*, Reprint Edition (Surat: Progressive Printing Press, 1977).

50. Abbasali Najafali, *Law of Marriage Governing Dawoodi Bohra Muslims* (Bombay: Times of India Press, 1943), 16.

51. Abdul Hussain, *Gulzare Daudi*, 73.

52. Najafali, *Law of Marriage*, 27, 58.

53. "The Pardah or Seclusion of Women," *Modern Review*, February 1937, 251.

54. "The Islamic Law," *Bombay Chronicle*, 13 February 1937, 6.

55. N. Hanif, "Appendix-V: Law and Communities," *Islamic Concept of Crime and Justice*, vol. 2 (New Delhi: Sarup and Sons, 1999), 290.

56. *Nar-e-haka* (Bombay: Dhī Daudī Vohrā vakf end trast velfar esosīeśannuṁ, 1940), 21–23.

57. Ashgar Ali Engineer, *The Bohras* (New Delhi: Vikas Publishing House, 1993), 197.

58. Engineer, *The Bohras,* 197.

59. "Interesting Judgment regarding Bohra Marriage," *Bombay Chronicle,* June 6, 1942, 7; Engineer, *The Bohras,* 200.

60. *Nar-e-haka,* 24.

61. Theodore P. Wright Jr., "Competitive Modernization within the Daudi Bohra Sect of Muslims and Its Significance for Indian Political Development," in *Competition and Modernization in South Asia,* ed. Helen E. Ullrich (New Delhi: Abhinay, 1975), 151–178.

62. Kutub E. Azad, *Barabādīnā paṁthe* (Bombay: Pukar Kāryālay, 1946).

63. Nile Green, *Terrains of Exchange: Religious Economies of Global Islam* (Oxford: Oxford University Press, 2015), 236.

64. Daleara Jamasji-Hirjikaka and Yasmin Qureshi, *The Merchant Knight: Adamjee Haji Dawood* (Karachi: Adamjee Foundation, 2004), 83.

65. Sugata Bose, *His Majesty's Opponent: Subhas Chandra Bose and India's Struggle against Empire* (Cambridge, MA: Harvard University Press, 2011), 272.

66. *Two Historic Trials in Red Fort; An Authentic Account of the Trial by a General Court Martial of Captain Shah Nawaz Khan, Captain P. K. Sahgal and Lt. G. S. Dhillon* (New Delhi: Moti Ram, 1946), 136.

67. Gregg Huff, *World War II and Southeast Asia: Economy and Society under Japanese Occupation* (Cambridge: Cambridge University Press, 2022), 20–21.

68. "Who Will Be the First Habeeb Here? Netaji's Challenge to Indians in Malai," *Azad Hind,* January 5, 1945, 1.

69. "Netaji Exhorts Indians Here to Make Maximum Sacrifice in Men & Money for India Liberation War," *Azad Hind,* December 25, 1945, 2.

70. "External Affairs: Far Eastern, 1945," NAI, Progs., Nos. 1073-F.E., 1945 (Secret), 8.

71. S. A. Ayer, *Unto Him a Witness: The Story of Netaji Subhas Chandra Bose in East Asia* (Bombay: Thacker, 1951), 196–199.

72. Stephen Philip Cohen, *The Idea of Pakistan* (Washington, D.C.: The Brookings Institution, 2004), 50.

73. For the broader context of this iconography, see Karen G. Ruffle, *Everyday Shiʿism in South Asia* (Hoboken, NJ: John Wiley and Sons, 2021), 138.

74. Srinath Raghavan, *India's War: World War II and the Making of Modern South Asia* (New York: Basic Books), 264, 326–327.

75. "Annual Report of Habib Bank, Ltd.," *Bombay Chronicle,* 21 April 1944, 3.

76. "Habib Bank Limited: Chart of Progress," *Bombay Chronicle,* 27 March 1947, 1.

77. M. A. H. Ispahani, *Qaid-e-Azam Jinnah as I Knew Him*, 2nd ed. (Karachi: Forward Publications Trust, 1967), 160.

78. "II. 2. Habib Bank Ltd., Delhi, to M.A. Jinnah," *Quaid-i-Azam: Mohammad Ali Jinnah Papers*, vol. 3, *On the Threshold of Pakistan, 1 July–25 July 1947*, ed. Z. H. Zaidi (Islamabad: National Archives of Pakistan, 1996), 728.

79. "Enemy Trading. New Delhi, The 4th May 1942," *The Calcutta Gazette*, 28 May 1942, 395.

80. "Proposal to Send a Mission to Tunis and Algeria Headed by Mullah Tahir Ud Din, Leader of Bohra Committee," NAI, Progs., Nos. 84-W, 1941(Secret).

81. Wright, "Competitive Modernization," 161.

82. "Dawoodi Bohra Conference," *Bombay Chronicle*, 22 January 1944, 4.

83. Mr. Tayabjee Abdulkaiyoom, "That Conference—Reform & Education," *Ummīd*, August 1944, 57–58.

84. "Haji Abdul Karim to M. A. Jinnah," in *Quaid-i-Azam: Mohammad Ali Jinnah Papers*, vol. 10, *Quest for Political Settlement in India, 1 October 1943–31 July 1944*, ed. Z. H. Zaidi (Islamabad: National Archives of Pakistan, 1993), 472.

85. Claude Markovits, *Merchants, Traders, Entrepreneurs: Indian Business in the Colonial Era* (Basingstoke, UK: Palgrave Macmillan, 2008), 81–82.

86. "M. A. Hassan Ispahani to M. A. Jinnah, Calcutta (3 April 1944)," in Zaidi, ed., *Quaid-i-Azam Mohammad Ali Jinnah Papers*, 10:252.

87. Markovits, *Merchants, Traders, Entrepreneurs*, 81–82.

88. Yahya Hashim Bavani, *Taḥrīk-i āzādī aur Meman barādarī: Jidd o jahd-i āzādī ke cand gum shudah tārīkhī aurāq* (Karachi: Vāḍāsāḍavālā Fā'ūnḍeshan, 1982).

89. "Aga Khan's Diamond Jubilee 1940–1949," https://www.britishpathe.com/video/aga-khans-diamond-jubilee. Accessed 21 December 2021.

90. Photo in author's personal collection. Available upon request.

91. "Not a Khoja or Bohra Candidate Selected," *Bombay Chronicle*, 9 January 1946, 3.

92. "Marshall Plan for Asian Countries," *Bombay Chronicle Weekly*, 27 June 1948, 12.

93. Denny D'Silva, *India: Reply to Her Critics* ([Bombay?]: n.p., [1946?]), 360.

94. "Representation from the All Parties Shia Conference regarding Protection to Safeguard Their Religion and Their Culture as Their Economic and Political Existence," NAI, Secretariat of the Governor General (Reforms), File No. 41 / 3 / 46-R.

95. "Enclosure: I," in *Hatim A. Alavi: Pillar of the Pakistan Movement*, ed. D. A. Pirzada (Karachi: Mehran Publishers, 1994), 131.

96. "46. Hatim Alavi to Mr. Liaquat Ali, Karachi, New Year, 1946, Sind, VIII: 32," in Pirzada, ed., *Hatim A. Alavi*, 144 (emphasis in the original).

97. "Saif Nambr," *The Tegh: Illustrated Urdu Weekly*, May 1946, 15, 18.

98. Blank, *Mullahs on the Mainframe*, 280.

99. “Annex to No. 112, Syedna Taher Saifuddin to M.A. Jinnah,” in *Quaid-i-Azam: Mohammad Ali Jinnah Papers*, vol. 2, *Pakistan in the Making, 3 June–30 June 1947*, ed. Z. H. Zaidi (Islamabad: National Archives of Pakistan, 1994), 197.

100. “Z. A. Bandukwalla to Jinnah,” in *Quaid-i-Azam: Mohammad Ali Jinnah Papers*, vol. 3, *On the Threshold of Pakistan, 1 July–25 July 1947*, ed. Z. H. Zaidi (Islamabad: National Archives of Pakistan, 1994), 109–110.

101. D.A. Pirzada, *Hatim A. Alavi, A Pillar of the Pakistan Movement* (Karachi: Mehran Publishers, 1994), 137–138.

102. “Akīdo Muslima Līg Che,” *Ummīd*, February 1946, 91–100.

103. “Exchange of Populations,” *Modern Review*, December 1946, 415, emphasis in the original.

104. “Jāhera vijñapati: Dhorājīni Hindu Musalamāna Prajā,” (Dhoraji, India: Māstar Press, 1947) [Handbill in Gujarati]. Author’s collection.

105. “Representations Received from Memon Muslims Residing in Burma and Ceylon regarding Their Property Left in Junagadh Which Has Been Taken Over by the Custodian as Evacuee Property,” NAI, Ministry of States: General, Progs., Nos. 6(47)-R, 1949.

106. “Copy of a telegram dated the 23rd December 1947 from President, Bohra Jamat, Indore addressed to Mahatma Gandhiji, New Delhi,” NAI, Gujarati Miscellaneous 1948, Digitized Sardar Patel Papers, 33.

8. Decolonization and Postcolonial Dilemmas in Asia and Africa, 1947–1975

1. S. F. Levin, “Ob ėvoli͡utsii musul′manskikh torgovykh kast v svi͡azi s razvitiem kapitalizma (na primere bokhra, memanov i khodzha),” in *Kasty v Indii* (Moscow: Nauka, 1965), 233–261. According to Levin (244), by 1961 Ismaili Khojas in India ran fifty-five cooperative banks.

2. Zulfikar Ali Bhutto, *Politics of the People: A Collection of Articles, Statements, and Speeches* (Rawalpindi: Pakistan Publications, 1974), 136.

3. *National Assembly of Pakistan Debates: Official Report*, vol. 2 (Karachi: Manager of Publications, 1965), 404.

4. Anuj Srivas, “The Messy Partition of the Reserve Bank of India,” The Wire, 14 August 2017, https://thewire.in/banking/partition-reserve-bank-of-india.

5. Tirthankar Roy, *A Business History of India: Enterprise and the Emergence of Capitalism from 1700* (Cambridge: Cambridge University Press, 2018), 150.

6. B. R. Ambedkar, *Maharashtra as a Linguistic Province: Statement Submitted to the Linguistic Provinces Commission* (Bombay: Thacker, 1948), 20–21.

7. Prof. M. L. Dantwalla, "Bombay City & Maharashtra," *Bombay Chronicle*, 2 November 1948, 8.

8. Partha S. Ghosh, *The Politics of Personal Law in South Asia* (New Delhi: Routledge, 2007), 76.

9. S. M. Naqvi, *The Law and Procedure of Income-Tax in Pakistan* (Lahore: Taxation, 1955), 34.

10. Sardar Patel, *Economic Situation in the Country*, vol. 2, *Private & Confidential*, September 17, 1949, NAI, Digitized Private Papers, Sardar Patel, File No. 2 / 274.

11. Morarji Desai to Sardar Patel, 12 January 1950, NAI, Activity of Mullaji Saheb of Dawoodi Bohra Community, Digitized Private Papers, Sardar Patel, File No. III-1-41.

12. Sardar Patel to Jawaharlal Nehru, 8 April 1950, NAI, Activity of Mullaji Saheb of Dawoodi Bohra Community, Digitized Private Papers, Sardar Patel, File No. III-1-41.

13. Jawaharlal Nehru to Sardar Patel, 9 April 1950, NAI, Activity of Mullaji Saheb of Dawoodi Bohra Community, Digitized Private Papers, Sardar Patel, File No. III-1-41.

14. Sardar Patel to Morarji Desai, 10 April 1950, NAI, Activity of Mullaji Saheb of Dawoodi Bohra Community," Digitized Private Papers, Sardar Patel, File No. III-1-41.

15. Ashgar Ali Engineer, *The Bohras* (New Delhi: Vikas Publishing House, 1993), 201–207.

16. For more on the concept of institutional voids, see Tarun Khanna, Krishna G. Palepu, and Richard J. Bullock, *Winning in Emerging Markets: A Road Map for Strategy and Execution* (Boston: Harvard Business Review Press, 2010), 7.

17. "Short Notice Questions and Answers: Restoration of Karachi Bohra Gymkhana," in *The Constituent Assembly (Legislature) of Pakistan Debates: Monday, the 29th March, 1954, Official Report* (Karachi: Government of Pakistan Press, 1954), 1205.

18. "Demands for Supplementary Grants for 1951–1952; Mr. Ahmad E. H. Jaffer," in *The Constituent Assembly (Legislature) of Pakistan Debate: Official Report*, vol. 1, 1952 (Karachi: Government of Pakistan Press, 1952), 881.

19. Anas Malik, *Polycentricity, Islam, and Development: Potentials and Challenges in Pakistan* (Lanham, MD: Lexington Books, 2018), 239.

20. "The Tour Report Mr. K.C. Sahgal, Vice Consul. Part I," NAI, Disabilities of People of Indian Origin in Burma—Policy, Ministry of External Affairs: B.C. Section, 1955, File No. 48-2 / 55-BC, 7.

21. "Memorandum of Memon Association of Ceylon," in *Constituent Assembly (Legislature) of Pakistan Debates, Saturday, the 28th August 1954, Official Report* (Karachi: Government of Pakistan Press, 1954), 1635.

22. "Quazis [*sic*] and Board of Quazis," *Administration Report of the Registrar-General*, 1969–1970 (Ceylon: Registrar General, 1970), 33.

23. Thomas Blom Hansen, "A History of Distributed Sovereignty: Trade, Migration and Rule in the Global Indian Ocean," in *Beyond Liberal Order: States, Societies and Markets in the Global Indian Ocean*, eds., Harry Verhoeven and Anatol Lieven (London: C. Hurst & Co., 2021), 53–54.

24. Brannon Ingram, *Revival from Below: The Deoband Movement and Global Islam* (Berkeley: University of California Press, 2018), ch. 7.

25. Howard Schwartz, *The Rise and Fall of Philanthropy in East Africa: The Asian Contribution* (London and New York: Routledge, 1992), 172.

26. *Āfrikā tathā kōngōmā̃ kōmī birādarōnā vasāhatanā itihāsanī rūparēkhā tathā vyavasāya nirdēśikā* (Arusha: Dhī suprīm kāunsīl . . . ōph āfrikā, 1960); *Mālagāsī rīpablīka, mōrīśī'asa, sōmālīyā tathā rīyunī'anamāṃ kōmī birādarōnā vasāhatanā itihāsanī rūparēkhā tathā vyavasāya nidrēśikā* (Arusha: Dhī suprīm kāunsīl . . . ōph āfrikā, 1960); S.K. Raik, ed. *Gulaśane Malumāta* (Ujjain: Kalim Kutub Khana, 1975). Faruq Ahmad Chotani, *Memons International* (Bombay: Memons International 1971). For a further analysis of the Bohra volume see Jonah Blank, *Mullahs on the Mainframe*, 297.

27. A. A. Aziz, *Zahure Haqqa, yāne 'Haydarī'nā khaṃdanno javāba* (Dar es Salaam: Īsmailīā Majalise Razākārāna, 1948), 6–7.

28. John Iliffe, *A Modern History of Tanganyika* (Cambridge: Cambridge University Press, 1979), 374.

29. Colette Le Cour Grandmaison, "Indian Africa: Minorities of Indian-Pakistani Origin in Eastern Africa," in *Indian Africa: Minorities of Indian-Pakistani Origin in Eastern Africa*, ed. Michael Adam (Dar es Salaam: Mkuki na Nyota, 2015), 214.

30. Farhad Daftary, *The Isma'ilis: Their History and Doctrines*, 2nd ed. (Cambridge: Cambridge University Press, 2007), 497–498.

31. Soumen Mukherjee, "Universalizing Aspirations," in *The Shi'a in Modern South Asia: Religion, History and Politics*, ed. Justin Jones and Ali Usman Qasmi (Cambridge: Cambridge University Press, 2015), 124.

32. Robert G. Gregory, *The Rise and Fall of Philanthropy in East Africa: The Asian Contribution* (New Brunswick, NJ: Transaction, 1992), 50, 172, 31.

33. Jean-Claude Penrad, "Sauti ya Bilal, ou les transformations de l'islam shi'ite missionnaire en Afrique orientale," *Islam et Sociétés au Sud du Sahara* 2 (1988): 17–33.

34. Sana Aiyar, *Indians in Kenya: The Politics of Diaspora* (Cambridge, MA: Harvard University Press, 2015), 288–289.

35. Aiyar, *Indians in Kenya*, 281.

36. *Kenya National Assembly, Official Report*, vol. 5 (Nairobi: Government Printer, 1965), 101, 907.

37. D. R. Mankekar, *Pak Colonialism in East Bengal* (Bombay: Somaiya, 1971), 22.

38. Sergey Levin, "The Upper Bourgeoisie from the Muslim Commercial Community of Memons in Pakistan, 1947 to 1971," *Asian Survey* 14, no. 3 (1974): 231–243.

39. Farzana Shaikh, *Making Sense of Pakistan* (Oxford: Oxford University Press, 2018), 124.

40. Hanna Papanek, "Pakistan's Big Businessmen: Muslim Separatism, Entrepreneurship, and Partial Modernization," *Economic Development and Cultural Change* 21, no. 1 (1972): 28.

41. Papanek, "Pakistan's Big Businessmen," 22, 26.

42. Laurent Gayer, *Karachi: Ordered Disorder and the Struggle for the City* (Oxford: Oxford University Press, 2014), 136.

43. Faisal Devji, *Muslim Zion: Pakistan as a Political Idea* (London: Hurst, 2013), 65.

44. Nasir Tyabji, *Forging Capitalism in Nehru's India: Neocolonialism and the State, c. 1940–1970* (Oxford: Oxford University Press, 2015), 83.

45. Ayesha Jalal, *Democracy and Authoritarianism in South Asia: A Comparative and Historical Perspective* (Cambridge: Cambridge University Press, 1995), chap. 4.

46. Papanek, "Pakistan's Big Businessmen," 27.

47. Zeeba Zafar Mahmood, *The Shaping of Karachi's Big Entrepreneurs: 1947–98, a Socio-Political Study* (Karachi: City Press, 2003), 106.

48. Sanaa Riaz, *New Islamic Schools: Tradition, Modernity, and Class in Urban Pakistan* (New York: Palgrave Macmillan, 2014), 103–110.

49. All Pakistan Women's Association, *Women's Movement in Pakistan* (Karachi: All Pakistan Women's Association, 1963), 48.

50. *An Account of the Khoja Sunnat Jamat, Bombay* (Karachi: Oxford Book House, 1967), 31.

51. *Anjuman-i Khuddām al-Kurān: Karācī, silvara jyubīlī soveniyar* (Karachi: Anjuman-i Khuddām al-Kurān, 1966).

52. Gopika Solanki, *Adjudication in Religious Family Laws: Cultural Accommodation, Legal Pluralism, and Gender Equality in India* (Cambridge: Cambridge University Press, 2011), 296.

53. Theodore P. Wright Jr., "Competitive Modernization within the Daudi Bohra Sect of Muslims and Its Significance for Indian Political Development," in *Competition and Modernization in South Asia*. ed. Helen E. Ullrich (New Delhi: Abhinay, 1975), 158–159.

54. Indian High Commissioner in Pakistan, "Pakistan's Decision Not to Devalue Its Currency," NAI, File No. 2 / 130, 1947–1950, n. p.

55. "Note on Political and Economic Conditions in Pakistan," 15th October 1948" NAI, Digitized Private Papers, Sardar Patel, Letters & Proceedings, File No. 19, 4.

56. Willi Frischauer, *The Aga Khans* (London: Bodley Head, 1970), 194.

57. Lawrence J. White, *Industrial Concentration and Economic Power in Pakistan* (Princeton, NJ: Princeton University Press, 1974), 74, 76.

58. Stephen Philip Cohen, *The Idea of Pakistan* (Washington, D.C.: The Brookings Institution, 2004), 50.

59. J. Russell Andrus and Azizali F. Mohammed, *The Economy of Pakistan* (Stanford, CA: Stanford University Press, 1958), 390.

60. Joe Studwell, *How Asia Works: Success and Failure in the World's Most Dynamic Region* (New York: Grove, 2013).

61. Andrus and Mohammed, *The Economy of Pakistan*, 361–362.

62. Gustav Papanek, *Pakistan's Development: Social Goals and Private Incentives* (Cambridge, MA: Harvard University Press, 1967), 88.

63. Tapan Das, *Pakistan Politics* (Delhi: People's Publishing House, 1969), 12.

64. Nadeem Malik, *Corporate Social Responsibility and Development in Pakistan* (Abingdon, UK: Routledge, 2015), 43.

65. Levin, "The Upper Bourgeoisie," 243.

66. Paul J. Kaiser, *Culture, Transnationalism, and Civil Society: Aga Khan Social Service Initiatives in Tanzania* (Westport, CT: Praeger, 1996): 42, 46.

67. G. Thomas Burgess, "The Zanzibar Revolution and Its Aftermath," in *Oxford Research Encyclopedia of African History Online*, 28 March 2018, https://oxfordre.com/africanhistory/display/10.1093/acrefore/9780190277734.001.0001/acrefore-9780190277734-e-155;jsessionid=224389D409504D55CF77FEDB30091323. Accessed 01 March 2022.

68. Iqbal Akhtar, *The Khōjā of Tanzania: Discontinuities of a Postcolonial Religious Identity* (Leiden, Netherlands: Brill, 2016), 52–53.

69. "New Facts on the Baghdad Murders," *Jewish Observer and Middle East Review* 18 (1969): 7.

70. "Talkback: Profile of Gulf Shipping," *Marine Week*, 28 July 1978, 40.

71. Philip Shenon, "B.C.C.I.'s Best Customer Is Also Its Worst Customer," *New York Times*, August 6, 1991, D1.

72. The history is briefly chronicled at Anjuman e Faiz e Panjetani, "Welcome to Faiz e Panjetani," accessed 1 June 2020, https://www.faizepanjetani.com/.

73. The event was a front page story in the official organ of the Hindu nationalist organization, the RSS. "Tanzania Expels Indian Muslim Leader," *The Organiser*, 7 September 1968, 1.

74. *Dawoodi Bohra Commission (Nathwani Commission)* (Ahmedabad: Nathwani Commission, 1979), 156.

75. "Asian Muslim Institutions Handed Over to Chief Qadi," Translations on Africa No. 1265, Arlington, VA, Joint Publications Research Service, 16 February 1973, 48.

76. Muhammad Abdul Mazid, "Industrialising Bangladesh: The Pioneering Role of A. K. Khan," *Financial Express*, 31 March 2018, https://thefinancialexpress.com.bd/views/industrialising-bangladesh-the-pioneering-role-of-ak-khan-1522509635.

77. Mahbub ul Haq, "Employment in the 1970's: A New Perspective," Haq, Mahbub ul—Articles and Speeches (1971–1977), 1651847, World Bank Group Archives, Washington, D.C., United States. 5.

78. Kalim Siddiqui, *Conflict, Crisis and War in Pakistan* (London: The Macmillan Press, 1972), 137.

79. Bawany Group, "Bawany Group History," accessed 15 May 2019. http://bawany.com/group-history/.

80. *Year Book of the Karachi Stock Exchange Ltd.* (Karachi Stock Exchange, 1968), 160, 173, 517.

81. Bawany Group, "Bawany Group History," http://bawany.com/group-history/

82. Renata Holod and Hasan-Uddin Khan, "Bait ul-Mukarram, Dhaka, Bangladesh," in *The Contemporary Mosque: Architects, Clients, and Designs since the 1950s* (New York: Rizzoli, 1997), 204–208.

83. Rakibuddin Ahmed, *Progress of the Jute Industry and Trade, 1855–1966* (Dhaka, Pakistan: Central Jute Committee, n.d. [1966]), 404.

84. Tariq Omar Ali, *A Local History of Global Capital: Jute and Peasant Life in the Bengal Delta* (Princeton: Princeton University Press, 2018), 181.

85. Mohammad Ayub Khan, "Adamjee Science College: An Example for Other Industrialists," in *Speeches and Statements*, vol. 4, July 1961–June 1962 (Karachi: Pakistan Publications, 1962), 65–66.

86. Syedur Rahman, "Adamjee Jute Mill," in *Historical Dictionary of Bangladesh* (Lanham, MD: Scarecrow, 2010), 5.

87. Kamran Asdar Ali, *Communism in Pakistan: Politics and Class Activism 1947–1972* (London: I. B. Tauris, 2015), 142.

88. Jyoti Sen Gupta, *History of Freedom Movement in Bangladesh, 1943–1973* (Calcutta: Naya Prokash, n.d. [1974]), 55.

89. Syed Humayun, *Sheikh Mujib's 6-point Formula: An Analytical Study of the Breakup of Pakistan* (Karachi: Royal, 1995), 301; Throughout 1972, thanks to its enormous campus, Adamjee Jute Mills supplied a haven for Bangladesh's suffering Bihari populations; see "The Biharis in Bangladesh," *United States of America Congressional Record: Proceedings and Debates of the 92d Congress, Second Session*, vol. 118, pt. 7, March 13, 1972 to March 21, 1972 (Washington, DC: GPO, 1972), 8274.

90. Farzana Shaikh, *Making Sense of Pakistan* (Oxford: Oxford University Press, 2018), 116–117, 123–125.

91. Gayer, *Karachi: Ordered Disorder*, 136, 300n8; Mahmood, *The Shaping of Karachi's Big Entrepreneurs*, 135.

92. For a brief discussion see Michael O'Sullivan, "Interest, Usury, and the Transition from "Muslim" to "Islamic" Banks, 1908–1958," *International Journal of Middle East Studies* 52 (2020): 261–287.

93. "Pakistan Prime Minister Urges Truman Aid Plan for Middle East," *Pakistan Affairs,* vol. 3, No. 2 (September 9, 1949): 3.

94. See the passing reference to this work in Abdul Azim Islahi, "The Legacy of Muhammad Hamidullah in Islamic Economics," MPRA Paper No. 80149, Munich Personal RePEc Archive, 13 July 2017, https://fdocuments.us/document/munich-personal-repec-archive-uni-personal-repec-archive-introduction-dr.html?page=1.

95. Fazlur Rahman, "Islam and the New Constitution of Pakistan," in *Contemporary Problems of Pakistan,* ed. J. Henry Korson (Leiden, Netherlands: Brill, 1974), 32.

96. "President Ayub Khan's Definition of Islamic Socialism," *Muslim World* 2 (1964): 18.

97. Siddiqui, *Conflict, Crisis, and War,* 123.

98. "Islam Needs No Crutch of Socialism," *Pakistan Review* 18 (1970): 9, 15.

99. Ebrahim Bawany, *Revolutionary Strategy for National Development* (Karachi: Muslim News International, 1970), ch. 8.

100. Elisa Giunchi, "The Political Thought of Abul Aʿlā Mawdūdī," *Il Politico* 59 (April–June 1994): 370–371.

101. Siddiqui, *Conflict, Crisis and War in Pakistan,* 60.

102. Mahbub ul Haq, *The Poverty Curtain: Choices for the Third World* (New York: Columbia University Press, 1976), 6.

103. W. Eric Gustafson, "Economic Reforms under the Bhutto Regime," in Korson, ed., *Contemporary Problems of Pakistan,* 81–119.

104. Ayub Khan, quoted in Gustafson, "Economic Reforms," 7.

105. Lawrence J. White, *Industrial Concentration and Economic Power in Pakistan* (Princeton, NJ: Princeton University Press, 1974), 66.

106. Saeed Shafqat, *Civil-Military Relations in Pakistan: From Zufikar Ali Bhutto to Benazir Bhutto* (Boulder, CO: Westview, 1997), 129; Shafqat cites White, *Industrial Concentration.*

107. Zaffar Hassan, "The magic number 22," *Pakistan Economist* (November 11, 1972), 13.

108. Stanley Kochanek, *Interest Groups and Development: Business and Politics in Pakistan* (Bombay: Oxford University Press, 1983), 184.

109. "Monday, the 21st June, 1965," *Assembly Debates: National Assembly of Pakistan,* 21 June 1965, 303.

110. "Economic Reforms Order 1972: President's Order 1 of 1972," The text of the order can helpfully be consulted at the following site legal site: https://joshand

makinternational.com/resources/laws-of-pakistan/land-property-acquisition-and-conveyancing-laws-of-pakistan/economic-reforms-order-1972-presidents-order-1-of-1972-gazette-of-pakistan-extraordinary-3rd-january-1972/ Accessed 27 May 2019.

111. "Economic Reforms Order 1972: President's Order 1 of 1972," 3 a.

112. Chamber of Commerce and Industry, *Economic Revival and Private Enterprise in Pakistan: Proceedings of the Businessmen's Conference, Karachi, May 14–17, 1973* (Karachi: Chamber of Commerce and Industry, n.d. [1973]), 35.

113. Mircea Raianu, *Tata: The Global Corporation That Built Indian Capitalism* (Cambridge, MA: Harvard University Press, 2021).

114. Mary C. Carras, *Indira Gandhi: In the Crucible of Leadership; A Political Biography* (Boston: Beacon, 1979), 147.

115. Cohen, *The Idea of Pakistan,* 83.

116. James P. Sterba, "Bhutto Picks Up the Pieces of Pakistan," *New York Times,* 25 June 1972, 7.

117. Nadeem Malik, *Corporate Social Responsibility and Development in Pakistan* (Abingdon, UK: Routledge, 2015), 44.

118. Seyyed Vali Reza Nasr, *The Vanguard of the Islamic Revolution: The Jamaʿat-i Islami of Pakistan* (Berkeley: University of California Press, 1994), 173.

119. "International Muslim Bank for Trade," in *Story of Islamic Summit in Lahore,* ed. Aziz Beg and Nasim Ahmad (Lahore: Babur and Amer, 1974), 250.

120. Nasr, *The Vanguard,* 59–60.

121. Seyyed Vali Reza Nasr, *Mawdūdī and the Making of Islamic Revivalism* (New York: Oxford University Press, 1994), 46.

122. Ayesha Siddiqa, *Military Inc.: Inside Pakistan's Military Economy,* 2nd ed. (London: Pluto, 2017), chap. 6.

123. Shahid-Ur Rehman, *Who Owns Pakistan? Fluctuating Fortunes of Business Mughals* (Islamabad: Shahid-ur-Rehman, 1998), 80.

124. Michael O'Sullivan, "Interest, Usury, and the Transition from "Muslim" to "Islamic" Banks, 1908–1958," *International Journal of Middle East Studies* 52 (May 2020): 261–287

125. Daryoush Mohammad Poor, *Authority without Territory: The Aga Khan Development Network and the Ismaili Imamate* (New York: Palgrave Macmillan, 2014); Jonah Blank, *Mullahs on the Mainframe: Islam and Modernity among the Daudi Bohras* (Chicago: University of Chicago Press, 2001), 181, 197.

126. All India Memon Jamat Federation, "Economic Upliftment," accessed 05 Sept6mber 2021, https://www.memonfederationindia.in/EconomicUpliftment.asp; *The Memon: Commemorative Publication of the First Ever Memon Alami Milan at Karachi, Pakistan, from 18th to 20th September, 1986* (Karachi: United Memon Jamaat, 1986), 83.

127. Rodney J. Wilson, "Economy," in *A Companion to Muslim Ethics,* ed. Amyn B. Sajoo, (London: I. B. Tauris: 2010), 146–147.

128. The most famous is M. Umar Chapra, a great popularizer of Islamic economics; see M. Umer Chapra, "Mawlana Mawdudi's Contribution to Islamic Economics," *Muslim World* 92, no. 2 (2004): 163–180.

Conclusion

1. Karim Muhammad Mastar, *Mahāgujarātanā Musalamāno* (Vadodara, India: Prācyavidyā Mandira, Majārājā Sayājīrāva Viśvavidyālaya, n.d. [1969]), 5–6.

2. The work was actually a partial translation of the second edition of a translation he completed in 1937 of the colonial gazetteer *Muslims of Gujarat.*

3. Kate Smith, "Amidst Things: New Histories of Commodities, Capital, and Consumption," *The Historical Journal,* 61, 3 (2018): 853.

4. Emma Rothschild, *An Infinite History: The Story of a Family in France over Three Centuries* (Princeton, NJ: Princeton University Press, 2021), 2–3.

5. Vali Nasr, *Meccanomics: The March of the New Muslim Middle Class* (Oxford: One World, 2010).

6. Stephen Kotkin, *Stalin: Waiting for Hitler, 1929–1941* (New York: Penguin, 2018), 296.

7. This is done very well in Melissa Macauley, *Distant Shores: Colonial Encounters on China's Maritime Frontier* (Princeton, NJ: Princeton University Press, 2021).

8. Peter Brown, *The Ransom of the Soul: Afterlife and Wealth in Early Western Christianity* (Cambridge, MA: Harvard University Press, 2015), 29.

9. One example of this view is Wael B. Hallaq, *The Impossible State: Islam, Politics, and Modernity's Moral Predicament* (New York: Columbia University Press, 2014), 146–152.

10. R. H. Tawney, *Religion and the Rise of Capitalism* (New Brunswick, NJ: Transaction, 1998), 4.

11. Timur Kuran, *The Long Divergence: How Islamic Law Held Back the Middle East* (Princeton, NJ: Princeton University Press, 2012).

12. Christophe Jaffrelot, *Religion, Caste, and Politics in India* (New York: Columbia University Press, 2011), 381–382.

13. Charlotte Proudman, *Female Genital Mutilation: When Culture and Law Clash* (Oxford: Oxford University Press, 2022), 130–132.

14. Abd al-Reşid Ibrahim, *ʿĀlem-i İslām ve Jāponyāda intişār-ı İslāmīyet,* vol. 2 (Istanbul: Ḳadr Maṭbaʿası, 1911), 38–39.

15. Thomas Kuttner, "Russian Jadīdism and the Islamic World: Ismail Gasprinskii in Cairo, 1908. A Call to the Arabs for the Rejuvenation of the Islamic World," *Cahiers du Monde russe et soviétique,* Vol. 16, No. 3 / 4 (July–December 1975): 383–424.

Acknowledgments

WHEN I BEGAN my professional training as a historian, I never imagined I would have the inclination or the training to write a book of this sort. After all, the sheer unpredictability of the research path is one of the most delightful and underrated aspects of being a historian. Even once a project is embarked upon—particularly a project such as this, where the sources are so dispersed and the archives in a sense must be constituted by the researcher—the method of acquiring material follows no straight course. And even at the very end of my writing process I discovered new material that made me rethink select parts of the book. If the historian R. G. Collingwood was right to say that no book is truly ever finished—citing reasons from editorial / print deadlines to authorial resignation—he failed to acknowledge the sheer irrepressibility of the archives, their refusal to play by the production timetable.

That I ever completed this book is due to the generous backing of family, friends, editors, teachers, and several academic institutions, though none of them is responsible for the contents of this manuscript.

Thanks go first and foremost to my academic mentors. Nile Green has been a bastion of incredible support over the past decade, a model scholar and human being in equal measure. Sanjay Subrahmanyam has likewise been a stalwart advocate of my scholarly development, and I am honored to have his support. Naomi Andrews and George Giacomini, my undergraduate mentors, were the first to give me the confidence to pursue this career. Sebouh Aslanian taught me how to be a historians' historian and to leave no archival stone unturned. Fahad Bishara stands in a league of his own, as interlocutor, collaborator, and supplier of materials. This book could not have been written were it not for his personal friendship or the paradigm shift he initiated in the study of Indian Ocean economic and legal history with his *Sea of Debt*. Christine Philliou and James Gelvin supplied generous critical feedback on the studies that formed the initial kernel of this book.

This book would have been dead on arrival without the scores of language teachers and learning partners who have tolerated me over the years. For help with Gujarati sources, I heartily thank Yusuf; in the case of Ottoman and modern Turkish I am indebted to Beyza Lorenz and Mehmet Taha Ayar; Domenico Ingenito and Sahba Shayani got me up to speed with Persian; to the staff at the Zabaan Language School in Delhi goes the credit for teaching me how to read Urdu. Kaleb Herman Adney, Sohaib Baig, Roy Bar Sadeh, Walter Lorenz, and Marjan Wardaki—whose individual linguistic acumen I will always envy—were vital lifelines when I got stuck. I owe them more than they could know. All mistakes of interpretation or translation remain entirely my own.

Several friends have been champions of this book. Herman Adney and Walter Lorenz were stalwart companions and unrivaled sources of counsel long before and throughout its writing. Dong Yan has been a tremendous confidant, alternatively acting as a source of pleasant distraction and a spur to carry on with the writing, even when things got dicey. Koh Choon Hwee is a great source of counsel. Sohaib Baig supplied three crucial manuscript sources, for which I am forever in his debt, and along with Marjan Wardaki, years of selfless encouragement.

I wrote this book while a Junior Research Fellow at the Center for History and Economics at Harvard University. It is an absurd understatement to say that being a fellow at the center has been the greatest professional privilege of my career, and much that is good in this book is due to what I learned from my colleagues there. Emma Rothschild has been a source of great encouragement and someone I immensely admire. Aditya Balasubramanian, Elsa Gerard, Mallory Hope, Ian Kumekawa, Jennifer Nickerson, Kalyani Ramnath, Salmaan Mirza, Joan Shaker, Tara Suri, David Todd, and Lola Zappi have all been the most wonderful friends. For all its eccentricities, I hope they find this book a worthwhile reflection of how I grew as a historian during our time together and how much they taught me. For their support over the years, I thank Ceren Abi, Roii Ball, Kate Creasey, Samuel Dolbee, Sam Keeley, Sean Heath, Marc Herman, Pauline Lewis, Nana Osei-Opare, Nicole and Aaron Gilhuis, Naveena Naqvi, Hasan Siddiqui, Sona Tajiryan, and Murat Yıldız. For the privilege of a year-long fellowship, I would also like to recognize the faculty and staff of the Abdallah S. Kamel Center at Yale Law School, whose influence shaped this book in diverse ways.

Even if I tried, I could not conjure up better editors than Sharmila Sen and Emily Marie Silk at Harvard University Press. In a series of initial conversations Sharmila helped shape my embryonic ideas of what this book would be. I am so grateful for the chance she gave me. From the moment she was assigned it, Emily has been a steadfast and (very, very) patient champion of this work. Throughout the writing process she has supplied brilliant critical feedback worthy of the finest specialists of South Asia. Her advice has repeatedly dug me out of many an interpretive rut. I can only pray that this book is a suitable testament to what she taught me about book writing. Also at Harvard University Press, Jillian Ann Quigley supplied fantastic editorial support and showed a superhuman tolerance while preparing the art. Last, but definitely not least, Sherry Gerstein and Brian Bendlin did a phenomenal job copyediting this book, for which I will always be grateful.

My sincere gratitude also goes to the three anonymous reviewers of this manuscript. In their individual ways each supplied badly needed insights on how I might improve my initial draft. I trust they will be pleased with the changes I have implemented and find a measure of their inspiration in this manuscript.

I would be remiss to leave out the many librarians, booksellers, archivists, bibliographers, and mapmakers—the unsung heroes of all research—who supplied the raw material for this book. The team at The Map Archive deserve high praise for creating the maps used in this book. The staff of the British Library's Asian and African Studies Reading Room, the affiliate libraries of the Center for Research Libraries, the Institute of Ismaili Studies in London, the digitization team at McGill University, the interlibrary loan departments at Harvard University, the University of California–Los Angeles, and Yale Law School, and the digital library collections of Florida International University and Southern Methodist University, contributed more than they could ever know to this project. I would also like to single out the booksellers in India and Pakistan who helped me track down material. A special word of appreciation is reserved for the many Indian institutions and individuals who regularly post scans of rare books at Archive.org and yumpu.com. The free material they supply to the site has proven a gold mine for this monograph. Those fastidious, although sadly anonymous, individuals who scanned volume after volume of long out-of-print Gujarati books will always merit my respect and thanks. Should they ever have doubted the value of what must have been hour upon hour of punishing work, I offer this book as proof of what their work has made possible, even amid a global pandemic.

Chapter 1 furthers scholarship first presented in "Vernacular Capitalism and Intellectual History in a Gujarati Account of China, 1860–68," *Journal of Asian Studies* 80, no. 2 (2021): 267–292. Chapter 3 builds on ideas first presented in "'Indian Money,' Intra-Shīʿī Polemic, and the Bohra and Khoja Pilgrimage Infrastructure in Iraq's Shrine Cities, 1897–1932," *Journal of the Royal Asiatic Society,* 3rd ser., 32, no. 1 (2022): 213–250. Chapter 4 expands on work presented in "Pan-Islamic Bonds and Interest: Ottoman Bonds, Red Crescent Remittances and the Limits of Indian Muslim capital, 1877–1924," *Indian Economic and Social History Review* 55, no. 2 (2018): 183–220.

And finally, my family. My grandmother, Patricia Dooley, has served as interlocutor, critic, and promoter of my work since my teenage years. My parents, James and Anne, sacrificed an enormous amount so that I could become a historian and supplied all sorts of parental and grandparental support throughout the writing of this book. My in-laws, Rosario and Elisabetta, have done the same and always encouraged me to get on with the writing. In similar fashion, my siblings and their families have kept me grounded, reminding me not to give into fatalism or self-absorption.

That brings me to Giuseppina and Hugh, to whom this book is dedicated. They have borne the burden of this work for the past few years, sharing space with a growing collection of Gujarati books and the commercial ephemera of some of the firms studied in this monograph, and moving from California to Connecticut, Massachusetts, and Italy. Even if they never read a word of what follows, they left their mark on every page.

Index